DATE DUE

DEC 0 5 2019	
	PRINTED IN U.S.A.

Moral Constraints on War

Moral Constraints on War

Principles and Cases

Second Edition

Edited by
Bruno Coppieters and Nick Fotion

LEXINGTON BOOKS

A division of
ROWMAN & LITTLEFIELD PUBLISHERS, INC.
Lanham • Boulder • New York • Toronto • Plymouth, UK

6/4/09
Lon
$80 —

LEXINGTON BOOKS

A division of Rowman & Littlefield Publishers, Inc.
A wholly owned subsidiary of The Rowman & Littlefield Publishing Group, Inc.
4501 Forbes Boulevard, Suite 200
Lanham, MD 20706

Estover Road
Plymouth PL6 7PY
United Kingdom

British Library Cataloguing in Publication Information Available

Library of Congress Cataloging-in-Publication Data

Moral constraints on war : principles and cases / edited by Bruno Coppieters and
Nick Fotion. — 2nd ed.
　　p. cm.
　Includes index.
　ISBN-13: 978-0-7391-2129-0 (cloth : alk. paper)
　ISBN-10: 0-7391-2129-4 (cloth : alk. paper)
　ISBN-13: 978-0-7391-2130-6 (pbk. : alk. paper)
　ISBN-10: 0-7391-2130-8 (pbk. : alk. paper)
　eISBN-13: 978-0-7391-2991-3
　eISBN-10: 0-7391-2991-0
　1. War—Moral and ethical aspects. 2. Military history, Modern—20th century.
I. Coppieters, Bruno II. Fotion, N.
　U22.M5924 2008
　172′.42—dc22　　　　　　　　　　　　　　　　　　　　　　　　2008009971

Printed in the United States of America

♾️™ The paper used in this publication meets the minimum requirements of
American National Standard for Information Sciences—Permanence of Paper
for Printed Library Materials, ANSI/NISO Z39.48-1992.

Contents

Preface   ix
Bruno Coppieters and Nick Fotion

Introduction   1
Nick Fotion, Bruno Coppieters, and Ruben Apressyan

Realism   1
Militarism   5
Pacifism   7
Just War Theory   10
Questions of Terminology: Justice, War, and Theory   14

PART I: *Jus ad Bellum*

1   Just Cause   27
Bruno Coppieters, Carl Ceulemans, and Anthony Hartle

A General Approach   27
Individual and Collective Self-Defense   29
Humanitarian Intervention   43

2   Legitimate Authority   55
Bruno Coppieters

Background   55
Collaboration and Resistance: *La France Libre*   58
Revolutionary Movements   61
Anticolonial Struggles: Algeria, 1954–1962   62
The Security System of the United Nations   66
Conclusion   70

3   Right Intentions   73
    Bruno Coppieters and Boris Kashnikov

    The Just War Tradition   75
    Testing the Principle   78
    Bangladesh, 1971   80
    Hitler's Occupation of Czechoslovakia, 1938   83
    Hitler's Occupation of Poland, 1939   85
    The Soviet Occupation of Poland, 1939   86
    A Four-Step Approach to the Iraq War, 2003   88

4   The Likelihood of Success   101
    Nick Fotion and Bruno Coppieters

    Problems   101
    Luxembourg, 1940   103
    Belgium, 1940   104
    Thailand, 1940 and 1941   105
    Cuba in the 1950s   106
    Hezbollah   108
    Mini and Maxi   110
    Czechoslovakia, 1968   111
    North Korea   114
    Afghanistan and Iraq Compared   117
    Sacrifice and Mobilization   120

5   Proportionality   125
    Nick Fotion

    A Relational Principle   125
    Luxembourg and Belgium Again   128
    Mini and Maxi Again   128
    Divergence between Success and Proportionality Principles   130
    North Korea and the Bomb Again   132

6   Last Resort   139
    Bruno Coppieters, Ruben Apressyan, and Carl Ceulemans

    The United Nations   140
    Nuclear Crisis Management: The Cuban Missile Crisis
    of 1962   142
    Humanitarian Crisis Management: Bosnia, 1992–1995   147

PART II: *Jus in Bello*

    A Historical Overview of the *Jus in Bello* Constraints   155
    Guy Van Damme

7 Proportionality 159
Guy Van Damme and Nick Fotion

Underlying Assumptions 159
The Conduct of War 160
Nuclear Arms 164
Biological Arms 165
The Principle of Double Effect 167
Conclusion 169

8 Discrimination 171
Anthony Hartle

Noncombatant Immunity 171
Nuclear Weapons 178
Land Mines 181
Targeting 183
Economic Sanctions 184
Counterterrorism 186
Conclusion 188

PART III: Cases

9 The NATO Intervention in the Kosovo Crisis:
March–June 1999 195
Carl Ceulemans

Presentation of the Case 195
Just Cause 198
Right Intentions 199
Legitimate Authority 201
Last Resort 203
Likelihood of Success 206
Proportionality (*ad Bellum*) 210
Discrimination 212
Proportionality (*in Bello*) 213
Conclusion 215

10 NATO's Intervention in the Kosovo Crisis: Whose Justice? 219
Boris Kashnikov

Just Cause? 219
Legitimate Authority? 221
Right Intentions? 223
Likelihood of Success? 225
Last Resort? 227

Proportionality (*ad Bellum*)?   229
Winning Ugly: Discrimination and Proportionality (*in Bello*)   231
Conclusion   233

11   Kosovo and the Question of a Just Secession   237
     Bruno Coppieters

     Three Debates on Kosovo   237
     Military Intervention: The Case of Abkhazia   240
     International Administration: The Case of Chechnya   242
     Unilateral Independence: The Case of Kosovo   245
     Conclusion   254

12   Terrorism   261
     Nick Fotion

     The Nature of Terrorism   261
     The Morality of Terrorism   264
     Terrorist Arguments   265
     Assessing the Arguments   268

13   The War in Iraq: 2003 and Beyond   279
     Nick Fotion

     Background   279
     Just Cause   282
     Right Intentions   285
     Last Resort   286
     Likelihood of Success   287
     Proportionality (*Jus ad Bellum*)   289
     Legitimate Authority   289
     Proportionality (*Jus in Bello*)   290
     Discrimination   292
     Later Developments   295
     Conclusion   297

14   Concluding Comments   303
     Nick Fotion and Bruno Coppieters

     Realism, Pacifism, and Militarism Revisted   303
     Just War Theory and Excessive Optimism   308
     Excessive Pessimism   312
     A Universal Theory?   314

Index   317

About the Contributors   327

Preface

Bruno Coppieters and Nick Fotion

War! The idea has historically evoked widely varying emotions, from wild enthusiasm to brutal viciousness to heart-stopping fear. War has built empires, extended civilizations, and produced terrible suffering and destruction. It has had its horrors from its inception when the main weapons were the spear, dagger, mace, sling, and bow.[1] The bloody business of stabbing and hacking someone to death at close quarters enthralled some. But others wearied or were repelled by such acts. Often, after the battle, war exhibited still other horrors such as the slaughter of the elderly, women, and children. Then there were the horrors that followed in the wake of war, such as starvation and disease, which often put more people in their graves than the war itself.

These horrors have always been more than occasional human experiences. There have been thousands of wars since the Bronze Age, and even back at the time of the Mongols the killings were in the hundreds of thousands, sometimes in the millions.[2] In the twentieth century, World Wars I and II caused 10 million and 55 million deaths respectively.[3] And even today there are scores of little but nonetheless shockingly bloody wars in progress throughout the world. Thus it is not surprising that people have been thinking about war since it came into existence. Some of this thinking, for example by Sun Tzu in *The Art of War*[4] (written more than 2,000 years ago) and by Clausewitz in *On War*[5] (first published in 1832), focus mainly on how to wage war. Because war is such a nasty activity, these authors were presumably encouraged to make sure that their state was not on the losing side. Others were concerned with the rights and wrongs of war. The horrors of war encouraged them to think about what role, if any, morality has to play in war. The authors of this book share this moral concern.

The present volume is about justice and war. Teachers of ethics at universities and military academies in Belgium, Russia, and the United States are its authors. Seen from this perspective, it is not a common type of book. Literature on the subject of war ethics is generally written for a domestic public as the issues at stake are those morally relevant to a particular culture. That discussions on the ethics of war remain strongly constrained within domestic borders is demonstrated by national debates on any international crisis. As we will see, these debates employ different arguments in discussing for instance NATO's intervention in Kosovo in 1999 or the 2003 Iraq war.

Finding the discussion of war-ethics compartmentalized nationally contrasts sharply with the international tenor of political discussions pertaining to human rights. It also contrasts with the increasingly international nature of certain military activities such as peacekeeping operations under the auspices of the UN. And finally, it contrasts with the moral approach to war as embodied in Just War Theory viewed strictly as a theory. As this book will make clear, this theory has its roots in transcultural experiences, concepts, and principles.

The concern of the scholarly community with domestic discussions on the ethics of war reflects the concerns of their public opinion. Scholars do not stand outside the body politic, and their contributions to national debates often reflect the political concerns of the nation in which they work. The moral attitude of the public and political elites in Russia, Western Europe, and the United States to the issues of war and military intervention vary significantly. This compartmentalization may be highlighted by the different reactions of different states to security issues. Since the beginning of the 1990s, Russia, Western Europe, and the United States have confronted four types of threat, against which the institutionalization of their security cooperation has often failed to provide adequate international responses.

The first type is interstate in nature and emerged between the United States and its Western allies, on the one hand, and a number of states that were accused of infringing the rules of international order, on the other. Afghanistan, Iran, Iraq, Libya, North Korea, Sudan, and Syria have been accused in the past or are still accused of either attacking neighboring states or developing military capacity in weapons of mass destruction or supporting terrorist activities. The conflict was worst with Iraq. After the Iraqi invasion of Kuwait on 2 August 1990, Western members of the UN Security Council persuaded their Soviet partner to develop a coercive approach toward Iraq by supporting a UN sanctions policy and the use of "all necessary means" to restore Kuwait's sovereignty. After the Gulf War in 1991, there was no lifting of sanctions. In the ensuing years, however, disagreements emerged among Russia, some Western European states, and the United

States concerning the legitimacy of this method.[6] Such disagreements largely reflected not only conflicts of national interest but also the increasingly widespread understanding that the embargo regime had failed to achieve concrete results. The dictatorship of Saddam Hussein remained strongly entrenched in power. The embargo policies caused the gradual but relentless destruction of the economy and infrastructure of what had been a relatively wealthy country. The consequences of the 1991 war, such as the breakdown in water supply and sanitation and the destruction of hospitals and schools, were worsened by the Iraqi inability to repair those services. According to a study conducted at Columbia University, between 100,000 and 227,000 children under five died between 1991 and 1998 as a result of the Gulf War and sanctions. A UNICEF report estimated that half a million children under five had died.[7] The sanctions targeting Saddam Hussein's regime struck mainly civilians, and first and foremost the most vulnerable of these—children and the old. Thus one of the basic Just War Theory principles—the Principle of Discrimination between combatants and noncombatants—was infringed.

Such disagreements concerning the right method for dealing with the governments of Iran, Iraq, or North Korea became even more prominent after the terrorist attacks on the United States on September 11, 2001. The Americans received widespread support for their policies toward Afghanistan, which had provided shelter to al-Qaeda, but not for other foreign policy priorities. In January 2002, President George W. Bush appealed to law-abiding nations to use all means possible to stop the production of weapons of mass destruction by rogue states and, in addition, to halt their support to terrorist groups. He said that Iran, Iraq, and North Korea constituted an "axis of evil." This demonizing language was strongly opposed by a number of European Union governments, such as France and Germany. They considered that a political dialogue with the governments of some of those states, such as Iran, might encourage them to cooperate in the struggle against terrorism.

The international community was deeply divided on the need to use force against the Iraqi regime of Saddam Hussein. The United States and the United Kingdom declared that disarming Iraq of all weapons of mass destruction had to be regarded as a just cause for the use of force. This war was preceded by intensive—and often also passionate—debates among the members of the UN Security Council on the right way to prevent the proliferation of weapons of mass destruction. The American administration thought that intervention against Iraq would act as a deterrent to all rogue states engaged in the illegal acquisition of these weapons. But other members of the UN Security Council did not agree with the American and British position that a war against Iraq could be considered as a war of self-defense. The United States and United Kingdom claimed that they had strong evidence of Iraq's unwillingness to destroy all its stocks of weapons of mass destruction, as ordered by UN Security Council resolutions for more than a decade. The two governments claimed they were convinced that Saddam Hussein's regime not only possessed some of these weapons but also had the firm intention of developing them further and using them against the Western world. In their view, all attempts at further negotiations with Iraq in order to achieve its disarmament were doomed to fail. This debate was not only pursued in diplomatic circles: public opinion all over the world was heavily engaged in political mobilization for or against the war. The present volume will deal with the basic Just War Theory principles as they arise in such debates.

The second type of new conflict confronting Russia, China, Western Europe, and the United States is intrastate in nature. The security regime developed after World War II with the creation of the United Nations, the Conference on Security and Cooperation in Europe (CSCE), and the Organization of African Unity (OAU) was designed to address classic cases of sovereign states warring against each other (interstate conflicts). But such organizations were quite helpless in dealing with violent internal conflicts. The disintegration of the federal systems of the Soviet Union and Yugoslavia at the beginning of the 1990s led to the creation—and the recognition by the international community—of new sovereign states (the fifteen Union republics of the Soviet Union and the five republics of Yugoslavia). It also led to demands for sovereign statehood by several ethnic minorities in these new states. This process of disintegration generated secessionist conflicts in the Caucasus, Moldova, and the Balkans. Tajikistan was confronted with disintegration along regional lines in a civil war that threatened its survival as a state (1992–1997). Russia started two wars against secessionist Chechnya (in 1994 and 1999), while NATO intervened militarily in Bosnia (1995) and Kosovo (1999).

In Rwanda, the conflict between Hutus and Tutsis escalated in 1994 to become one of the worst examples of genocide of the twentieth century. There were some 800,000 people butchered among the Tutsi population. The failure of the United Nations to intervene in this conflict, and in particular the failure of countries such as Belgium and France to address this crisis with the necessary military means, has generated a good deal of criticism. It is now assumed that a relatively small military contingent could have halted the murdering.

In most of these cases, it was extremely difficult for Russia, China, Western Europe, and the United States to agree on common principles for intervention. The most serious international crisis over an intrastate conflict occurred in 1999 with NATO's intervention in Kosovo, a region of Serbia where the Albanian majority was striving to secede. The escalating conflict with the Serbian authorities led to widespread violence and ethnic cleansing, which was used as the main argument for NATO to intervene in 1999. The Russian and Chinese governments criticized NATO's lack of legitimate authority to intervene militarily in Kosovo since, it was said, NATO was interfering in the internal affairs of Serbia. Basing their criticism on international law, the Russian and Chinese governments claimed that only the UN Security Council could take such a decision. As we will show in this volume, where this case is discussed in depth, such criticism relates to the application of classic principles of Just War Theory.

The third security issue to which Russia, China, the member states of the European Union, and the United States respond differently is nuclear arms control and the proliferation of other weapons of mass destruction. The nuclear powers have not honored their commitment under the Nuclear Non-Proliferation Treaty (NPT)—which seeks to inhibit the use of nuclear energy for military purposes—to reduce their nuclear arsenals. Under this multilateral treaty they all solemnly declared "their intention to achieve at the earliest possible date the cessation of the nuclear arms race and to undertake effective measures in the direction of nuclear disarmament."[8] Mohamed ElBaradei, director-general of the International Atomic Energy Agency (IAEA), blamed these powers for not having done enough in this respect in recent years.[9] The major nuclear powers further disagree about how to deal with the question of proliferation of nuclear and other weapons of mass destruction (WMD). This issue is closely linked to the first one mentioned above, namely the attitude of the American administration toward what it calls "rogue states." In this volume, it will be shown how the arguments put forward in the international debates on Iran's nuclear program are related to the Just Cause Principle in Just War Theory.

Fourth, the international community remains deeply divided in its attitude to terrorism, all the more so as it is closely linked to all three of the other divisive issues mentioned above. There is broad agreement that terrorist movements constitute a threat that needs an international response, but there is no consensus on the definition of terrorism, its root causes, or on what an appropriate response would be. For some countries, terrorist attacks have led to a complete paradigm shift in their thinking (and spending) on security and defense, while other countries have not given these attacks such a prominent place on their national security agenda. International cooperation in criminal investigations related to terrorism and the exchange of information remains a problem. Some authoritarian governments now label nonviolent opposition groups as terrorist in order to outlaw them, in the expectation that the universal condemnation of terrorism will give them a free hand in their repression. But such governments do not always manage to avoid condemnation by other countries, particularly when the improvement of their human rights record and the democratization of their society are seen by other nations as a far better remedy for improving their security than authoritarianism. Repression of terrorism also involves questions of International Humanitarian Law. During the last few years the United States and the United Kingdom, which are close allies in the "war against terror," have repeatedly disagreed on the question of how to treat prisoners of war from Afghanistan and the concrete application of the principle of discrimination on the Iraqi battlefield.

A first edition of *Moral Constraints on War* was published in 2002. Since then there have been significant worldwide changes in how wars are started and how they are fought. The questions of armed conflicts within states, of nuclear proliferation, of asymmetry between warring parties, and of guerrilla tactics and terrorism are not new questions in the ethics of war, but they became even more prominent with the Iraq war of 2003 and other discussions on the use of force. This second edition takes account of these recent discussions. It also gives an account of the Iraq war that started after the original publication of this book. It has therefore been largely rewritten to reflect the shifts in our thinking about security, and in particular the greater emphasis on issues pertaining to terrorism and the proliferation of nuclear weapons.

Like the first edition, the second is divided into three parts. Before the first part, an introductory chapter situates Just War Theory among contending approaches to the ethics of war, such as Realism, Militarism, and Pacifism. It then outlines some of the main methodological problems in writing a book on Just War Theory. Some terminological problems, such as the definition of war and the conception of justice in Just War Theory, are also analyzed. The Introduction finally raises the question of the extent to which such an approach may claim to constitute a theory, as opposed to merely a tradition.

As in the first edition, Part I here deals with the six principles of *jus ad bellum*, the principles that determine the conditions on which a war may be started. Part II analyzes the two *jus in bello* principles of Just War Theory, that is, the ones dealing with the principles to be followed once a war begins. Each principle is analyzed in a separate chapter, its length depending roughly on its importance in the systematic framework of Just War Theory. The analysis of each principle is illustrated by a variety of historical examples.

Part 3 applies the various principles of parts 1 and 2 to military interventions. In this second edition, chapters devoted to the Gulf War (1990–1991), the First Chechen War (1994–1996), and the U.S.-led intervention in Afghanistan (2001) have been deleted in order to make room for three new chapters, one on the application of Just War Theory to the question of the international status of Kosovo, one on terrorism, and one chapter on the Iraq war. Two chapters on NATO's intervention in Kosovo (1999) are retained. As before, the final chapter is titled "Concluding Comments."

The contributors to this volume do not necessarily share the same opinion concerning the legitimacy of using force in the different cases. They do not even necessarily share the same opinion on how to interpret the various just war principles, or the theory itself. Such differences in approach are a natural consequence of the specifically pluralistic character of Just War Theory. Agreeing with a verdict concerning the legitimacy of the use of force in a certain case is only possible if the same abstract principles are applied to a situation where there are no major differences concerning its interpretation. In our case, it was not so much the importance of the various principles that was an issue in the sometimes heated discussions we had in preparing this book, but rather their concrete meaning in a particular context, and whether particular conflicts had been correctly described and analyzed. Some disagreements about factual accuracy could be dealt with by a more thorough analysis of the literature available and by an appeal to various historical sources. But description and analysis are also the result of a large number of presuppositions and value orientations. Where differences of opinion remained, we have expressed them by mentioning the possibility of various ethical perspectives. This book includes two different applications of the Right Intentions Principle to the Iraq war and also diverging definitions of terrorism. Further, disagreements led to two opposed views on NATO's 1999 war on Kosovo. Most chapters of this book have been coauthored by different participants in the project, and the names of the authors are indicated at the beginning of each chapter.

This project received support from a great number of institutions and individuals in Belgium, China, Russia, and the United States. We would like to thank the Belgian Royal Military Academy, the Belgian Ministry of Defense, and the Vrije Universiteit Brussel for financing the project, including the Russian and Chinese versions of the first edition of this book.[10] Further support has been received from the Fund for Scientific Research (Flanders, Belgium), United States Military Academy of West Point, NATO, Institute of Philosophy of the Russian Academy of Sciences, Carnegie Moscow Center, Ryazan branch of the Moscow Institute of the Russian Ministry of Internal Affairs, U.S. Embassy in Belgium, Emory University, the Fulbright Scholar Program, and the American Council for International Exchange of Scholars (CIES). We are particularly grateful to Werner Bauwens, Pol De Witte, Knut Dörmann, Chris Donnelly, Michael Emerson, André Flahaut, Erik Franckx, Paul Georis, Andrea Huterer, Veronica Kelly, Anthony F. Lang, Nicu Popescu, Jean-Paul Salmon, Stefaan Smis, Xiaokun Song, Xinning Song, Neri Sybesma-Knol, Nathalie Tocci, Dmitri Trenin, Jan Van de Weyer, Marc Vankeirsbilck, Leo Vermaere, and Alexei Zverev for their comments on our drafts or other forms of support to this project. The reviews published in

Millennium, Review of International Studies, Journal of Peace Research, Journal of Military Ethics, Choice, and in the electronic *Ethics Today Newsletter* and *H-Net Reviews* were particularly helpful in preparing this second edition.

Finally, we extend our thanks to the anonymous reader for Lexington Books who looked upon our project with favor and to Martin Hayward, Jason Proetorius, Serena Krombach, and Joseph Parry at Lexington Books, who helped see the project through to its successful completion.

NOTES

1. Arther Ferrill, *The Origins of War: From the Stone Age to Alexander the Great* (London: Thames and Hudson Ltd, 1985), 18–19.

2. Luc Kwanton, *Imperial Nomads: A History of Central Asia 500–1500* (Philadelphia: University of Pennsylvania Press, 1979), 121.

3. Larry H. Addington, *The Patterns of War Since the Eighteenth Century* (Bloomington: Indiana University Press, 1984), 157, 248.

4. Sun Tzu, *The Art of War,* ed. James Clavell (New York: Dell Publishing, 1983).

5. Carl von Clausewitz, *On War,* trans. and ed. Michael Howard and Peter Peret (Princeton, N.J.: Princeton University Press, 1976).

6. Lakhadar Brahimi, "Foreword" to *Political Gain and Civilian Pain,* ed. Thomas G. Weiss, David Cortright, George A. Lopez, and Larry Minear (Lanham, Md.: Rowman & Littlefield, 1997), xiii.

7. *Economist,* 8–14 April 2000.

8. Treaty on the Non-Proliferation of Nuclear Weapons, www.iaea.org/Publications/Documents/Treaties/npt.html (accessed 14 February 2008).

9. Quentin Peel and Daniel Dombey, "A System Shaken: Pyongyang Deals a Blow to Nuclear Non-Proliferation," *Financial Times,* 10 October 2006, 11.

10. Bruno Coppieters, Nick Fotion, and Ruben Apressyan (obschaya redaktsiya), *Nravstvennie ogranicheniya vojny. Problemi i primeri* (Moscow: Gardariki, 2002), poli.vub.ac.be/ (accessed 8 February 2008) and Bruno Coppieters, Nick Fotion, and Yinhong Shi, eds., *Zhanzheng de daode zhiyue: lengzhan hou jubu zhanzheng de zhexue sikao* (Beijing: Law Press, 2003), www.cesruc.org/upload//moral.pdf (accessed 8 February 2008).

Introduction

Nick Fotion, Bruno Coppieters, and Ruben Apressyan

REALISM

The killing, the maiming, and the destruction associated with almost all wars has led to the development of four lines of thought about the ethics of war. One of these lines has come to be known as Realism.[1] Realists fully appreciate war's horrors and so, just like most others, try desperately to assess its costs, especially to their own nation. In this connection, they are fond of saying that war is hell. But realists also react to war in terms of its benefits. They know that at times war yields gains to a nation in the form of land and resources. However when they come to their concern about war, realists argue that war is a nonmoral activity. For them, war and ethics are two kinds of activity that have little or nothing to do with one another. More specifically, when the defenders of Strong Realism present their position they make two claims.

First, they say that even during peacetime there are no significant moral relationships between nations, the way there can be between people who live within one nation. Individual people within a nation or society can morally help or hurt one another in a variety of ways. When they plan to kill and then actually kill one another, we condemn them morally. But, according to strong realists, moral rules against planning and then deciding to kill, maim, steal, lie, and so on, have no application when nations are involved. Thus, when a nation is considering going to war with another nation, it does not have to consult moral reasons (i.e., those that take the interests of other nations and their people into account) before actually starting the war.

Second, strong realists claim that once a war starts, moral considerations remain inoperative. Thus warring nations cannot be criticized for how they point, they will likely employ their power overtly, and act in ways that are not even in accordance with the principles of morality.

The second comment pertains to the claim that Realism represents a non-moral stance with respect to war. This claim, it was said, needs qualifying. The reason is that some realists claim that their theory actually falls within the domain of ethics.[9] The form that their national ethics takes is of rulers doing their duty to protect the state and the people within it. In principle this position could be expanded to say that, overall, more good results are achieved when all nations look after the interests of their own people first and foremost. In this expanded form, then, these realists claim that they are indirectly taking account of the interests of "foreigners" in their thinking. Needless to say, this is dubious since in carrying out their duties to their own people, rulers could order attacks on and even order the elimination of those who are not their own.

The third, and final, comment on Realism has to do with more variations on the position. Because Realism is a two-part theory, dealing with conditions for starting a war and those for fighting it, the possibility arises that there are realists about one part but not the other. In this sense, a realist may very well say that his country's leaders should articulate a concept of national interest for their public, without ever declaring that in case such a concept leads to war, they should fight an immoral war.

In contrast, William Tecumseh Sherman, the American Civil War general fighting on the side of the Union, considered that the Civil War was the crime of those who started it. So once that war started, the transgressor must pay and soldiers can never be blamed for doing what they must to bring it to a quick end. When he was accused by a Confederate commander of committing a most cruel act of war in ordering the evacuation of and then the burning of Atlanta, he did not deny the charge. Rather, he stated that such cruelty was necessary. All acts of war are dark. Sherman was determined that Atlanta should never again serve as a military depot for the Confederates. In his view, the leaders of the Southern States were fully responsible for the war and they could restore peace only by obeying the Federal Constitution. Sherman is a not a realist before the war starts but seemed to be one after it does. Here is Sherman's classic statement of his version of Realism:

> You cannot qualify war in harsher terms than I will. War is cruelty, and you cannot refine it; and those who brought war into our country deserve all the curses and maledictions a people can pour out. . . . You might as well appeal against a thunderstorm as against these terrible hardships of war. They are inevitable, and the only way the people of Atlanta can hope once more to live in peace and quiet at home, is to stop the war, which can only be done by admitting that it began in error and is perpetuated by pride.[10]

In sum, Realism is a highly variant position that one way or another eliminates or diminishes the role of ethics in war. What it says is that anything is fair when it comes to war, which is a roundabout way of saying that fairness, justice, ethics, and so on, have nothing to do with war. Instead of ethics, Realism says that a nation's concern should be with its self-interest.

MILITARISM

A second line of thought in response to war's horrors is Militarism. It is easily confused with Realism since both positions seem to be permissive when it comes to war. It can also be confused because some forms of Militarism have a nationalistic basis, as does Realism.[11] As we will see, another reason for confusion is that some nations vacillate between following realist policies and militaristic ones, in large part because of the difficulties of implementing the militaristic doctrine. However, in spite of these reasons for confusion, there are significant differences between the two positions. Realists, such as Sun Tzu, try to avoid war or try to mitigate its costs and horrors.[12] One way they do this is to form alliances in order to achieve a balance of power against powerful and threatening nations. If this balancing strategy does not work, realists may recommend that their nation go to war. But they will do so reluctantly unless, of course, they see that their nation has a clear advantage that allows it to win the war easily.

Militarists are also aware of war's horrors but are convinced, in contrast to realists, that these horrors are much more than compensated for by the gains of war. For Militarists, war transforms individuals into what they were not, and perhaps could not be, before. It makes Men out of men. It gives those who participate in war a sense of identity and accomplishment. It also develops their character. The rigors of war teach those who participate in it such virtues as discipline, self-confidence, perseverance, loyalty, responsibility, and courage. So along with the costs of war, there are also important gains for the individual who lives in the militaristic society.

But there are gains for the nation as well. War turns the nation from a collection of individuals or members of this or that group into a single Community. It unites the people by giving them a common purpose. They now develop a sense of "we." They now think and talk in terms of "We fought hard, we won the war, and we will win the next one." This is how the Spartans began to think in the eighth century B.C.E. after they had conquered Messenia.[13] Outnumbered seven to one by the Messenians, whom they had turned into state slaves (helots), the Spartans were forced to develop and then sustain a military establishment to retain their dominance. The establishment was nourished by the work the helots were forced to do; which, in turn, served to keep the helots enslaved.

Militarism is, perhaps, easier to create and sustain in a small and relatively simple society such as Sparta. Still, in modern times, Japan evidently became a militaristic state after World War I.[14] Although already a complex society, it managed to become militaristic because it was culturally very homogeneous and had a divine-like leader to help focus its loyalties. Italy's Fascist Militarism was less successful. Mussolini found it difficult to convert farmer and worker thinking to the militaristic ideology.[15] These and other groups within Italy had their own agendas (e.g., land reform and higher wages) so they did not find the militaristic ideology particularly enthralling. To the extent that Mussolini succeeded in militarizing Italy, he did so with the military establishment itself (mostly the officer class) and with some but not all government officials. With others, he appealed to a realist doctrine. It was easier for Italy as a whole to respond to an appeal to the nation's self-interest than to the personal and social demands of Militarism. In contrast, Nazi Germany became more militaristic than Italy in part because of Hitler's strong leadership and because of the exigencies of a long and desperate war that Germany fought against Great Britain, the United States, the USSR, and other nations.[16]

Enemies of the militarist "crusade" are found not only abroad but at home as well. At home those who are labeled enemies are not just those who oppose the "crusade" but include those who are passive and thus do nothing to support it. Both must be treated ruthlessly. Indeed, there is reason to be more ruthless with the "enemies from within" since they are apostates and traitors who corrupt the society.[17] But ruthlessness is also the order of the day when dealing with enemies abroad. The cause for which the typical militarist fights is important, and even sacred, so halfway measures are not to be tolerated. More than that, the cause is said to be urgent. It is as if society and the world are suffering from an acute and dangerous illness that can be cured only by the radical surgery of war.

So there are two key differences between militarists and realists. The first is that the former is more prone to go to war than the latter. For militarists war is the first resort in dealing with the ills of society and the world, whereas for realists it is not. The second is that, with their talk about the virtues and fighting for some higher purpose, militarists leave war within the realm of ethics whereas realists do not. The militarist enmity toward Pacifism is likewise ethically motivated. In one of his pamphlets, Benito Mussolini rejected Pacifism and glorified war on moral grounds.

> Where the future and development of humanity are concerned generally speaking, and leaving aside any considerations to do with current policy fascism believes, above all, that perpetual peace is neither possible nor useful. It rejects Pacifism, which is a cover for fleeing in the face of struggle and cowardice in the face of sacrifice. War alone lifts all human energies to a state of

maximum tension, stamping the hallmark of nobility on those peoples who have the courage to confront it. All other ordeals are but secondary, and never bring man face to face with his own self, where he is forced to choose between life and death.[18]

PACIFISM

Pacifism represents the third line of thought in reaction to the horrors of war. Pacifism is a doctrine according to which war is morally wrong. It encourages everyone to reject immediately the ideas of war, Militarism, and violence. But Pacifism is often used in a broader sense. It may be thought of as a centuries-old ideological trend based on the belief that war is a phenomenon of human history that should be *eventually* eliminated. This desire to abolish war, going back to the philosophers Erasmus and Immanuel Kant, has found a practical expression in the development of international law and the foundation of the League of Nations and the United Nations.[19] But such a definition of Pacifism is probably too broad to say anything substantial about the use of force. No state leader of any respectable country would publicly deny that humanity should strive for a peaceful world where war will be banned forever. Most responsible Russian or Western citizens would likewise consider war as an absolute evil which humankind should try to abolish the way slavery was. At the same time, however, many of these same citizens think that their governments should build up an efficient military defense. They may have supported military involvement by their governments in the past, and may do so again in the future.

A similar problem arises when using Pacifism in a very narrow sense, as an opposition to the use of a particular category of weapons. Such a problem arises with the term of "nuclear pacifism." Many of the mass mobilizations in the United States and Western Europe after World War II against the escalation of nuclear arms have often been labeled in the media and history books as being pacifist. But this kind of antiwar movement was primarily opposed to nuclear deterrence policies that, in the view of the protesters, would inevitably lead to nuclear war and the destruction of the whole planet. These mobilizations were not directed at the legitimacy of military defense as such.[20] The participants were not necessarily motivated by moral concerns that can be considered pacifist in nature. Various other arguments ("it is not in the national interest to pursue nuclear deterrence policies any further") played a role as well. This narrow use of the term Pacifism is not appropriate to our purposes. We try to describe basic ethical attitudes toward problems of war and peace. In the following, we will therefore concentrate on two versions of Pacifism that: (a) defend a relatively coherent set of moral arguments on this issue, and (b) are qualitatively different from the other three basic lines of thought about the ethics of war discussed in this introduction. The first version may be labeled "religious Pacifism" and the second "nonviolent resistance." Those two versions are not mutually exclusive. Some Peace Churches and individuals—such as the Russian writer Leo Tolstoy—are part of the histories of both.

The first kind of Pacifism is motivated by religious and spiritual opposition to war. In the West, it is rooted in Christianity and was particularly strong in the first centuries of our era. Medieval heretical movements (such as the Czech Brethren), as well as Protestant Peace Churches in modern times, like the Quakers, the Mennonites, the Amish, and the Dukhobors (originally from Russia, but the majority now live in Canada) took up the initial Christian tradition. They based their pacifist views on the New Testament precepts such as those in the Sermon on the Mount but especially on such sayings as "Blessed are the peacemakers" (Matthew 5:9). These communities did not oppose the need for the state to organize military service or to defend the country with military means. For these religious communities, the state was a necessary vehicle of social order.[21] But their religious views prohibited them from assuming military duties or military service. This rule was based on a strict division between the "church" and the "world." The pacifist communities regarded themselves as a group of believers, whose nonviolent stance would ensure their salvation.

There are various kinds of religious Pacifism.[22] In spite of peculiarities in their moral foundation, they all urge individuals to abstain from the use of force based on certain universal principles. Among the principles that figure prominently are the inner light of a divine spirit present in everyone, charity, reason, and the initial openness of every human being to the transcendent world. Many of these principles are well expressed in the philosophical writings of Leo Tolstoy, one of the most famous figures in the history of religious Pacifism. He radicalized many of the moral prescriptions found in the religious pacifist tradition. Central in his thought was the biblical quotation "Ye have heard, it was said of old, An eye for an eye, a tooth for a tooth, but I say unto you, Resist not evil" (Matthew 5:38–39).[23] Tolstoy did not understand this phrase as an appeal to passive submission to evil, but as an injunction to moral resistance to violence. In his view, moral resistance consists primarily in not doing the evil you may be ordered to do by public officials. He opposed not only state policies but also the legitimacy of the state. The state is the instrument of violence and Christians should therefore not participate in politics and hold public office: "Government is violence, Christianity is meekness, non-resistance, love. And, therefore, Government cannot be Christian, and a man who wishes to be a Christian must not serve Government."[24] The maxim of nonparticipation in government politics, if raised to the level of a universal law, renders sovereign political power superfluous. Tolstoy considered armies to be the means by which governments:

accomplish the greatest atrocities, the possibility of perpetrating which gives them power over the people. The only means therefore to destroy Governments is not by force, but by the exposure of this fraud. It is necessary that people should understand . . . that in Christendom there is no need to protect the people, one from another; that the enmity of the peoples, one to another, is produced by the Governments themselves; and that armies are only needed for the advantage of the small number who rule.[25]

This Russian writer and philosopher had a tremendous influence on pacifist movements all over the world. Mohandas Gandhi's struggle for Indian independence and Martin Luther King Jr.'s actions for civil rights in the United States were inspired by his writings. Their political campaigns insisted upon the need for resistance against injustices, but resistance without using military or, broader, physical force against persons. Following Gandhi, those who favor nonviolent resistance use the word "opponent" rather than enemy to indicate an assailant. They further stress the need for continuing the dialogue with their "opponents."

This last point can be taken as the starting point for understanding the thinking of a contemporary American pacifist, or nonviolentist as he prefers to call himself. Robert Holmes argues that indeed the dialogue with one's opponent must be kept going.[26] Talking things over furthers understanding. On his view, wars start in large part because we do not understand one another very well. We, as individuals and representatives of government, have limited knowledge especially in situations of conflict. Efforts to enhance our knowledge of war's dangers and of the "other side's" views cannot help but delay, and perhaps delay indefinitely, the onset of war. In contrast, efforts to resolve the problem by use of threats and other strong-arm tactics cannot help but make matters worse. If the dialogue is allowed to continue, then there is every reason to believe that wars could in theory become extinct. Of course, there is no guarantee that this will happen. So Holmes is no absolute pacifist. He allows for the theoretical possibility that war could be justified. So he calls himself a conditional pacifist or nonviolentist. But short of making a far greater effort to foster understanding than most nations are willing to do, going to war cannot, on his view, be justified.

Acting nonviolently, as Holmes proposes, does not exclude acting assertively.[27] Nonviolent resistance has traditionally been associated with reform movements on the domestic level, such as the campaign against racial discrimination in the United States or the overthrow of authoritarian regimes in Eastern Europe. The Serbian leader Slobodan Milosevic was ousted from power in October 2000 by a vast political mobilization organized in protest against falsified parliamentary elections. This mobilization was led by the student movement Otpor, which followed a nonviolent strategy. This example was followed in Georgia, where the government of Eduard Shevardnadze, accused of corruption, was brought down by nonviolent means in the so-called Rose Revolution in 2003.[28] But nonviolent resistance has also significance for defense policies. Thus when negotiations with aggressors fail and all attempts at negotiation prove fruitless, a nation may still have capabilities for *civil*, that is, nonviolent, resistance—the second version of Pacifism. For its pacifist advocates, civilian-based defense (CBD)[29] may become a full alternative[30] to ordinary (i.e., military means) of repulsing aggression. CBD may be defined as a system of deterrence based upon the capability of a population to defend itself with nonviolent means.[31] A policy of nonviolent action attempts to weaken the occupation regime by withdrawing cooperation. This can be done openly by such means as strikes and sit-ins or more clandestinely by work slowdowns, the destruction of information useful to the invader, boycotts, and so forth. All these actions aim at denying an oppressor the fruits of his wrongdoing and supremacy.[32] CBD's possible application depends primarily upon psychological and social factors, such as the moral determination of the citizens to refuse collaboration with the enemy, their ability to organize nonviolent resistance, their technical training, and discipline. The effectiveness of CBD further assumes that an aggressor is not prepared to use all means necessary to achieve its goals. CBD will, for instance, not reach its goals if the aggressor has no interest in the economic potential of the country and is ready to destroy it completely. It also assumes that the aggressor has a certain interest in having the population maintain a positive or at least a neutral attitude. Finally, it assumes that the aggressor is concerned about its public opinion at home and on the international stage.[33]

JUST WAR THEORY

If Pacifism represents a line of thought at one extreme in saying that wars are immoral, and Realism the other in saying that they are nonmoral, Just War Theory sits in the middle. It says that some wars are, while others are not, immoral. Sitting in the middle makes the position vulnerable to attack from both sides. On one side, pacifists claim that just war theorists are permissive of war; on the other, realists claim that just war theorists take nations to the wrong wars for the wrong reasons.

Just war theorists are vulnerable for another reason. They are also subject to attack from militarists who insist that their advocacy of war is also moral (ethical) in nature. But these theorists have a totally different view on the ethics of war. Putting it crudely, whereas militarists see much moral good coming from war and thus advocate it as a means to the nation's moral rebirth, just war theorists are more aware of war's danger and thus strive to place moral constraints on the use of force. Insofar, then, as just war theorists have to defend themselves from criticism from various sides, the task they face is daunting.

The tradition of Just War Theory is a long one. In the West it goes back at least to the Christians and the writings of St. Augustine.[34] Faced with the reality of supporting a recently Christianized Roman Empire, Augustine found that he had to come to terms with war. He could not easily adopt a pacifist stance as some of the earlier unempowered Christians did. Since the Empire was at that time under attack from "heathens" of all kind, he had to consider urging Christians, who were champions of peace, to go to war. So he faced this reality and, in the process, articulated some of the principles of Just War Theory, as we know them today. These include the Principle of Just Cause (i.e., a nation or empire must have good reasons for going to war) and Principle of Legitimate Authority (i.e., only certain legally situated officials can take a nation into war), among others. Later, St. Thomas Aquinas developed Just War Theory still more but did so, as did Augustine, within the framework of the Church. Still, later, especially with the work of Hugo Grotius, that tradition became secularized.

However, the Just War Tradition has a history even before Augustine. St. Ambrose wrote on the subject, but before him the tradition goes back to the Romans and even to the Greeks. Cicero, with the former, and both Plato and Aristotle with the latter, wrote about the moral issues facing leaders and soldiers when they go to war. But it would be misleading to suppose that the Just War Tradition is wholly Western. In ancient China, Mo Tzu[35] and Mencius[36] both wrote about the injustices facing people and the necessity, at times, of taking up arms to remedy them. And in India we find a discussion of war and the ethics of war in *The Laws of Manu*[37] and *The Bhagavad Gita*.[38] So the tradition of Just War Theory is truly intercultural.

As we know it today, Just War Theory possesses a certain degree of uniformity. Most contemporary followers of the theory agree, on the surface at any rate, on the structure of the theory and what the principles constitute. About the structure, a division is made between *jus ad bellum* (justice having to do with starting a war) and *jus in bello* (justice once the war has started). Just war theorists argue that criteria for helping a nation determine when it is morally justified in going to war (*jus ad bellum*) and how that war is to be morally fought (*jus in bello*) are needed. The principles or criteria related to *jus ad bellum* usually come to six. A brief discussion of each follows. Each criterion will be discussed in more detail in separate chapters of this work.

The first criterion or principle, already anticipated in the earlier reference to Augustine, is Just Cause. This criterion can also be called righteous cause, or the very good reasons criterion. None of these names is especially helpful in understanding what concrete reason will morally permit a nation to go to war. Realizing this, just war theorists add substance to this principle by saying that any one of the following subcriteria will satisfy it. If nation A aggresses and thus victimizes nation V in the sense that A's military forces cross the border into V uninvited, engage in wholesale destruction, and occupy parts of V, then V is justified in responding militarily. So, national self-defense counts as a good reason for entering into war. Or, if A aggresses against F, a friend or ally of V, then V can justifiably enter into the war even if it is not been attacked itself. Another subcriterion concerns A's aggressive behavior against its own people. If A, in consort with a large ethnic group within A, practices genocide on another group, then the international community can justifiably enter the war on humanitarian grounds.

Although within Just War Theory, Just Cause is a necessary condition for going to war, it is not sufficient. The other five criteria must be applied as well. One of these five is the Principle of Legitimate Authority. It is quite different from the rest in that it does not directly tell us how to deal with an impending war. Rather, it tells us that only certain people are authorized to make the decision whether to go or not go to war. The authorized ones are not private citizens, private organizations, generals, business leaders, or philosophy professors, but instead they are national officials and institutions of a certain sort (e.g., presidents and legislatures). However, others besides national leaders can count as legitimate authorities. For instance, in certain circumstances, the Security Council of the United Nations may act as a legitimate authority if there is a threat to the peace, a breach of the peace, or an act of aggression. National liberation movements opposing colonial regimes can, in certain circumstances, also be considered to have legitimate authority to defend their right to self-determination with the use of force. However, the legitimate authority of violent movements for secession in a noncolonial context has been contested. It is also questionable under what conditions and to what extent revolutionary movements may be considered to have legitimate authority to use force for a just cause.

The third criterion of Just War Theory is the Good Intentions Principle. In the past this principle was read as saying that a nation, especially its fighters, would not enter a war with hate in their hearts. Nowadays, the Right Intentions Principle usually means something a little easier to measure and a little less demanding. It now means that the nation should enter a war with the intent of acting in accordance with the just cause that prompted it to go to war in the first place. So if nation V responds to an aggression, the good intentions of V would simply be to stop the aggression and, perhaps, punish the wrongdoers. V would not use the war as an excuse to gain territory that it has always coveted.

The fourth criterion, Principle of Likelihood of Success is related to the fifth, the Principle of Proportionality. These two prudential principles refer directly to how the Just Cause Principle is to be realized. The Likelihood of Success Principle says that if there is no reasonable chance for a country to successfully prevent or to correct severe injustices by going to war, then its leaders should not go to war.

The Principle of Proportionality says that the anticipated evils or moral costs of fighting the war should not be out of line with the goods or moral benefits. But what this principle means precisely is often not clear. Does it mean that a war is just only if the anticipated benefits are greater than the anticipated costs? Or is it good enough that the costs and benefits are about equal? There is another problem having to do with how costs and benefits are measured. How, for instance, are the benefits of going to war in order to deter future aggressors to be measured? Then there is the related problem of predicting how long the war will last, and how nasty it will become. The expression "the fog of war" clearly expresses the difficulties inherent in the application of this principle.

The sixth and final criterion under the *jus ad bellum* heading is the Last Resort Principle. Some take this principle as urging the move to war only after "no stone has been left unturned." But that is probably more hyperbole than good advice since the process of looking at all the options is literally endless. There is always another negotiating move, sanction, political maneuver, boycott, and so on, to be tried before firing the guns and unleashing the missiles. So probably the Last Resort Principle should be taken as meaning something like last reasonable resort. Before resorting to war, it should be perfectly clear that all further diplomatic efforts are meaningless. In effect, the Last Resort Principle discourages trigger-happy responses in response to provocations. The principle favors cool over hot heads.

In contrast to the *jus ad bellum* war criteria that do their work before the war starts, the *jus in bello* criteria do theirs after it starts. Theorists usually cite two criteria. The first is Discrimination. Somehow or other those in war are supposed to discriminate so that some of the enemy are targets of a legitimate attack while others are not. A not wholly satisfactory, but still serviceable, way of discriminating is in terms of who is and is not in uniform. If an enemy force attacked only those in uniform, it would attack chaplains and medical personnel, as well as fighters. But at least this interpretation of the Principle of Discrimination would leave the aged, (civilian) women, and children alone. In short, if followed, it would significantly curtail the slaughter of war.

However, some have argued that not only should chaplains and medical personnel not be targeted, but certain groups who are not in uniform should be. These might include guerrilla fighters not in uniform, but also those who work in factories that produce military equipment and supplies. Railroad workers who help bring this equipment and supplies to the front lines are also said by some to be legitimate targets.

The second *jus in bello* principle is called Proportionality, once again, only now with respect to moral costs and benefits of doing things in war. According to this principle, battle plans to cross a certain river directly and immediately are condemned if they lead to a victory but do so with high costs to both sides that could have been avoided had some other reasonable plan been adopted.

QUESTIONS OF TERMINOLOGY:
JUSTICE, WAR, AND THEORY

When speaking about Just War Theory, we are first of all speaking about justice. For our purposes, justice means fairness. Fairness, in turn, means that people, groups, cultures, and nations are treated as equals in at least two ways. First, they are treated with equal concern and, second, with equal respect. With the former, thought and action focus on their welfare, with the latter on their wishes and choices. The idea is that when acting justly, somebody in a position of power is not permitted to take advantage of someone else who has no power. What Just War Theory teaches, then, is that the powerful should be constrained by the principles of the theory, be attentive to, care for, be concerned about, and respect the wishes and choices of those who are not so powerful. Because the subject matter of this work is war, and war is a group activity, the plea for justice is addressed to state, political, and social leaders. It is addressed to these leaders because they make decisions that can very quickly lead to mass injustice. But it is addressed to individuals as well because in war, when their leaders put modern weapons in their hands, individuals too can very quickly commit serious acts of injustice.

War is the second term whose meaning needs to be clarified if one speaks about Just War Theory. War is one of the many central concepts in politics that has seen its meaning profoundly changed over the last few centuries.[39] Eighteenth- and nineteenth-century scholars writing on war and peace considered both concepts to be sharply distinguished. Times of war and peace could be easily differentiated. They referred to contrasting conditions of human existence. Hostilities did not necessarily start with declarations of war, but such declarations were generally made as public announcements that state behavior appropriate for times of peace had given way to behavior appropriate for war activities. In previous centuries, scholars produced an impressive amount of legal literature to regulate the behavior of states toward each other in wartime as distinguished from peacetime.

No such clear distinction exists today. It faded away during the twentieth century, and peace treaties have largely been replaced by more limited ways of terminating violent conflicts such as the simple cessation of hostilities, cease-fires, armistices, truces, accords, or the introduction of peacekeeping forces. These ways of settling violent conflicts do not necessarily end them. A cease-fire does not preclude the continuation of the armed conflict by other military means, such as terrorist attacks. According to the United States Secretary of State Condoleezza Rice, there is a continuum between war and peace and it is not possible to say simply that the war has ended or that the peace has started in Afghanistan or Iraq. According to Rice, the United States has to deal simultaneously with the sources of insecurity and with the forces that are trying to rebuild these states. For her, this contradictory process may be viewed as nation building.[40]

Like the transition from war to peace, the transition from peace to war also lacks a clear distinction. The term "war" is avoided in violent conflicts that are regarded by one side as intrastate in nature, such as civil wars, secessionist struggles, anticolonial wars, or proxy wars. In secessionist conflicts, central governments have no interest in granting a kind of recognition to the secessionist party by using the term "war," since that term is generally understood to be reserved for interstate conflicts between sovereign entities. To call the struggle a war would be tantamount to legitimizing the secession. In international law, the category of "belligerent status" has therefore been introduced for open rebellions and secessionist conflicts. This category aims to bring the law of international armed conflict into play for both sides. To be granted this status, the rebels or the secessionist party have to control territory by well-organized armed forces and must also be recognized as such by the central government. Unfortunately, the introduction of this legal category does not resolve the problem. Governments fighting against a rebellion or secession often refuse to grant belligerent status to the rebellion, as the granting in effect concedes the loss of a significant portion of their territory to the rebels.

Confronted with this refusal, international law has provided that minimum standards of humanitarian law will be triggered by a factual situation on the ground. In this way, the sensitive issue of recognition of sovereignty is sidestepped. The term "internal armed conflict" is used in international law when a particular set of criteria is met. This does not include the criterion of recognition. A confrontation between two groups is considered an internal armed conflict when "the fighting is intense, organized, and protracted enough to be beyond temporal disturbances and tensions. Additionally, the conflict must be confined within a State's borders and generally not involve foreign parties."[41] Once such a situation occurs, Article 3 Common to the Four Geneva Conventions of 1949 and Additional Protocol II apply regardless of the legal standing of the parties. These rules include the classic *jus in bello* Principles of Proportionality and Discrimination from the Just War Tradition.

The complex constitutional requirements of democratic states concerning the declaration and initiation of war, and the highly restrictive articles of the Charter of the United Nations concerning the use of force, have induced nations to be extremely careful in their use of terminology also in interstate military conflicts. For the use of the term "war" has direct legal consequences both in domestic decision-making (which may include the need to obtain the approval of a legislative body, for instance) and on the international scene. In general, "war" has been avoided. There was no declaration of war by the United States in Vietnam, by the United Kingdom when it sent troops to the Falkland Islands against Argentina, or by NATO members in their military interventions in Kosovo. The terms "Vietnam War," "Falklands War," and "Kosovo War" are favored by the media and by scholars, but are not part of the officially acknowledged descriptions of these conflicts by the United States, United Kingdom, or NATO members respectively.

There was a radical turnaround after the terrorist attacks on the United States on September 11, 2001, when the Bush administration described its political and military measures against terrorists and states supporting terrorism as a "war on terror." It labeled the Afghan campaign of 2001 as the first and the Iraq war of 2003 the second phase in a global war on terror. Such wording has far-reaching consequences, going far beyond metaphorical use.[42] For the Bush administration, the use of this concept had a variety of objectives. It expressed their perception of international terrorism as having reached a destructive capacity on a par with the military capacity of states, their strong resolve to fight terrorism with military means, their firm refusal of any compromise with such evil, their determination to draw clear lines in the confrontation with a hidden enemy, and their need for massive mobilization of public opinion behind the American leadership.

Expressions such as "war on terror" have not, however, been adopted by all governments. These expressions have been strongly criticized as inappropriate when applied to antiterrorist operations. First, Gilles Andréani has pointed out that their use inadvertently increases the status and even legitimacy of terrorist groups. Terrorists themselves have traditionally justified their struggle as being part of a war. Right-wing and left-wing terrorists proclaim their murderous activities to be part of a domestic or international ideological war. Similarly, terrorists with a nationalistic program regard themselves as legitimate warriors against foreign occupiers in anticolonial wars and, finally, Islamic terrorist groups speak about a holy war against unbelievers and "apostate" Muslim regimes. All these groups seek to have a state of war acknowledged by the authorities they are fighting against. They regard their imprisoned members as heroes to whom the status of prisoner of war should be granted. But state authorities have rejected these claims by treating terrorism as a criminal act and terrorists as criminals. In effect, the use of the term "global war on terror" by the Bush administration unwarrantedly acknowledges the state of war as defined by the terrorists themselves. It confers on the terrorists a degree of dignity they fervently seek.

Second, viewing antiterrorist operations as part of a global war has, according to Andréani, strategic consequences. In the past, successful fights against terrorism were mostly based on a mixture of military operations, intelligence activities, police repression, and political openings. This mixture persuaded terrorists, for instance in Northern Ireland, to abandon the use of violence and to rely exclusively on a negotiated political process to reach their aims. Negotiations and engagement are thus an integral part of such an antiterrorist policy, while the military has a subordinate role. By contrast, the American description of its antiterrorist struggle as a war on terror puts an overly heavy stress on the role of military forces in fighting global terrorism and its causes; and, as a result, it does not leave much room (if any) for negotiations with terrorist groups. A number of Western governments considered that such an emphasis should not be put on military means and that, instead, roads should be kept open for political dialogue with terrorist groups. The hope here is that this dialogue would encourage the more moderate members of these groups to abandon the use of force. This is the second reason why these Western governments oppose a terminological shift to "war on terror."

Different problems are raised with the use of the term "civil war." In November 2006, President Bush still denied that Iraq was in a state of civil war, contrary to a vast majority of analysts, media, and politicians from both the Republican and Democratic parties in the United States.[43] The use of this term indicates that the military situation in Iraq has largely spiraled out of the control of the Iraqi government and the occupying forces, thus diminishing the sense that they still could achieve a significant success in their fight against the different insurgent groups. Calling the conflict between Shiite and Sunni groups a civil war implies that it is less likely that agreements between the religious communities can be achieved and implemented. It not only acknowledges the failure of the military intervention against Iraq but also implies that it is unlikely that correcting its tragic humanitarian consequences will be possible. According to a report by the United Nations High Commission for Refugees (UNHCR) in October 2006, 100,000 people have been leaving Iraq every month. By October of that year, more than 1.5 million people had been displaced within Iraq itself and up to 1.6 million Iraqis had left their country (most of them having gone to Jordan and Syria).[44] To admit that the conflict in Iraq is a civil war, in effect, concedes that these millions of Iraqi refugees will not be able to return to their homes for the foreseeable future.

There are strong arguments for not using the term "civil war" to characterize the sectarian strife taking place in Iraq. U.S. National Security Adviser Stephan Hadley countered the majority view among scholars, journalists, and politicians by claiming that the Iraqi government, the army, and the police have not really fractured along sectarian lines, which would be characteristic of a civil war.[45] John Keegan and Bartle Bull underline the importance of the debate on civil war terminology in the search for an appropriate military strategy. They acknowledge that the use of such a term has direct implications for the likelihood of success of further American involvement in Iraq. In their view, the term "civil war" is appropriate on three conditions. The violence should be "civil," meaning that the struggle must take place mainly between the people of a national territory and with popular participation. Second, the violence has to be characterized as a "war," which means a "hostile contention by means of armed forces."[46] Furthermore, the parties should defend clear war aims and the combatants should be clearly identifiable. Third, the aim should be "the exercise or acquisition of national authority" as opposed to other motives such as revenge, criminality, or economic gain.

In the view of these two scholars, few violent conflicts can be characterized as civil wars. Only the English (1642–1649), the American (1861–1865), the Russian (1918–1921), the Spanish (1936–1939), and the Lebanese (1975–1990) civil wars would pass this test. In the case of Iraq, only the first condition had been met, as the violence takes place within national boundaries and mainly between local people. According to this definition, the insurgency and widespread terrorism in Iraq cannot be considered to be a war, as the fighting is still taking place largely with militias that lack even a minimal degree of formal organization. Moreover, the leaders of the various communities have not called for war against each other, in an attempt to seize control over the state, but on the contrary, have appealed for unity and an end to the bloodshed—even if they have failed to implement such policies. The authors conclude that the situation thus far falls short of a civil war and may be described rather as a combination of extreme factionalism and massive criminality. This means that, in their view, the U.S. forces still have some reasonable chance of success—defined as the stabilization of a "unified Iraqi Arab state with moderate internal violence and a smooth electoral cycle," and they should not leave, "unless things get much better or much worse."[47]

Scholars working in the Just War Tradition do have to take such arguments about the use of "war on terror" and "civil war" into account, but they have no reason to stick to official terminology or acts of recognition in deciding whether armed conflicts constitute wars or civil wars. They do not share the same disciplinary perspective as historians or international lawyers, and so remain quite free to define their own terminology. In any case, the problems raised by all these discussions among politicians, journalists, historians, and legal scholars can be analyzed within the framework of Just War Theory with the help of *jus ad bellum* and *jus in bello* principles. Questions to do with the use the term "war on terrorism"—such as how military forces should be used against terrorist threats and whether political negotiations with terrorists are legitimate—can be discussed within the framework of the Just Cause, Legitimate Authority, Last Resort, and Discrimination Principles. Where the discussion of the term "civil war" is concerned, an analysis of the motives for going to war may be conducted from the perspective of the Right Intentions Principle, while the combatants' degree of formal organization will have consequences for the application of the Legitimate Authority and Discrimination Principles.

Where the definition of "war" is concerned, many sorts of wars have been discussed within the long history of Just War Theory, which requires a very broad definition of this expression. We need a definition of war that makes no distinction between interstate and intrastate conflicts or between conflicts between recognized and nonrecognized states. Hedley Bull proposes a definition of war that is broad enough to include all of these kinds of conflict: "Violence is not war unless it is carried out in the name of a political unit; what distinguishes killing in war from murder is its vicarious and official character, the symbolic responsibility of the unit whose agent the killer is. Equally, violence carried out in the name of a political unit is not war unless it is directed against another political unit."[48]

Theory is the third and final concept whose meaning should be clarified before discussing Just War Theory in detail in the following chapters. When we speak of Just War Theory, we do not mean theory in the same way as in the natural or empirical sciences. A distinction has to be made here between a more and a less demanding concept of theory.[49] A demanding view of theory sees it as encompassing explanatory principles, which are able to generate a set of testable hypotheses. The construction of specific scenarios then makes it possible to predict future events and thereby to test the validity of these hypotheses. When we speak about Just War Theory, we understand theory in a far weaker sense. This "thin theory" gives a certain structure to the field of research, systematizes the research questions, and includes a coherent set of concepts. A practical "thin" theory does not deliver the choices to be made. These need to be filled in by individuals.[50] Theory has a quite modest meaning as a way of exploring what is morally at stake when dealing with the use of military force.

Some authors avoid using the term "theory," preferring instead to speak about a Just War Tradition.[51] One of their arguments is that a moral analysis of the use of force should not be guided by principles that are invariably applied to various situational settings, but that their use should remain highly context-sensitive. For this reason, the term "theory" is, in their view, not appropriate. The present book does not share the opinion that we should speak exclusively about a Just War Tradition and not about a Just War Theory. The use of the term "theory" presupposes, on the contrary, that a systematic approach may remain attentive to the significance that a particular context may have for the use of general moral principles. How general principles should be applied in specific historical situations very much depends on the particular features of contextual variables. It is moreover appropriate to use the *ad bellum* set of principles of Just War Theory in dealing with other political problems, such as those concerning the legitimacy of unilateral forms of secession. The diplomatic recognition of a state that has seceded from a central government without its authorization is an exception to the general rule that the territorial integrity of states has to be preserved. The theoretical framework constituted by the six *jus ad bellum* principles may be fruitfully applied in order to assess the legitimacy of such recognition of independence, as will be demonstrated below in the discussion of the case of Kosovo (see chapter 11).

Further, in focusing on the content (the What-portion) of Just War Theory, very little has been said thus far about the Why-portion. Indeed, some would argue that there is no theory without the why. Theory, it is said, involves not only pulling together many aspects of a subject but also explaining why the parts pulled together, and not other parts, belong in the theory. But when talking about justifying a theory we face a problem. On reading the literature on the topic of Just War Theory, it quickly becomes apparent that there is little agreement on the why-question. One writer justifies a version of the theory by appealing to a particular religious tradition,[52] while another takes a rights-based approach.[53] A third appeals to some medium-level "intuitive" principles,[54] and yet another to some version of a contract theory.[55] There are also utilitarian defenses of Just War Theory.[56]

One consoling aspect of the justification problem is that it does not plague Just War Theory alone. Realism and Pacifism have the same problem. Some pacifists arrive at their convictions by appealing to the New Testament, others by appealing to rights, or to general moral principles, and still others to utility. Beyond that, this why-problem plagues all of ethics in a way it does not affect science. This variety of available theories at any one time does not mean that theories are worthless.[57] The fact that several general justification-type theories of ethics converge on Just War Theory (or Pacifism) no more shows that they and Just War Theory are worthless than the fact that several highways converge on Moscow shows that they are worthless. Theories are useful instruments for ordering our thinking, and thus we do not need to insist that only one overarching theory does this best. So Just War Theory can be justified or explained in many different ways, with one way, perhaps, emphasizing one aspect of the theory and another emphasizing another.

NOTES

1. Some passages in this section on Realism and in the one on Just War Theory borrow from Nick Fotion, "Reactions to War: Pacifism, Realism, and Just War Theory," in *Ethics in International Affairs*, ed. Andrew Valls (Lanham, Md.: Rowman & Littlefield, 2000), 15–32.

2. Nicholas J. Spykman, *America's Strategy in World Politics: The United States and the Balance of Power* (New York: Harcourt Brace & Company, 1994), 18. Quoted in Jack Donnelly, *Realism and International Relations* (Cambridge: Cambridge University Press, 2000), 162.

3. In his *Politics* (reprinted *Readings in Western Civilization: 1500 to the Present*, ed. George H. Knoles and Rixford K. Snyder [Philadelphia and New York: J. B. Lippincott Co., 1968], 417), Heinrich von Treitschke writes: "It is a further consequence of the essential sovereignty of the State that it can acknowledge no arbiter above it, and must ultimately submit its legal obligations to its own verdict." Actually this statement sounds more like a prescription rather than a description of how things are. In some sense of "should" he thinks the state should not allow a higher authority to make decisions for it.

4. During a visit to Israel in 1995 an Israeli official said to Nick Fotion: "We would have no choice if we were attacked. We would do anything and everything to keep Israel from going under."

5. See Joel Rosenthal's *Righteous Realists: Political Realism, Responsible Power, and American Culture in the Nuclear Age* (Baton Rouge: Louisiana State University Press, 1991) for a general statement about the ethics involved in the realist position. As to the realists themselves, see E. H. Carr *Twenty Years of Crisis, 1919–1939: An Introduction to the Study of International Relations* (New York: Harper Torchbook, 1964; MacMillan, 1951); George Kennan *American Diplomacy, 1900–1950* (Chicago: University of Chicago Press, 1951); and Hans Morgenthau, *In Defense of the National Interest* (New York: Alfred A. Knopf, 1952).

6. On Carr and Morgenthau, see Donnelly, *Realism and International Relations*, 166–67.

7. Robert Holmes in his *On War and Morality* (Princeton, N.J.: Princeton University Press, 1989), 57, calls some of these thinkers soft realists. These realists "honor morality when they can. But . . . believe that when it is expedient to do so, morality should be abandoned."

8. Sun Tzu, *The Art of War*, ed. James Clavell (New York: Dell Publishing, 1983), 14.

9. Reinhold Neibuhr in *Moral Man and Immoral Society* (New York: Charles Scribner's Sons, 1932), 83 seems to be arguing that the rules of the collective (the nation, state) transcend those of the individual.

10. William Tecumseh Sherman, *Memoirs*, 4th ed. (New York: Charles L. Webster and Co., 1892), 2:126. On Sherman, see Michael Walzer, *Just and Unjust Wars* (New York: Basic Books, 1977), 32–33.

11. As for instance, see the realist author Heinrich von Treitschke, *Politics*, abridged (originally published as two volumes in 1916) and ed. Hans Kohn (New York and Burlingame: Harcourt Brace & World, 1963), 12–15.

12. Sun Tzu, *The Art of War*, chaps. 2 and 3.

13. *The New Encyclopaedia Britannica*, 13th ed., *Macropaedia*, "Greek and Roman Civilization" (Chicago, 1998), 20:225–27.

14. Robert B. Edgerton, *Warriors of the Rising Sun* (New York and London: W. W. Norton and Company, 1977), 234–39.

15. Alexander De Grand, *Italian Fascism: Its Origins and Development* (Lincoln and London: University of Nebraska Press, 1982), 138–39, 143, 147.

16. Aristotle A. Kallis, *Fascist Ideology: Territory and Expansionism in Italy and Germany 1922–1945* (London and New York: Routledge, 2000), 5–9.

17. John Kelsay, *Islam and War: A Study of Comparative Ethics* (Louisville, Ky.: Westminster/John Knox Press, 1993), 100–104.

18. Benito Mussolini, *La Doctrine du Fascisme* (Firenze: Vallecchi Editore, 1936), 28–29 (our translation).

19. See Thomas J. Koontz, "Christian Nonviolence: An Interpretation," in *The Ethics of War and Peace: Religious and Secular Perspectives*, ed. Terry Nardin (Princeton, N.J.: Princeton University Press, 1995), 318–19.

20. One can also distinguish, as Robert Holmes puts it, absolute and conditional Pacifism. According to absolute Pacifism, there are no such circumstances under which war might be allowable. According to conditional Pacifism, war is inadmissible in certain types of circumstances. *Nonviolence in Theory and Practice*, ed. Robert Holmes (Belmont, Calif.: Wadsworth Publishing Company, 1990), 114.

21. See Bruno Coppieters, "Die pazifistischen Sekten, die Bolschewiki und das Recht auf Wehrdienstverweigerung," in *Lehren aus der Geschichte? Historische Friedensforschung*, ed. Reiner Steinweg (Frankfurt: Suhrkamp Verlag, 1990), 308–60, and Alexei Zverev and Bruno Coppieters, "V. D. Bonch-Bruevich and the Doukhobors: On the Conscientious Objection Policies of the Bolsheviks," *Canadian Ethnic Studies/Etudes Ethniques au Canada* 27, no. 3 (1995): 72–90.

22. Following pacifist literature John Yoder distinguishes over twenty different kinds of religious Pacifism. John H. Yoder, *Nevertheless; Varieties of Religious Pacifism* (Scottsdale, Pa.: Herald Press, 1976).

23. See David Stephens, "The Non-violent Anarchism of Leo Tolstoy," in *Leo Tolstoy, Government Is Violence: Essays on Anarchism and Pacifism*, ed. David Stephens (London: Phoenix Press, 1990), 7–19.

24. Tolstoy in an undated letter to Dr. Eugen Schmitt, quoted in Stephens, "The Non-violent Anarchism," 13.

25. Leo Tolstoy, "How Can Governments Be Abolished?" in *Leo Tolstoy, Government Is Violence*, 147.

26. Robert L. Holmes, "The Morality of Nonviolence," *Concerned Philosophers for Peace Newsletter* 15, no. 2 (Fall 1995): 5–16.

27. Holmes, *On War and Morality*, 277.

28. *Statehood and Security: Georgia After the Rose Revolution*, ed. Bruno Coppieters and Robert Legvold (Cambridge, Mass.: MIT Press, 2005).

29. Different authors use different concepts and definitions such as "*social defense*" (Johan Niezing) and "*nonviolent civilian defense*" (George Crowell). The term "civilian-based defense," proposed by Gene Sharp, has become by our days the most familiar. See Gene Sharp, *Civilian-Based Defense* (Cambridge, Mass.: Harvard University Press, 1990); Johan Jorgen Holst, *Civilian-Based Defense in a New Era*, Monograph Series 2 (Cambridge, Mass.: The Albert Einstein Institution, 1990); Gene Sharp, *The Dynamics of Nonviolent Action*, 3 vols. (Boston: Porter Sargent, 1973); Gene Sharp, *Self-reliant Defense without Bankruptcy or War: Considerations for the Baltic, East Central Europe, and Members of the Commonwealth of Independent States* (Cambridge, Mass.: The Albert Einstein Institution, 1992). See also George Crowell, *The Case for Nonviolent Civilian Defence against External Aggression* (Waterloo, Ont.: Ploughshares Working Paper), 90–94.

30. For some advocates, elements of CBD against external aggression might be gradually incorporated into a state's doctrine of defense side by side with military means. A certain conception of CBD was included in the defense doctrines of such nations as Switzerland and Sweden along with usual military and guerrilla means of resistance. Rudolf A. Epple, *Terminological Make-up—the Ideas of Swiss Military Strategies about the Role and Meaning of Non-violent Actions of Resistance as Part of the Total Defense in Western Europe* (Brussels: Free University of Brussels, 1977).

31. Johan Niezing, *Sociale verdediging als logisch alternatief: Van utopie naar optie,* (Antwerpen: EPO, 1987), 9.

32. On practical examples of nonviolent resistance, see the website of the pacifist organization War Resisters International at wri-irg.org/from-off.htm (accessed February 14, 2008).

33. Johan Niezing, *Sociale Verdediging,* 43–46.

34. See Augustine's *City of God,* especially books 17 and 19 (*Basic Writings of Saint Augustine,* ed. Whitney J. Oates [New York: Random House, 1948]). For commentaries on Augustine's role in developing Just War Theory in the West, see Paul Christopher's *The Ethics of War and Peace: An Introduction to Legal and Moral Issues,* 2nd ed. (Englewood Cliffs, N.J.: Prentice Hall, 1999), chap. 3. See also Robert L. Holmes's *On War and Morality,* chap. 4. Inclined as he is in the direction of Pacifism, Holmes's account of Augustine is negative.

35. Mo Tzu, *Basic Writings,* trans. Burton Watson (New York and London: Columbia University Press, 1963), 50–61.

36. Mencius, *The Works of Mencius,* bk. 1, pt. 1, chaps. 4–7, pt. 2, chap. 8; bk. 2, pt. 1, chaps. 2–3, vol. 2 of the *Chinese Classics,* ed. James Legge (Oxford: Oxford University Press, 1894).

37. *The Laws of Manu,* trans. Wendy Doniger and Brian K. Smith (New York and London: Penguin Books, 1991), 137.

38. *The Bhagavad Gita,* trans. Eliot Geutsch (New York: Holt, Rinehart and Winston, 1968). See also Nick Allen, "Just War in the Mahābhārata," in *The Ethics of War: Shared Problems in Different Traditions,* ed. Richard Sorabji and David Rodin (Aldershot: Ashgate, 2006), 138–49.

39. Geoffrey Best, *War and Law Since 1945* (Oxford: Oxford University Press, 1997), 228 ff.

40. Edward Luce, Lionel Barber and Guy Dinmore, "A Return to Realism?" *Financial Times,* April 23, 2007, 7.

41. Ewen Allison and Robert K. Goldman, "Belligerent Status," in *Crimes of War,* ed. Roy Gutman and David Rieff (New York and London: Norton & Company, 1999), 42.

42. The following description of the political consequences of the use of the term "war on terror" is based on Gilles Andréani, "The 'War on Terror': Good Cause, Wrong Concept," *Survival* 46, no. 4 (Winter 2004–2005), 31–50.

43. Edward Luce, "Bush Denies Iraq Is in State of Civil War," *Financial Times,* November 29, 2006, 8; Julian Borger, "White House on Defensive as U.S. Media Breaks Taboo to Declare Conflict 'Civil War,'" *Guardian,* November 29, 2006, 7.

44. "Iraq Displacement," Global Policy Forum, October 13, 2006, at globalpolicy.igc.org/security/issues/iraq/attack/consequences/2006/1013displace.htm (accessed April 9, 2008).

45. Borger, "White House on Defensive."

46. John Keegan and Bartle Bull, "The Definition of 'Civil War' Is Critical to Iraq's Future," *Financial Times*, November 20, 2006, 13.

47. Keegan and Bull, "The Definition of 'Civil War.'"

48. Hedrey Bull, *The Anarchical Society: A Study of Order in World Politics* (London: Macmillan, 1977), 184, quoted in Best, *War & Law since 1945*, 4.

49. On the following see Bruno Coppieters, Ivan Myhul, and Michel Huysseune, introduction to *Secession, History, and the Social Sciences*, ed. Bruno Coppieters and Michel Huysseune (Brussels: VUB Brussels University Press, 2002), 12–13. See also Barry Buzan and Ole Waever, "Security Complexes: A Theory of Regional Security," paper presented at the conference "Central Asia in a New Security Context," organized by the Swedish Institute of International Affairs in Stockholm on September 2–3, 1999.

50. Jeremy Waldron, "Minority Cultures and the Cosmopolitan Alternative," in *The Rights of Minority Cultures*, ed. Will Kymlicka (Oxford: Oxford University Press, 1996), 98.

51. In his review of the first edition of this book, Nicholas Rengger denies that the Just War Tradition constitutes a theory, saying instead that it should be considered a moral practice. In his view, such a practice can be reflected upon (meaning theorized), but it cannot lead to a theory claiming universality. See his book review in *International Affairs* 79, no. 3: 643–44.

52. U.S. Catholic Bishops, "The Just War and Non-violent Positions," in *War, Morality, and the Military Profession*, 2nd ed., ed. Malham M. Wakin (Boulder, Colo., and London: Westview Press, 1989), 239–55.

53. Walzer, *Just and Unjust Wars*.

54. James F. Childress, "Just-War Theories: The Bases, Interrelations, Priorities and Functions of Their Criteria," in *War, Morality, and the Military Profession*, 256–76. Childress appeals to what might be called mid-level principles such as nonmaleficence (do not harm), beneficence (help others), and justice to generate the principles of Just War Theory.

55. John Rawls, "The Law of Peoples," in *On Human Rights: The Oxford Amnesty Lectures 1993*, ed. Stephen Shute and Susan Hurley (New York: Basic Books, 1993), 41–82.

56. Richard Brandt, "Utilitarianism and the Rules of War," in *War, Morality, and the Military Profession*, ed. Malhan Wakin (Boulder, Colo.: Westview Press, 1981), 393–413; R. M. Hare, "Rules of War and Moral Reasoning," in *Essays on Political Morality*, ed. R. M. Hare (Oxford: Clarendon Press, 1989), 45–61. See also Nick Fotion, "A Utilitarian Defense of Just War Theory," *Synthesis philosophica*, Zagreb, 12, fasc. 1 (1997): 209–25.

57. Such a conclusion is drawn, however, by Annette Baier. Annette Baier, "Doing Without Moral Theory?" in *Anti-theory in Ethics and Moral Conservatism*, ed. Stanley G. Clarke and Evan Simpson (Albany: State University of New York Press, 1989), 33–34.

I

JUS AD BELLUM

1

Just Cause

Bruno Coppieters, Carl Ceulemans, and Anthony Hartle

This chapter is concerned with the first and no doubt the most important *jus ad bellum* principle. In order to get an overall sense of the Just Cause Principle, we will proceed in three steps. We will begin by taking a general approach to the just cause concept. In the process, a definition of the Just Cause Principle will emerge. With the second and third steps, we will discuss two substantial just cause categories: self-defense and the defense of others. Each of these two categories will be analyzed and illustrated with a number of examples.

A GENERAL APPROACH

Those who wish to be considered justified in the use of military force need to have what the Just War Tradition calls a just cause. This means literally that one has to have a good reason for starting a war. The next obvious question is, of course, what constitutes a good reason? What reason is serious enough for starting something with such terrible consequences? In order to answer this question it is helpful to turn to what some of the most influential just war thinkers have said on the subject.

Saint Augustine (354–430), who is widely recognized as the father of the Just War Tradition, gives us some idea about the content of just cause. As quoted by Thomas Aquinas, Augustine says: "A just war is wont to be described as one that avenges wrongs, when a nation or state has to be punished for refusing to make amends for wrongs inflicted by its subjects, or to restore what has been seized unjustly."[1] For the Dominican Francisco de Vitoria (1480–1546), another innovative just war theorist, a nation has a *causa justa* when it tries to correct a violation of its rights.[2] Vitoria adds that such a violation of rights not only constitutes a just cause for those who suffered the injustice but also for the international community as a whole. For the Jesuit Francisco Suarez (1548–1617) the right to *punish* those who are responsible for the injustice is generated by the fact that those who underwent an injustice acquire jurisdiction over those who are responsible for the injustice.[3]

For Hugo Grotius (1583–1645) and Emmerich de Vattel (1714–1767), the preemption of an injustice also constitutes a just cause.[4] But here Grotius adds that fear of future wrongdoing cannot be a legitimate ground for killing. He refers to an observation made by Cicero in his first book of *Offices*, that many wrongs proceed from fear. Grotius also refers to Xenophon, who wrote about misrepresentations and suspicions that may lead men, "in order to prevent the supposed intentions of their adversaries, . . . [to commit] the most enormous cruelties against those who neither designed, nor wished them any harm."[5] Grotius rejects the use of military force against distant or potential dangers and asserts that we have to accept the idea of living without enjoying full security. He further states that we have to rely on defensive precaution rather than on a preventive use of force against another state that does not express any intention to harm:

> Some writers have advanced a doctrine which can never be admitted, maintaining that the law of nations authorizes one power to commence hostilities against another, whose increasing greatness awakens her alarms. As a matter of expediency such a measure may be adopted, but the principles of justice can never be advanced in its favor. The causes which entitle a war to the denomination of just are somewhat different from those of expediency alone. But to maintain that the bare probability of some remote, or future annoyance from a neighbouring state affords a just ground of hostile aggression, is a doctrine repugnant to every principle of equity. Such however is the condition of human life, that no full security can be enjoyed. The only protection against uncertain fears must be sought, not from violence, but from the divine providence, and defensive precaution.[6]

De Vattel expresses similar caution concerning what would be later labeled a preemptive use of force. This measure may in principle be justified, but one has to be very careful not to base one's case on "vague and uncertain suppositions, in order not to become an unjust aggressor oneself."[7]

Based on these propositions and this distinction between a justified preemptive and an unjustified preventive use of force, one might say that having a just cause is essentially about the *correction* and/or the *punishment* of an injustice that has been done, or about the *preemption* of an injustice that is about to happen. The use of force with the aim of preventing another state from strengthening itself may never be considered a just cause, as such an action does not aim to correct, to punish, or to preempt any injustice.

Let us try to clarify the concept of a just cause a little further. A basic element in the definition of just cause is the presence (actual or in the near future) of an injustice. Now what kind of injustice are we talking about? When we say that we are the victims of an injustice, we mean that someone has wronged us, or put differently, that someone has not treated us as they should have. From this it follows that an injustice presupposes the idea that individuals and/or groups of people (e.g., a state) possess certain rights, the protection of which may require the use of force. The violation of a state's political sovereignty and territorial integrity, an act we commonly label as an aggression, is a clear example of such an injustice. But the Just War Tradition clearly stipulates that the use of military force is not restricted to the protection of one's own rights (self-defense). The protection of the rights of others is also a valid just cause. Let us look at both of these just cause categories (self-defense and the defense of others) in detail.

INDIVIDUAL AND COLLECTIVE SELF-DEFENSE

When we are asked to give an example of a reason sufficient to justify the use of military force, the first thing that comes to mind is self-defense. Indeed, most of us are convinced that a state, just like an individual, has a right to use force when its rights (to political sovereignty and territorial integrity) are being violated. Belgium had a just cause in defending itself militarily against the German invasion during World War I. On August 2, 1914, Germany handed Belgium (which was neutral) an ultimatum demanding free passage for the German armies on their way to attack France. Belgium refused, and the next day German forces entered Belgian territory. In this case the justification for resisting militarily was so obvious that the Germans did not even bother to hide the fact that what they were doing was a breach of international law.[8] The self-evident character of self-defense does not mean, however, that this issue is without difficulties.

A less obvious form of self-defense that goes well beyond resistance against an ongoing aggression is the taking back of something that has been wrongfully seized. Once a fight is over, and the enemy has unjustly obtained its objective, self-defense no longer seems to be the apt concept. Corrective military action to reestablish territorial integrity must now be situated in the realm of delivering justice and must have therefore a more offensive character. Once an initial victim-state tries to recover the unjustly taken parts of its territory by attacking the initial aggressor, it risks being labeled as an aggressor itself. In order to avoid this consequence, there is a tendency to include the retaking of what has been wrongfully taken in an enlarged concept of self-defense. But this label of self-defense tends to fade gradually as the interval grows longer. The longer one waits to respond to a wrong, the more likely it will be that the eventual response will be regarded as an aggressive rather than a defensive act, particularly when the UN Security Council (UNSC) is dealing with the issue and when it has not authorized the use of force.

The Iraqi president Saddam Hussein claimed that Kuwait was part of Iraq when he invaded that country on August 2, 1990.[9] He stated that Iraq's use of force was therefore justified. But the international community condemned him as an aggressor against a sovereign country. What does history tell us about such competing claims? Kuwait had existed as an independent state since 1961 and had been admitted to the United Nations, but its status as a separate geopolitical entity was the result of boundaries imposed by Great Britain after World War I.[10] Under varying circumstances, the al-Sabah family had ruled Kuwait since 1752.[11] Part of the Ottoman Empire for centuries until 1913, the regime became fully autonomous under the treaty signed that year with Britain (autonomy dominated by British interests, needless to say).

The country of Iraq itself existed largely because Great Britain had so decreed, carving the state out of Mesopotamia in 1921 over the objections of Turkey. Under the Ottoman Empire, Iraq was not a unified entity. Three separate provinces existed: Mosul, Baghdad, and Basra, with present-day Kuwait a part of Basra.[12] As Sir Anthony Parsons, former British ambassador to the United Nations, observed in 1990, "We, the British, cobbled Iraq together. It was always an artificial state; it had nothing to do with the people who lived there."[13] But Iraq's claim that Kuwait was properly part of Iraq was nonetheless one of long standing, dating back to 1932 when Iraq formally became an independent member of the international community.[14] Iraqi rulers from King Ghazi in 1938 to Abd al-Karim Qassem in 1961 declared that Kuwait was a part of the province of Basra and threatened to seize the region using force.[15] The long-standing nature of the claim and its equally long-standing dismissal by the international community probably explains why Saddam Hussein's blustering threats in 1990 were not taken seriously. In addition to the larger issue of Kuwait's status, Iraq had tried since 1973 to obtain Warbah and Bubiyan, two Kuwaiti islands in a position to deny Iraq's only access to the Persian Gulf if held by a hostile government. Kuwait had refused to transfer or lease the islands.[16]

On the day following the invasion, August 3, 1990, the United Nations condemned Iraq's seizure of its neighbor to the south and called for the immediate withdrawal of Iraqi forces. Three days later, the UNSC imposed an economic embargo on all Iraqi oil exports and on all imports other than certain humanitarian items (Resolution 661). Iraq's response was uncompromising. On August 8, Hussein's government sent home all foreign diplomats in Kuwait City and formally annexed Kuwait as the nineteenth province of Iraq. United Nations condemnation remained constant thereafter, culminating with the UNSC action on November 29, 1990, that authorized the use of military force to eject the Iraqis from Kuwait if they had not complied with United Nations demands by January 15, 1991 (Resolution 678). Iraq did not comply, despite the fact that the buildup of a U.S.-led Allied Coalition in the region proceeded at an accelerating pace. By January, forces from twenty-eight nations were positioned in Middle Eastern countries. The war began at 0300 hours on January 17, 1991 with massive Coalition air strikes. The Iraqi troops were overwhelmed and had to retreat from Kuwait. On February 27, 1991, President George H. W. Bush declared that the sovereignty of Kuwait had been fully reestablished.

The war expressed two opposing views on just cause. Many Iraqis who reflected on the matter undoubtedly felt that Iraq was the victim of injustice inflicted by the imperious nations of the West. But the fact that the world had recognized Kuwait as a sovereign nation made its independent status and borders inviolable. International recognition implied that it was impossible to undo or to correct the injustice implied in the colonial imposition of borders. Iraq's invasion was consequently perceived by the world community as aggression by one state against another.

Individual and collective forms of defense against an ongoing attack, such as against the Iraqi occupation of Kuwait, are considered a legitimate form of self-defense. But what if a country decides to attack another at the very moment it knows with certainty that an attack from this country is imminent? Can such a preemptive military action still be regarded as a legitimate act of self-defense? It can. The legitimacy of a *preemptive strike* as a just cause is derived from the fact that a presumed injustice is about to occur. Needless to say, given that the *actual* injustice has not taken place yet, the self-defense quality (and thus also the just cause quality) of the preemptive strike will most likely remain somewhat suspect. Indeed, how credible is the threat, and does it really justify an anticipatory military response? Proponents of the preemptive strike as an act of self-defense support this view in quite a straightforward manner: Why should I wait for an injustice to be inflicted on me, when I have better chance of defending myself if I can prevent it from happening in the first place?

International lawyers will cite the 1837 *Caroline* incident as the modern classic exposition of a case of what they call "anticipatory self-defense." The British had destroyed an American steamship in U.S. territorial waters, claiming that this ship had been used, and would probably be used again, to support a Canadian rebellion against their colonial rule. In the debate on this act of war, the American secretary of state Daniel Webster defined the circumstances in which anticipatory action may justifiably be taken. He stated that such an action was to be regarded as an exception to the general rule concerning self-defense and "should be confined to cases in which the "necessity of that self-defense is instant, overwhelming, and leaving no choice of means, and no moment for deliberation.'"[17] Here Webster was articulating a highly restrictive rule concerning the right to use force preemptively.

Some international lawyers deny the value of the *Caroline* incident as a precedent for contemporary conflicts. This is because of its anachronistic character. The incident dates from a period when states could lawfully wage war.[18] These opponents of the existence of a customary right of self-defense refer to Article 51 of the UN Charter, which recognizes the right of individual or collective self-defense only where there has been an armed attack.

The question whether the right to self-defense exclusively allows defensive wars against ongoing attacks is also debated in the ethics of war. Michael Walzer is in favor of a restrictive use of a preemptive right of self-defense but stresses that one must be careful not confuse the *preemptive* with the *preventive* use of force. When talking about the preventive use of force Walzer is referring to the eighteenth-century realist idea that a war initiated to prevent a neighbor from "overgrowing," and thereby destabilizing the balance of power, is legitimate. The realist argument is that such a war would not only help restore the balance of power but also, and more importantly, greatly reduce the cost of defense. According to this view, waiting would not mean avoiding war but merely fighting on a larger scale and against heavier odds.[19] Walzer rejects this consequentialist argument. International relations, he says, have a dynamic character. Indeed, there is no such thing as perfect equilibrium, because shifts in the power configuration happen all the time. This means that if states decided to initiate a war whenever such a power shift occurs, war would become an "ordinary and all too frequently used" instrument of statecraft.

The preemptive use of force can be considered justified, Walzer continues, only if it constitutes a response to a *sufficient threat*. This concept is vaguer than Webster's concept of anticipatory self-defense, which includes the criterion of an imminent attack. It does, however, include three other conditions for drawing the line to show when there is sufficient threat to make a first strike legitimate:

1. the potential aggressor has a manifest intent to injure;
2. the potential aggressor exhibits a degree of active preparation that makes that intent a positive danger;
3. a general situation in which waiting, or doing anything other than fighting, greatly increases the risk to the victim nation.[20]

Walzer illustrates this notion of justified preemptive strike by referring to the Six Day War (1967).

This war began on June 5 with a first strike by Israel against Egypt and its allies (Syria, Jordan, and Iraq). Walzer analyses the narrow time frame (three weeks) that preceded the actual attack and concludes that there were abundant reasons for believing that Israel was faced with what he calls a sufficient threat. First, there was a manifest intent to injure. In a speech on May 29, Egyptian president Nasser made it clear "that if war came, the Egyptian goal would be nothing less than the destruction of Israel."[21] Second, there were clear signs that Egypt and its allies were making active preparations to substantiate their hostile intentions toward Israel. On May 14, the Egyptian government began to move its troops into the Sinai. Egypt also ordered the United Nations Emergency Force to leave, and announced that the Straits of Tiran would no longer be accessible to Israeli shipping. By the end of May, Syria, Jordan, and Iraq had formed a military alliance with Egypt. Finally, there existed what Walzer calls "a basic asymmetry of forces."[22] Egypt had the military capacity to deploy a large army over a long period of time at the Israeli border. Israel, in contrast, had to mobilize its reserve troops each time a crisis occurred. These reserves could be used only for a short period of time, which meant that Israel could not "sit out" the crisis in the same way as Egypt could. In other words, Israel did not have the luxury of postponing its military actions indefinitely without seriously jeopardizing its chances of defense. But it is not absolutely certain that Egypt intended to start a war. Nasser would have regarded it as a victory if the Egyptians merely denied Israel the right to use an international waterway and put the Israeli defense system under the strain of knowing it could be attacked at any time.[23] Even this was unacceptable to Israel. According to Walzer, it had to strike first against Egypt if it did not want to put its territorial integrity, or even its existence as an independent state, at risk.

At the time, the majority view within the UN and in international law opposed a right to anticipatory or preemptive self-defense. Israel was itself reluctant to invoke such a legal right openly. In its address to the General Assembly it described the threatening language and military mobilization by its Arab neighbors but also stated that it had acted in response to an attack before engaging in military operations. Nasser's closing of the Straits of Tiran had to be seen as a blockade, which was "by definition an act of war, imposed and enforced through violence."[24] Thus Israel itself did not consider its waging of the war as a model for affirming a right to anticipatory self-defense.[25] This demonstrates how difficult it was at the time to invoke a right to self-defense on any legal ground other than a direct response to an armed attack.

During the Cold War period the issue of preemptive strike became hotly debated in the terminology of a first and second nuclear strike.[26] The particular nature of strategic nuclear weapons brought a whole new dimension to the discussion on the anticipatory use of force. Indeed, the injustice one sought to prevent in the nuclear context was nothing less than the partial or total annihilation of one's own society as the result of a nuclear attack. Another innovative aspect of this change was the constant presence of the nuclear threat. Unlike in the case of a conventional preemptive strike, there is no need for a buildup in a nuclear scenario because of the constant and direct availability of the strategic nuclear arsenal. Now, as long as each of the nuclear opponents is convinced that its military capacity has sufficiently deterred the other party, there is no immediate danger of a preemptive strike. The relevance of the anticipatory use of nuclear weapons becomes dangerously clear, however, in a scenario where both actors are convinced that they themselves have a first-strike capacity, but *also* believe that the other party has a similar capacity. This could very well lead to a situation where each side begins to suspect that the other is bound to launch a surprise attack, which preemption would in turn have to be preempted, and so on.[27] It should be obvious to everyone that such a "Do it to them before they do it to us" scenario would have disastrous consequences and must therefore be avoided at all costs.

With the end of the Cold War, the United States was confronted with a series of new threats. But it was the 9/11 experience that most radically changed the American perception of international security. In the view of the U.S. government, al-Qaeda's attack on the United States showed that terrorists were an elusive enemy who were able to hide their future actions and that their capacity to do so was significantly increased by rogue states. The Taliban government of Afghanistan was ready to offer them sanctuary while they prepared their terrorist operations against America. The need to preempt such actions was central to the 2002 National Security Strategy of the United States (NSS).[28]

According to this strategy, the core new threat came from a combination of two actors—terrorists and so-called rogue states—which have traditionally been considered separate. The cooperation between al-Qaeda and the Taliban was only one example among many. The transnational terrorist movements that had always used statelessness as a protection now received support from what the United States views as rogue states, such as Iran, Syria, and Iraq. Rogue states disregard international law, brutalize their own populations, and intimidate their neighbors. Both terrorists and rogue states seemed determined to obtain weapons of mass destruction (WMD), which were hitherto available only to a limited group of nations. Their possession by terrorists or rogue states increases the threat to the United States and the civilized world. According to the 2002 strategy, the risk of mass civilian casualties ruled out the option of inaction.

Confronted with such threats, the United States felt it should no longer rely on a reactive posture, as it did with the policy of deterrence in the Cold War period. Nor should it consider itself bound by a restrictive interpretation of preemptive self-defense, which limits justified forms of preemption to imminent threats. The U.S. government implicitly rejected Webster's doctrine of anticipatory self-defense, mentioned above, which confines preemptive action to "cases in which the necessity of that self-defense is instant, overwhelming, and leaving no choice of means, and no moment for deliberation." Such a doctrine was in its view inappropriate to address the threat of terrorists and rogue states that intended to use WMD. These new types of security issues narrow the gap between imminent and nonimminent threats and between preemptive and preventive forms of self-defense.

The NSS stated that the main new threat to American security was created by the combination of the threats of terrorism, rogue states, and the proliferation of WMD. If we agree to set Webster aside, the three conditions listed by Walzer that define what he calls a "sufficient threat" are useful in considering how to respond to the NSS's perception of threat. The NSS had something to say about each of these conditions. It assumed that the first condition—the intention to harm—is always present in the case of terrorist groups and rogue states. The intention to harm the United States at any price puts terrorist groups and rogue states in a special category. The second condition—the mobilization of military forces by the hostile party, demonstrating its intent to go to war—does not have the same meaning in the case of covert operations by terrorist forces with the support of rogue states as it does in the traditional use of conventional or nuclear military forces. The third condition—that any form of inaction short of using force greatly increases the risk to the victim nation—is always met in the case of potential attacks by terrorists or rogue states using WMD. Such weapons may always be used without warning, but they are a particular danger in the hands of terrorists or rogue state leaders who cannot be deterred in the same way as traditional state actors. According to the NSS, emerging threats must be addressed long before they are fully formed and capable of threatening the United States and its allies.

For the U.S. administration, the cooperation between terrorist groups and rogue states aiming at mastering WMD technology constituted a sufficient threat for it to act preemptively (to use Walzer's and NSS terminology), or a just cause for the use of force (to use the terminology of the Just War Tradition). But this threat perception did not necessarily mean that force had to be used against threats from rogue states. It was stated explicitly in the NSS that the United States would "not use force in all cases to preempt emerging threats."[29] The United States would always proceed deliberately and weigh the consequences of its actions. This prudential consideration is in accordance with the Last Resort and Proportionality Principles in Just War Theory. The NSS document further referred to the need to coordinate its positions with its allies, with the aim of arriving at a common assessment of the threat. The United States would, moreover, build alliances and, wherever possible, rely on regional organizations. But the United States might have to act alone and does not require the authorization of others, such as a decision by the United Nations. These prescriptions refer to the Legitimate Authority Principle in Just War Theory. In relation to the just war Principle of a Likelihood of Success, the NSS stated that the fight against terrorism was different from any previous war in American history. It needed to be fought on a variety of fronts, over an extended period of time, and in conditions where progress was not always visible.[30]

The NSS radically challenged traditional legal and ethical notions about how to restrict the use of military force at an international level. It explicitly acknowledged the fact that states may use preemption as a pretext for aggression against other states, but the document did not respond to the question of how, when justifying preemptive military action, to replace the traditional criterion of an imminent threat with more appropriate normative criteria. This omission makes it difficult to understand how these policy prescriptions can be generalized to other states in the world community and how to ensure that preemption is not abused to justify aggression.

The 2002 NSS stated that preemptive self-defense is a long-accepted right (a claim that has been challenged by many legal scholars), and it reinterpreted this right by broadening it. It was the first time that a state has tried to change the legal restrictions on the use of force by openly asserting a right to start military operations against nonimminent threats. What was referred to as a preemptive use of force in this document is therefore in a sense preventive, as it is directed in an offensive mode against distant and therefore only potential dangers. But contrary to the traditional concept of a preventive war, the NSS doctrine of preemptive war assumes that the use of force is legitimized by the clear intent and actual capacity of hostile forces to inflict massive harm, and by the argument that any delay in addressing growing threats to national security would increase the risk to an intolerable level. This means that the distinction between preemptive and preventive has partly lost its previous normative meaning.

The 2002 doctrine has been put into practice in the war against Iraq.[31] In international diplomatic circles, the war itself was argued for in more traditional terms. In its legal justification before the UN at the start of the war on March 20, 2003, the United States put forward Iraq's noncompliance with its disarmament obligations concerning weapons of mass destruction. This included Baghdad's failure to present a full declaration of all aspects of its WMD programs. The letter claimed that the United States was taking the necessary steps to defend itself and the international community from the threat posed by Iraq.[32]

But the new doctrine on preemption had already been outlined in several public statements by the Bush administration in the run-up to the war. Iraq's possession of WMD and its support to international terrorist networks such as al-Qaeda were presented as aspects of the same threat to the United States, and the war against Iraq as part of the war against terror. On October 7, 2002, President Bush outlined the Iraqi threat as follows:

We know that Iraq and the al Qaeda terrorist network share a common enemy—the United States of America. We know that Iraq and al Qaeda have had high-level contacts that go back a decade. . . . We've learned that Iraq has trained al Qaeda members in bomb-making and poisons and deadly gases. And we know that after September the 11th, Saddam Hussein's regime gleefully celebrated the terrorist attacks on America. Iraq could decide on any given day to provide a biological or chemical weapon to a terrorist group or individual terrorists. Alliance with terrorists could allow the Iraqi regime to attack America without leaving any fingerprints.[33]

On October 2, 2002, the joint resolution by Congress authorizing U.S. military action in Iraq included a just cause description close to the terms used in the 2002 National Security Strategy:

Whereas Iraq's demonstrated capability and willingness to use weapons of mass destruction, the risk that the current Iraqi regime will either employ those weapons to launch a surprise attack against the United States or its Armed Forces or provide them to international terrorists who would do so, and the extreme magnitude of harm that would result to the United States and its citizens from such an attack, combine to justify action by the United States to defend itself.[34]

In the aftermath of 9/11 the American public was ready to accept the kind of threat scenario described in the National Security Strategy document, and in particular the assessment of the support potentially given to terrorist groups by rogue states such as Iraq. According to a Pew Research Center poll in October 2002, 79 percent of the U.S. population believed that Iraq was close to having or already had nuclear weapons and 66 percent believed that Saddam Hussein had helped the terrorists in the 9/11 attacks.[35]

The American and British troops occupying Iraq failed to find proof of Iraq's possession of WMD programs or weapons. Nor was there any compelling evidence of its cooperation with international terrorist groups such as al-Qaeda. Thus, despite popular beliefs, despite Saddam Hussein's repeated blustering threats, and despite concerns in the intelligence agencies of Western nations, Iraq apparently had no plans to use WMD and had no technical capacity to develop such capability rapidly. Accordingly, waiting to use force would not in fact have represented unacceptable costs. These intelligence failures did not lead to a revision of the 2002 strategy, and claims about cooperation between states radically opposed to U.S. policies and nonstate terrorist groups continued. The Bush administration persisted in using the threatening language of regime change when talking about North Korea and Iran. President Bush stated in an interview in February 2004 that such threats cannot be dealt with when they become imminent, as then it is simply too late.[36] The 2006 National Security Strategy repeats most of the 2002 doctrine on acting preemptively in exercising the right of self-defense, including the threat constituted by rogue states' support for terrorist groups and the need to preempt attacks by terrorist networks before they occur.[37] The new doctrine on preemptive defense has again been put to the test in the response to Iran's nuclear program. In this case, too, the three conditions listed by Walzer as defining what he calls a "sufficient threat" are central to the Western threat perception. First, there is the question whether an Iranian intention to breach its obligations concerning nuclear proliferation can be proven. Second, there is the question of Iran's actual capacity to acquire nuclear weapons. And there is finally the third question, the cost of refraining from using forceful means to prevent such acquisition. Would military abstinence and the exclusive use of nonforceful means greatly increase the risk of a future nuclear war? Just War Theory, as articulated today, requires the answer to these three questions in order to determine the justice of using forceful means against Iran.

There is no clear proof that Iran intends to build nuclear weapons. According to a National Intelligence Estimate (NIE)[38] made public by the U.S. intelligence agencies in November 2007, Iran was working on the development of nuclear weapons until the program was halted in 2003. Although Tehran did not appear to have any nuclear weapons program in mid-2007, the American intelligence community could not know whether it intended to resume plans for development later on. According to a declaration by President Bush on 4 December 2007, the fact that Iran had stopped one covert nuclear weapons program did not mean that it could not start another one.[39]

What could convince us that Iran has a clear intention to produce nuclear weapons? Intelligence assessments such as the NIE report on Iran are formulated in probabilistic terms as they are based on incomplete and fragmentary information. It is not possible in such a case to speak about hard facts or proofs.[40] But there is a long list of arguments critical of the view that Iran has no intention to build nuclear weapons.

First of all, Iran has breached the Nuclear Non-proliferation Treaty (NPT). Iran has been a party to this multilateral treaty since 1970. The NPT, which has been joined by 187 states since it was opened for signature in 1968, limits the spread of nuclear weapons and other nuclear explosive devices and favors international cooperation in the field of peaceful nuclear activities. Iran, as a non-nuclear-weapon state party to the NPT, accepted safeguards that it had negotiated and concluded with the International Atomic Energy Agency (IAEA), the UN body responsible for ensuring that signatory states live up to their commitments to the NPT. Since the 1980s, however, Iran has failed to declare to the IAEA what work it has conducted on uranium enrichment and plutonium separation. Tehran admitted this concealment only in 2003, after IAEA investigations. The Pakistan scientist A. Q. Khan, the father of the Pakistani nuclear weapons program, admitted that he had sold sensitive technology to Iran, as well as to Libya and North Korea.[41] This intensified the suspicion that Iran was working on a secret nuclear weapons program.[42] Owing to this past subterfuge, the onus is now on Iran to prove its peaceful intentions.[43] Some who are skeptical of Iran's good intentions argue that it may have had to stop its program on the weaponization of nuclear energy in 2003 but it has not relinquished its intention to resume this program when it has the chance.

One of the main arguments put forward in the discussion on Iran's intentions is that Iran has strong security reasons for acquiring nuclear technology. The 1980–1988 war with Iraq, in which the latter used chemical weapons, is one of the key factors likely to have prompted Iran to start a secret program to acquire nuclear weapons in the 1980s.[44] During this war, Saddam Hussein's regime received massive support from the Soviet Union, the Arab world, and Western countries—including the United States—whereas Iran remained internationally isolated.[45] The threat from Iraq was removed in 2003 as a result of the invasion of that country by American and British forces, but the escalating conflict between Iran and the United States created deep fears of another war.

The conflict between Iran and the United States has a long history. Iran has confronted the United States since the Iranian Revolution of 1979. For more than two decades U.S. diplomacy tried to isolate and punish Iran, primarily because of the hostage crisis of 1979, when some seventy U.S. diplomats and American citizens were held captive in Tehran for over fourteen months. In addition, Iran has given support to Hezbollah and other groups labeled by the Americans as terrorists. The conflict was heightened by the American description of Iran as a rogue state and part of the "axis of evil," by its appeals for regime change in Tehran, and by its increasing military presence at Iran's borders. There is a long-standing U.S. military presence in the Gulf region, and the military pressure on Iran was intensified by the opening of new military bases in Central Asia in 2001, the deployment of thousands of troops in Afghanistan in the same year, and the occupation of Iraq in 2003. Under such conditions, Iran may well have an interest in deterring an attack from the United States or from any other country that possesses WMD. This defensive security interest would be a strong motive for acquiring nuclear weapons.

A further argument in support of the view that Iran intends to build nuclear weapons runs as follows: not only does Iran have an interest in defending itself against its enemies, it also has a record of conflicts with its neighbors. Possessing a nuclear bomb would also help Iran in its attempt to play a hegemonic role in the Gulf region. Where Israel is concerned, Iran's spoiler's role in the Middle East peace process and its support for the Lebanese Hezbollah and the Palestinian Hamas has brought Tehran into confrontation with Jerusalem. The troubling statements by its president,

Mahmoud Ahmadinejad, questioning the occurrence of the Shoah and call-ing for the Israeli regime "to vanish from the page of time," has reinforced international concerns about the Iranian policy.[46]

Iranian support of terrorist groups has been seen as a serious threat by Western governments. The French nuclear doctrine presented by President Jacques Chirac in January 2006 threatened any state using terrorist means against France with reprisals up to the use of the *force de frappe* (nuclear strike force).[47] Such deterrence would not work against Iran if it possessed nuclear weapons, a fact considered by some to be a further potential motive for Tehran to move in that direction.

Tehran's use of Hezbollah as a surrogate in the struggle against Israel and the United States also has implications for the stabilization of Iraq. Britain officially complained to Tehran that explosive technology used by the Iran-ian-backed Hezbollah had been found in the hands of a Shiia militia.[48] There is widespread fear in the West that the reckless policies of the most radical currents within Iran may be pursued more easily once the country has nuclear capability with which it can deter any reprisal.[49]

The striving for international prestige and enhanced status makes nuclear capability desirable. As Iraq was eliminated as a strong regional power in 2003, Iran has the opportunity to take a leading role in a region that in-cludes some two-thirds of proven reserves of oil and 40 percent of the world's natural gas reserves.[50] This need for status became even stronger with the election of the conservative Mahmoud Ahmadinejad as president in June 2005. Ahmadinejad defends a radical agenda in domestic and in-ternational affairs.[51] Those who mistrust his intentions in the nuclear field point out that his formative political years were during the bitter war against Iraq. In Ahmadinejad's view, this was also an age of comradeship, self-sacrifice, and unity.[52] This experience may have led to his undeclared in-tention to be better prepared for any future military confrontation, which would be optimized with a nuclear deterrence capacity.

None of these arguments amounts to real proof that Iran intends to de-velop nuclear weapons. These various assumptions and observations only indicate that Iran may have a security interest in obtaining nuclear weapons and that it might use such weapons to pursue policies that go beyond strictly defensive needs.

But the question of the perception of threat goes beyond Iranian inten-tions. The discussion also concerns its capacity to acquire such weapons in the future. Even if Iran does not at present intend or have the capacity to build nuclear weapons, it may very well develop civilian nuclear capacity now and redefine its intentions later on. The so-called Japanese option—having full mastery of nuclear technology by staying below the military threshold—would therefore entail a security risk that Western countries consider unacceptable.

Some Western voices have expressed skepticism concerning the need for Iran, which possesses vast wealth in oil and gas, to invest so heavily in the civilian nuclear sector. It would be more rational for it to use its limited resources to modernize its oil and gas industry. But Iran justifies its nuclear energy policy with economic and ecological arguments. It needs electricity from nuclear plants to make better use of its oil reserves. A petrochemical industry can generate greater added value for oil than its use as fuel for power stations. According to Tehran, nuclear energy is also cleaner than oil.[53] Western governments, including the United States, accept that argument. They do not question Iran's right to acquire civilian nuclear plants—such as the one Russia is currently building in Bushehr—or to master nuclear capacity. They deny, however, that Iran needs to master the full nuclear cycle, including the uranium enrichment necessary for nuclear weapons. Mastering this technology would mean that Iran would be able to produce both nuclear fuel for civilian plants and weapons-grade material. Even if there is no proof of the claim that Iran intends to acquire nuclear weapons, its "past failure to comply with the NPT regime should lead to the permanent suspension of all uranium enrichment activities."[54] Western governments have put strong pressure on Tehran to obtain such guarantees, particularly in 2003, when it became public knowledge that Iran had an undeclared nuclear program.

As a result of this pressure, Iran became a signatory of an additional protocol with the IAEA in December 2003. This protocol obliges Tehran to provide an inventory of nuclear activities and gives the IAEA greater access to nuclear sites. It facilitates the verification of the civilian nature of Iran's program under the NPT.[55] Iran also agreed, voluntarily, not to work on a full enrichment and recycling capacity.

Iran felt compelled to make this compromise. There was economic pressure from countries such as Japan, which would invest in the oil sector only if Tehran agreed to give additional guarantees in the nuclear field.[56] Russia and China also insisted that their assistance to Iran in the nuclear field should benefit peaceful uses only.[57] And there was a strong military threat. American and British troops were deployed in Iraq. The Coalition's initial effort appeared to be quite successful at that point, and it might very well have been coupled with a military attack against Iran.

But in August 2005, Iran suddenly withdrew from the Additional Protocol and declared that it would proceed with uranium enrichment plans. It stated that it had the right to master the full nuclear cycle, as explicitly mentioned in the NPT.[58] It refused to have the nuclear fuel processed outside its borders, preferring to be independent of outside pressure in times of international crisis. It also used the argument of national pride. Iranians do not wish to be regarded as a second-class nation that is not entitled to access advanced nuclear technology, including uranium enrichment.[59]

Western governments do not consider Iran's participation in the NPT to be a sufficient guarantee that it would use nuclear energy exclusively for civilian purposes. On the contrary, being a party to this treaty has given Iran a number of significant advantages in the field of international nuclear cooperation. By acceding to this treaty, Iran has received benefits that have never been given to Israel, Pakistan, or India, all of which became nuclear powers without ever signing the NPT.[60] Thus it may be that Iran is building military nuclear capacity under the cover of a civilian nuclear program. There is moreover the fear that Iran is using the NPT to cross the nuclear threshold and that it will then withdraw from the treaty, after giving six months' notice, and develop a military nuclear program.[61] It is true, of course, that this claim could be made for all countries in possession of nuclear research or power reactors,[62] but it is a powerful argument in the context of a country that has had to admit to breaches to the NPT in the past and is so deeply mistrusted by the UNSC.

The lack of confidence in Iran was clearly expressed in the UNSC Resolution 1696 of July 2006. The council noted "with serious concern" that "the IAEA Director General's report of February 27, 2006 (GOV/2006/15) lists a number of outstanding issues and concerns on Iran's nuclear programme, including topics which could have a military nuclear dimension, and that the IAEA is unable to conclude that there are no undeclared nuclear materials or activities in Iran." It further notes that "after more than three years of Agency efforts to seek clarity about all aspects of Iran's nuclear programme, the existing gaps in knowledge continue to be a matter of concern, and that the IAEA is unable to make progress in its efforts to provide assurances about the absence of undeclared nuclear material and activities in Iran."[63]

In contrast to its estimates on WMD in Iraq, American intelligence did not exaggerate the degree of preparation of Iran. The U.S. intelligence community has been more moderate than its British, French and, certainly, its Israeli counterparts.[64] This is manifest in the NIE of 2007, which concluded that the work on weaponization was put on hold in 2003. But the report also estimated "with moderate confidence" that Iran would have the technical capacity to produce enough highly enriched uranium for a nuclear weapon between 2010 and 2015.[65] In addition, Iran is improving its missile technology. As there are three crucial elements in judging the Iranian capacity to build a nuclear weapon—the fissile material, the missile, and missile weaponization[66]—many conclude that Iran is significantly strengthening its capacity to master the full nuclear cycle and that it is developing new missile technology, without necessarily having the intention of developing nuclear weapons at the present stage. But this strengthened capacity in relation to the first two elements would give Iran greater freedom to make a radical shift in relation to the third.

What would be the consequences of such a shift, if Iran decided to withdraw from the NPT to build nuclear weapons? This question leads us to the more general problem of the risks involved in a wait-and-see attitude, which would refrain from using military force against Iran's development of a nuclear enrichment capacity. Should this increasing capacity be regarded as an imminent danger, where doing anything other than waging war greatly increases the risk of nuclear proliferation and even nuclear war?

Iran's withdrawal from the NPT—which would be the second in the treaty's history, after the withdrawal of North Korea in 2003—and particularly its acquisition of nuclear weapons would give a major impetus to nuclear proliferation, especially in the Middle East. Saudi Arabia, Egypt, and Turkey would probably try to follow suit.[67] Seen from this regional perspective, the negative consequences of acquiring nuclear weapons for regional stability would even be greater than in the case of North Korea. It would moreover have detrimental consequences for the prospect for a settlement between Israelis and Palestinians, taking into account the strengthening of the radical positions of the Iranian-backed Hezbollah in Lebanon and Hamas in the occupied territories.

This proliferation risk and the other consequences of Iran's nuclear policy for international security explain why the UNSC decided to use coercive means against Iran. It wants to obtain strict guarantees concerning the use of nuclear energy for exclusively peaceful purposes, including the suspension of enrichment-related and reprocessing activities. The UNSC further wants Iran to take concrete steps to increase confidence in its compliance with safeguard agreements with the IAEA. The UNSC has, however, limited its measures against Iran to so-called smart or targeted sanctions, aiming at the parts of Iran's nuclear program related to uranium enrichment—steps that will not have severe consequences for the Iranian population as a whole.

As we have seen, there is no manifest Iranian intention to produce nuclear weapons. Without clear proof of such intentions, its increased capacity to master nuclear technology—including those parts which would permit it to produce weapons-grade material—may not be considered sufficient to justify forceful measures that go beyond targeted sanctions. There is a risk that Iran may cross the military threshold once it has civilian nuclear capacity, but there is no consensus that this risk justifies measures beyond the art of diplomacy. Just War Theory provides no justification for the use of military force against Iran in these circumstances.

HUMANITARIAN INTERVENTION

According to Walzer, the right to use force in the defense of others, whose sovereignty and/or territorial integrity are being violated, is not so much an act of charity as it is simply an act of necessity. Because the rights of the members of international society cannot be enforced by a police force (as in a domestic society), police powers are distributed among its members. If the rights of states, Walzer says, cannot be upheld by those states, "international society collapses into a state of war or is transformed into a universal tyranny."[68]

In the Just War Tradition "other," as in "defense of others," does not have to be another state, it can also be a group of individuals belonging to another state whose fundamental rights are being violated. For just war theorists like Vitoria, Suarez, Grotius, and Gentilis, the concept of intervention for humanitarian reasons was certainly not unknown. On the contrary, the idea that the responsibility of political leaders does not stop at state borders follows logically from their natural law perspective. The belief in the existence of a universal moral order that unifies all of humanity establishes the right for states to intervene in the affairs of another state for the protection of innocent citizens belonging to that state.

One of the central post–Cold War debates in the domain of ethics and international relations is that of the legitimacy of humanitarian interventions, where, to use the definition of Paul Christopher, the intervening actor "uses its armed forces in a coercive role to cause some effect in the internal affairs of another state, and withdraws its armed force once the humanitarian objective has been met."[69] When we want to translate the subject of humanitarian interventions in terms of our general just cause definition, it is fairly obvious that a massive violation of human rights constitutes an injustice, the preemption, punishment, or correction of which can be considered to be a just cause.

Moreover, it may be argued that when states violate the most fundamental rights of their own population in a systematic and gross way, they forfeit their sovereignty. This line of argument is rooted in social contract theory. State sovereignty, so it is said, ultimately derives its legitimacy from the rights that the individuals gained in a social contract that led to the formation of the state. And so once a state stops respecting the contract of its citizens, it can no longer be considered as a legitimate political organization.

But anti-interventionists will argue that humanitarian intervention violates basic principles of international law, particularly the sovereignty and the territorial integrity of that state. The target-state might well argue that it is not being treated as it should be (others should not interfere with its internal affairs) and that in defending its sovereignty it has a just cause. Opening the door for intervention will put nations on a very slippery slope. Allowing intervention for humanitarian reasons will ultimately undermine the cornerstone of our international order.

What is more, states have a primary responsibility toward their own people and have no obligation to go to the rescue of populations in need all over the world. The idea of humanitarian intervention, so anti-interventionists may say, seems to instill us with some kind of universal guilt as experienced by Father Zossima's younger brother in *The Brothers Karamazov*, who was convinced that "every one of us is responsible for everyone else in every way, and I most of all."[70]

Who is right then? The intervening actor who wants to protect the fundamental rights of people belonging to another country or the state that wants to defend itself against an intervention? Although each of these two positions concerning humanitarian intervention has a long history and has always been defended in some way, Bryan Hehir notices that over time there seems to have been a pendulum movement between these two extremes.[71] Throughout the Middle Ages until the middle of the seventeenth century, the dominant normative perspective was in favor of intervention. The medieval political community was built on the universal values of Christianity. When a ruler committed a grave injustice against the citizens of the state, that injustice was not just the business of that ruler alone. Other rulers of the "Republica Christiana" had a right to intervene in order to come to the rescue of the oppressed people.[72] With the Peace of Westphalia in 1648, the normative perspective of sovereignty and nonintervention replaced this universal moral foundation. In order to put an end to all the religious wars and chaos, all parties thought it more prudent that all states keep to their own affairs. In that view, nonintervention became the proclaimed (although not necessarily respected) rule.

The meaning of sovereignty changed in the post–World War II period. Although sovereignty and nonintervention were still the dominant values in the UN Charter, individual human rights became an increasingly important part of international moral reality. This became even more evident at the end of the Cold War in the 1990s. While the number of humanitarian interventions during the Cold War period was limited for the fear of escalation, one of the major trends in the post–Cold War era was an increasing demand for international humanitarian interventions in intrastate conflicts, particularly those conflicts where massive human rights violations were taking place.[73]

Another just cause–related problem concerns the definition of the *scope* of the intervention. How far should such an intervention go? Should the intervening actor limit himself to the delivery of humanitarian assistance or should such an operation be more substantial by trying to create an environment safe for democracy and human rights? We enter here the whole field of state and nation building. One might defend the first position by arguing that even when we intervene for humanitarian purposes, we should always refrain as much as possible from interfering in the internal affairs of another community. We must never forget that the conflict in which we intervene is not *our* conflict. It is therefore advisable not to influence the outcome in any way.

For John Stuart Mill, who is a strong anti-interventionist, this position implies the ultimate respect for the principle of self-determination. "The members of a political community must seek their own freedom" and "they cannot be set free by external force."[74] In contrast, Robert Phillips is a strong defender of the more interventionist stance. He argues that "it would be morally retrograde to bring someone back from the brink of death only to resubmit him to the political regime whose ineptness or malice consigned him to starvation in the first place."[75] Now although it *feels* right to say that this humanitarian assistance approach constitutes a definite just cause, from a more conceptual point this is strangely enough not so self-evident. The international intervention in the Bosnian conflict (1992–1995) illustrates this point nicely.[76]

When the Bosnian war started in the spring of 1992, the international community had already recognized Bosnia as a sovereign state. The official Muslim-led government of Bosnia tried to keep Bosnia together as an independent state, whereas the Bosnian Serbs and Bosnian Croats were eager to join Serbia and Croatia respectively. The Bosnian government desperately asked the international community to intervene on its behalf to stem sectarian violence. Although the UNSC several times condemned all the attempts to violate Bosnian integrity, the Council was very reluctant to send in peacekeeping troops to stop the fighting.[77] What the UNSC was willing to do, however, was to provide troops in order to distribute humanitarian assistance. Indeed, from the very beginning of the hostilities, the international community witnessed the most atrocious and inhumane acts committed by all the parties to the conflict. The main objective of these acts was to get rid of those persons who did not belong to the "right" ethnic group. This process of ethnic cleansing had many faces: harassment, dispossession of property, detainment in concentration camps, mass rape, and execution, among others. It goes without saying that all this created an enormous problem of refugees and displaced persons in the former Yugoslavia itself as well as in neighboring countries. In August 1994, the United Nations High Commissioner for Refugees estimated the number of refugees in Bosnia and Herzegovina alone to be more than two million. In order to do something about this humanitarian catastrophe, the UNSC authorized the use of force to ensure the security of the humanitarian personnel,[78] to protect the humanitarian convoys,[79] and to ensure the compliance with the ban on flights in the airspace of Bosnia.[80] In the course of the Bosnian conflict, the international community also created six so-called safe areas (Sarajevo, Srebrenica, Zepa, Gorazde, Bihac, and Tuzla).[81] These areas were to be free from any armed attack or hostile act. Despite its humanitarian concerns, the international community had no intention of defending these areas militarily.[82] The UN forces stationed in these areas were intended to have only a deterrent effect. But as the tragedy of Srebrenica in July of 1995 shows, where the Bosnian Serbs slaughtered several thousand male Muslims without encountering resistance from Dutch UN troops, this safe-area policy failed miserably.[83]

Now, the essence of the act of humanitarian assistance in the Bosnian conflict was in fact quite simple, viz., try to reduce the amount of human suffering by providing for the most urgent needs, such as food, shelter, and health care. This means that the ground of humanitarianism was not about the correction, prevention, or punishment of the injustices, but about the mitigation of the consequences of these injustices. Given this ground for the use of force as provided by the UNSC resolutions, it was possible for the international community to use military force in order to deliver humanitarian assistance, but not, for instance, to stop the practice of ethnic cleansing. Nor could this ground have been used to arrest and punish those who gave orders for and those who executed these heinous crimes. The fact that the ground of humanitarian assistance lacked the corrective, punitive, or preventive nature means, *stricto sensu*, that it did not satisfy the requirements of the Just Cause definition, and therefore could not be considered to be a just cause. One might argue in this respect that the Just Cause definition seems to imply the presence of a relatively robust ambition. The alleviation of human suffering alone, it appears, is not enough. According to our general Just Cause definition more than that needs to be achieved.

A number of authors have commented negatively about the minimalist nature of humanitarian assistance during the Bosnian war. Rosalyn Higgins, for instance, pointed out that the international community simply did not do enough in the Bosnian conflict: "We have chosen to respond to major unlawful violence not by stopping that violence, but by trying to provide relief to the suffering. But our choice of policy allows the suffering to continue."[84] David Rieff formulated this view even more sharply: "The UN fed people and allowed them to be shelled."[85] For Thomas Weiss it was clear for all to see that the UN concentrated far too much on the consequences of the conflict. He said "the United Nations has collectively downplayed tasks such as protecting fundamental rights and gathering information about war crimes or even assertively and routinely investigating alleged abuses."[86]

Finally, it is also important to realize that the discussion on the scope of humanitarian interventions does not limit itself to the Just Cause Principle alone. It also has serious consequences for those *jus ad bellum* criteria that are closely related to the Principle of the Just Cause. Think for instance of the Likelihood of Success or the Proportionality principles. The results for these two principles will probably be very different when we choose either a minimal or a more substantial intervention. One could even argue that the authority that has the right to decide in both scenarios does not necessarily have to be one and the same (Principle of Legitimate Authority). One could indeed easily claim that an intervention with wide-ranging political and social implications will no doubt require a much broader basis of legitimacy (e.g., the UNSC) than an intervention with pure humanitarian assistance purposes.

The question of humanitarian intervention, which had been so passionately debated during the 1990s in respect to the Balkans, was addressed again a decade later in the framework of the discussions on the reform of the UN security system. At the UN World Summit of September 2005, the participating states endorsed a new concept, called "the responsibility to protect," which vests the international community with a special responsibility for the protection of the people within a state's territory from genocide, war crimes, ethnic cleansing, and crimes against humanity. According to this concept, the international community has to take up this responsibility if that state is unable or unwilling to meet its obligations as a sovereign state.[87]

The concept of a "responsibility to protect" should not be seen as a challenge to the principle of sovereignty but as a clarification of its limits and as part of an enlarged concept of security. It does not amount to a legal norm that would legitimize unilateral intervention in domestic affairs by individual states or regional organizations, but refers on the contrary to the encouragement and support the international community has to give to states so that they exercise this responsibility. It also refers to the special responsibility of the UNSC to use appropriate means if states fail to act responsibly. But the new concept does not include a legal obligation on the UNSC to intervene.

The UN document illustrates the profound shift in the attitude to sovereignty, which has moved from meaning control over national territory to being viewed in terms of responsibility toward a state's own population.[88] The culture of sovereign impunity, characteristic of older views of the principle of nonintervention in domestic affairs, is likewise slowly moving toward a culture of international accountability. In such a context, the concept of a "responsibility to protect" has some advantages over the use of the traditional term "right to intervene." According to Gareth Evans and Mohamed Sahnoun, the point of view of those considering intervention is replaced by the perspective of those seeking or needing support. It is moreover implicit in this formulation that the state retains the primary responsibility to protect its own population and that the international community can act in its place only if it fails to fulfill its duty in this regard. Where the traditional concept of humanitarian intervention put strong emphasis on the "responsibility to react," the new concept of "responsibility to protect" also stresses the "responsibility to prevent" and the "responsibility to rebuild."

There is no easy and straightforward answer when we are confronted with cases in which Just Cause is, apparently, found on both sides. This problem has been analyzed in depth by just war theorists. The U.S. Catholic bishops for instance, are all too conscious of the tendency of some theorists to trea

Just Cause as an absolute principle. In their pastoral letter, "The Challenge of Peace, God's Promise, and our Response," they state that "every party should acknowledge the limits of its Just Cause and the consequent requirement to use only limited means in pursuit of its objectives."[89] This principle or doctrine, which is seldom mentioned as a separate *jus ad bellum* criterion, is generally referred to in the Just War Tradition as that of comparative justice. Because the adversary is not all bad and one's own side is not wholly righteous, Just War Theory urges governments not to exaggerate accusations against other states and to avoid the excessive use of force in pursuit of perceived just cause.

NOTES

1. Thomas Aquinas, *Summa Theologica (II–II)*, pt. 3, q. 40 (Paris: CERF, 1985), 280.

2. Gregory M. Reichberg, Henrik Syse, and Endre Begby, eds., *The Ethics of War: Classic and Contemporary Readings* (Oxford: Blackwell Publishing, 2006), 315–16.

3. Reichberg, Syse, and Begby, *The Ethics of* War, 343.

4. Emmerich de Vattel, *The Law of Nations or Principles of the Law of Nature Applied to the Conduct and Affairs of Nations and Sovereigns*, bk. 3, chap. 3, § 26, ed. Joseph Chitty (Philadelphia: T. & J. W. Johnson & Co., 1883), at www.constitution.org/vattel/vattel.htm (accessed February 17, 2008); "A just cause then of war is an injury, which though not actually committed, threatens our persons or property with danger." Hugo Grotius, *The Rights of War and Peace*, bk. 2, chap. 1, sec. 2, trans. A. C. Campbell (Washington, D.C., and London: M. Walter Dunne, 1901), at www.constitution.org/gro/djbp.htm (accessed February 17, 2008).

5. Grotius, *The Rights of War and Peace*, bk. 2, chap. 1, sec. 5.

6. Grotius, *The Rights of War and Peace*, bk. 2, chap. 1, sec. 17.

7. Vattel, *The Law of Nations*, bk. 2, chap. 4, § 50.

8. See Michael Walzer's discussion of what he calls "the rape of Belgium." Michael Walzer, *Just and Unjust Wars: A Moral Argument with Historical Illustrations*, 2nd ed. (New York: Basic Books, 1992), 240–42.

9. The following example is taken from Anthony Hartle's contribution to the first edition of this book: Anthony Hartle, "The Gulf War," in *Moral Constraints on War*, ed. Bruno Coppieters and Nick Fotion, 1st ed. (Lanham, Md.: Lexington Books, 2002), 161–62.

10. Richard J. Regan, *Just War: Principles and Cases* (Washington, D.C.: Catholic University of America Press, 1996), 172.

11. Steve A. Yetiv, *The Persian Gulf Crisis* (Westport, Conn.: Greenwood Press, 1997), xvii.

12. Yetiv, *The Persian Gulf Crisis*, 7.

13. Glenn Frankel, "Imperialist Legacy: Lines in the Sand," *Washington Post*, April 2, 1990, A20, as quoted in Alan Geyer and Barbara G. Green, *Lines in the Sand: Justice and the Gulf War* (Louisville, Ky.: Westminster/John Knox Press, 1992), 34.

14. Frankel, "Imperialist Legacy," 33.

15. Lawrence Freedman and Efraim Karsh, *The Gulf Conflict, 1990–1991: Diplomacy and War in the New World Order* (Princeton, N.J.: Princeton University Press, 1993), 43.

16. U.S. Department of Defense, *Conduct of the Persian Gulf War* (Washington, D.C.: U.S. Government Printing Office, 1992), 7.

17. See David B. Rivkin Jr., Lee A. Casey, and Mark Wendell DeLaquil, "Preemption and Law in the Twenty-first Century," *Chicago Journal of International Law* 5, no. 2 (Winter 2005): 467–99.

18. Jan Wouters and Tom Ruys, "The Legality of Anticipatory Military Action after 9/11: The Slippery Slope of Self-Defence," in *The Impact of 9/11 on European Foreign and Security Policy*, ed. Giovanna Bono (Brussels: VUB Press / Brussels University Press, 2006), 61–63.

19. Walzer, *Just and Unjust Wars*, 77.

20. Walzer, *Just and Unjust Wars*, 81. The two first principles refer to the Just Cause Principle and the third one to the Proportionality and Last Resort Principles.

21. Walzer, *Just and Unjust Wars*, 83. This claim that Nasser himself appealed for Israel to be destroyed is denied by the French historian Henry Laurens, who states in an interview that Nasser was far more moderate in his attacks against Israel than the Egyptian media and the Egyptian propaganda machinery, who did indeed call for the destruction of Israel. Nasser was thus a victim of his own propaganda. See "Une guerre par inadvertence," *Courrier International* no. 865, May 31–June 6, 2007, 39.

22. Walzer, *Just and Unjust Wars*, 83.

23. The Israeli army, which had been trained to move quickly and to attack, was not prepared for such a long-term defensive task. See the interview with the French historian Henry Laurens: "Une guerre par inadvertence," 39.

24. Statement to the General Assembly by Foreign Minister Eban, June 19, 1967, at www.mfa.gov.il/MFA/Foreign%20Relations/Israels%20Foreign%20Relations%20since%201947/1947-1974/ (accessed February 14, 2008).

25. Wouters and Ruys, "The Legality of Anticipatory Military Action after 9/11," 65.

26. For more information on the distinction between "first strike" and "second strike," see Steven Lee's contribution in *An Encyclopedia of War and Ethics*, ed. Donald A. Wells (Westport and London: Greenwood Press, 1996), 140–42.

27. Paul Ramsey, *The Just War: Force and Political Responsibility* (Littlefield, Texas: Adams Quality Paperbacks, 1983), 68.

28. The National Security Strategy of the United States, September 2002, on the Internet at www.whitehouse.gov/nsc/nss.pdf (accessed February 14, 2008). On the Bush doctrine of preemptive war, see Rivkin, Casey, and DeLaquil, "Preemption and Law in the Twenty-first Century"; Gilles Andréani, "The 'War on Terror': Good Cause, Wrong Concept," *Survival* 46, no. 4 (Winter 2004–2005): 31–50; Wouters and Ruys, "The Legality of Anticipatory Military Action after 9/11," 67–72; Alan M. Dershowitz, *Preemption: A Knife that Cuts Both Ways* (New York and London: W. W. Norton & Company, 2006).

29. The National Security Strategy of the United States, 15.

30. The National Security Strategy of the United States, 5.

31. On the following, see Andréani, "'The War on Terror,'" 45–46.

32. Letter dated March 20, 2003, from the permanent representative of the United States of America to the United Nations, addressed to the president of the security council, UN Doc. S/2003/351 (Mar. 21, 2003).

33. "President Bush Outlines Iraqi Threat, Remarks by the President on Iraq," October 7, 2002, at www.whitehouse.gov/news/releases/2002/10/print/20021007-8 .html (accessed February 14, 2008).

34. "Joint Resolution to Authorize the Use of United States Armed Forces Against Iraq," October 2, 2002, at www.whitehouse.gov/news/releases/2002/10/20021002 -2.html (accessed February 14, 2008). See also Andréani, "'The War on Terror,'" 45–46

35. Lee Feinstein, "Most Americans Support War with Iraq, Shows New Pew/CFR Poll," Council on Foreign Relations, October 10, 2002, at www.cfr.org/publication .html?id=5051 (accessed February 14, 2008).

36. Michael Byers, *War Law* (London: Atlantic Books, 2005), 80.

37. The National Security Strategy of the United States of America, March 2006, at www.whitehouse.gov/nsc/nss/2006/ (accessed February 14, 2008).

38. National Intelligence Estimate, *Iran: Nuclear Intentions and Capabilities*, National Intelligence Council, November 2007, at www.dni.gov/press_releases/ 20071203_release.pdf (accessed February 14, 2008).

39. Andrew Ward, Daniel Dombey, and Demetri Sevastopulo, "Tehran Remains a Threat, Insists White House," *Financial Times*, December 5, 2007, 4.

40. *Iran: Nuclear Intentions and Capabilities*.

41. See Wyn Q. Bowen and Joanna Kidd, "The Iranian Nuclear Challenge," *International Affairs* 80, no. 2 (2004): 262; Daniel Dombey and Guy Dinmore, "Iranian Defiance Reveals Weakness in West's Lobbying," *Financial Times*, September 19, 2005, 4.

42. Bowen and Kidd, "The Iranian Nuclear Challenge," 257–60; François Heisbourg, *Iran, le Choix des Armes?* (Paris: Stock, 2007), 44–45.

43. Gareth Smyth and Raphael Minder, "EU Fears as Iran Gets Set to Resume Atomic Research," *Financial Times*, January 9, 2006.

44. On Iran's threat perceptions, see Bowen and Kidd, "The Iranian Nuclear Challenge," 263–65.

45. Heisbourg, *Iran, le Choix des Armes?* 61.

46. John J. Mearsheimer and Stephen M. Walt, *The Israel Lobby and U.S. Foreign Policy* (New York: Farrar, Straus and Giroux, 2007), 280–81.

47. Heisbourg, *Iran, le Choix des Armes?* 71. David S. Yost, "France's New Nuclear Doctrine," *International Affairs* 82, no. 4 (2006): 702.

48. Christopher Adams and Roula Khalaf, "UK Accuses Iran over Iraqi Rebels," *Financial Times*, October 6, 2005, 5.

49. Bertelsmann Group for Policy Research and Center for Applied Policy Research, *Europe and the Middle East—New Ways and Solutions for Old Problems and Challenges?* (Munich: Center for Applied Policy Research, September 2006), 19.

50. Heisbourg, *Iran, le Choix des Armes?* 59.

51. Heisbourg, *Iran, le Choix des Armes?* 58.

52. Gareth Smyth, "Humble Son of Revolution," *Financial Times*, January 14–15, 2006, 7; Ray Takeyh, "Diplomacy Will Not End Iran's Nuclear Programme," *Financial Times*, December 21, 2005, 13. There are unproven accusations against Ahmadinejad that he has a terrorist background and was even implicated in the occupation of the U.S. embassy in Tehran. According to Bernard Lewis, an American scholar on Islam with influence on the Bush administration's views on the Middle

East, Ahmadinejad thinks he is living in an apocalyptic age where a nuclear conflict with Israel, or even all infidels, may hasten the return of the Hidden Imam. Bernard Lewis, "August 22: Does Iran Have Something in Store?" *Wall Street Journal,* August 8, 2006, at www.opinionjournal.com/extra/?id=110008768 (accessed February 14, 2008). See also Harvey Morris, "Spectre of Nuclear Neighbour Leaves Israel Braced for Action," *Financial Times,* January 13–14, 2007, 2. Lewis' thesis that Iran has the intention not only of building nuclear weapons but also of provoking a nuclear war for religious reasons goes far beyond the traditional worst-case scenarios discussed in Western capitals.

53. Bowen and Kidd, "The Iranian Nuclear Challenge," 258.

54. Group for Policy Research and Center for Applied Policy Research, *Europe and the Middle East,* 21.

55. Bowen and Kidd, "The Iranian Nuclear Challenge," 257.

56. Bowen and Kidd, "The Iranian Nuclear Challenge," 266.

57. Bowen and Kidd, "The Iranian Nuclear Challenge," 261.

58. Article 4 of the NPT states that "Nothing in this Treaty shall be interpreted as affecting the inalienable right of all the Parties to the Treaty to develop research, production and use of nuclear energy for peaceful purposes." Treaty on the Non-proliferation of Nuclear Weapons, at www.iaea.org/Publications/Documents/Treaties/npt.html (accessed February 14, 2008).

59. Gareth Smith, "Defiant Tehran Warns Europe on Allocation of Oil and Gas Contracts," *Financial Times,* September 21, 2005, 7.

60. Heisbourg, *Iran, le Choix des Armes?* 78.

61. Bowen and Kidd, "The Iranian Nuclear Challenge," 267.

62. Alexander H. Montgomery, "Ringing in Proliferation. How to Dismantle an Atomic Bomb Network," *International Security* 30, no. 2 (Fall 2005): 167.

63. Resolution 1696, adopted by the Security Council at its 5500th meeting, on July 31, 2006.

64. Heisbourg, *Iran, le Choix des Armes?* 173–74.

65. National Intelligence Estimate, *Iran: Nuclear Intentions and Capabilities;* Ward, Dombey, and Sevastopulo, "Tehran Remains a Threat, Insists White House."

66. David Miliband, "Why We Must Not Take the Pressure off Iran," *Financial Times,* December 6, 2007, 11.

67. Heisbourg, *Iran, le Choix des Armes?* 142–43.

68. Walzer, *Just and Unjust Wars,* 59.

69. Paul Christopher, *The Ethics of War and Peace: An Introduction to Legal and Moral Issues,* 2nd ed. (Upper Saddle River, N.J.: Prentice Hall, 1999), 193.

70. Fyodor Dostoyevsky quoted in David Fisher, "The Ethics of Intervention," *Survival* 36, no. 1 (Spring 1994): 51.

71. J. Bryan Hehir, "Intervention: From Theories to Cases," *Ethics & International Affairs* 9 (1995): 5–6.

72. The right to intervene for humanitarian purposes can be found in the work of a number of just war theorists, such as de Vitoria, Suarez, and Grotius. See also James Turner Johnson, "Humanitarian Intervention, Christian Ethical Reasoning, and the Just War Idea," in *Sovereignty at the Crossroads? Morality and International Politics in the Post–Cold War Era,* ed. Luis Lugo (Lanham, Md.: Rowman & Littlefield, 1996), 127–43.

73. There is an extensive body of literature on this subject. Some examples: Jarat Chopra and Thomas Weiss, "Sovereignty Is No Longer Sacrosanct: Codifying Humanitarian Intervention," *Ethics & International Affairs* 6 (1992): 95–117; Peter Malanczuk, *Humanitarian Intervention and the Legitimacy of the Use of Force* (Amsterdam: Het Spinhuis, 1993), 69; Richard Lilllich, "Humanitarian Intervention through the United Nations: Towards the Development of Criteria," *Zeitschrift für ausländisches öffentliches Recht und Volkenrecht* 53, no. 3 (1993): 557–75; Fernando Tesón, *Humanitarian Intervention: An Inquiry into Law and Morality*, 2nd ed. (Irvington-on-Hudson, N.Y.: Transnational Publishers, 1997), 338.

74. John Stuart Mill quoted in Walzer, *Just and Unjust Wars*, 87.

75. Robert Phillips and Duane Cady, *Humanitarian Intervention: Just War vs. Pacifism* (Lanham, Md.: Rowman & Littlefield, 1996), 28.

76. For a just war analysis of the Bosnian war, see Carl Ceulemans, *Reluctant Justice: A Just-War Analysis of the International Use of Force in Former Yugoslavia (1991–1995)* (Brussels: VUB Brussels University Press, 2005).

77. International reluctance to get militarily involved in Bosnia would change somewhat after the fall of the safe area of Srebrenica in July 1995, and certainly after the mortar attack on a marketplace in Sarajevo on August 28, 1995, which killed forty-one people and injured eighty-four. In reaction to this mortar attack, NATO initiated an air campaign ("Deliberate Force") against Bosnian Serb targets in Bosnia. This air campaign, which was suspended indefinitely by the UN and NATO on September 20, 1995, would ultimately lead to the final talks in Dayton that in turn would result in a global agreement on Bosnia (November 1995).

78. In Security Council Resolution 761 (June 29, 1992) §4 and Security Council Resolution 770 (August 13, 1992) §6, the Security Council demanded for instance that "all parties and others concerned take the necessary measures to ensure the safety of United Nations and other personnel engaged in the delivery of humanitarian assistance."

79. In Resolution 770 (August 13, 1992) §2 the Security Council called upon states "to take, nationally or through regional agencies or arrangements, all necessary measures to facilitate, in co-ordination with the United Nations, the delivery by the relevant UN humanitarian organizations and others of humanitarian assistance to Sarajevo and wherever needed in other parts of Bosnia and Herzegovina."

80. In Resolution 816 (March 31, 1993) §4, the Security Council authorized "Member States, acting nationally or through regional organizations or arrangements, to take, under the authority of the Security Council and subject to close co-ordination with the Secretary-General and UNPROFOR, all necessary measures in order to ensure compliance with the ban in the airspace of Bosnia and Herzegovina."

81. See Security Council Resolution 819 of April 16, 1993 and Security Council Resolution 824 of May 6, 1993.

82. The key resolution in this respect was Security Council Resolution 836 of 4 June 1993. Here the Security Council authorized UNPROFOR "acting in self-defence, to take the necessary measures, including the use of force, in reply to bombardments against the safe areas by any of the parties or to armed incursion into them or in the event of any deliberate obstruction in or around those areas to the freedom of movement of UNPROFOR or of protected humanitarian convoys." At first sight these stipulations seem to support the fact that the protection of the safe

areas constituted a ground for the use of force: if a safe area is subjected to an armed attack, whether by means of bombardments or armed incursions, then it is authorized to use all necessary means to put an end to this attack. Now, this would no doubt be the case were it not for the fact that Security Council Resolution 836 explicitly mentioned "acting in self-defence." These three words make all the difference. By adding the expression "acting in self-defense," the international community restricted the possibility of resorting to military force to those cases where the armed attacks also represented a danger to the safety of UN personnel and the personnel of other agencies.

83. For a detailed account of this tragedy, see Jan Willem Honig and Norbert Both, *Srebrenica: Record of a War Crime* (London: Penguin Books, 1996), 204.

84. Rosalyn Higgins, "The New United Nations and Former Yugoslavia," *International Affairs* 69 (1993): 469.

85. David Rieff, *Slaughterhouse: Bosnia and the Failure of the West* (London: Vintage, 1995), 120.

86. Thomas Weiss, "UN Responses in the Former Yugoslavia. Moral and Operational Choices," *Ethics & International Affairs* 8 (1994): 5. For a more detailed study of the ethical implications and limitations of humanitarian assistance, see also Amir Pasic and Thomas Weiss, "The Politics of Rescue: Yugoslavia's Wars and the Humanitarian Impulse," *Ethics & International Affairs* 11 (1997): 105–31.

87. See Barbara Delcourt, "The Doctrine of 'Responsibility to Protect' and the EU Stance: A Critical Appraisal," in *The Impact of 9/11 on European Foreign and Security Policy*, 99–126; Anne Peters and Simone Peter, "Lehren vom 'gerechten Krieg' aus völkerrechtlicher Sicht," in *Der "Gerechte Krieg." Zur Geschichte einer aktuellen Denkfigur*, ed. Georg Kreis (Basel: Schwabe Verlag, 2006), 88–90.

88. On the normative implications of the language of "responsibility to protect" rather than the "right to intervene," see Gareth Evans and Mohamed Sahnoun, "The Responsibility to Protect," *Foreign Affairs* 81, no. 6 (November/December 2002): 99–110.

89. U.S. Catholic Bishops, "Pastoral Letter: The Challenge of Peace, God's Promise and our Response," in *Just War Theory*, ed. Jean Bethke Elshtain (Oxford: Basil Blackwell, 1992), 99.

2

Legitimate Authority

Bruno Coppieters

BACKGROUND

Throughout modern history, the state has been the main agent of war. States have engaged in military aggression, colonial expansion, and violent repression of minority populations. Even when states do not pursue these policies, they constitute a *threat* to other states. It has always been assumed that the old Roman maxim *Si vis pacem, para bellum* (If you want peace, prepare for war) constitutes a sound basis for wise statecraft. Even the most peace-loving statesmen have to act according to this maxim. Apparently, all states—even those not preparing for military aggression or expansion—have to be sufficiently armed to be able to defend their population and territory. Seen from this perspective, states do not restrain the use of military force but actually favor it. They are prone to the use of violence, it seems, regardless of the political intentions of their leaders.

The pacifying role of states should, however, also be taken into account.[1] States play prominent roles in restraining violence. One of the achievements of modern sovereign states has been to establish a monopoly on the use of force by outlawing vendettas and blood revenge, and confiscating weaponry from militias, local warlords, and medieval barons. The repression of all private forms of warfare was carried out in the name of the public interest. The German sociologist Max Weber, referring to a statement made by the Russian Bolshevik Leon Trotsky, therefore considered that the distinctive attribute of the state—as opposed to other forms of political organization—was its monopoly on the use of force.[2]

The distinction between a "private" and a "public" form of warfare helps to limit the recourse to violence. Private warfare is always illegitimate, but public warfare may be legitimate under certain circumstances. The principle whereby each person has the right to take justice into his own hands would make any legal order impossible. Private warfare would lead to an anarchic situation, in which each individual would constitute a threat to all other individuals. People would judge according to their own personal moral criteria, without any consideration for legal procedures. In the Old Testament, the last verse of the Book of Judges vividly describes such an anarchic situation: "In those days there was no king in Israel; every man did that which was right in his own eyes." (Judges 21:25).

From the just war perspective, public warfare is only to be used as a legal instrument, as part of the coercive power (*vis coactiva*) of a state to implement a just cause. Public institutions may be considered to have legitimate authority to use force when they need to correct and/or punish an injustice that has been perpetrated, or *preempt* an injustice that is about to happen. The Principle of Legitimate Authority thus refers to state institutions as the legitimate source of force. But legitimation does not derive only from a state's interest or its domestic concerns. The right of a state or an international institution to wage war may also be understood as deriving from its commitment, as part of the international community, to the common good and the rule of law. States and international organizations may use force only if doing so can be construed as a defense of international order and a means of ensuring peace and security.[3] Such an understanding of the state and the military presupposes the primacy of the rule of law in international relations. This just war concept is only one of many that have gradually emerged over the centuries. A very different conception of legitimate authority prevailed only a few centuries ago.

During the Middle Ages soldiering was seen as a mercenary enterprise, not a public service.[4] Those who soldiered fought on their own, with their own equipment and men, not as salaried servants of public interest. In the Hundred Years' War between France and England (1337–1453), it was often difficult to say what cause the various local warlords and bands of indigent knights were fighting for.[5] But they always fought in the name of some prince. Without this public sanction they could not fight according to the laws of war in use at that time. Without such a sanction they had, for instance, no title to the ransom and booty they captured.[6] In that period the question also remained, however, as to who could qualify as a public authority in a public space where power was fragmented among hundreds of different political entities. The pope? The king? The local princes? The cities? The lack of consensus on this question lasted until a monopoly on the use of force had been established in favor of a limited number of sovereign states.

The political map of Medieval Europe, where the boundaries of the political communities were not clearly defined geographically, was gradually redrawn. That state sovereignty, independent of any external authority, was the only way to prevent the wars of religion that had destroyed so much of Europe during the sixteenth and seventeenth centuries was an argument that increasingly gained ground. This secularization of the notion of Legitimate Authority included a rejection of the claims to universal authority made by the Catholic Church. The definition of who could legitimately use force was gradually narrowed down over the centuries. It was clearer in 1500 than in 1300 and even clearer after the Peace of Westphalia, which concluded the bitter Thirty Years' War (1618–1648). The principle of nonintervention in the internal affairs of sovereign states was clearly articulated at the end of the eighteenth century as the Westphalian system of international order.[7] The sovereign power exercised by states ruled out all other types of actors in the domestic and international order as being illegitimate.[8]

The modern just war Principle of Legitimate Authority is inextricably bound up with the modern legal principle of state sovereignty. Since the end of the eighteenth century the right of governments to represent final and absolute sovereignty, in effect denying the existence of any other final absolute authority,[9] has been seen as a widely accepted and feasible mechanism for organizing international society. But its meaning and scope has been constantly debated. In fact, the fundament of the Westphalian model—the principle of nonintervention in the internal affairs of other countries—has been repeatedly violated. The Holy Alliance, established by Europe's main powers after the defeat of Napoleon in 1815, invoked the right to intervene against revolutionary regimes in order to safeguard the traditional order.[10] The United States, a nation that had intervened repeatedly in Central America and the Caribbean, rejected the legal principle that "no state has a right to interfere in the internal affairs of another" until 1933.[11] Soviet troops were deployed in Hungary (1956) and Czechoslovakia (1968). When the United States invaded Panama in 1989, it invoked the problem of drug running.[12] Throughout the whole of the Cold War, the Soviet and American governments were active in supporting their respective allies in proxy wars in Africa and Asia. The Soviet intervention in Afghanistan in 1979 was followed by active military support from Western countries to the anti-Soviet Mujahiddin. But not even all these breaches led to the abolition of the institution of sovereignty: even those states that had, by their practical actions, violated the principle of nonintervention in internal affairs, had a basic interest in retaining sovereignty as the cornerstone of international security.

It is possible to distinguish a set of five problems linked to the question of when force may be used in the name of a legitimate authority. All these problems are directly related to the question of sovereignty. The principle of the internal sovereignty of states has been questioned in the domestic sphere by patriotic forces opposing collaborationist regimes, revolutionary parties, and anticolonial movements. And the principle of external sovereignty has been questioned at the international level by the security system of the United Nations. The question of secession lies at the boundary between domestic and international sovereignty. This will be dealt with in a separate chapter in this volume—chapter 11, which is a case study on the international status of Kosovo.

COLLABORATION AND RESISTANCE: *LA FRANCE LIBRE*

The Principle of Legitimate Authority should not be subordinated to the concept of state sovereignty, lest it be transformed into a purely formal and undemanding requirement. Such subordination might also undermine the right of resistance against tyrannical and otherwise unjust regimes.[13] According to a formalist interpretation of this principle, resistance movements against Nazi occupation in Western or Eastern Europe would not have had a legitimate right to defend their homelands because they were not acting under the orders of a regular government.[14] The case of France illustrates this problem.

On September 3, 1939, both France and Britain declared war on Germany.[15] Four and a half million Frenchmen were mobilized to serve either in France or in the French colonies. But the fighting did not start until spring. On May 10, 1940, the German army launched its offensive. The first weeks of the blitzkrieg were disastrous for the allied forces. Belgium capitulated on May 28. Two hundred and thirty-five thousand British and 115,000 French troops had to be evacuated to Britain, while 35,000 French soldiers were taken prisoner. On June 14, the German troops entered Paris. Three days later, Marshal Philippe Pétain, the new leader of the French government, acknowledged the French defeat. Pétain enjoyed wide popular support as one of the main architects of the French military victory in World War I. But, now, in World War II, he decided that further resistance against Germany was futile. An armistice was signed on June 22. More than a simple cease-fire, the armistice implied that France and Germany were no longer in a state of war with each other. The significance of this act was far-reaching. By putting their signature to the text of the armistice, the French authorities put all those who wanted to continue to fight against German occupation outside the law. As the government representing the French people had capitulated, no legitimate authority existed to pursue the war or any armed resistance.

The French official attitude was partly influenced by the experience of the previous war. Despite their firm resolution to achieve military victory over Germany at the beginning of the military operations, the French had strongly hoped that the tragedy of World War I, in which the country had lost 1.4 million people, could be avoided. Yet the number of victims of the war operations of 1940 should not be overlooked: by the end of June 1940, after some crushing military defeats, some 92,000 French and allied troops had been killed or reported missing, 200,000 had been wounded, and 1,500,000 taken prisoner. The German army had lost 45,000 troops in the war. These numbers testified to the fierceness of the battles.

In spite of France's crushing defeat, Pétain hoped that peace with Germany would lead to a moral renewal of French society. In accepting collaboration, Pétain was thinking about implementing his own political program. The ideal of the "révolution nationale," as he called it, was summarized in a few words: "God, Fatherland, Family, and Work." Pétain's ideology was in line with extreme right-wing European thought of the 1930s. It was both anti-Semitic and opposed to parliamentary democracy.

Not all French accepted defeat. On the BBC on June 18, 1940, a few days before the signing of the armistice, General Charles de Gaulle appealed to the French to continue the resistance. This officer, who was completely unknown to the public in France, called on the French—and in particular the French military—to choose between two authorities. He called on the military to break with their hierarchical superiors, and on other French citizens to distance themselves from their government. He asked them all to acknowledge the higher authority of "France libre" ("Free France").

The number of officers and soldiers who were ready to accept this call was modest. Of the 115,000 French troops who had taken refuge in Britain at the time, only a small minority did not ask to be repatriated to France. By the end of August only two generals and one admiral had accepted de Gaulle's call to arms. Youngsters and military personnel who had escaped from German prison camps came to join the Forces françaises libres (FFL or Free French Forces), but their numbers were not high. The number of troops rose from 7,000 in July 1940 to 50,000 in July 1943, but this figure represented only 2 percent of the strength of the regular French ground forces at the start of the war. The higher ranks of the French officer corps remained underrepresented in Free France. The officers who joined de Gaulle were mainly lieutenants and captains from the Légion étrangère (Foreign Legion) and colonial troops. Nor were members of the civil service eager to join Free France. Among the diplomatic staff, not a single ambassador or high-ranking diplomat joined de Gaulle before the end of 1940, the sole exception being the head of the French commercial representation in New York.

On August 7, 1940, de Gaulle and Churchill signed an agreement concerning the organization of the French troops. The question of legitimate authority was at the center of their discussions. De Gaulle insisted that la France libre had to be considered part of the Allies and that he and his FFL were reconstituting the *French* army. "We are France," he said to Churchill.[16] The British prime minister accepted the idea that the French units would keep their autonomy as far as possible.

In July and August 1940 some of the French colonies, such as New Caledonia, Tahiti, Chad, Cameroon, and French Equatorial Africa (AEF), joined *la France libre*. This was done by the local authorities or at the initiative of military units in favor of continuing the war. The authority of *la France libre* was greatly strengthened by this move, even though the support did not extend to all the colonies in Western or Northern Africa. This territorial expansion brought the government of de Gaulle new troops and—even more importantly—territorial sovereignty. The idea of a "Free France" had now become a territorial reality.

A further reflection of the legitimacy of Free France was the creation of a Defense Council in October 1940. This was followed in September 1941 by the creation of a government, the French National Committee (*Comité national français*, CNF) under the leadership of de Gaulle. The committee included colonial governors, leading military figures, and other well-known personalities. It was established "in name of the French People and Empire."[17] The British government recognized this institution as representing "*la France libre*," but did not go so far as to regard de Gaulle as a head of state.

In a declaration published in French Equatorial Africa in November 1941, the new authorities claimed that the "new French power" had been established on the basis of the free will of millions of French citizens all over the world.[18] The declaration denied the legitimacy and legality of the collaborationist Vichy regime. In the public statements de Gaulle made during the war, "*la France libre*" was presented not only as the liberated part of the French empire, but as its "spiritual reality," which had "preserved the honor of the fatherland."

Support from the resistance movement in France itself represented a decisive breakthrough for de Gaulle in his search for recognition as the legitimate military and political authority. The fact that, in 1942, the French resistance acknowledged the authority of de Gaulle meant that he was then leading a significant fighting force. On July 14, 1942, the name "*France libre*" was consequently changed to "*France combattante*." Leading members of the resistance were included in the French National Committee.

De Gaulle defended the worldwide involvement of France in the war. This view was already implied in his appeal of June 18, 1940: "This war has not been decided by the battle for France, this war is a world war. There are in the universe sufficient forces to crush our enemies . . ."[19] In practical terms this meant that de Gaulle had to disperse his weak military forces all around the globe. French pilots, for instance, were sent in April 1943 to the Eastern front, where they fought against the Germans in Kaluga. The involvement of French troops often amounted to no more than a symbolic presence, but their presence at the side of the Allies had great geopolitical value. De Gaulle in fact wanted to be involved in all decisions concerning the future of the French colonies. He therefore kept *la France libre* from being seen as a British protectorate, or a provisional authority. But the Americans and the British were not always eager to take French interests into account, since they had their own geopolitical interests to defend.

Pétain regarded those who had joined Free France as dissidents. But afterward he, not de Gaulle, was the one who would be condemned by the French courts for his behavior during the war. Pétain was accused of collaboration and treason. In the eyes of the whole world (and in the history books), the French troops under de Gaulle and the resistance in France itself (including the many communist resisters) would be seen as representing "the true France." The great difficulty de Gaulle experienced in gathering support among the French army and civil service shows, however, how hard it is to change traditional patterns of loyalty and discipline. The idea that the legal authorities constitute the only legitimate authority entitled to wage a war was well established in France, especially in its state institutions. Most of the support for de Gaulle's moral appeal to resist came from the periphery of the empire—where it was harder for the central authorities to keep full control of local events—and from outside the state structures. The fact that Pétain was a highly respected figure, and that he had come to power by legal means, added to that limited understanding of the Principle of Legitimate Authority.

REVOLUTIONARY MOVEMENTS

The existence of revolutionary movements represents the second problem for the Principle of Legitimate Authority. Revolutionaries challenge established power in the name of a higher authority, such as the popular will, the laws of history, or some ideological program. In 1917 the Russian Bolsheviks, taking advantage of a widespread movement of discontent, arrested the members of the Russian government and seized power in St. Petersburg. They claimed be acting in accordance with the historical interests of the laboring classes. In 1989, the communist regime of Ceaucescu in Romania was opposed by large mobilizations of the population and was eventually violently overthrown. The first example represents a revolutionary communist movement, the second a revolutionary anticommunist movement. What is common to them is that, in using force, mass movements appealed to the Principle of Legitimate Authority in the name of the sovereign popular will.[20]

Through their practice, revolutionaries demonstrate that the formalist identification of sovereignty and legitimate authority with an existing government is mistaken. This identification fails to assess the possibility that rebels may, through the use of force, become victorious, and constitute effective government. In the eyes of the revolutionaries, their authority is legitimate because it allows the people to recover the rights that they have been deprived of by an unjust regime. The concept of sovereignty, and more specifically of popular sovereignty, is at the heart of revolutionary thought. Their legitimacy does not depend solely, however, on their intentions or how they see themselves. In some cases, revolutionary movements have been able to build on popular legitimacy and thereby become recognized as a legitimate authority. This was the case for the Cuban revolutionaries who, in 1959, were able to overthrow the dictatorship of Batista thanks to popular support. In other cases, however, the revolutionary message failed to find acceptance among the population the revolutionaries wanted to mobilize. This was, for instance, the fate of Ernesto Che Guevara in his attempt to gather support for his guerrilla war among the poor peasants of Bolivia in the 1960s. Guevara and his fellow guerrilleros failed to build up a broad revolutionary movement, and remained isolated. Che was arrested and then executed by the Bolivian authorities (with the involvement of the CIA) in 1967.

ANTICOLONIAL STRUGGLES: ALGERIA, 1954–1962

The application of the Principle of Legitimate Authority exclusively to internationally recognized states and to the UN Security Council (UNSC) has been challenged by the emergence of various independence movements in the colonies. This represents the third problem for the Principle of Legitimate Authority. National liberation movements present their armed struggle as a legitimate form of resistance against colonial oppression, which implies a striving for recognition of their leadership as legitimate. These movements not only create new forms of political loyalty but also new forms of legitimacy. Before they came onto the UN agenda, the international community regarded them as insurgents that could receive the benefits and rights of international law only "when they had developed characteristics sufficiently analogous to those of States to be granted belligerent rights or to be recognized as the new government in power."[21]

Independence movements strove, however, for recognition as subjects of international law and, thus, raised the question of the conditions under which they could resort to the use of force to liberate their country. To base their claim on Article 51 of the UN Charter, national liberation movements had to use the plea of self-defense.[22] They succeeded in defending this claim by presenting themselves as movements resisting forcible action that was depriving them of their right to self-determination. The "Declaration on the Granting of Independence to Colonial Countries and Peoples" of the UN

General Assembly on December 14, 1960, formally stated that placing people under alien subjugation, domination, and exploitation constituted a denial of fundamental human rights. It was said to be contrary to the Charter of the UN, and to constitute an impediment to the promotion of world peace and cooperation.[23] It was then a small step from declaring that a people under colonial rule had the right to self-determination to declaring that the use of force was legitimate when that right was denied. This line of argument found acceptance among many UN members. In the language of the Just War Tradition, this line of argument means that anticolonial movements can, under certain circumstances, derive their legitimate authority to act as a public authority and to use force from a just cause—emancipation from colonial oppression and alien subjugation.

This debate was reopened with the 1970 "Declaration on Principles of International Law concerning Friendly Relations and Co-operation among States in Accordance with the Charter of the UN." According to one interpretation, this declaration legitimizes armed resistance to the denial of self-determination in a situation when colonial or alien domination is imposed or maintained by force. It has even been said that the declaration asserts that liberation movements have a *jus belli* (a right to wage war) under the charter. According to another interpretation, the use of force is legitimate only when used in defense against armed attack, rather than in the initiation of an armed struggle to achieve self-determination. The fact that the declaration makes no mention of *armed* resistance, but only of resistance, does not facilitate the interpretation of the rights of liberation movements. So, at the level of international law the problem of whether these movements could legitimately initiate the use of force, or use it only as a response, remained open.

The Algerian war for national liberation against French colonization started in 1954, the year in which the French army suffered a crushing defeat at Vietnamese hands in Dien Bien Phu.[24] The *Front de Libération Nationale* (FLN) launched its struggle in November with a number of military attacks in various parts of the Algerian territory. This campaign broke with the legalistic traditions of previous Algerian parties that had striven for the gradual political reform of the colonial system. The use of force was seen by the FLN as the best method of compelling the other political parties to take a clear position in the struggle for national liberation.

To repress this movement, the French authorities used military force. They also tried to isolate the FLN from the population by implementing limited political and social reforms, such as the integration of Algerians into the lower levels of the civil service, and land reforms. The French hoped that these policies would weaken and isolate the FLN and thereby lead to the emergence of a "third force," making any negotiations with the FLN superfluous. The leading military French officers were strongly opposed to any compromise solution. The defeat in Indochina and the threat of communism created a mood in which political solutions were difficult to accept. From the French perspective, Algeria—*l'Algérie française*—was an inalienable part of French territory, and the principle of territorial integrity was not open to negotiation. The vast majority of the French population supported this position. There were roughly a million French colonists in Algeria, the so-called *pieds noirs*, whose whole future was at stake. Seen from this perspective, Algeria was far more important to France than any other French colony.

The French authorities failed to undermine the authority of the FLN. At the military level, they failed to annihilate its military apparatus; at the political level, they failed to delegitimize the movement in the eyes of the population. The French military did manage to evict the FLN from the cities, but it could not eradicate them from the countryside. It then tried to strip the FLN guerrilla forces of their civilian cover and support by relocating hundreds of thousands of villagers to "regroupment camps." This forced displacement was carried out under deplorable and often inhuman conditions, and led to a further strengthening of the popularity of the FLN. The repression by the French authorities against Algerian nationalists also enhanced its authority in the eyes of the local population.

The French government's refusal to recognize the FLN as a legitimate authority had direct consequences for the way in which the war was fought. Guerrilla fighters were refused belligerent status, so they could not benefit from the treatment accorded by the Geneva Conventions. For the French government, the war was the result of an internal rebellion led by terrorist forces. These terrorists had to be crushed using all necessary means. The French authorities at first refused to apply Article 3, common to all conventions regulating noninternational conflicts, or to follow basic humanitarian rules. But it moved away from this position in March 1956, when it agreed to abide by Common Article 3 and to allow the International Committee of the Red Cross to visit detainees.[25] But this change of position did not prevent further large-scale violations of human rights. Torture was widely practiced in what the French public from the beginning called *"une sale guerre"* ("a dirty war"). The methods used during the war—including the setting up of concentration camps and the granting of immunity to French military personnel who violated the laws of war—did, however, discredit the aims of the war itself. It became deeply disturbing to French public opinion that the *"patrie des droits de l'homme"* could be involved in a barbarous war. In the case of torture, the French military violated not only the Geneva Conventions but also French domestic law and the Universal Declaration of Human Rights.

The FLN had hoped for a military victory, as had been achieved by the Vietnamese at the battle of Dien Bien Phu. But the French government had a far greater interest in defending Algeria than Indochina. So it sent ever larger contingents of troops to the region. By 1956, some 350,000 troops were stationed in Algeria. The French authorities managed to close the borders with Morocco and Tunisia, which made it difficult for the FLN to obtain military hardware. As a result, the FLN found it increasingly difficult to confront the French at a military level, and achieved successful results only by employing guerrilla tactics. In 1958, a Provisional Government of the Algerian Republic was created, which strove for recognition by the international community. It received support from Third World countries such as Egypt.

In France, the government of de Gaulle, installed in 1958, had to change the policies of its predecessors. He implicitly recognized the belligerence in official statements.[26] Some two million people, or one-fifth of the entire Algerian population, had been forcibly displaced. De Gaulle tried to modernize the Algerian economy, in order to gain support from the Algerian elites. But this policy failed. The French position toward the war gradually changed as it became increasingly burdensome for the French economy. The war made modernization difficult. It diverted the attention of the political leadership from the necessary political and economic reforms. A large part of the French elite, confronted with the need to strengthen the French position in the processes of international competition and European integration, felt that Algeria should have a lower priority.

In September 1959, de Gaulle acknowledged the right to national self-determination of the Algerian people and declared that the citizens of Algeria had three alternatives: the full integration of Algeria into France, full independence, or autonomy in association with France. The decision would have to be taken by a referendum. Within the French military, opposition to a compromise solution led in April 1961 to a putsch that was quickly repressed by the French authorities. For its part, the FLN organized huge demonstrations in Algeria, which showed that it had to be recognized as the only legitimate authority on Algerian territory. Pro-French Algerian politicians were thus excluded from the negotiating table. In the end, the negotiations between the two warring parties led to an agreement on Algerian independence which received the support of an overwhelming majority both in France (90 percent) and in Algeria (99 percent). For a time, however, fighting continued between French underground fighters (*Organisation de l'Armée Secrète*, OAS) who rejected both the agreement and the FLN. But eventually, in July 1962, Algeria became independent.

As is the case in so many wars, the *jus ad bellum* considerations of the French authorities marginalized the *jus in bello* principles. The French authorities in Algeria claimed they were on a *mission civilisatrice* (civilizing mission) in enforcing a policy that violated basic humanitarian norms. The criticism directed against the French authorities by increasingly large currents of domestic public opinion and by the international community weakened their position and contributed decisively to their defeat.

THE SECURITY SYSTEM OF THE UNITED NATIONS

Even if, over the last three centuries, sovereignty has remained the central principle in international relations, after World War II decisive steps were taken to restrain the use of force by sovereign states. The restraints set by the United Nation's Charter on the use of military force, and more specifically the role of the UNSC, constitute a fourth problem for the traditional Principle of Legitimate Authority. The United Nations' Charter binds member states to "settle their international disputes by peaceful means in such a manner that international peace and security, and justice, are not endangered" and to refrain from the threat or use of force against any other state. The member states retain the right of individual or collective self-defense, however, if there is an armed attack against them or against other members. When a dispute is brought before it, the UNSC will recommend to the parties that they should reach an agreement or, if a dispute leads to fighting, it will try to bring the conflict to a peaceful end.

The UN security system does not exclude intervention against or in the territory of a sovereign state when the actions of a government constitute a threat to peace. Here the UN Charter grants the SC broad discretion to determine the scope of its own powers.[27] The basic condition is that none of the five permanent members of the UNSC should oppose such a step. Under chapter 7, the UNSC may take measures to enforce its decision. This may be done in the event of a threat to peace, a breach of the peace, or an act of aggression. The measures may include the implementation of economic sanctions or other nonmilitary measures and even—when all other means of settling a dispute have been exhausted—the authorization for member states or regional organizations to use "all necessary means"—including military action—to deal with a conflict.[28] This means that the UNSC legalizes or legitimizes the use of force by others.[29]

The endorsement of the UN Charter by almost all the states in the international community has not put an end to the debates about who is qualified to use force as a legitimate authority. In academic discussions on the use of force in humanitarian intervention, a large number of authors have endorsed the position that the UNSC has exclusive authority.[30] They are convinced that the authorization of the use of force by an organization in which the representatives of the world's leading nations are represented constitutes the best guarantee of resolving a conflict. They also share the conviction that the legal order of the UN security system, as it was established after World War II, constitutes the best guarantee against unilateral actions by one single power or by an alliance of states. According to this view, the moral values used to justify humanitarian intervention should remain subordinate to the legal norms of the UN Charter.

A second group of authors, however, think that this right lies primarily but not exclusively with the UNSC. Regional organizations such as the Organization of African States (OAS) or the Organization for Security and Cooperation in Europe (OSCE) may, in certain cases, legitimately act autonomously. This group, however, would exclude the possibility of unilateral intervention by individual states—unlike a third group of authors, who feel that, despite the existence of the UN, sovereign states retain the right to use force for humanitarian interventions. The authors of the second and third groups give various reasons for deeming the use of force by regional security organizations or by sovereign states legitimate. These reasons have to do with the lack of an "exercise of real power" by the UNSC (Paul Ramsey) or the failure of the UN to act as an organization "willing and able" to intervene in grave humanitarian crises (Michael Walzer).

This academic discussion became very real during the 1999 Serbia/Kosovo crisis, when the members of the UNSC failed to defend a common position on the humanitarian catastrophe in Kosovo. On March 24, 1999, NATO started military operations against Serbia, to end its repression of the Kosovo Albanian population, without the authorization of the UNSC. This case is examined in more detail in chapters 9 and 10 of this book.

A new discussion on the authority of the UNSC took place a few years later, during the buildup to the 2003 Iraq war. The United States and United Kingdom tried to get international support for the decision to invade Iraq, particularly from the UNSC. However, the other permanent UNSC members—France, Russia, and China—strongly opposed the use of force to overthrow the Iraqi regime and would have vetoed any proposed resolution legitimizing such a move. The United States and the United Kingdom started the war without UN authorization.

All the *jus ad bellum* principles are to be found in the UNSC debates on Iraq. The critics of the U.S. and British position did not agree that there was strong evidence that Iraq still possessed vast quantities of weapons of mass destruction, that that country was still able to develop such an armaments program, or that Saddam Hussein had the firm intention of using such weapons (Just Cause Principle). In their view, the UN weapons inspectors, whose task it was to verify the accuracy of these accusations, needed more time and resources in order to complete their inspection work. The countries opposed to the use of military force also disagreed with the assessment that it did not make sense to continue to use diplomatic pressure to facilitate the inspectors' work (Last Resort Principle). France, Germany, Russia, and China, unlike the United States and the United Kingdom, were convinced that the moral and political costs of the war would far outweigh its benefits (Proportionality Principle) and did not believe that Saddam Hussein's regime could be replaced by a stable government through the use of force (Likelihood of Success Principle). Furthermore, in their view, the American and British motives for going to war had more to do with their geopolitical interests in the region than their right of self-defense (Principle of Right Intentions).

With regard to the Principle of Legitimate Authority, there was a discussion on the right of states to decide unilaterally what constitutes a sufficient cause for war. Washington and London did not regard a UNSC decision as decisive. British prime minister Tony Blair even used the expression "unreasonable veto"[31] to disqualify the view that the UNSC had exclusive authority in a decision on the use of military force against Iraq. This attempt to delegitimize the UNSC increased the risk of an arbitrary decision, particularly in the context of the new American doctrine of preemptive self-defense. As we have seen in the previous chapter on the Just Cause Principle, there was already a danger that this doctrine—formalized in the 2002 National Security Strategy (NSS)—would open the door to a situation in which it would no longer be necessary to provide solid proof of an impending attack. Proof of aggressive intention and capacity could be provided *ex post*. The Americans and British were convinced that the occupation of Iraq would uncover undeclared stocks of WMD and plans to use them. But such a conviction—expressed in intelligence reports based on fears, guesses, and incomplete information[32]—did not amount to clear, objective proof of aggression, as traditionally required in a legal justification of the use of force in self-defense. In its application of the Last Resort Principle to nonimminent threats, the NSS doctrine of starting a preemptive war in self-defense also increased the risk of arbitrary decision-making. According to the NSS, these perceived threats needed to be addressed long before they became imminent—which implied the predominance of military over diplomatic instruments. From the perspective of the Principle of Proportionality, it is far more difficult to estimate the costs and benefits of a preemptive war than those of a traditional war fought in self-defense.

It may be concluded that the lack of authorization from the UNSC increased the risk that the decision would be made arbitrarily.[33] It is important to notice in this context that, in the UNSC debate before the war, the main arguments put forward to oppose the American and British positions referred, implicitly or explicitly, to the lack of a just cause and to a violation of the other just war principles. The prudential considerations implied in this criticism were proved right after the invasion. There was thus no good reason to dismiss a potential veto by the UNSC as "unreasonable," as the British prime minister Tony Blair had done.

As had been the case in NATO's war on Kosovo, the United States and Britain considered that they had legitimate authority—both in moral and in legal terms—to act on their own. In the case of Iraq, however, some of the NATO countries that had taken part in the 1999 Kosovo war opposed this view. What then are the differences between these two wars from the point of view of the Legitimate Authority Principle?

The Kosovo war was depicted as a humanitarian intervention, whose aim was, by definition, the defense of others. The Iraq war, on the contrary, was claimed to be a war of self-defense. As a result, the justification for military intervention in Kosovo was framed mainly in moral terms. Little was advanced in terms of its legal justification. UNSC resolutions had identified the situation in Kosovo as a threat to international peace and security. Those who favored going to war in Kosovo without explicit UNSC authorization used the argument that these resolutions implicitly authorized the use of force.[34] But such legal arguments were not prominent in the debate, unlike the moral arguments pointing to the need to preempt massive human rights violations such as ethnic cleansing and the threat of genocide. The fact that individual NATO countries justified their position in terms of their domestic public debates largely explains why their governments found it easier to make use of moral rather than legal arguments to justify the fact that they were acting without UNSC authorization. President Clinton did not even refer to international law in his statement on March 24, 1999, announcing the beginning of air strikes against Serbia,[35] in which he called the ending of the Kosovo tragedy a "moral imperative." The German government went even further, pointing to the contradiction between the formal stipulations of international law concerning UNSC authorization and the duty of the permanent members to uphold the standards of common humanity in exercising their responsibilities. In the case of Kosovo, morality was seen as rightly breaking the law.[36] The interpretation of the Principle of Legitimate Authority in favor of a unilateral decision to wage war on Kosovo was thus mainly done on the basis of a moral imperative, and not in terms of formal legal principles. It was widely argued that international law had to be adapted and revised in the light of moral requirements, such as the right of the international community to intervene forcefully in cases of severe human rights violations.

Less space was given to moral principles in the buildup to the Iraq war. The supporters of a preemptive war invoked the need for such wars against the new security threats constituted by terrorist groups, rogue states, and WMD. They preferred to strengthen their case using legal rather than moral arguments. The United States and the United Kingdom wanted to show that they based their position on international law and not on particular political views or security interests. This type of argumentation is also fully in line with the definition of a "rogue state" as one that does not respect international law. Compared with the Kosovo debate, they therefore made far more use of the argument that Iraq's lack of compliance with its obligations under various UNSC resolutions justified the use of force without explicit UNSC authorization.[37]

CONCLUSION

The Principle of Legitimate Authority has been applied throughout history to many different types of political authorities. When St. Augustine first framed this Just War principle, he associated it with the institutions of the Roman Empire. In the Middle Ages, kings, nobles, and cities claimed the right to act as a public authority in waging war.[38] The institution of sovereignty established itself only slowly over the centuries as the sole principle in determining which political institutions had the right to redress grievances or to avenge wrongs. Despite the fact that sovereignty is still the basic regulatory institution in international relations today, and that established governments are perceived to be the sole depositories of the right to wage wars, competing forms of legitimate authority have manifested themselves throughout modern history. Revolutionary, secessionist, and anticolonial movements have challenged the right of established governments to be the sole authority legitimately entitled to use force. After World War II, the UN Charter limited the rights of states to wage war or to threaten the use of force. It gave the UNSC primary responsibility for maintaining international peace and security. All these different expressions of the Principle of Legitimate Authority demonstrate that the just war principles are not unvarying and ahistorical, but, on the contrary, deeply historical in that they respond to varying cultural and political needs.

NOTES

1. See Michael Ignatieff, *The Warrior's Honor: Ethnic War and the Modern Conscience* (New York: Henry Holt, 1998), 160.

2. On the principle of legitimate authority, see Anthony Joseph Coates, *The Ethics of War* (Manchester: Manchester University Press, 1997), 123–45. See also Max Weber, "Politik als Beruf," in *Gesammelte Politische Schriften* (Tübingen, Ger.: Mohr, 1980), 506.

3. Coates, *The Ethics of War*, 126–28.

4. On the transformation of the notion of public authority in warfare, see Robert C. Stacey, "The Age of Chivalry," in *The Laws of War: Constraints on Warfare in the Western World*, ed. Michael Howard, George J. Andreopoulos, and Mark R. Shulman (New Haven, Conn., and London: Yale University Press, 1994), 27–39.

5. Stacey, "The Age of Chivalry," 31.

6. Stacey, "The Age of Chivalry," 32.

7. The belief that the norm of nonintervention in internal affairs was implemented after the Peace of Westphalia is historically inaccurate. See Stephen D. Krasner, *Sovereignty: Organized Hypocrisy* (Princeton, N.J.: Princeton University Press, 1999), 19.

8. On the notion of sovereignty, see Adrian Hyde-Price, "Reflections on Security and Identity in Europe," in *Security and Identity in Europe: Exploring the New Agenda*, ed. Lisbeth Aggestam and Adrian Hyde-Price (Basingstoke, Eng.: Macmillan, 2000),

30–31; Sovereignty has both an internal and an external dimension. Internal sovereignty refers to the supremacy over all other authorities in a given territory. External sovereignty is independence of outside authorities. See Krasner, *Sovereignty*, 47.

9. Krasner, *Sovereignty*, 11.

10. Krasner, *Sovereignty*, 69.

11. The United States accepted this principle at the seventh International Conference of American States in 1933. Krasner, *Sovereignty*, 21.

12. Krasner, *Sovereignty*, 69.

13. Coates, *The Ethics of War*, 125–29.

14. The formalist interpretation has been challenged by official practice. During World War II, for instance, the British government had good reasons for giving practical support to Tito's communist partisans in their resistance against the German occupation of Yugoslavia, all the while recognizing the royalist government of Yugoslavia as the only legitimate government. George J. Andreopoulos, "The Age of National Liberation Movements," in *The Laws of War*, 197.

15. On the following, see P. M. H. Bell, *The Origins of the Second World War in Europe* (London and New York: Longman, 1986); Christian Bachelier, "L'Armée française entre la victoire et la défaite," in *La France des années noires*, ed. Jean-Pierre Azéma and François Bédarida (Paris: Seuil, 2000), 75–101, and the following chapters in the same volume: Jean-Pierre Azéma, "Le choc armé et les débandades," 105–37; Jean-Louis Crémieux-Brilhac, "La France libre," 191–242; Robert Frank, "Pétain, Laval, Darlan," 307–48; Jean-Pierre Azéma, *De Munich à la Libération. 1938–1944* (Paris: Seuil, 1979).

16. Quoted in Crémieux-Brilhac, "La France libre," 201.

17. Quoted in Crémieux-Brilhac, "La France libre," 208.

18. Quoted in Crémieux-Brilhac, "La France libre," 209.

19. Crémieux-Brilhac, "La France libre," 192.

20. In 1917 this popular will was called the dictatorship of the proletariat.

21. Heather Wilson, *International Law and the Use of Force by National Liberation Movements* (Oxford: Clarendon Press, 1988), 105, quoted by Andreopoulos, "The Age of National Liberation Movements," 197.

22. On the following, see Andreopoulos, "The Age of National Liberation Movements," 199 ff.

23. *Basic Facts about the United Nations* (New York: United Nations Department of Public Information, 1998), 277.

24. On the following, see Andreopoulos, "The Age of National Liberation Movements," 191–213; Benjamin Stora, *Histoire de la guerre d'Algérie (1954–1962)* (Paris: La Découverte, 1995); Bruno Coppieters, "De Algerijnse Onafhankelijkheidsoorlog," in *Diskussiedossiers Derde Wereld*, ed. Els Witte (Brussel: Centrum voor Sociale Structuur en Economische Conjunctuur van de Vrije Universiteit Brussel, 1979), 38–94.

25. Stephen C. Neff, *War and the Law of Nations: A General History* (Cambridge: Cambridge University Press, 2005), 369–70. "In Algeria the Front de Libération Nationale (National Liberation Front) in 1956 acknowledged that Article 3 was applicable. Actually it was at that time that Pierre Mendès-France, who was the cousin of the International Committee of the Red Cross (ICRC) delegate posted in Paris, called him and said "I am going to resign in one week, can I do anything for you?"

The answer of the ICRC delegate was "'Yes, recognize the applicability of Article 3' and the French prime minister granted the ICRC delegate his wish. I mention this anecdote to stress the role of the human factor and how personal links can sometimes lead to positive developments": Michel Veuthey, "Learning from History: Accession to the Conventions, Special Agreements, Unilateral Declarations," at www.veuthey.org/mv/ActesColloqueVeuthey.1.doc (accessed February 14, 2008).

26. Neff, *War and the Law of Nations*, 370.

27. Michael Byers, *War Law* (London: Atlantic Books, 2005), 25–6.

28. *Basic Facts about the United Nations*, 76.

29. Thierry Tardy, "'Conflict Prevention' versus 'Coercive Prevention': Where Does the EU Stand?" in *The Impact of 9/11 on European Foreign and Security Policy*, ed. Giovanna Bono (Brussels: VUB Brussels University Press, 2006), 149.

30. On these discussions, see Carl Ceulemans, *Reluctant Justice: A Just-War Analysis of the International Use of Force in Former Yugoslavia (1991–1995)* (Brussels: VUB Brussels University Press, 2005), 135–52.

31. Warren Hoge, "Blaming France, Blair Says Passage of Iraq Resolution Unlikely," *New York Times*, March 13, 2003. See also Byers, *War Law*, 1.

32. In his speech to the UN on February 5, 2003, Colin Powell stated the following: "My colleagues, every statement I make today is backed up by sources, solid sources. These are not assertions. What we are giving you are facts and conclusions based on solid intelligence." But his statements about Iraqi chemical and biological weapons programs proved false. See Douglas Kellner, "Preemptive Strikes and the War on Iraq: A Critique of Bush Administration Unilateralism and Militarism," in *The Politics of Empire: War, Terror, and Hegemony*, ed. Joseph G. Peschek (London and New York: Routledge, 2006), 155.

33. The doctrine of preemptive defense is criticized from an international legal perspective in Jan Wouters and Tom Ruys, "The Legality of Anticipatory Military Action after 9/11: The Slippery Slope of Self-Defence," in *The Impact of 9/11 on European Foreign and Security Policy*, 79.

34. Byers, *War Law*, 42–43.

35. See Shirley V. Scott and Olivia Ambler, "Does Legality *Really* Matter? Accounting for the Decline in U.S. Foreign Policy Legitimacy Following the 2003 Invasion of Iraq," *European Journal of International Relations* 13, no. 1: 81.

36. Nicholas J. Wheeler, *Saving Strangers: Humanitarian Intervention in International Society* (Oxford: Oxford University Press, 2000), 277–78.

37. See Scott and Ambler, "Does Legality *Really* Matter?" 75–81.

38. On the laws of war in the Middle Ages, see also Geoffrey Parker, "Early Modern Europe," in *The Laws of War*, 40–58.

3

Right Intentions

Bruno Coppieters and Boris Kashnikov

The Principle of Right Intentions is closely related to the Just Cause Principle. This principle directs attention to the subjective dimension of the use of force. It must, however, be regarded as a moral principle that stands on its own. A nation may have a just cause, for instance, but no intention of going to war. Furthermore, the intention to go to war may have very little to do with a just cause, even if such a reason is, in some sense, objectively present. Throughout history, war has been waged with the intention (among others) of

1. seeking glory in war (wars of chivalry);
2. promoting colonial expansion (colonial wars);
3. promoting the interests of this or that religion (crusades and religious wars);
4. acquiring domestic state authority (civil wars);
5. seceding or opposing secession (wars of secession);
6. exporting revolution to other countries (revolutionary wars);
7. avenging a wrong (wars of revenge);
8. defending one's own country from aggression (self-defense wars);
9. defending another country from aggression (collective defense);
10. preventing the strengthening of a potential military adversary (preventive wars);
11. striking first, before the inevitable strike by the other power reaches you (preemptive wars);
12. protecting people threatened with genocide or gross human rights violations (humanitarian intervention).

Intuitively, most of us tend to think that several of the twelve war aims listed above are wrong while others are right. For instance, the intention of defending one's country from aggression, thus causing a defensive war, is considered right. Intuitively correct as such a judgment seems to be, however, we realize that our moral intuitions are not always reliable guides to moral knowledge in more complex situations. One reason they are not is that they are subject to the influence of a particular political culture. The Principle of Right Intentions should therefore be based on more solid ethical grounds than intuitions.

Unfortunately, there are a number of problems involved in providing a sound moral basis for the Right Intentions Principle and in applying this principle to the concrete circumstances of war. Most wars are fought in the name of high-sounding ideals that do not necessarily tell us much about real intentions. One state may officially declare war to protect another country from aggression (which objectively constitutes a just cause), but may actually go into that war with the intention of exploiting that country's resources. The presence of such an intention is difficult to discern. One of the main problems with the Right Intentions Principle is indeed its subjective character. One's good or bad intentions cannot be assessed by others unless they are made objective in one way or another by external behavior. Yet even that is not easy to do since any single example of public behavior may be open to a variety of interpretations. Often, assessments can be made only after tracking a nation's behavior over long periods of time. Indeed, this approach is what we use to uncover the intentions of individuals. Their public actions over time reveal their private morality and character.

However, even if state intentions are assessed over long periods of time, this assessment is far more complicated than an assessment of individual intentions. State actions result from the intentions of very different political actors. In every country (including autocratic regimes), various political currents, pressure groups, and organizations defend different views of the national interest. Often, political actions result from the rivalry of many political wills. State behavior will therefore not necessarily be consistent—which is one of the reasons the real intentions of a state are difficult to uncover. Moreover, actors who determine military policies do not typically reveal their intentions to the public. Political deliberations on questions of war and peace often take place behind closed doors, and the documents that would give scholars some clue about the real intentions of politicians are often not publicly available for decades.

One may be discouraged by the huge methodological problems involved in the application of this principle and declare that what is really needed to put the principle to work in politics is the watchful eye of Almighty God. He at least would be able to disclose the subjective motives at work behind all decisions to wage war. Such confidence in an all-knowing supreme power surely dominated the thought of St. Augustine, who was the first to articulate the Principle of Right Intentions (in its Christian interpretation). In spite of these problems, we will apply the Right Intentions Principle in the remaining portion of this chapter as it has been interpreted in the Just War Tradition.

THE JUST WAR TRADITION

As a philosophical principle, the Principle of Right Intentions emerged along with Christianity—a movement that laid emphasis on the inner life of the agent. St. Augustine, who was critical of the Christian pacifist tradition, wanted to explain to Christians the necessity to use force under certain circumstances, so that they could go to war with a clear conscience. For Augustine, just wars should be waged with the intention of achieving peace. "It is therefore with the desire for peace that wars are waged."[1] Peace is something for which any sound person would wish.

For Augustine, the desire of Christians to be faithful to the Christian message of nonviolence had to be reconciled with the need for a state to base its defense on loyal and obedient citizens. He thus remained mainly concerned with the personal intentions of the various individuals who were responsible for military policies. He defended the state as an instrument for maintaining peace and order, but expressed mistrust of human intentions in waging war. He wrote in "Contra Faustum" that "the real evils of the war are love for violence, revengeful cruelty, fierce and implacable amenity, wild resistance and lust for power and such like. . . ."[2] The intentions of the individual who is waging war may only be considered right if it is waged "in obedience to God or some lawful authority" and if he is not dominated by the inherently evil motives of hatred of the enemy or lust for violence.[3] This means that the Principle of Right Intentions was linked no less to the Principle of Legitimate Authority—and in particular to the holder of a divinely sanctioned office of ruler—than to the Just Cause Principle.[4]

Augustine understood that his attempt to define right intentions in terms of the desire to reach peace needed a precise understanding of this concept. He therefore introduced the concept of a peace of the just, or a just peace: "He then who prefers what is right to what is wrong, and what is well organized to what is perverted, sees that peace of unjust men is not worthy to be called peace in comparison with peace of the just."[5] So it is not only an intention to reach peace that is needed but also an intention to reach just peace.

The formulation of the Principle of Right Intentions was undoubtedly very important. Wars had previously often been justified by the open and frank intention of killing, raping, robbing, seeking revenge, or seeking glory. Augustine banned such intentions. His understanding of this principle paved the way for a philosophical justification of religious wars. Augustine considered wars just when they were aimed at restoring justice and doing what God has ordained. "Just wars are usually defined as those that avenge injuries, when the nation or city against which warlike action is to be directed has neglected either to punish wrongs committed by its own citizens or to restore what has been unjustly taken by it. Further, that kind of war is undoubtedly just which God Himself ordains."[6]

Critics pointed out that Augustine's last argument in this quotation would lead to arbitrary decisions. Some wars would be just because they are perceived by religious believers as ordained by God.[7] Moreover, the combination of a theological interpretation of the Just Cause Principle with an arbitrary claim to act in line with the Principles of Right Intentions and Legitimate Authority could easily lead to a conception of war where the other principles of *jus ad bellum* and *jus in bello* would be overruled. The many religious wars waged throughout the centuries—which, indeed, did not respect the three other *jus ad bellum* principles of Proportionality, Chance of Success, and Last Resort, or the two *jus in bello* principles of Proportionality and Discrimination—demonstrate that such a possibility is more than a theoretical one.

But there is also a pacifist touch to Augustine's theory about war. Augustine justified the use of force in the defense of the general good, but denied that individual Christians are justified in using force for their individual self-defense, for instance when they are attacked by robbers. He banned the use of force in self-defense as being triggered by the motive of self-love: "As to killing others in order to defend one's life, I do not approve of this, unless one happens to be a soldier . . . acting in defense of others according to the commission lawfully given him."[8] That thought was no doubt a remnant of the traditional Christian ideas on nonresistance to evil and stands in opposition to his political views on a just war.

The Islamic tradition of just war (*jihad*), which emerged some centuries after Augustine, is based on a number of similar considerations. The only right intention possible in a war is the desire to serve Islam. All selfish motives, be they hatred, lust, greed, or glory, are strictly prohibited and are unjust.[9]

Hugo Grotius' secular and juridical reinterpretation of Just War Theory opposed the Right Intentions Principle. In his efforts to base international law on truly objective criteria, Grotius rejected the use of this principle as incompatible with his approach. He argued that the other *jus ad bellum* principles are objective in the sense that they apply to relationships between states. Intentions refer, however, to the internal attitudes of individual agents, which may or may not be blamable, but do not ultimately affect the just or unjust character of the war itself: "But such motives, though blamable, when even connected with a just war, do not render the war itself unjust, nor invalidate its conquests."[10] Every state has, for instance, the right to resist foreign invasion, regardless of the intentions of the state leaders when they wage a war in self-defense. Objective rights exist independently of subjective intentions. Such intentions will only be helpful for assessing whether the actions are to be labelled unjust: "It may happen indeed that neither of two belligerent powers may act unjustly. For no one can be charged with acting unjustly unless he knows that he is doing so; but there are many, who are not aware of the nature, extent, and consequences of their measures."[11]

The distinction between an objective and a subjective concept of just war had a strong impact on the development of the ethics of war and international law during the eighteenth and the nineteenth centuries.[12] It led to the pragmatic attempt to divorce the moral question of substantive justice from the legal question of rights in war. This distinction implied that even if only one side could be just, both warring parties might subjectively believe that they may have a just cause.[13] This led to an emphasis on the equality of the parties, irrespective of the question of a just cause. As a consequence, the party that did not have just cause on its side was seen as retaining certain rights in war, despite its mistaken beliefs. This was particularly true in the field of *jus in bello*. As an ultimate consequence of this line of thought, in the course of the eighteenth and nineteenth centuries, "international law denied itself any authority for pronouncing upon the substantive issue of justice of cause. It was no longer deemed to be the business of international law so to pronounce because this was but a fragmentary remnant of a natural law tradition that was no longer credible in the age of legal positivism."[14] This line of thought also strengthened the argument for a realist and nonmoral approach in international relations.

To this day, the debate on how international law and the ethics of war should assess subjective intentions has not ended. In the field of law, the Genocide Convention of 1948 defines the crime of genocide partly by its intention.[15] Contemporary philosophical and theological discussions still largely make use of the arguments found in the Just War Tradition. One contemporary interpretation of the Right Intention Principle can be found in a pastoral letter on war and peace by the National Conference of Catholic Bishops in the United States. This states that good intentions in the use of force should aim at achieving a just cause,[16] which is specified as confronting "a real and certain danger." Just cause further includes the protection of innocent life, the preservation of the conditions necessary for a decent human existence, and the defense of basic human rights.[17] But other participants in the debate on the Just War Principle still question its validity. Robert Holmes, for instance, considers that this principle impedes a cool, dispassionate assessment, which is one of the moral constraints on the use of force.[18]

TESTING THE PRINCIPLE

There are three different interpretations as to how the Right Intentions Principle should be applied. All three agree that having the right intention when using force involves upholding a just cause. That is, all agree that a state must have the intention of correcting the injustices that led to its claim that it has a just cause for being involved in war. But they disagree in their judgment as to what extent other intentions have a role to play in the decision to use force. The first interpretation says that the intention should be aimed exclusively at upholding a just cause. The second says that although other intentions may be present when applying force in a war setting, the intention of acting in accordance with the Just Cause Principle must override all the others in being the most powerful. The third says that even though many powerful intentions are at play in the decision to go to war, so long as the intention to uphold a just cause also influences the decision, the Right Intentions Principle has been satisfied.

According to the first interpretation, the Right Intentions Principle prescribes that only the just cause intention should be present when a nation goes to war. Any creeping in of intentions not directly linked to upholding it leads invariably to the verdict that the Right Intentions Principle has not been respected and, therefore, that the war is unjust. On this interpretation, the purity of the intentions is the moral ideal we seek. Thus, in the case of the Gulf War of 1991, since oil interests obviously played a role in the motives of the United States and its allies for undoing the Iraqi invasion of Kuwait by force, the Right Intentions Principle was not satisfied.

This view of the Right Intentions Principle has been criticized as being too demanding[19]—as demanding perfectionism. And perfectionism, it is said, overlooks the limited nature and purposes of political morality. The morality of the public sphere deals with the less-than-perfect world of politics and so should not be based on the same standards that we apply to private morality. In many settings in the private or personal sphere, we consider an act to be moral only when it is done with the intention of benefiting others *and* when it is not tainted by motives of self-interest. But, the critics say, such a view of morality cannot be transferred to the political sphere because public authorities are required to acknowledge the autonomy and specific needs of the community. These authorities are responsible for satisfying not only the needs of other peoples but also, and especially, the needs of the society they represent. Their intentions in the decisions they make concerning the use of force in war, the critics conclude, should reflect this attitude.

This leads to the second interpretation of the Right Intentions Principle. According to this interpretation, the diversity of intentions in the sphere of public decision-making should be acknowledged. We cannot suppose that everyone in a state involved in deciding on war will have the same "pure" just cause intention and no other. But so long as the just cause intention dominates the other intentions, the Right Intentions Principle has been satisfied. Actually this interpretation allows for some flexibility. It acknowledges that some of the remaining intentions can contribute to acting with good (right) intentions and in this way help to support the primary intention. In the Gulf War of 1991, then, one could assume that the coalition forces had as their primary intention to undo the Iraqi aggression against Kuwait. However, such an interpretation allows the coalition forces to argue that it was also their intention to secure the self-interest of the world economies, including their own, of course, by not letting Saddam Hussein take over an even bigger share of the world's oil supplies. Exhibiting such additional intentions would not make the coalition forces fail the test. What this interpretation forbids are actions intended to serve primarily the interests of big oil companies, the coffers of political leaders, and the like. These intentions may be present, but they cannot play a "lead" role in the decision-making process.

According to the third interpretation, it is sufficient if, among the many intentions involved in the decision to wage a war, the just cause intention is present. On this interpretation, there is little or no need to examine the relative weights of the various intentions to determine whether the just cause intention and any other supporting intentions are stronger than the bad ones. Thus if the aim of restoring Kuwait's sovereignty was among the significant intentions of the coalition, then the Principle of Right Intentions is satisfied. Even if a bad intention was present or was even predominant in the mix (e.g., such as going to war in order to secure oil interests or to test new missile technology), the question of whether the principle was satisfied will not have to be answered differently. This third interpretation makes it relatively easy to show that the coalition forces had good intentions. It is so easy, in fact, that it becomes difficult to separate this interpretation of right intentions from Realism. The intentions of realists, recall, are of the self-interest variety. If the right intentions of the coalition forces include a spectrum of self-interest intentions, a blurring of just war with realist thinking seems likely even though the former makes an ethical appeal for going to war in terms of just cause while the latter does not.

Of these three interpretations the second, in our view, is most in line with the Just War Tradition. According to what has already been written in the chapter on the Just Cause Principle, there are two basic forms of just cause, each of which may be differentiated further. First, under the general heading of self-defense, we differentiate between force as used to stop an ongoing aggression, to remedy a past aggression, and to initiate preemptive actions against a potential aggressor. Second, under the heading of helping others, we differentiate between military actions undertaken to help a friendly nation or an ally being subjected to ongoing aggression, or to remedy a past aggression, and military actions for humanitarian reasons. The Principle of Right Intentions is supposed to ensure that these just causes are the primary objects of our intentions.

A war of self-defense seems to pose the fewest problems in this respect. If a country is the victim of an unjust aggression, there is no question but that the intention to repel the aggressor is right. But the case of a preemptive war in self-defense may raise questions about the rightfulness of those who claim to act in self-defense. The intentions of a state that assists an ally in repelling an aggressor and then withdraws its military forces without gaining any territorial advantage may generally also seem to be right. It goes without saying that most historical cases are often not clear-cut. What follows are five case studies that raise interesting questions in this respect.

BANGLADESH, 1971[20]

Before 1971, the country now known as Bangladesh was a province of Pakistan and was known as East Pakistan. At the end of the 1960s, a strong movement for greater autonomy was in place. The local Bengali population was kept from playing much of a role in government and also from having much say about the economic policies adopted by the central government. Discontent among the Bengalis was rampant thanks to economic policies regarded as discriminating against East Pakistan. The nationalist leaders of the Awami League in East Pakistan demanded that the powers of taxation be vested in their own province. They also demanded that steps be taken to protect their national language, bring about political reform, and foster friendly relations with India. They opposed the military rulers of Pakistan, who were not eager to accept any such reforms.

In 1970, floods and a major cyclone in East Pakistan left hundreds of thousands of victims. The military administration proved incapable of organizing relief operations. This increased the discontent of the local population. Not surprisingly, national elections on December 7 gave a sweeping victory to the Awami League, which won 160 out of 162 National Assembly seats allocated to East Pakistan. In contrast, in West Pakistan, the People's Party captured a large majority of the votes.

The programs of the Awami League and of the People's Party were diametrically opposed. Ali Bhutto of the People's Party championed centralized government, while Sheikh Mujibur Rahman of the Awami League demanded that the central government be responsible only for defense and foreign affairs. The talks between the two parties brought no concrete results. Demonstrations and strikes took place in East Pakistan, where the nationalist movement openly began to discuss the option of independence. In response, the central government took repressive measures against the population there. Sheikh Mujibur Rahman accused the army of killing unarmed people and behaving like an occupation force. But he also made proposals for power sharing that would preserve the territorial integrity of Pakistan. He was still convinced that political reform could give a decisive voice to the population of East Pakistan, which was larger than that of West Pakistan, and also put an end to the oppression. But the central government refused to negotiate or to lift martial law.

March 25, 1971, was a fateful day for the future of Pakistan. Sheikh Mujibur Rahman was arrested. The Pakistani president Yahya Khan said that law and order would be restored, by all means available to him. On the same day, the military embarked on a general massacre. It began at the University of Dacca. After the dormitories had been shelled at point-blank range, any students remaining alive were shot or bayoneted. Major-General Fazal Muqeem Khan, the official historian of the Pakistan Army, wrote: "The army had to use rocket launchers to break open some rooms of the halls (Dacca University). From the sound of fire during that fateful night in Dacca, it appeared as if there was an actual war on with modern weapons."[21] A "death list" of professors living in the neighborhood had been drawn up and raiding parties were sent out. Western journalists expressed their outrage at the extent of the killing. In their reports, they ruefully referred to the military equipment and supplies that Pakistan had received from the United States. The correspondent from the British *Daily Telegraph* newspaper reported on March 30: "Led by the American-supplied M-24 World War II tanks, one column of troops sped to Dacca University shortly after midnight. Troops took over the British Council library (situated within the campus) and used it as a fire base from which to shell nearby dormitory areas. Caught completely by surprise, some 200 students were killed in Iqbal Hall, headquarters of the militant anti-government students' union, I was told. Two days later bodies were still smouldering in burnt-out rooms, others were scattered outside, more floated in a nearby lake."[22]

The attack on the university was part of a concerted plan to wipe out the intellectual and political life of the country. The massacre continued for months in all parts of East Pakistan. The central authorities were determined to destroy any forces that might challenge their authority. By May, the army had regained control over the whole territory. According to Sheikh Mujibur Rahman, three million people had been killed. Public opinion in the world was shocked by this appalling tragedy.

During that summer of 1971 India lived through a nightmare. While the massacre of the Bengalis continued, refugees poured over its frontier in astronomical numbers. According to several sources, up to ten million people took refuge in India. After a five-day tour of the refugee camps the American senator Edward Kennedy declared that "he was now convinced that the

Pakistan Army had committed genocide in East Pakistan."[23] The cost of supporting the refugees, even on a minimal subsistence level, reached staggering proportions. That cost threatened the weak Indian economy. The Indian government could not remain passive in the face of the tragedy. In contrast, the Pakistani military appeared completely out of touch with the political and military realities. It was confident that it had definitively crushed the secession movement in East Pakistan, and that it would be able to face and defeat any Indian threat of intervention.

The security situation at the Pakistani-Indian borders deteriorated quickly, with frequent border clashes between the two countries. On December 3, 1971, Pakistani planes made a surprise attack on Indian air bases. The radio at Islamabad proclaimed that Pakistan was waging a *jihad*, a holy war, against India. However, it quickly became clear that the Pakistani military had grossly overestimated its capabilities and the extent of the foreign support it might receive. The Indian army, supported by the local guerrillas, advanced into East Pakistan with astonishing speed. The front rolled up like strips of leather. By December 13, the Indian army came close to the capital, Dacca. The permanent American representative at the UN, George H. W. Bush, claimed that India was clearly "the major aggressor." The American Seventh Fleet steamed into the Bay of Bengal in an attempt to intimidate the Indian government. But by now there was no longer any way to help the Pakistani army, which surrendered on December 17. Bangladesh was soon recognized by the world community as an independent state. Until the disintegration of Yugoslavia twenty years later, Bangladesh was the only case of unilateral secession in a noncolonial context that was acknowledged internationally as being morally and politically legitimate. Indian troops were withdrawn, letting the new Muslim nation of Bangladesh take care of itself.

The Indian Representative to the United Nations stated at the time that India had "on this particular occasion absolutely nothing but the purest of motives and the purest of intentions; to rescue the people of East Bengal from what they are suffering."[24] We have every right to believe that India's real intentions were in accord with the just cause officially proclaimed: viz., to stop the massacre in East Pakistan and to defend India from aggression. Indeed, the Indian military did stop the massacre before it withdrew. This does not mean that the Indian intentions were "pure," as claimed by the Indian ambassador to the UN, and that we should neglect the geopolitical advantages India took from the dismemberment of its main rival in the region. But nor does this interest in weakening Pakistan mean that India's intentions were in fact different from the just cause it proclaimed for using force. It had the right to save the lives of millions of innocent people, in a situation where all possibilities of negotiation had long been exhausted, and also where the basic security interests of India itself were at stake. The destabilizing effects of millions of refugees, including the economic burden it represented for an exhausted economy, and the increased tensions at its borders, should indeed not be neglected in a moral assessment of the Indian intervention.

Some authors, such as G. W. Choudhury,[25] criticize both the Pakistani atrocities and the Indian military intervention, which, of necessity, also supported the secession of Bangladesh. At the time, such criticism was shared by many U.S. officials. However, it remains unclear how further massacres in East Pakistan could have been prevented without the Indian intervention. The UN Security Council was not ready to act. The American condemnation of the Indian policies was, it seems, inspired more by Cold War politics than by Just War considerations. For the United States, India was an ally of the Soviet Union whereas Pakistan was an ally of the West, so that the strengthening of India's geopolitical position in the region had to be prevented, despite any right intentions India might have had in this particular case.

HITLER'S OCCUPATION OF CZECHOSLOVAKIA, 1938[26]

Czechoslovakia, with its plentiful economic resources, had been included in Hitler's annexation plans long before the outbreak of World War II. In a speech to the Reichstag on February 20, 1938, Hitler declared that 10 million Germans lived "separated from us on the immediate borders of the Reich." Out of those 10 million, 6.5 lived in Austria. Another 3.2 million lived in Czechoslovakia. Hitler had repeatedly expressed his hatred and contempt for the Slavic people and from 1937 onward he had also repeatedly stated that his final goal was to destroy the multiethnic state of Czechoslovakia. One of his options was to annex the Sudetenland, where the bulk of the German population lived, and then to take over the remainder of the country. He planned to use the national-socialist *Heimatpartei* of the Sudeten Germans, under the leadership of Konrad Geinlein, for these purposes. The demand for autonomy was a useful political slogan in this context. Geinlein's party proved a great success among the German population in the Sudetenland. In the elections of May 1935, it garnered nearly 1.2 million votes. Early in 1937 Geinlein started to demand autonomy for the German areas. The government refused his demands, as it feared similar demands from the many other nationalities within the country. In March 1938, Geinlein conferred with Hitler and agreed with him that "we must always demand so much that we can never be satisfied."[27]

At the time, both Britain and France were determined to avoid war with Germany, even at the expense of Czechoslovakia. They did not feel sufficiently prepared for an armed confrontation, and hoped to reach a separate arrangement with Hitler without involving the Soviet Union. At a conference in London in April 1937, British and French leaders agreed that they would put as much pressure as possible on the government of Czechoslovakia to meet the Sudeten German demands. In May, there were riots in the Sudetenland. On May 21, two Germans were killed while assaulting Czech policemen. The German media immediately unleashed anti-Czech hysteria, accusing the Czechs of unspeakable atrocities against the Germans in the Sudetenland.

The government of President Benesh succumbed in September to the combined pressure from Germany, France, and Britain and agreed to nearly all of Geinlein's party's demands. But the German irredentists[28] staged an incident in the town of Moravska-Ostrava that resulted in the arrest of two of their deputies. They then used the arrests to break off negotiations. On September 12, at a Nazi Party rally in Nuremberg, Hitler declared that he could not leave the Sudeten Germans defenseless. The same night, riots were organized in the main towns in the Sudetenland.

Chamberlain was convinced that war was imminent, and so went to Berchtesgaden to meet Hitler. There he agreed in principle that the Sudetenland would be attached to Germany, though he said that he would have to consult his cabinet and the French. He did not mention any right of the Czechoslovak government to be involved in this decision. But once Chamberlain had received support from his cabinet and from the French government, Hitler put forward new demands, including autonomy for the Slovak minority. He also wanted to occupy the Sudetenland at once. It became increasingly clear that Hitler would never be satisfied with any compromise solution, and that any arrangement would be followed by new threats and new bullying. Britain and France decided then to start military mobilization. They had demonstrated their readiness to sacrifice the interests of Czechoslovakia for the sake of stability in Europe, but this did not mean that they were also ready to buy peace at the cost of having the whole of Europe dominated by Germany.

Faced with this crisis, a conference of four states (England, France, Germany, and Italy) was held in Munich at the end of September. The Soviet Union was not invited. Hitler made a speech in which he accused Czechoslovakia of oppressing the German population and reiterated his demands for the immediate annexation of the German-populated regions "for the benefit of international peace and stability." He declared that, whatever the outcome of the conference, German troops would be deployed in the Sudetenland on October 1. Again, France and Britain decided to reach an agreement at the expense of Czechoslovakia. On September 30, 1938, the Munich Agreement was signed by the four states. Sudeten German territories were to be ceded to Germany at once. German occupation was to begin on October 1. Plebiscites would be held in some other territories with large German populations. The final frontier would be fixed by the four countries at a later time. The Czechoslovak government had no choice but to accept.

With the signing of the Munich Agreement, the second stage in the plan to destroy the statehood of Czechoslovakia began. There were roughly 3.3 million Slovaks and half a million Ruthenes in Czechoslovakia. Slovak politicians were told that Germany would support Slovak independence, and Germany also put pressure on Ruthenia. In March 1939 the Czechoslovak government dismissed the governments of Ruthenia and Slovakia and proclaimed martial law. Hitler then invited the Slovak premier to Berlin in order to prepare a declaration of independence. On the night of March 15 Hitler met the Czechoslovak president Emil Hacha in Berlin and declared that the Czechoslovak state no longer existed. Hacha had to agree virtually at gunpoint, faced with the threat of the destruction of Czechoslovakian cities by the German air force if he refused. Hitler told him he had a choice between resistance, which would be crushed at once, and peaceful occupation. That same night, German troops crossed the border. The newly "independent" Slovakia accepted German protection, and Ruthenia was handed over to Germany's ally Hungary. It became clear that Germany's next move would be eastward, toward Poland. As France Miller wrote, "Hitler had stated in *Mein Kampf* that he intended to move the Slavic races bodily out of central Europe to regions in the East. In the first two years the German occupation authorities specified five large areas of Bohemia and Moravia from which all Czechs were forced to move by certain dates to make way for German colonists. By September 1, 1941, these areas were emptied of their Czech population, and Germans moved in. The Czechs were forbidden to take with them anything except clothing. Their farm tools and stock, their businesses, even their kitchen utensils, had to be left for the German settlers."[29]

Hitler's intentions in the war against Czechoslovakia were pretty clear. They were to seize new territories and populations, and to prepare for future wars. These real intentions had nothing to do with the officially proclaimed intention of protecting German minorities from oppression and atrocities. The rights of national self-determination of the Sudetenland and Slovakia were understood in a purely ethnic sense, and used to justify territorial expansion. The Western democracies would have had a just cause in defending Czechoslovakia. But their intention was not that of acting justly and, in so doing, supporting a victim of aggression. Instead, they were intent on preserving their own geopolitical interests and avoiding war for as long as possible.

HITLER'S OCCUPATION OF POLAND, 1939[30]

After Czechoslovakia, Poland became the primary target of further German expansion. Adolf Hitler started World War II with the deliberate purpose of subjugating Europe for the sake of the supremacy of the Aryan race. At dawn

on September 1, 1939, without a declaration of war, German warplanes attacked Poland. Within the next few hours more than thirty cities were in
flames. Homes, hospitals, churches, and schools were indiscriminately
bombed along with military objectives. Hitler's perfidy shocked the moral
conscience of the world. The invasion of Poland had been preceded by a
concerted campaign of propaganda against the Polish people. Poland was
blamed for carrying out aggressive plans against Germany and the German
attack was declared to be a preemptive strike. In fact, the occupation of
Poland, located just west of the Soviet Union, had a strategic significance.
In the long run, the Soviet Union was an even more valuable target for German expansion, since it had oil, iron, manganese, and other natural resources in abundance.

The Polish army was totally overmatched. The firepower ratio in
weaponry was 72 to 1 in favor of Germany. The Polish Army resisted heroically, but it was doomed. Within a month the war in Poland was over. We
are fully entitled to believe that the just cause proclaimed by Hitler in this
war had nothing to do with his real intentions of expansion and conquest.
But what about the next case, which also involves Poland?

THE SOVIET OCCUPATION OF POLAND, 1939[31]

On the seventeenth day of Poland's resistance against the Germans, another
bombshell struck: the Soviet Union entered the war. On September 17, the
Soviet army moved into Poland from the east. Within two days Soviet
troops, meeting no resistance, occupied nearly half of Poland, cutting Hitler
off from the rich oil wells of Galicia and blocking his direct route to Ru-
mania. Passing quickly to Lwow and reaching Brest, the Soviets took their
stand close to the Russian border of 1918.

The intentions of the Nazis in the Polish war were obvious. Nobody took
seriously the German claim that it had to strike "in the face of Polish aggression," or with the intention of protecting the German minority. The intentions of the Poles in that war were also obvious. They were defending
their country as effectively as they could. But what about the Soviet intentions in intervening in Poland? Were they good in the sense of being in accord with Just War Theory?

The Soviets had signed a pact with Hitler on August 23, 1939. The Secret
Protocols to this pact provided for the division of Poland between Germany
and Poland. The Soviet Union was given the further option of annexing Es-
tonia, Latvia, and Lithuania. This pact came about partly because of Soviet
disillusionment with Western policies: Stalin had made several attempts to
organize a broad coalition of states to oppose Nazi Germany, but the Western democracies had failed to respond positively. Moscow expected that the

pact with Germany would give the USSR some respite in preparing its military defense against future German aggression.

But the Soviet Union, when it invaded Poland, also claimed to be reconquering territories that had been part of the Czarist Empire. These territories, populated by millions of Ukrainians and Belorussians, had, in its view, been unjustly taken away from the Soviet republics of Ukraine and Belorussia by Poland in the Soviet-Polish war of 1920. But it is striking that the Secret Protocols to the German-Soviet Pact of 1939 made no mention of Soviet claims to Polish territories on the basis of Ukrainian and Belorussian national aspirations.[32] The Soviet Union's decision to invoke the principle of self-determination as a justification for its occupation of Poland was apparently made at the last minute. When, on September 3, the German foreign minister von Ribbentrop invited the Soviet Union to take its share of Polish territory (in accord with the Secret Protocols), Soviet Minister for Foreign Affairs Molotov answered that it was the Soviet Union's intention to declare first that it was necessary to come to the aid of the Ukrainians and Belorussians. This would make the justification of the Soviet military intervention plausible to public opinion. An article in the leading Soviet newspaper *Pravda* complained about the condition of minorities in eastern Poland. Following its own military intervention on September 17, the Soviet government then presented a further justification to the Polish ambassador in Moscow and to the international public in which it was said that the Polish state had virtually ceased to exist. This condition was viewed as creating a serious problem for the Soviet Union insofar as it created a power vacuum in the area—one that the Nazis would certainly fill if they were allowed to do so. Intervention, it was said, was further necessary in order to protect its Ukrainian and Belorussian nationals after the collapse of the Polish state.

The Soviet population accepted the justifications of the creation of a better defense against Germany, self-determination for Ukrainian and Belorussian nationals, and the restoration of just borders. This view was not shared by all, however. Many observers claimed that the real Soviet intentions had to do with political expansion and political domination. They pointed out that the Soviet secret service had murdered thousands of Polish officers in the Katyn Forest near Smolensk in 1940, a crime that was acknowledged officially only half a century later by the post-Soviet Russian government. The intention of destroying the Polish army, which had resisted heroically against German invasion, could not be justified in terms of the self-defense of the Soviet Union. Moreover, 1.5 million Poles, in particular members of the intelligentsia, were deported to Soviet labor camps.[33]

Many historical cases resemble this one. Scholars are not able to give a quick answer to the question: what are the real intentions of those who use military force? Any interpretation must be based on an examination from a variety of perspectives. But moral abuse of the Principle of Right Intentions is a real risk. This is one reason why Grotius' skepticism about the Right Intentions Principle should not be dismissed lightly.

A FOUR-STEP APPROACH TO THE IRAQ WAR, 2003

The literature on the Iraq war has dealt extensively with the American and British governments' intention to wage a "preemptive war" against Iraq. Their motives have also been at the center of political disputes between government and opposition in these two countries. The antiwar movement and the media have added their own arguments to these discussions. The two governments have been accused of having sacrificed the national interest, regional stability in the Middle East, and numerous lives for the sake of motives that had nothing to do with the threat of weapons of mass destruction or any other just cause. Despite the failure of their war policies, the American president George W. Bush and British prime minister Tony Blair remained unrepentant and firm in their belief that they had done "the right thing."[34]

Much is at stake in the discussion on whether the intentions behind the war were in line with a just cause or not. Decision-makers have been accused of promoting immoral policies and have fiercely defended their respectability. The discussion further involves the future role and intentions of these countries in the stabilization of Iraq. It also challenges the United States's claim to moral leadership. The debate is highly emotional and the literature on the subject highly controversial. The far-reaching political consequences of these debates do not make it any easier to assess the subjective intentions that pushed for war.

In June 2003, U.S. Deputy Defense Secretary Paul Wolfowitz, one of the most influential advisers of President Bush and a strong advocate of going to war against Iraq, made an interesting statement on the decision-making process on the war. When he did so, it had already become clear that the American invasion had failed to uncover any secret WMD program. Wolfowitz wanted to convince the American public that the destruction of Iraq's WMD had been only one of several reasons for going to war, and not necessarily the main one: "The truth is that for reasons that have a lot to do with the U.S. government bureaucracy, we settled on the one issue that everyone could agree on, which was weapons of mass destruction."[35] In his view, there had been a variety of good motives, such as putting an end to the criminal mistreatment of the Iraqi people. What is interesting about this statement is not so much the attempt to find a new justification for the Iraq campaign, but rather the frank acknowledgment that the moral justification of the war in terms of a preemptive strategy resulted in the first place from the inability of the Bush administration to agree on a common definition of its own objectives.

There were a variety of motives for the Iraq war, and a step-by-step approach may be helpful in disentangling them. As a first step, we need to make a list of the various intentions to be found in literature and in the media. Here we may take all possible arguments into account. It is not necessary to assess these intentions critically at this stage. An overview of the main theses concerning intentions—limited in this case study to the American ones—can be found in box 3.1.

In a second step, we can classify all these intentions. Some items duplicate each other or are so closely related that they can be replaced by a single item. But one has to be careful not to omit necessary distinctions. In its

---

Box 3.1

- preventing the production of weapons of mass destruction
- preventing Iraq's development of nuclear weapons
- preempting the use of weapons of mass destruction
- destroying Iraq's stock of chemical and biological weapons
- preventing Iraqi support to international terrorism
- defending human rights in Iraq
- keeping the United States on a war footing to ensure Republican majorities
- defending human rights in the Middle East
- enhancing the popularity of President Bush for a second presidential term
- stabilizing the Middle East
- confronting the Islamic world
- democratizing Iraq
- maintaining U.S. control over access to oil
- democratizing the Middle East
- preempting the use of weapons of mass destruction against Israel
- affirming U.S. hegemony over the Middle East
- strengthening the security of Israel
- achieving the regime change that Bush Senior failed to achieve in 1991
- gaining U.S. control over Iraq's oil resources
- favoring the arms industry and corporations such as Halliburton
- affirming U.S. hegemony over other world powers
- increasing electoral support at home
- testing new military technology
- affirming U.S. hegemony over its allies

---

public statements the Bush administration has, for instance, lumped together Iraq's capacity to use chemical and biological weapons with the development of nuclear weapons by referring to WMD in general. The administration did not have an interest in focusing on the differences between different kinds of WMD in its mobilizing appeals for war against Iraq. It did not possess strong evidence of Iraq's development of nuclear weapons, and tried to convince the public that one could deduce—from Iraq's previous use of chemical weapons against its own population—that Saddam also intended to acquire nuclear weapons. But these threats have to be distinguished, as they are of a different magnitude and demand different political and military responses.[36] The American administration was of course conscious of this distinction. Its intention to destroy existing Iraqi stocks of chemical and biological weapons cannot be equated with its policy of preventing the development of a nuclear weapons production program. For this reason, it is not correct to refer to the threat of WMD generally, as the American administration did for mobilizing purposes. It is preferable to make a distinction in this list between chemical and biological weapons on the one hand and nuclear weapons on the other.

There is furthermore a major distinction to be made between the defense of human rights and the spreading of democracy. Both are generally closely related, but their moral value is very different in Just War Theory terms. The remedying or prevention of massive human rights violations can constitute a just cause for the use of force in a humanitarian intervention, but the improvement of state structures cannot. This is particularly true for the expectation that the war against Iraq would lead to a wave of democratic political reforms throughout the whole of the Middle East. Political reforms are not a just cause for war. Democratization is a necessary requirement for postwar reconstruction in a country where military humanitarian intervention has taken place for a just reason, but on its own it is not a valid reason for such intervention.

In its strategy of preemptive wars, analyzed in the previous chapter on the Just Cause Principle, the U.S. government used the term "rogue state" which confused the defense of human rights with democratization, but it did not entirely deny the difference between them. It considered the political regime of Saddam Hussein to be unjust, because it violated the rights of its population and threatened international security. It did not pass the same judgment on the other undemocratic regimes in the Middle East that are loyal U.S. allies. These states were supposed to benefit in the long term from Iraq's democratization by being pushed toward political reform, but they were not presented as threats to their populations or to international law.

The Bush administration—and particularly its neoconservative members—linked the security interests of the United States with those of Israel.[37] The destruction of the stocks of chemical and biological weapons by Iraq and the intention to spread democracy in the Middle East through regime change in Baghdad were in the direct interest of Israel. But the American government still considered that the possession of chemical and biological weapons by Iraq constituted a different type of threat for Israel than for the United States. It is therefore necessary to consider these issues separately.

Box 3.2 gives a more systematic overview of the various intentions at stake in the war against Iraq. Some of the intentions mentioned in the previous list have been deleted, such as those referring to WMD in general. The remaining ones are ordered according to their mutual affinity. Some of the intentions deal with military security, others with the questions of human rights, democratization, conflict resolution, and political stability. Intentions may further be related to geopolitics, economics, or domestic politics. Psychological factors or ideological concepts belonging to Western civilization may also play a role and are listed separately.

Box 3.2

- preventing Iraq's development of nuclear weapons
- destroying Iraq's stock of chemical and biological weapons
- preventing Iraq's support to international terrorism
- affirming U.S. hegemony over the Middle East
- affirming U.S. hegemony over other world powers
- affirming U.S. hegemony over its allies
- preempting the use of chemical and biological weapons against Israel
- strengthening the security of Israel
- defending human rights in Iraq
- democratizing Iraq
- defending human rights in the Middle East
- democratizing the Middle East
- stabilizing the Middle East
- controlling Iraq's oil resources
- controlling access to oil
- favoring the U.S. arms industry and corporations such as Halliburton
- testing new military technology
- keeping the country on a war footing to ensure Republican majorities
- increasing electoral support at home
- confronting the Islamic world
- achieving the regime change that Bush Senior failed to achieve in 1991

As a third step in our analysis, we need to assess these objectives morally. This should not necessarily be done in contradiction to the moral views of the decision-makers themselves. But it is also true that the good of one's own nation—including one's own economy and one's own arms industry—may easily be confused with what is morally just, or, to speak with reference to ethical traditions, the nonmoral language of Realism is easily confused with the moral language of the Just War Tradition. The Bush administration, however, made great efforts to frame its war objectives in a universal moral language, particularly in public statements addressed to an international audience. International diplomatic negotiations on the use of force refer to broader security interests than those of a single state. It is possible, on this basis, to determine what the U.S. administration thought the world community would find morally acceptable as a just cause.

Box 3.3 gives a moral evaluation of the various intentions behind the decision to go to war. A distinction is made between intentions that are subjectively in line with a just cause for war (+) and intentions that are subjectively not in line with a just cause for war (-). It has to be borne in mind that we are dealing not with morally good or bad intentions in general, but with the moral intentions for a decision to go to war. The potentially fateful consequences of the Iraqi invasion were widely discussed before the beginning of the war, and the moral nature of the intentions of those who decided on this war has to be assessed accordingly. We may, for instance, consider the objective of democratizing the Middle East as an acceptable objective of American foreign policy, but not as a morally acceptable ground for war. This is in line with what the United States itself considered to be internationally acceptable as a just cause for war.

It should further be noted that the search for domestic support cannot be a morally acceptable motive for going to war. It is of course to be expected that a government will attempt to obtain domestic support for a war that it wages for good reasons, but this does not mean that such an attempt is a proper motive for going to war.

In our fourth step, we have to assess the presence of each of these objectives in the decision-making process leading to the war. Concerning the items regarding Israel, John J. Mearsheimer and Stephen M. Walt assert that among the many factors influencing U.S. foreign policy, the pressure of Israel and its lobby in the United States have to be taken into account. Without this pressure, combined with the pressure coming from the American neoconservatives, "America would probably not be in Iraq today."[38]

Flawed intelligence reports have been widely acknowledged as one of the main causes of the Iraq war. Officials used raw intelligence before it had been seriously tested and analyzed.[39] Some of the critics state that political pressure was put on the intelligence community to justify decisions already taken. Intelligence agencies in the United States and Britain had to find ev-

---

Box 3.3

- preventing Iraq's development of nuclear weapons (+)
- destroying Iraq's stock of chemical and biological weapons (+)
- preventing Iraq's support to international terrorism (+)
- affirming U.S. hegemony over the Middle East (-)
- affirming U.S. hegemony over other world powers (-)
- affirming U.S. hegemony over its allies (-)
- preempting the use of chemical and biological weapons against Israel (+)
- strengthening the security of Israel (-)
- defending human rights in Iraq (+)
- democratizing Iraq (-)
- defending human rights in the Middle East (-)
- democratizing the Middle East (-)
- stabilizing the Middle East (-)
- controlling Iraq's oil resources (-)
- gaining access to oil (-)
- favoring the U.S. arms industry and corporations such as Halliburton (-)
- testing new military technology (-)
- keeping the country on a war footing to ensure Republican majorities (-)
- increasing electoral support at home (-)
- confronting the Islamic world (-)
- achieving the regime change that Bush Senior failed to achieve in 1991 (-)

---

idence of the existence and potential use of WMD by Saddam Hussein's regime and by presenting worst-case scenarios as factual proof.[40] It is said that the just cause for a preemptive war was largely fabricated, and that the real motives for going to war were other than to respond to an imminent threat. Leading American politicians, such as John Kerry, the Democratic presidential candidate in 2004, stated that George W. Bush had misled the American public.

But the war policies of Bush are open to alternative interpretations. They may be the consequence of self-deception. Some sources state that the consensus of the intelligence community on Iraq's efforts to develop WMD—a consensus including even the foreign intelligence agencies of countries opposed to the Iraq war—was overwhelming.[41] There does not seem to be hard proof that the Bush administration intentionally misled the public about the existence of an Iraqi threat and the need to react preemptively. It may very well be that the administration, by its way of managing intelligence agencies and handling intelligence information, favored such self-deception.

Iraq's share of world oil reserves is estimated at about 11 percent, the second largest after Saudi Arabia. The importance of oil in the American decision to go to war has been assessed in various ways.[42] According to one interpretation, the Bush administration wanted to control these oil reserves. It could then hand over licenses to U.S. oil companies after the war. American policies after the invasion seemed to confirm this view. By putting itself in the role of a decision-maker in the oil sector, the United States raised suspicions about its previous intentions.[43]

Such an interpretation of the role of oil in American war policies is challenged by the argument that the United States does not generally aim at direct military control of oil-producing countries and that there was no economic reason to invade Iraq because of its oil as long as the regime of Saddam Hussein did not withhold it from world markets. Moreover, American oil companies had not lobbied for the war but had pushed, on the contrary, for an end to the sanctions on Iraq.[44]

After his retirement, Alan Greenspan, who had been chairman of the Federal Reserve, stated in an interview that the Iraq war was largely about oil and that his own support for regime change in Baghdad through the use of force was mainly economically motivated. He considered the need to ensure oil for the world markets to be even more important than the threat of WMD, which he had nevertheless taken very seriously before the war. But in saying this he did not mean that the aim of the war was the establishment of American control over Iraq's oil fields. Greenspan feared that Saddam Hussein would be able to control the Straits of Hormuz, which see a throughput of up to 19 million barrels a day. A disruption of even three or four million barrels a day could push oil prices to levels as high as \$120 a barrel, which would lead to a breakdown of the global economy. He thought that the war and regime change had to guarantee the smooth operation of the existing oil market.[45] Of course, this view is not in line with a just cause for war, but defends the right of preventive wars to improve guarantees of economic stability.

Still another view of the importance of oil for the war policies has been provided by Paul Wolfowitz. He was asked at a security conference in Singapore in May 2003 why a nuclear power such as North Korea was being treated differently from Iraq. He answered that one of the factors to be taken into account was the fact that North Korea is on the edge of economic collapse, which gives the Americans a point of leverage in negotiations with the regime. The United States had, on the contrary, "virtually no economic options with Iraq because the country floats on a sea of oil."[46] In Wolfowitz view, Iraq's oil wealth was thus a reason that military force had to be used—but this does not mean either that control over oil reserves were the major reason for war.

There has been also a broad discussion in the international business community and the media on the economic consequences of the Iraq war and the economic motives for going to war. Business leaders and economists have pointed out that lingering uncertainty about war depresses markets and boosts oil prices. Economic historians have observed that most wars in U.S. history have stimulated the economy through massive government spending on defense, but this does not rule out exceptions, such as the economic recession that resulted from the 1990 Iraqi invasion of Kuwait. In February 2003, a few weeks before the beginning of the new military operations against Iraq, the world business community expressed contradictory feelings about the future of the war. Business leaders hoped that the uncertainty surrounding a potential war would end and at the same time they feared that, once the action started, the fog of war and the geopolitical consequences of the invasion of Iraq would worsen the world's economic prospects.[47]

The reconstruction of Iraq as a result of the 2003 war was to involve a multibillion-dollar program. According to a study carried out before the war by the Baker Institute for Public Policy at Rice University, to achieve pre-1991 production levels the oil industry would need 5 billion dollars' worth of investment.[48] Such prospects were of major interest to engineering companies such as Halliburton, which was headed by Dick Cheney before he became vice president of the United States in 2001.[49] The search for personal profit should not be overlooked in an analysis of war—as already indicated by the classics in the Just War Tradition—but it would be wrong to overestimate this type of motive. Nor can the intentions of European countries opposed to the Iraq war, such as France and Germany, be reduced to their fear of losing lucrative contracts or business relations with Iraq. It was first and foremost a conflict about ideas and principles, and about the fear of U.S. hegemony and unilateralism.[50]

Box 3.4 weighs up the importance of the various intentions in American decision-making. Their degree of prominence has been rated on a scale from 0 to 3. Such an overview gives of course only a raw picture of the situation and is open to criticism. There is a lack of hard evidence for the various arguments in the debate, and these figures should not give the (wrong) impression that it is possible to quantify decision-making precisely.

We can conclude that, in the mix of intentions leading to the decision to go to war, the bad ones prevailed. The Bush administration failed to act in accordance with the Right Intentions Principle. The lack of strong evidence cannot be used against this historical interpretation of events. It is quite true that lack of evidence—as seen in this type of interpretation—would rule out a conviction in court proceedings. But we are not dealing with legal procedures, but with a *jus ad bellum* principle that is not and cannot be enforced by any international court. The United States claimed to act in defense of its own interests and in defense of the interests of the world community, but it failed to provide evidence not only of a just cause for a preemptive war

---

Box 3.4

- preventing Iraq's development of nuclear weapons (+) (2)
- destroying Iraq's stock of chemical and biological weapons (+) (3)
- preventing Iraq's support to international terrorism (+) (2)
- affirming U.S. hegemony over the Middle East (-) (3)
- affirming U.S. hegemony over other world powers (-) (3)
- affirming U.S. hegemony over its allies (-) (2)
- preempting the use of chemical and biological weapons against Israel (+) (3)
- strengthening the security of Israel (-) (3)
- defending human rights in Iraq (+) (1)
- democratizing Iraq (-) (2)
- defending human rights in the Middle East (-) (0)
- democratizing the Middle East (-) (2)
- stabilizing the Middle East (-) (3)
- controlling Iraq's oil resources (-) (2)
- controlling access to oil (-) (3)
- favoring the U.S. arms industry and corporations such as Halliburton (-) (1)
- testing new military technology (-) (1)
- keeping the country on a war footing to ensure Republican majorities (-) (0)
- increasing electoral support at home (-) (1)
- confronting the Islamic world (-) (0)
- achieving the regime change that Bush Senior failed to achieve in 1991 (-) (1)

---

but also of its own righteousness. To prove its right intentions, the United States should have clarified from the start what its long-term prospects in Iraq were.[51] It should also have clarified from the start which policies on oil exploitation it wanted to pursue, particularly with regard to the interests of the Iraqi people. But it failed to do so, which is fully consistent with its lack of an overall strategy on the occupation and reconstruction of Iraq. Wolfowitz's frank statement that the threat of WMD was put in a prominent place in the justification for war as a result of bureaucratic wrangling within the administration does not contradict this moral judgment. As a consequence of its failure to respect the moral rules of war, the Bush administration aroused worldwide opposition to American leadership. But at the domestic level, American voters kept their confidence in the American president and in 2004 they renewed his term in office.

NOTES

1. Saint Augustine, "The City of God," bk. 19, chap. 12, trans. Marcus Dods, in *Great Books of the Western World* (Chicago: Encyclopaedia Britannica, 1990), 16:506.

2. Saint Augustine, "Contra Faustum," in *The Works of Aurelius Augustine*, vol. 6, *Writings in Connection with the Manichaean Heresy*, trans. Richard Stothert, ed. Marcus Dods (Edinburgh: T. and T. Clark, 1872), bk. 22, chap. 74.

3. Saint Augustine, "Contra Faustum," 74.

4. See Colm McKeogh, *Innocent Civilians: The Morality of Killing in War* (Basingstoke, Eng.: Palgrave, 2002), 25.

5. Saint Augustine, "The City of God," bk. 19, chap. 12, 587.

6. Paul Christopher, *The Ethics of War and Peace*, 2nd ed. (Boulder, Colo.: Westview Press, 1999), 40.

7. Christopher, *The Ethics of War and Peace*, 41.

8. Christopher, *The Ethics of War and Peace*, 46.

9. John Kelsay, *Islam and War: A Study in Comparative Ethics* (Louisville, Ky.: Westminster/John Knox Press, 1993), 29.

10. Hugo Grotius, *The Rights of War and Peace*, bk. 2, chap. 22, 17, trans. A. C. Campbell (London: B. Boothroyd, 1814), at www.constitution.org/gro/djbp.htm (accessed February 8, 2008).

11. Grotius, *The Rights of War and Peace*, bk. 2, chap. 23, 13.

12. On the following see Ian Clark, *Waging War: A Philosophical Introduction* (Oxford: Clarendon Press, 1988), 42–43.

13. According to Francisco de Vitoria (1486–1546), there was "no inconsistency, indeed, in holding the war to be a just war on both sides, seeing that on one side there is right and on the other side there is invincible ignorance." Quoted in McKeogh, *Innocent Civilians*, 84.

14. Clark, *Waging War*, 42.

15. See George P. Fletcher, *Romantics at War: Glory and Guilt in the Age of Terrorism* (Princeton, N.J., and Oxford: Princeton University Press, 2002), 67.

16. "U.S. Catholic Bishops' Pastoral Letter, the Challenge of Peace: God's Promise and Our Response," in *Just War Theory*, ed. Jean Bethke Elshtain (New York: New York University Press, 1992), 100.

17. "Catholic Bishops' Pastoral Letter," 98.

18. Robert Holmes, *On War and Morality* (Princeton, N.J.: Princeton University Press, 1989), 196.

19. For the criticism of a morally too demanding approach to Just War Theory, see the discussion of this theme by Anthony Coates, "The New World Order and the Ethics of War," in *The Ethical Dimension of Global Change*, ed. Barry Holden (London: Macmillan, 1996), 205–25.

20. See Damodar P. Singhal, *Pakistan* (Englewood Cliffs, N.J.: Prentice-Hall, 1972); Louis Baeck, *Van Pakistan tot Bangla Desh* (Antwerpen, Utrecht: De Nederlandsche Boekhandel, 1972); Robert Payne, *Massacre* (New York: Macmillan, 1973); G. W. Choudhury, *The Last Days of United Pakistan* (London: Hurst & Co, 1974); Lawrence Ziring, *Pakistan: The Enigma of Political Development* (Folkestone, Eng., and Boulder, Colo.: Dawson & Westview, 1980); Vladimir Puchkov, *Politicheskoje razvitije*

Bungladesh (Moscow: Nauka, 1986), 9–14; Francis Robinson, ed., *The Cambridge Encyclopedia of India, Pakistan, Bangladesh* (Cambridge: Cambridge University Press, 1989).

21. Choudhury, *The Last Days*, 184.

22. Choudhury, *The Last Days*, 185.

23. *Times*, August 17, 1971, quoted in Singhal, *Pakistan*, 199.

24. Quoted in Nicholas J. Wheeler, *Saving Strangers: Humanitarian Intervention in International* Society (Oxford: Oxford University Press, 2000), 64.

25. Choudhury, *The Last Days*, 202–27.

26. On the following see: *Istoriya Vtoroi mirovoi voiny 1939–1945 v dvenadtsati tomakh* (Moscow: Voenizdat, 1974), 2:90–99; P. M. H. Bell, *The Origins of the Second World War in Europe* (London and New York: Longman, 1986); Martin Kitchen, *Europe between the Wars: A Political History* (London and New York: Longman, 1988); Roger Maria, *De l'accord de Munich au pacte germano-soviétique du 23 août 1939* (Paris: L'Harmattan, 1995).

27. Bell, *The Origins of the Second World War*, 231.

28. The difference between secession and irredentism may be defined as follows: "Secession involves the withdrawal of a group and its territory from the authority of a state of which it is a part. Irredentism entails the retrieval of ethnically kindred people and their territory across an international boundary, joining them and it to the retrieving state." Donald Horowitz, "Self-Determination: Politics, Philosophy, and Law," in *National Self-Determination and Secession*, ed. Margaret Moore (Oxford: Oxford University Press, 1998), 182.

29. France T. Miller, *History of World War 2* (Philadelphia and Toronto: The John C. Wenston Company, 1945), 117.

30. Miller, *History of World War 2*, 120–27; *Istoriya Vtoroi mirovoi voiny*, 3:13–35.

31. Miller, *History of World War 2*, 355–58.

32. On this issue, see Vernon V. Aspaturian, *The Union Republics in Soviet Diplomacy: A Study of Soviet Federalism in the Service of Soviet Foreign Policy* (Geneva and Paris: Librarie Droz and Librairie Minard, 1960), 59–71.

33. Richard Sakwa, *Soviet Politics in Perspective* (London: Routledge, 1998), 257.

34. On Tony Blair, see "Beating the Retreat From a Broken Iraq," *Financial Times*, December 18, 2007, 10.

35. Transcripts, Live from the Headlines, "Wolfowitz: WMD Chosen as Reason for Iraq War for 'Bureaucratic Reasons,'" aired May 30, 2003, at transcripts.cnn.com/TRANSCRIPTS/0305/30/se.08.html (accessed February 6, 2008). See also Mark Huband and Stephen Fidler, "No Smoking Gun: How Intelligence May Have Been Exaggerated, Misinterpreted, and Manipulated," *Financial Times*, June 4, 2003, 11.

36. Edward Alden, "Democrats Face Struggle to Win Support for Iraq War 'Lie' Claim," *Financial Times*, November 16, 2005, 6.

37. On this issue, see John J. Mearsheimer and Stephen M. Walt, *The Israel Lobby and U.S. Foreign Policy* (New York: Farrar, Straus & Giroux, 2007), 229–62.

38. Mearsheimer and Walt, *The Israel Lobby and U.S. Foreign Policy*, 233. This pressure does not reflect the opinion of American Jews. According to Pew Research Center polls, American Jews were less supportive of the war (52 percent) just after it had

started than the American population in general (62 percent). Mearsheimer and Walt, *The Israel Lobby and U.S. Foreign Policy*, 243.

39. David E. Sanger and Steven Lee Myers, "U.S. Says Details in Military Notes Led to Shift on Iran," *New York Times*, December 6, 2007, A12.

40. Mearsheimer and Walt, *The Israel Lobby and U.S. Foreign Policy*, 250–53.

41. Alden, "Democrats Face Struggle", 6.

42. "Not a War for Oil," *Financial Times*, February 22–23, 2003, 6.

43. Jeffrey Sachs, "American Intentions are Tainted by Iraq's Oil," *Financial Times*, May 22, 2003, 13.

44. Mearsheimer and Walt, *The Israel Lobby and U.S. Foreign Policy*, 254–55.

45. Matthew Sheffield, "Alan Greenspan: I Never Said Iraq War Was about Oil," *NewsBusters*, September 17, 2007, at www.newsbusters.org/blogs/matthew -sheffield/2007/09/17/alan-greenspan-i-never-said-iraq-war-was-about-oil (accessed February 7, 2008).

46. U.S. Department of Defense, News Transcript, Deputy Secretary Wolfowitz Q&A Following IISS Asia Security Conference, May 31, 2003, at www .defenselink.mil/transcripts/transcript.aspx?transcriptid=2704 (accessed February 18, 2008).

47. "Calculating the Consequences," *Economist*, November 30, 2002, 67; Andrew Hill and Dan Roberts, "The World's Companies Wait in Hope for the Fog of War To Clear," *Financial Times*, February 22–23, 2003, 7.

48. Joshua Chaffin and Andrew Hill, "How Often Do Countries Change Regimes—Especially Ones that Have the World's Second Largest Oil Reserves?" *Financial Times*, April 28, 2003, 11.

49. Chaffin and Hill, "How Often Do Countries Change Regimes," 11.

50. Gerard Baker et al., "The U.S. Has Come to See the Status Quo as Inherently Dangerous," *Financial Times*, May 30, 2003, 13.

51. Samuel Berger and Bruce Riedel, "America Must Pull Out of Iraq to Contain Civil War," *Financial Times*, July 23, 2007, 7.

4

The Likelihood of Success

Nick Fotion and Bruno Coppieters

PROBLEMS

The Likelihood of Success Principle has a relatively short history. To someone like St. Augustine, for example, the outcome of a war was a matter for God to determine.[1] So, for him, the likelihood of success did not constitute a separate principle. Hugo Grotius, early in the seventeenth century, was one of the first to identify it explicitly as a principle of Just War Theory.[2] Since then, most writers have listed it as one of the six or so principles of the *jus ad bellum* portion of the theory. However, it has also been argued that the principle should be subsumed under Principle of Proportionality and thus that it is not a basic principle.[3] See the next chapter for a discussion of this argument.

The principle carries more than one name. Some call it the Hope of Success, others the Reasonable Hope of Success Principle.[4] However, none of these names tells us whether the anticipated level of success should be one chance in two, two in three, three in four, or what. It seems that different just war theorists choose different standards of likelihood so that one person says that the likelihood of success when entering into a particular war is not high enough, while another says it is.

But a more serious problem with this principle is not with the concepts of "likelihood" or even "reasonable," but with "success." It might be supposed that this is not so. To many, perhaps the powerful, success in war means victory in attacking the enemy or in defending themselves against an attack. Lack of success means something less. But in some wars, success can mean simply stopping the enemy's invasion somewhere near the border where the war began, or even stopping the enemy short of losing everything. One may think of success even if one's army is obliterated because it and the nation have gained respect by putting up a noble fight. Beyond that, success can be characterized not with an immediate, but with a long-term positive result.

Another problem with "success" is the tendency of nations to redefine it as the war progresses. When it starts, the leaders bravely say that success means complete victory. Once the realities of war set in, these same leaders often say that their armed forces and their nation have been successful in just repelling aggression or achieving something short of complete victory in their attack.

There is yet another problem with the notion of success as it is found in the Likelihood of Success Principle. It can mean success in military endeavors quite apart from the justice of these endeavors. With this meaning, a nation calculates its likelihood of success in a war without considering if its cause is just or not. A nation may, for instance, consider that its military superiority gives it the opportunity to aggress its neighbor and to enlarge its territory. We can call this the military interpretation of the principle.[5] But success can mean something different. Success, in this second interpretation, is tied to just cause. With this meaning, a nation calculates its likelihood of success after having determined that it has just cause on its side. Success then means not just military success but success in undoing or preempting severe injustices in the short or long term. We can call this the just cause interpretation of the principle. Thus, if a nation has been the victim of aggression, success means that that nation has dealt effectively with that aggression. If, in contrast, a nation achieves its goals in its unjust conquests, it can only say that it has succeeded militarily. This distinction is important for a better understanding of the cases below, even if both interpretations are at work in most of them.

Historical research demonstrates that states generally exaggerate their capacity to control events and entertain positive illusions concerning their chances of being militarily successful.[6] They tend to overestimate their own abilities and underestimate the potential of their enemy. According to Dominic D. P. Johnson, overconfidence in conflict is an adaptive trait in the evolution of humanity which facilitates survival. Exaggerated confidence is a mechanism of self-deception that brings greater advantage in challenging or combat situations than excessive cautiousness. Napoleon famously stated that, in war, morale was three times more important than physical strength. In the case of conflict, high self-confidence increases performance by boosting resolve or bluffing the enemy into submission. It may thus be rational to be overconfident. If a decision to go to war under these circumstances leads to victory, everyone will forget about the exaggerated expectations and the original decision to confront the enemy will look as if it had been based on a reasonable chance of success. But positive illusions make it difficult for the parties in a conflict to negotiate a prewar bargain that reflects their real power. This aspect of human psychology is thus a factor that often leads to success but also largely contributes to causing unnecessary wars.

LUXEMBOURG, 1940

A sense of the difficulty involved in applying the success principle can be given even by citing a seemingly simple and straightforward case from World War II. During that war, Luxembourg found itself in the Wehrmacht's path. Geographically, Luxembourg is a nation of about 1,000 square miles (a bit over 2,500 square kilometers). Its population back then was 300,000.[7] Its army was not really an army, but a frontier guard of about three hundred.[8] When Nazi Germany decided to attack France in 1940, it did not make military sense to attempt to do so straight into and through the powerful Maginot Line stretching from Switzerland north to the borders of Belgium and Luxembourg. As in World War I, it made more sense to go around France's main defenses. But this necessitated traveling through Luxembourg, and also Belgium and The Netherlands. When it became evident to the people of Luxembourg in 1940 that the Germans were about to move through the country to attack France, the question was: How should that country respond to the German aggression?

One response compatible with the Likelihood of Success Principle is to say to the Germans "Be our guests" and allow them, and perhaps even help them, move quickly and efficiently west toward France. A second response (also) compatible with the principle is to treat the Germans as unwelcome guests. With this response, the German army is offered neither resistance nor cooperation. In World War II evidently this was the policy of the Luxembourg government—which in fact fled to England as the Germans moved in. But either way, whether the Germans were treated as welcome or unwelcome guests, the Likelihood of Success Principle (under both interpretations) makes it clear that the Luxembourg government and its people should not have resisted the Germans. It does so by in effect asking what hoped-for success might be forthcoming with resistance. Was there any likelihood that the three hundred lightly armed border guards would defeat the German army? Hardly! Was there any likelihood that those guards, even if they could not defeat the Germans, could have delayed them long enough to help the Belgians and the French resist German invasion? That is, was it likely that they could have succeeded by helping others in some significant way, even if they could not help themselves? Again, hardly!

Finally, could Luxembourg have succeeded in gaining self-respect and honor by resisting the Germans and thereby, for example, inspiring those in exile—who were few in number—to fight harder? That is, could it have succeeded in achieving some higher moral purpose by standing up to the Wehrmacht? Answering these questions with a "Yes" sounds strained to say the least.

It is not at all clear that, later, those in exile would have fought harder just because of the sacrifice of the three hundred and just because of the corresponding gain in honor and respect. If the exiles felt that their country had been unjustly invaded, they would likely have fought just as hard, with the help of the Allies, to recover their lost nation with or without the sacrifice of the three hundred. Further, it is not clear that honor or self-respect is lost in the first place when a nation surrenders in the face of absolutely overwhelming odds.

In a different situation, the conclusion that a hopelessly overmatched nation should not fight might be less clear. Consider a hypothetical setting where the invading force threatens to destroy everything and everybody in its path whether there is resistance or not. The choice of the victimized people then is to die without resisting or die resisting. Here it might be argued that it is proper to offer resistance since there is some sense of success left in keeping one's honor (for future generations to be proud of) and there is thus little or nothing to lose. But clearly Luxembourg in World War II was not in this situation. The Germans were not out to eliminate the people of Luxembourg. So Luxembourg's meager forces did the right thing by following the recommendation of the Likelihood of Success Principle. In effect, that principle told them that they should not resist the Germans *at the time* of the invasion. But later, it sent a different message about resistance. Once the Allied forces gained strength, the Likelihood of Success Principle now recommended resistance.

BELGIUM, 1940

It is instructive to compare the military interpretation of the Success Principle when applied to Luxembourg and to Belgium. During World War II, Belgium was a nation of some 8 million people that possessed a twenty-two-division army.[9] Its air force was not formidable, but it was not negligible either. In addition, although Belgium was not formally allied with Great Britain and France, it had every expectation that, if attacked, it would receive help. Indeed, with that help, the Allied forces were larger than Germany's. These forces contained more men and tanks, for example, and probably an equal number of airplanes. It is true that coordination between Belgium and the Netherlands, on the one side, and Britain and France, on the other, was not ideal. For one thing, the Belgians did not want to be associated too closely with the Allies for fear of provoking the Germans. Still, the forces arrayed against Germany were large enough and of high enough quality for the Belgians to conclude that if a war started, they should follow the recommendation of the Likelihood of Success Principle and offer resistance to the Germans.

As it turned out, they were not successful. At that time, the Germans understood better than the Allies how to use modern military equipment such as tanks and airplanes. As a result, they quickly overcame not only the armies of Belgium, but also those of France and Great Britain. Twenty thousand military personnel and civilians died in the eighteen-day battle in May 1940.[10] What success the Belgians had came later, largely through the efforts of its allies. But just before the war started, and soon after, the Belgians had a choice of fighting or not. The point is that if that choice had been made in accordance with the Likelihood of Success Principle, that principle would have encouraged Belgium to fight.

THAILAND, 1940 AND 1941

Another example of the application of the same version of the principle appears in World War II, this time in Asia. As the war was about to spread in Asia, Thailand found itself in a situation somewhere between that of Luxembourg and that of Belgium. Thailand, unlike Luxembourg, had an army, but it was not so strong as Belgium's. At most, its army numbered 50,000.[11] Thailand had 150 airplanes, but their quality was not uniformly high. The Thai navy was weak, composed of one vintage destroyer and a number of smaller craft. Politically, Thailand found itself in an uncomfortable situation. The Thai government feared Great Britain and France since it suspected that one or the other aspired to add Thailand to its empire. Great Britain had colonized Burma to its west, while France had colonized Laos and Cambodia to its east. The fear the Thais felt was thus not unreasonable.

Nonetheless, Thai fear was somewhat mitigated when Thailand and both Great Britain and France together signed a nonaggression pact in 1940.[12] The pact guaranteed Thai neutrality should war break out in that part of the world. However, by the next year, the situation had changed. Late in 1940, France had been defeated on the Western Front, so now Thailand found itself dealing with a weakened Vichy French government. The Thais took advantage of the situation by attacking the French. They wanted to gain some disputed lands in Laos and Cambodia. Before this little war was over, the Thais had occupied most of the disputed land but, in the process, lost a good portion of their dilapidated navy.

Japan actually mediated an end to this war.[13] The agreement arrived at formally granted to Thailand possession of the disputed land it had won in battle. While acting as mediator, the Japanese gained something for themselves as well. They extracted permission from the Vichy government to use its Indochina colonial territories as staging posts for any attacks Japan might want to initiate in the direction of Malaya, Singapore, and the Dutch colonies to the south. Japan also suggested that if the Thais would permit some of their territory to be used as staging posts as well, Thailand would be rewarded with still more French-held land in Cambodia and Laos. Understandably, the Thais were tempted by these offers but, at the same time, were fearful that they were now being threatened by another colonial power—this time one from Asia.

Matters came to a head on December 8, 1941. The Japanese war against the United States and Great Britain had begun the day before. The very next day the Japanese began their move south and thus were looking to use whatever staging posts they could find to help them reach Singapore and beyond. The Thais wondered how they should react to the Japanese aggression. On the one side, if they cooperated and granted the Japanese their staging posts, they would gain more French colonial territory. They might also receive better treatment than if they slowed the Japanese advance.[14] On the other side, if they resisted, their prospects were not good. Their army may have been strong enough to maul the weakened French forces, but they were no match for the Japanese. Their likelihood of success was nil or almost so. Thus, if they applied the Principle of Likelihood of Success, the Thais would have allowed the Japanese free passage. This is what they did. There evidently was token resistance by some forces, but it lasted less than one day. Overall, then, the Thais chose to let the Japanese through.

The Thais very likely made their decision not to oppose the Japanese *in accordance with* the military and not with the just cause interpretation of the Likelihood of Success Principle. It is even doubtful whether they were thinking in Just War Theory terms at all. The following passage on Thai relations with Japan well after December 7, 1941, suggests as much. The passage is quoted from Sar Desai's book *Southeast Asia*.

> Despite a treaty of friendship and cooperation with Japan that allowed Thailand a greater internal autonomy than enjoyed by most other Southeast Asian countries, there was no love lost between the two Asian allies. The prime consideration of Thai leadership was the preservation of their independence. As Phibun Songkhram [the prime minister] told his chief of staff in 1942: "Which side do you think will be defeated in this war? That side is our enemy."[15]

Judging by his comment, Songkhram sounds more like a realist than a just war theorist. Self-interest is the mover here rather than justice. But a realist approach does not exclude prudential constraints on the use of force. It was indeed in the national interest of Thailand not to oppose Japan.

CUBA IN THE 1950S

As difficult as it is to apply the Likelihood of Success Principle in conventional wars, it is even more difficult in civil and guerrilla wars. Cuba in the 1950s is a case in point. Between 1952 and 1958 Cuba was ruled by the thoroughly corrupt regime of General Fulgencio Batista. Understandably opposition to this regime developed quickly. The most promising opposi tion group was led by the young and charismatic Fidel Castro. Even so, there seemed to be little likelihood of military success for Castro's efforts to overthrow the Bastista regime. His efforts on July 26, 1953, to seize the Moncada barracks in Oriente Province and thus start the revolution were a failure.[16] Castro himself ended up in prison as a result. There were other failures and setbacks, not the least of which was a landing in 1956 when Castro and some of his people returned to Cuba in still another attempt to overthrow Batista.[17]

> Logistically, indeed, the invasion turned out to be a disaster. Setting sail on 25 November on a yacht which was intended to carry less than half the load, the eighty-two-man expedition ran into a storm, had mechanical break-downs, was forced to jettison supplies, lost its way, and landed at the wrong place on the wrong day. Two days before the yacht *Granma* beached in a muddy estuary on 2 December, Frank Pais' [one of the leaders of the 26 July Movement] armed group had attempted to stage an uprising in Santiago, but after some thirty hours of sporadic gunfire against the police and the army they had been forced to abandon the enterprise. Forty-eight hours later, wad-ing painfully through a mangrove swamp, the ragged and exhausted invaders finally landed on dry ground. Castro announced grandly to the first peasant they came across, "I am Fidel Castro and we have come to liberate Cuba." Four days later, another peasant betrayed them to the Rural Guard, who were searching the area for the expeditionaries. In a devastating ambush that fol-lowed, Castro's expedition was all but destroyed. Of the eighty-two men who had set out, only sixteen (though legend conveniently has it that there were twelve) remained alive or free to start the war against the modern army of the Batista regime.[18]

It was not until sometime in 1958 that anyone could claim that Castro's forces had a reasonable chance of success. By then they had settled into the Sierra Maestra mountains in Eastern Cuba, had won the support of the peasants there, and had also won some modest battles against the Batista forces. But before that, between 1953 and even as late as 1957, the outlook for Castro's revolution was grim. Indeed, if either the military or the just cause version of the Likelihood of Success Principle had been applied dur-ing this period, Castro would have been advised to fold his tent and aban-don his revolutionary ways. His likelihood of success seemed so remote that Just War Theory would simply not have sanctioned the revolution. As it turned out, Castro's likelihood of success was so remote that even he was surprised when the Batista regime suddenly collapsed, some say, from the weight of its own corruption.

This kind of scenario poses a problem for Just War Theory. At a certain point in time, early in many revolutions (e.g., the American Revolution), suc-cess can only be thought of as at most remote. If that is the case, it would seem that Just War Theory has a built-in bias in favor of establishment governments as against revolutionary movements. Even if they satisfied the other criteria of Just War Theory, these movements would seem incapable of satisfying the Likelihood of Success Principle.

This suggests that in cases like those of Castro's revolution the principle should not be honored. That is, if revolutionary groups satisfy all of the other *jus ad bellum* principles, but not the Likelihood of Success Principle, they should still be judged as having engaged in war justly simply because that principle does not apply to them. This suggests, further, that Just War Theory should not be thought of as composed of a fixed set of criteria to be applied to any and all situations. Instead, it should be treated in a more adaptable fashion so that in certain situations a criterion can be eliminated, modified somewhat, or even added to the list. The need for adaptability is exemplified in the following case, which differs significantly from those we have already discussed.

HEZBOLLAH

Hezbollah or the "Party of God" was created in Lebanon in 1982, during the civil war (1975–1990), as a resistance movement against Israeli occupation. It waged guerrilla operations in Lebanon and across the border in Israel itself. Over the years, it gradually moved into parliamentary work by mobilizing the Shiite electorate. The organization has strong links to the Iranian regime. Despite its condemnation of al-Qaeda and the terrorist acts of September 11, 2001, it is considered by the United States as a "terrorist group"—as a consequence of its suicide operations in Israel and Lebanon itself. There is no agreement within the European Union (EU) on this label. For some, only some individuals, or parts of Hezbollah, should be branded as terrorist.

Hezbollah's conception of a *jihad* or "holy war," as described by Naim Qassem, one of its main leaders,[19] includes several *jus ad bellum* principles, even though they are not explicitly labeled as such. They have a specifically religious meaning. Moral constraints on the use of force are legitimate only if are ordained by God, which has direct consequences for the application of the Legitimate Authority Principle. This principle refers to the jurisdiction of a Jurist-Theologian, who has the "task of evaluating the objective circumstances, weighing the advantages and hardships and exercising the *jihad* option."[20] Hezbollah's conception of a just war may be described as a radical one, to the extent that its understanding of the Legitimate Authority Principle further excludes governmental control over its resistance activities. Hezbollah argues, for example, that the path of resistance should not be subject to any negotiation process between Lebanon and Israel.[2]

The theological conception is also visible in the way the Likelihood of Success Principle is applied in the analysis of *jihad*, sacrifice, and martyrdom.

Jihad literally means "to struggle" or "to strive." It does not refer only to the defense by Muslims against aggression and occupation. It also embraces "the struggle against man's internal foes as represented by the soul's insinuations and temptations to evil or satanic calls to falsehood."[22] Such a broad understanding of *jihad* has direct consequences for the understanding of martyrdom and how success should be defined.[23] In Qassem's view, in each case it will be the task of the highest religious authority—what he calls the Jurist-Theologian—to weigh the circumstances, capabilities, and other factors that will determine the right decision. But the requirements of *jihad*, in general, include the defense of basic rights or the mobilization of the nation, without necessarily achieving immediate results. Success may be achieved in various stages, according to a long-term plan, until final victory.

According to Qassem, the meaning of victory in a traditional understanding of a military conflict differs from its meaning in a *jihad*, which leaves room for martyrdom. In a tradition of military conflict, a man may abandon his struggle if there is no clear prospect of success because he lacks material resources. With *jihad*, by contrast, martyrdom may open up new horizons for victory, despite a lack of material resources:

> When a man is cultivated to seek victory, making it the sole purpose of his actions, his quest ceases as soon as the possibility of victory seems vague or difficult to achieve. But when brought to learn of *jihad* and martyrdom, his sacrifice would be of the highest order, his actions effective, his martyrdom a fulfillment of desire, and thus victory would be but a worldly blessing and reward for his efforts. Cultivating victory does not assure it, and may weaken the strengths of a nation, while cultivation of martyrdom invests all resources to achieve either martyrdom or victory or both, opening up the horizon to all possibilities and carrying the hope for victory. Cultivation of victory requires reliance on material capabilities, while martyrdom bears on human morale and on an individual's relationship with God, and therefore requires few resources.[24]

Martyrdom may help to compensate for an asymmetric relationship of military forces. It renders military threats ineffective and may achieve deadly results with few technological resources. According to Hezbollah, the Israeli decision to withdraw its troops from Lebanon by July 2000 was the result of successful martyrdom and *jihad* operations. These had, moreover, led to "a surge of patriotic fervor across the region" and strengthened particularly the Palestinian resistance in the occupied territories.[25] All these victories, as stated by Hezbollah leader al-Sayyid Hassan Nasrullah, were the work of God and not the work of their own hands.[26]

According to Quassem, martyrdom expresses one's love for God, and so, by implication, shows us how "martyrdom" differs from "suicide." The former is a "voluntary act undertaken by a person who has every reason to live, love life, and cling to it, and who also possesses the means for living. It is thus the act of one who does not suffer from any reason compelling him to commit suicide."[27] It is further defined by Qassem as "the supreme manifestation of self-giving" by a believer; whereas suicide, on the contrary, is an "expression of despair, hopelessness, frustration and defeat," usually committed by a nonbeliever.

There is no agreement about what to call this type of struggle. Those who champion Hezbollah's religious interpretation of the Likelihood of Success Principle use the term "martyrdom." They would not agree with the term "suicide attack," often used in the Western press to describe that form of self-sacrifice.

MINI AND MAXI

There are still other atypical scenarios that need to be considered for a fuller understanding of the Likelihood of Success Principle. These are scenarios in which a nation is prepared to say "No" to war but still has another option besides that of total capitulation. Consider the following fictional scenario. A nation, let us call it Mini, realizes that it is very likely to be invaded soon by Maxi, and that it has no chance of stopping the invasion. So, listening to the Likelihood of Success Principle, Mini decides not to put up a fight. But rather than be totally passive, its leaders devise a civilian-based defense (CBD) plan.[28] With this plan in hand, Mini's leaders organize and train their civilian population to resist the invasion, whenever it comes, through noncooperation. The training is disciplined in that Mini's population is asked to spend a good deal of time before the invasion learning what nonviolent resistance is and how to implement it. So, once Maxi's forces peacefully occupy Mini, Mini's civilians do such things as provide inefficient road repair, food, and telephone services, turn street signs around, block traffic, spread misinformation, and try to convince Maxi's soldiers that occupation is wrong. In general, they do whatever they can nonviolently to make the lives of the occupiers anything from unpleasant to miserable.

How, then, is the likelihood of success of *this* program of resistance to be assessed? The right answer is "Not easily." If Maxi is a *democratic* country with armed forces inclined to operate according to International Humanitarian Law or having a government responsive to international public opinion, it will not be able to retaliate with a policy of noncooperation of its own by, among other things, cutting off the food supplies of Mini's population. Nor will Maxi be able to resort to violence by, for example, executing those Min civilians caught not cooperating. So, in time, over a span of a year or two, the political leaders of Maxi might count the costs of an unhappy occupation and conclude that they must negotiate with those who organize Mini's resistance and perhaps even return home. But Maxi might reject these options, especially if it has sufficient political and military reasons for staying. It also might not tire since Maxi's military would soon learn to adjust, for example, to the inconvenience of a bad local phone service by using their own network of cell phones. At best, if Mini's population triumphed over Maxi's occupiers they would do so in what might be called a long nonwar of attrition.

However remote or likely success might be for Mini's people in dealing with a *liberal* Maxi, the chances of success are likely to be significantly slimmer if it is forced to deal with an *authoritarian* Maxi. This version of Maxi is not likely to be so forgiving of the civilian-based defense plan with which they are dealing on a day-to-day basis. Food and medical supplies would likely be curtailed to induce cooperation. Noncooperators would be arrested and many of their leaders executed. Maxi could organize labor camps. No doubt, this nonwar of attrition would affect both sides in significant ways. Maxi's forces would still be living in a miserable environment, but Mini's population would be suffering too—by way, for example, of increased illness among its children and the aged. It is an open question as to which side would buckle first, and thus an open question as to how the Principle of Likelihood of Success would be applied to Mini's CBD plan.

CZECHOSLOVAKIA, 1968

The application of the Principle of Likelihood of Success in the context of the occupation of Czechoslovakia in August 1968 shows in more concrete terms that the refusal to use force in self-defense does not necessarily condemn a population to inevitable disaster. Indeed, a significant part of the Czechoslovak population demonstrated that civilian resistance can be relatively efficient and effective.[29]

Several months prior to the occupation, the party leadership in Czechoslovakia began a determined program of de-Stalinization and democratization. Pluralism was introduced into the party structure. The leadership strove to decentralize the decision-making process and also promote the implementation of legal reforms.

These changes aroused great suspicion in Moscow. In time, the suspicion turned into open hostility. The relaxation of censorship and the emergence of new political groups with their own programs did not fit the Soviet view of socialism. The Moscow leadership feared that the appeal for socialist reforms would be followed by more appeals from other countries of the socialist bloc that, in turn, would strengthen "counterrevolutionary forces."

On August 21, 1968, Soviet troops, supported by contingents of other Warsaw Pact countries, invaded Czechoslovakia to put an end to the reform movement and to restore a pro-Soviet regime. The leading Soviet newspaper, *Pravda*, wrote that each nation may take its "own separate road to socialism," but added as a condition that this "must damage neither socialism in their own country nor the fundamental interests of the other socialist countries, nor the worldwide workers' movement, which is waging a struggle for socialism."[30] According to this declaration (which was soon nicknamed the "Brezhnev doctrine"), the other socialist countries had the right and the duty to intervene if this condition was not fulfilled.

Confronted with this invasion, the Czechoslovak government did not appeal to the army to resist the advance of occupation troops. Armed resistance did not make sense. According to the Czechoslovak leadership, all violent confrontation between citizens and occupying forces had to be avoided. But numerous officials, reformist party members, journalists, students, and blue-collar workers started nonviolent resistance against the occupation. They disseminated newspapers and news bulletins informing the population about the real situation in the country. Through a clandestine radio network, people received instructions about what to do, how to communicate with the occupation troops, and how to resist them without provoking repression. Traffic signs were destroyed or changed to halt the progress of the troops. Nonviolent resisters tried further to convince the soldiers that the occupation was unjust. In order to interact with them, they brought them food, tea, and coffee. It was not difficult to establish a dialogue. Young Czechs and Slovaks by that time had been studying Russian at school.

Moscow justified the military operation as a kind of "brotherly help" for the Czechoslovak people who were said to be victims of the "revisionism of some Czechoslovak Communist party leaders" and of "world imperialism." It was not too difficult for the nonviolent resisters to explain to the Soviet soldiers and officers that this was not the case. These explanations were successful enough that the Soviet command had to rotate a certain number of the occupation troops away from Czechoslovakia. According to the historian Geoffrey Hosking, the resistance among the workers was especially strong. A secret Communist Party congress was even organized in one of the factories in the suburbs of Prague. At the congress, reformist Communist Party members condemned the invasion.

This nonviolent resistance did not lead to victory. Instead, the Soviet government came to an agreement with the Czechoslovak reformist leadership. First Secretary Alexander Dubcek was allowed to return to power, but had to agree that political life would be "normalized" in Czechoslovakia. This meant that the previous communist regime had to be restored. This normalization took place gradually. Dubcek was replaced in April 1969 by the conservative Gustav Husak. The Communist Party was screened and purged. One third of its 1.5 million members left or were expelled. Similar purges took place in the media, scientific institutions, and educational establishments.

Thanks to this repression, the new regime stabilized itself. But this does not mean that the nonviolent resistance movement was just a futile gesture. Those who opposed to the occupation had effectively managed to make the best of a bad situation. In retrospect, it would have been surprising that a country living under an authoritarian regime for twenty years could have organized a nonviolent resistance movement as efficiently as it might in a democracy. Since the movement was largely spontaneous, it missed having the impact that civilian-based defense organized in advance by the authorities might have had. The resistance leaders rightfully behaved according to the Principle of Likelihood of Success and thereby managed to avoid senseless violent confrontations with the Soviet troops. They made clear, nevertheless, that the Soviet troops were not welcome guests. Their resistance belied official propaganda that claimed that the military's intervention was in the population's interest. As a result, it was then extremely difficult for the "normalized" regime to make its ideology credible.

Although the short-term effects of the Czechoslovak resistance were limited, there is evidence that the long-term effects were not. The resistance had a tremendous influence on communist parties all over the world. A whole series of West European communist parties protested openly against the Soviet invasion and definitely distanced themselves from the Soviet leadership. In Western Europe, these parties started to propagate an "eurocommunist" program of socialism, which was highly critical of the Soviet model. The Czechoslovak resistance also had great ideological influence on those communist reformers and dissidents who, two decades later, would start democratic reforms in Poland, the Soviet Union, and the other countries of the socialist bloc. These reform movements would refer positively to the Czechoslovak model. The democratization of the 1980s would eventually lead to the end of the occupation of Czechoslovakia by a foreign power.

If compared to the previous imagined models of Mini resisting the occupation of Maxi, we see that Czechoslovakia of 1968 and 1969 falls somewhere in between. The Soviet regime was highly authoritarian. It did not respond to civilian-based defense in a way that a democratic state might have by negotiating, compromising, and then withdrawing its forces. But neither was the Soviet regime so repressive that it executed resistance leaders or created labor camps in order to control the local population. The Soviet regime was indeed authoritarian, but it relied heavily on a peculiar ideology that claimed it was in the best interest of the local population to have Czechoslovakia occupied. This ideological motivation limited the extent of the repression the regime was able to impose. Nonviolent resistance demonstrated effectively that this pretense of a democratic argumentation was fallacious. On a short-term basis, then, nonviolent resistance did not prove very efficient. It avoided bloodshed, but remained highly symbolic. In the long term, however, it proved to be a most powerful weapon in undermining the legitimacy of the occupation.

NORTH KOREA

The various problems associated with applying the success principle can also be illuminated by considering what might happen in a future war with a country such as North Korea. The North Korean government has been difficult to deal with ever since the Korean War (1950–1953). Under the leadership first of Kim Il Sung and then of his son Kim Jong Il, it adopted a variety of political, economic, and military programs that harmed its own people and, at the same time, threatened other nations (especially South Korea). North Korea's nuclear program, which led to the creation of "the bomb," is one such example. The program siphoned off resources that could have been used to help its own people. It also frightened neighboring states, including its former allies China and Russia.

But, now, what if, for whatever reason, a war broke out in the Korean peninsula? If it did, it would be because North Korea attacked South Korea, or South Korea attacked North Korea. In the former case, two scenarios can be imagined: one where the Chinese would add their military might to the mix, as they did in the 1950s Korean War, and one where they would abstain from intervening in an intra-Korean military conflict. In the first case, North Korea would seem to have a high likelihood of success (under the military interpretation of the Success Principle). After all, its military establishment is almost twice the size of South Korea's (1.2 million military personnel vs. 650,000).[31] When combined with the Chinese army, the sheer force of numbers would propel its military deep into South Korea or even enable North Korea to occupy all of South Korea. Together they could do this well before South Korea's allies could come to its aid. And, most probably, they could do it without using whatever nuclear weapons are available to them.

A more likely scenario is one where North Korea attacks alone, within the framework of its official policy of self-reliance (*Juche*). On their own, however, it is difficult to imagine that North Korea's forces would be successful in their endeavor. By themselves they might at first penetrate into South Korea perhaps as far as Seoul (the capital of South Korea), which is only about thirty or thirty-five miles from the border separating the North from the South. But because satellite and other intelligence would detect the imminence of the invasion well before it started, the North Koreans would meet an enemy ready to fight. This invasion would not be the surprise it was in 1950. Being forewarned, American airpower, most notably from its aircraft carriers, would severely punish the North Korean ground forces as soon as they crossed the North/South border. That same airpower, supported by a strong South Korean air force, would likely sweep the North Korean planes from the sky in short order. On the ground, most of the task of blunting the North Korean attack would fall to a well-trained and well-equipped South Korean army. With the help of American and perhaps other forces (e.g., from Australia), the battle would turn against the North Koreans if not immediately, then certainly quite soon. Thus, under the military interpretation of the Likelihood of Success Principle, the North would be advised against attacking the South. In the end, a North Korean attack would lead to a South Korean victory.

But what would the principle say to the South if it invaded the North? Again one can imagine scores of scenarios, each with its measure of possible success or failure. One of the most likely would be where the attack would come only if the South Koreans had an assurance from the Chinese (however unlikely that might be) that they would not intervene. Similar assurances would be required from the Russians. Without these assurances, it would be difficult to imagine how an invasion of the North could avoid being turned into a wider, less predictable, war. Without these assurances, then, the Success Principle would advise against an invasion.

If, in fact, the war were confined to being primarily between the North and the South, but with the South receiving direct military aid from the Americans, success would be conceivable. The success might be costly (see next chapter), but there could still be success. There are at least three reasons for saying this. First, South Korea would have the advantage of having struck the first blow and therefore being ahead in inflicting damage. Second, it would have the advantage of using military technologies (most of it American) unavailable to the North. Third, being pounded from the air and thus having problems of supplying troops at the front, the North Korean forces would soon be faced with fighting a war with diminishing resources. By contrast, the South Koreans, and their American allies, would have an open-ended resupply chain. So if South Korean success is characterized as the overthrow of the North Korean government (i.e., in purely military terms), and if the war between the North and the South were restrained as explained above, the success principle would say that war is permissible.

However, factoring the nuclear weaponry capability of the North Koreans into the mix complicates the South Korean calculations of likelihood of success. This is so even after one realizes that the nuclear device the North Koreans exploded on October 9, 2006, was mostly unsuccessful.[32] Its yield (4 kilotons) was perhaps one-tenth of what the North Koreans expected.[33] Further, the explosion device was just that, a device. It was not an operational bomb. To go from a device to a bomb requires further development.

But that was then. Now, things may be different. Until, and if, the North Koreans test other nuclear devices, the world will be left wondering what kind of bombs, if any, North Korea actually possesses. But assuming the worst from the South Korean point of view (i.e., that the North Koreans have developed operational bombs), the situation becomes more complicated. The use of such bombs by North Korea would certainly affect the Principle of Proportionality (again, see the next chapter) but it would also affect their chances of success.

> North Korean troops [could] detonate a nuclear device in one of the many large tunnels they've dug beneath the DMZ [demilitarized zone]. The resultant explosion would instantaneously breach allied forward defenses and blanket forces downwind beneath a radioactive cloud. Electromagnetic pulse would incapacitate radio communications and computers. Communist troops then could pour south over high-speed routes on both flanks while confusion reigned following the first-ever use of nuclear weapons against ground forces. A second weapon, delivered by an inconspicuous truck or cargo ship, could easily level the port of Pusan [the main port, where U.S. forces would be expected to land] while ballistic missiles and special operations forces simultaneously hit air bases and other critical positions throughout South Korea.[34]

This worst-case scenario could get worse. Under their nuclear umbrella the North Koreans could capture Seoul and then hold that city hostage. They might also employ missile strikes against South Korean and American bases in South Korea and even in Japan. The overall damage they could do makes it conceivable that they might be successful in their endeavor.

However, North Korea's enemies would not sit idly by waiting for the next blow to fall. Instantly, there would be a demand to punish those who had ordered the use of nuclear weapons. Almost instantly, nuclear weapons carried by the U.S.'s Trident submarines could rain on North Korea and its concentration of military forces. Whatever chaos North Korea's use of bombs had created in starting the war would be matched, swiftly, with even greater chaos in North Korea. In retaliating against the North Koreans it might not even be necessary to use nuclear weapons. U.S. aircraft carriers positioned far enough away from the radiation effect of the North Korean bombs could cause fearful damage. Whether nuclear weapons would be needed to stop the North Koreans or not, there is no way that the North Koreans could succeed in their effort to conquer South Korea.

One can conclude, then, that even with North Korean nuclear weapons in place, it is possible to imagine scenarios in which the South Koreans could satisfy the Likelihood of Success Principle (but not necessarily the Proportionality Principle). They could gain satisfaction not only if they were the first to attack but also if they were attacked first. These scenarios are limited in scope in the sense that other scenarios can be imagined that would not lead to success if a war started. Further, all of the success scenarios presuppose that the South Koreans would, in fact, get generous support from their American allies whereas the North Koreans would remain internationally isolated. Without those two conditions, the principle of success would speak in a different tone. It would say to the South Koreans, don't get involved in a war with the North.

AFGHANISTAN AND IRAQ COMPARED

Wars do not necessarily end with the defeat of one of the armies or even with the surrender of one of the parties. There are plenty of examples of military defeats of armed forces that were followed by a new phase in a war, a phase in which guerrilla fighters, or other forms of resistance, replaced the troops. In the chapter on the Legitimate Authority Principle we described the French capitulation to Germany, one of the major events at the start of the Second World War. French Marshal Philippe Pétain signed an armistice with Germany on June 22, 1940, which implied that France and Germany were no longer at war with one another. But the resistance against the German occupation continued, under the leadership of General de Gaulle, up until the liberation of Paris in August 1944.[35] To apply the Likelihood of Success Principle to each of these phases we have to analyze such factors as the military balance of forces, the mobilizing force of an appeal to national resistance and the international alliances behind the parties. This constellation of factors differs greatly in the two phases, which means that the application of the Likelihood of Success Principle needs to be assessed differently for each of them.

Where present-day wars are concerned, we have likewise to distinguish between two phases in the wars in Afghanistan and Iraq.[36] The first phase in the war against Afghanistan started on October 7, 2001, and ended with the triumphant entry of the Northern Alliance into Kabul on November 13, 2001. The first phase in the war against Iraq started on March 20, 2003, and ended with the defeat of the Iraqi army and the conquest of Baghdad and other Iraqi cities by American and British troops in April 2003. The second phase in both wars started after the takeover of the Afghan and Iraqi capitals. Neither of them is over yet. In Afghanistan the war is being fought against Taliban troops and in Iraq against insurgents from the Sunni and Shiite communities, many jihadis among them. In both cases, the insurgents want to drive out the American troops and their allies, and then try and bring down a regime they consider to be collaborationist. In both cases, the governments will probably not be able to win the war by military means alone, but will have to find a political compromise or series of compromises with the insurgents. Alternatively, the war may end in Afghanistan or Iraq with the eviction of Western troops and the defeat of the local governments.

From an American perspective, each phase in these wars has a distinct likelihood of success. In the first phase, the United States had unparalleled "power to destroy." Buster Glosson, the American air force general who led the bombing campaign in the 1991 war against Iraq, declared in the run-up to the 2003 Iraq war, "We have the armaments now to accomplish in 24 or 36 hours what it took seven days to accomplish in the Gulf war."[37] The Afghan and Iraqi troops were no match for the American forces and their allies. The Taliban regime in Afghanistan and the Baath regime in Iraq were easily overthrown. The second phases in both wars, on the other hand, should be judged according to a far more demanding criterion of success. In order to be successful in establishing democratic pro-Western regimes, the Americans need the "power to control."[38] The two types of power do not necessarily go hand in hand. It has become conventional wisdom that the capacity of the United States to destroy the Afghan or Iraqi regimes did not give them sufficient power to control Afghanistan or Iraq politically or militarily, or to create the conditions for stability.

Here we applied the military interpretation of the Likelihood of Success Principle to the two phases of the Afghan and Iraq wars. This interpretation does not take into account the question of just cause. If we tie the Likelihood of Success principle to the Just Cause Principle, we see that the two phases in the Afghan war have been fought for much the same cause but that each phase in the Iraq war has been fought for different just causes. Both phases in the Afghan war have been about the disruption of Afghanistan as a base of operations for terrorists. This just cause makes it necessary to establish a pro-Western democratic regime, but this latter objective is not strictly speaking a just cause for the war. Establishing democracy in Afghanistan was not even mentioned in the Presidential Address to the Nation of October 7, 2001, where President Bush announced the start of the military operations in Afghanistan. The first phase of the Iraq war was about preventing Saddam Hussein from developing or using weapons of mass destruction. This was officially its just cause for the American and British governments. It has been stated that this war has also been waged to liberate the Iraqi people from a dictatorial regime, but this cause was not included in the letters addressed by the United States and the United Kingdom to the UN Security Council to justify the start of their military operations.[39]

In Afghanistan, the first stage of the war was a success in military and in just cause terms. The fall of the Taliban regime meant that al-Qaeda and other terrorists groups could no longer rely on the protection of a government. The international community—including all the permanent members of the UN Security Council—had also been convinced of the war's just cause.[40] The American government could further count on military help from a large number of allies. It is true that the second phase of the war is proving far more difficult to win than had been expected. There have been serious setbacks and even total failures in particular policy domains such as the eradication of heroin production and the drug trade. It has not been easy for a society that had been through so many decades of civil strife, anarchy, and dictatorship to devise a formula for power sharing. The Taliban receives support from a wide number of sources, including opposition groups in neighboring Pakistan, and can rely on the population's dissatisfaction with government policies. They control substantial parts of the country. It was often difficult for the Americans to get the minimum number of troops from allied countries, but they did eventually manage to get both troops and machines, although in insufficient numbers. Despite all the failures and setbacks, the successful fulfillment of the just cause principle during the first phase of the war increased the chances of success in the second phase. There is a broad consensus within the international community that failure is not an option in Afghanistan. The destabilization of the country could benefit terrorist forces operating worldwide. The risk that an Afghan failure might have a spillover effect on the weak and failing states in its neighborhood, such as Pakistan, heightens the determination of all the countries involved.

Success in the fulfillment of a just cause in the first phase of the Afghan war contrasts with its failure in Iraq. The announcement by the American and British governments that the first ground forces had advanced into Iraq on March 20, 2003, was echoed by loud condemnation from around the world. The Russian president Vladimir Putin said in a television address that this "military action . . . is a big political error. This military action is unjustified."[41] French president Jacques Chirac and the German government condemned the decision in similar terms. Many other countries, including the majority of the permanent members of the UN Security Council, also did not think that the war had a just cause. And indeed, "there were no weapons of mass destruction to be dismantled."[42] American and British government propaganda then replaced the official *casus belli* by the liberation of Iraq, as if Saddam's dictatorship had constituted an unacceptable threat to peace, security, and international order.[43] The Bush administration claimed that the first phase of the war had enabled the Iraqi people to elect a parliament democratically. But this representative body failed to create a government capable of providing the Iraqi population with security or other basic public goods such as economic development.

The global failure to achieve a just cause in the first phase of the war had far-reaching consequences for the likelihood of success of the second phase of the war, both in military and in just cause terms. And there is at present such a cause in Iraq, which can be described as follows: failure to succeed would risk creating a situation far worse than the injustices their military intervention claimed to correct. In terms of the prevention of future injustices, the second phase of the Iraq war is indeed about preventing a fully fledged civil war, or even overlapping civil wars, between the various nations and religious communities. The second phase of the war is further being waged to prevent al-Qaeda from gaining a new operational base from which to start terrorist activities, since they lost their Afghan sanctuary in October 2001. A disorderly retreat of American troops would draw Syria, Iran, Turkey, and Saudi Arabia more deeply into these domestic conflicts, increasing the risk of regional military escalation and reducing the chances of stabilizing the Middle East.[44]

The distinction between the two phases makes it understandable that once the war had started some European governments—such as France and Germany, who were among the severest critics of the decision to go to war against Iraq—argued against any form of disorderly retreat which would fail to guarantee future security in the region. But it is impossible for such governments—or for the European Union as a whole—to be committed to the success of the second phase in the Iraq war with military or other concrete forms of support, unlike their present active involvement in Afghanistan. Other governments that supported the American and British decision to go to war against Baghdad, such as those of Madrid and Rome, were confronted with strong antiwar protests and have since withdrawn their troops from Iraq. The failure of the American government to start the Iraq war with a just cause has thus created insurmountable hurdles in the creation of a broad international coalition that would increase its chances to succeed in the second phase, even though it is widely acknowledged within the international community that such a just cause now exists.

The failure to succeed in just cause terms in the first phase of the Iraq war has negatively affected not only the likelihood of success in the second phase in Iraq but also the likelihood of success in both military and just cause terms in the second phase in Afghanistan. Some of the domestic criticism in the United States directed against Bush's war policies was based on the argument that the invasion of Iraq had made it more difficult to commit sufficient American troops and other necessary forms of support to Afghanistan. Furthermore, the now broadly held view that the Iraq war started as an unjust war has made it more difficult for public opinion in the United States and other countries to view the Afghan war as a just war, with all the negative consequences of such diminished public support for its likelihood of success.

SACRIFICE AND MOBILIZATION

The Likelihood of Success Principle may either be subordinated to the Just Cause Principle—which we call the just cause interpretation of that principle—or be considered independently of it—the military interpretation of that principle. Applications according to the first interpretation are more demanding than those of the second. Cases that satisfy the former interpretation will thus logically also satisfy the latter, but the reverse is not necessarily true. All the cases analyzed in this chapter, with the sole exception of those Korean scenarios where war is assumed to take place without good reason, deal with instances of military or nonviolent resistance against injustices where both interpretations apply.

A further distinction between the various applications of the Likelihood of Success Principle could be made according to the relevance of the political mobilization needed to achieve military success. This is particularly important in asymmetrical conflicts, characterized by great discrepancies of material resources and military manpower. The significance of political mobilization in each case has direct implications for the sacrifices that can be required from the combatants or from the population at large. The Luxembourg government decided not to fight a hopeless war against the German invader as it did not believe that even the fiercest resistance by its "troops" or its population would in any way alter the balance of forces between its allies and Germany. No substantial benefit could be expected, even in the long run, from such a sacrifice. A brief war against the Wehrmacht would not have led to the kind of popular resistance that might have been helpful in liberating the country or achieving any other form of military success. The government did not even have the moral right to order its frontier guards to fight until the very end. It decided not to accept defeat either, but to flee to London and continue the war from there. According to the Likelihood of Success Principle, this decision to continue moral resistance against the aggressor was highly symbolic but not meaningless. It was fully in line with the policies of the Polish, Belgian, Norwegian, and Dutch governments. They had also been driven out of their capitals by the German occupier, but had decided to stay firmly on the side of the Allies. The policy of the Luxembourg government thus helped to mobilize external support at a minimal cost in human lives.

In the case of the Czechoslovak resistance to Soviet occupation in 1968, political mobilization with the aim of achieving internal and external support also played a major role, while the type of resistance—it was nonviolent—kept the number of sacrifices to a minimum. Political mobilization was also a key strategic issue in the overthrow of the Batista dictatorship in Cuba by a revolutionary movement. In this case, however, the revolutionaries had to make far greater sacrifices for their cause. Revolutionaries at war may have an even greater sense of duty than ordinary soldiers. Their morals are underpinned by historical optimism, a firm belief that it is possible to eradicate the sources of exploitation and social conflict through a radical transformation of state and society. For these revolutionaries, historical progress is the final guarantor of the Likelihood of Success Principle.

An even greater demand for self-sacrifice is made by Hezbollah when it prescribes martyrdom as an expression of love for God and a sign of trust in His power. It will be up to God to decide about Hezbollah's ultimate success. In the meantime, Hezbollah may count on the mobilizing effects of martyrdom in its war against Israel.

The greatest sacrifices, however, are made in the event of a nuclear war, as illustrated by the various war scenarios involving Korea. In these scenarios the readiness of a country or its allies to use such weapons, and to sacrifice a large part of its own population in a war that respects no moral restraints, is expected to have a strong deterrent effect. Unlike in the previous cases discussed in this chapter, these sacrifices are required not only from combatants but also from the population at large. The sacrifices required by a nuclear war also differ from the others as regards their consequences for political mobilization. No favorable consequences can be expected from these sacrifices made in mobilizing for a just cause or a military victory.

More will be said about the Likelihood of Success Principle in the next chapter, which is devoted to Proportionality, but this is so close to the Success Principle that it is difficult to complete what should be said about the latter principle without considering the former.

NOTES

1. Adam Roberts, "Just Peace: A Cause Worth Fighting For," in *What Is a Just Peace?* ed. Pierre Allan and Alexis Keller (Oxford: Oxford University Press, 2006), 61.

2. Hugo Grotius, *The Rights of War and Peace*, bk. 2, 24, secs. 4–8, trans. A. C. Campbell (Washington, D.C.: M. Walter Dunn, 1901), 280–84.

3. A. J. Coates, *The Ethics of War* (Manchester: Manchester University Press, 1997), 179.

4. James F. Childress, "Just-War Theories: The Bases, Interrelations, Priorities and Functions of Their Criteria," in *War, Morality and the Military Profession*, ed. Malham Wakin, 2nd ed. (Boulder, Colo.: Westview Press, 1986), 264.

5. The military interpretation of the Likelihood of Success Principle also applies to nonviolent forms of struggle that replace military means. It is possible to struggle nonviolently for causes that cannot be regarded as just.

6. Dominic D. P. Johnson, *Overconfidence and War: The Havoc and Glory of Positive Illusions* (Cambridge, Mass., and London: Harvard University Press, 2004), 4–14.

7. *The New Encyclopaedia Britannica: Macropaedia* (Chicago: Encyclopaedia Britannica Inc., 1998), 314–18.

8. *Collier's Encyclopedia* (New York: Collier's, 1996), 121.

9. *The Oxford Companion to World War II*, ed. I. C. B. Dear and M. R. D. Foot (Oxford: Oxford University Press, 1995), 118.

10. Theo Luykx, *Politieke Geschiedenis van België* (Brussels, Amsterdam: Elsevier, 1964), 395.

11. *Oxford Companion*, 1106.

12. *Oxford Companion*, 1107.

13. *Oxford Companion*, 1107.

14. D. R. Sar Desai, *Southeast Asia: Past and Present*, 4th ed. (Boulder, Colo.: Westview Press, 1997), 186.

15. Sar Desai, *Southeast Asia*, 186.

16. Sebastian Balfour, *Castro* (London: Longman, 1990), 38–40. See also Sheldon B. Liss's *Fidel!* (Boulder, Colo.: Westview Press, 1994), 16.

17. Balfour, *Castro*, 47–48.

18. Balfour, *Castro*, 48.

19. Naim Qassem, *Hizbollah: The Story from Within* (London: Saqi, 2005). This book, authored by the Hezbollah's deputy secretary-general, describes clearly its political program and conception of a *jihad*. It applies a number of *jus ad bellum* principles, even it does not refer explicitly to the Just War Tradition or to the various *jus ad bellum* or *jus in bello* principles.

20. Qassem, *Hizbollah*, 40.

21. Qassem, *Hizbollah*, 106–7.

22. Qassem, *Hizbollah*, 34.

23. Qassem, *Hizbollah*, 40.

24. Qassem, *Hizbollah*, 44–45.

25. Qassem, *Hizbollah*, 50. See also Amal Saad-Ghorayeb, *Hizbu'llah: Politics and Religion* (London: Pluto Press, 2002), 118–19.

26. Saad-Ghorayeb, *Hizbu'llah*, 127.

27. Qassem, *Hizbollah*, 47.

28. See the introduction to this volume for more information on civilian-based defense.

29. Geoffrey Hosking, *The First Socialist Society: A History of the Soviet Union from Within* (Cambridge, Mass.: Harvard University Press, 1990), 368–74; Philip Windsor and Adam Roberts, *Czechloslovakia 1968: Reform, Repression & Resistance* (New York: Columbia University Press, 1969); Gene Sharp, *The Dynamics of Nonviolent Action* (Boston: Porter Sargent), 98–101.

30. Hosking, *The First Socialist Society*, 372.

31. Wikipedia, "North Korea," at en.wikipedia.org/wiki/North_Korea (accessed June 5, 2007).

32. Jacques E. C. Hymans, "North Korea's Nuclear Neurosis," *The Bulletin of the Atomic Scientists*, May/June 2007, 45–49, 74.

33. The bombs dropped on Hiroshima and Nagasaki weighed roughly 20 kilotons (20,000 tons of TNT). The North Korean bomb did not even reach the level of power achieved by the Americans in World War II. Most modern nuclear weapons usually start at the 100,000-ton level and go up, steeply, from there.

34. John M. Collins, "North Korea: The Case against Preemption," in *U.S. Naval Institute Proceedings*, November 2006, 29.

35. See the analysis of this case study from the perspective of the Legitimate Authority Principle in the second chapter of this volume.

36. On the likelihood of success in the Iraq war, see Philip Stephens, "A Change of Course Would be the Least Worst Option in Iraq," *Financial Times*, October 21, 2005, 13; Jacob Weisberg, "An International Way Forward in Iraq," *Financial Times*, November 30, 2006, 13.

37. Peter Spiegel, "We Now Have the Armaments to Accomplish in 24 or 36 Hours What Took Seven Days in the 1991 War," *Financial Times*, March 20, 2003, 13.

38. On the distinction between power to destroy and power to control, see Philip Stephens, "How America Allowed Disorder to Rule," *Financial Times*, April 16, 2007, 12. This article is a review of Zbigniew Brzezinski's book, *Second Chance: Three Presidents and the Crisis of American Superpower* (New York: Basic Books, 2007).

39. On whether or not there was just cause for the Iraq war, see the Just War and Iraq chapters of this volume. We will exclusively take such official justifications and objectives into account in the following application of the Likelihood of Success Principle (following the just cause interpretation) to the first phases of the wars in Afghanistan and Iraq.

40. Cuba opposed the war with the argument that the use of force was not effective against terrorism and was unjustified under international law.

41. See Peter Spiegel, Paul Eedle, and Victor Mallet, "U.S. and UK Forces Invade Iraq," *Financial Times*, March 21, 2003, 1.

42. Jacob Weisberg, "The Democrats Face another Vietnam," *Financial Times*, August 10, 2006, 9.

43. An attempt to justify this shift is to be found in Gerard Baker, "War Was Justified by Saddam's Removal," *Financial Times*, July 17, 2003.

44. Here we are referring exclusively to those potential consequences of an American retreat from Iraq that are related to the correction or prevention of injustices. But we may also think about consequences for American interests in the region that are not directly related to a moral cause. A defeat in the second stage of the Iraq war would make it more difficult for the United States to keep a leading role in the Middle East and would strengthen the resolve of regional powers opposed to the West, such as Iran, to act against American interests in the region.

5

Proportionality

Nick Fotion

A RELATIONAL PRINCIPLE

Proportionality is a relational principle. Nothing is proportional by itself. Rather, something is proportional in relation to something else. In law, for example, it is often said that the punishment should be proportional (i.e., related in a certain way) to the crime. What this means is not always clear, but almost everyone agrees that it would be disproportional (i.e., unjustly so) if a person received the death penalty for committing a first-time crime of stealing a car. However, many would agree that putting this person in jail for a certain period is a proportional penalty. Similarly, rewarding a young man with a million dollars for helping an old lady cross the street would be disproportional, but thanking him would not be. Another example. It certainly would be disproportional to merely give a soldier a verbal commendation (e.g., "Well done!") for putting his life at great risk, and thereby saving the lives of some of his comrades; but proportional to give him a medal and/or a promotion.

When it comes to the *jus ad bellum* portion of Just War Theory, real and imaginary examples of disproportionality are equally easy to find. It would be disproportional for a nation to start a major war that brings about thousands of casualties in order to stop the damage a few drunken soldiers do, on the other side, when they rather regularly stumble across the border. It would also be disproportional to start a major, or even a minor, war over a border dispute involving a dozen or so houses or over fishing rights in a small area of the ocean. It is somewhat more difficult to identify examples on the proportional side. Still, it is generally agreed that it is proportional to go to war when a relatively strong nation is attacked by an equally strong nation, and when a very strong nation responds to an attack by a relatively strong nation on a weak ally (e.g., the 1990–1991 Gulf War).

But even if these intuitive judgments about starting a war are treated as unproblematic, applying the Principle of Proportionality requires more clarity and precision. Otherwise these judgments about war take on a subjective character. Also, without an explicitly and precisely stated principle, it would seem almost impossible to make more difficult judgments about whether to go to war or not.

Explicit mention of the principle takes us back to ancient China. Perhaps the best-known Chinese champion of the principle was Mo Tzu.[1] This philosopher and practitioner of war was quite naturally concerned with costs and benefits since his basic stance in ethics is Utilitarian—a theory that advocates maximizing overall benefits and minimizing overall losses for *all* who are affected by whatever actions are taken.[2] However, the Proportionality Principle did not receive much attention during the early Just War Tradition in Christianity. St. Augustine and many of his followers were more concerned with the Right (Good) Intentions Principle. Much later, St. Thomas Aquinas makes reference to Proportionality, but he does not treat it as a major principle alongside such principles as Legitimate Authority, Just Cause, and Right Intentions.[3] By the time of Hugo Grotius, however, the Proportionality Principle is thoroughly embedded in Just War Theory as a full-fledged member.[4]

Unfortunately, neither the ancient nor the recent literature is of much help in stating the Principle of Proportionality clearly. Many writers talk about this principle without explicitly specifying its content.[5] They merely name it, and then go on to apply it in *jus ad bellum* settings as if everyone understood its meaning. There is a good reason for being so coy. It is, in fact, difficult to articulate a defensible version of the principle. Does it mean that the good (consequences) of going to war must be equal to or greater than the bad? Or does it mean that the good of going to war must be two-thirds greater when compared with the bad, at least three-fourths greater, or what?

Notice in this connection how unhelpful it is when, on rare occasions, commentators attempt to explain the principle. In the Pastoral Letter of the National Conference of Catholic Bishops, the principle is explained as follows: "The damage to be inflicted and the costs incurred by war must be proportionate to the good expected by taking up arms. . . ."[6] Similarly, Sheldon Cohen tells us that the principle says that "the harm done by military action be in proportion to the military gain."[7] Far from explicating proportionality, these formulations merely use the word that needs explaining. Paul Ramsey is more helpful. He says that a nation achieves proportionality when "more good will be done than undone or a greater measure of evil prevented."[8] W. V. O'Brien expresses the same thought as follows: "The probable good to be achieved by successful recourse to armed coercion in pursuit of the just cause must outweigh the probable evil that the war will produce."[9] The suggestion is that if the chance of good consequences outweighing the bad is 51 percent or more, while the chance of the bad consequences dominating is 49 percent or less, it is proper to go to war, other things being equal. Evidently for Ramsey and O'Brien, even a 50 percent/50 percent measure is not good enough to send the troops into action.

However, putting it this way poses a problem that casts doubt on this reading of the principle. Even if the Principle of Proportionality could be stated in some specific way so as to give concrete guidance about when to go to war, it suffers from a severe measurement problem. What sense does it make to talk about a 51 percent, 52 percent, or 53 percent chance of having a good outcome when it is often difficult to know whether a war will last a few weeks or years? Think here of the American Civil War and World War I. Many thought these wars would "be over by [the] Christmas [of the year the war started]." What sense do such measurements make when, before the war starts, it is often not even clear who will be involved in it? Think here of the Korean War. North Korea, the USSR, and China were evidently all convinced that the United States (along with other UN nations) would not intervene. Also, one might ask, will the war be between two nations or between two coalitions? Will it be a local or a world war? What turn will the war take with the introduction of new technologies? If a nation goes to war, will aggression actually be deterred in the future? And if deterred, just how much of this precious commodity will be gained?

So where do all these seemingly unanswerable questions leave the Principle of Proportionality? Keep in mind that the purpose of the *jus ad bellum* portion of Just War Theory is to place restraints on the start of war. What these questions suggest is that as a principle, Proportionality will be best applied at the extremes. If the amount of good that might come from a war is clearly going to be overwhelmed by the bad, then the principle will not countenance going to war. Conversely, if it is clear that the good will overwhelm the bad, then the principle will countenance war. These kinds of recommendations are appropriate because measurements can be made where great disparities exist between what is good and bad. Putting it differently, the principle can deal with easy cases. In contrast, when measurements are "too close to call" or can be made only with the greatest difficulty because of the lack of information, the Proportionality Principle will tend to be permissive. Those who are considering going to war will say to themselves something like, "Since there is no clear-cut evidence forbidding war, we can in good conscience go to war." So both with regard to dealing with easy and not-so-easy cases, the Proportionality Principle operates in Just War Theory much like the Likelihood of Success Principle.

LUXEMBOURG AND BELGIUM AGAIN

Recall from the previous chapter the situation that Luxembourg found itself in during World War II. It had no likelihood of success, and so Just War Theory indicates that it should not have done anything during the initial invasion to thwart the German advance over its land and into Belgium and France. But, equally, resisting German aggression in this case would have been disproportional. The harm done to its three-hundred-man police force and to the civilian population, who would have gotten in the way of the shooting, would not be compensated for by any good.

The Belgian situation in World War II, also described in the previous chapter, follows the same pattern. The Proportionality Principle recommends that the Belgians fight, just as did the Likelihood of Success Principle. Given the information available before the Germans attacked, Belgian calculations of costs and benefits would not forbid resisting the Germans. It was not obvious before the battle was fought that the Germans would win decisively. Rather, at the time, it seemed obvious that Belgium and its allies had a fighting chance to stop the German aggression.

It should be made clear how the assessment of costs and benefits is made and, in this case, how the Belgians could say that more good would come from resisting the Germans rather than not. Like the Just Cause interpretation of the Likelihood of Success Principle, Proportionality is a measure of overall benefits and harms. Neither principle measures benefits and harms from the point of view of one side only. Rather, they both take everyone's interests into account—including the potential enemy. In this sense, both principles are ethical as such. A war is said to be just (other things being equal) if engaging in it is likely to bring about more overall good than harm. In this spirit, one good in having the Belgians and their allies resist the Germans is to teach them a lesson that aggression is costly. Learning this lesson may be painful but, in the long run, it is supposed to be beneficial to the Germans. The lesson will even apply to nations not involved in World War II, but who are contemplating aggression. On the other side, World War II is said to be just because it helps to maintain freedom for the people of Belgium, France, Great Britain, Luxembourg, and the Netherlands. It is also just because the freedom of other nations will be maintained who would have been victims of aggression had it not been made clear that aggression does not pay. So everybody's good and harm is taken into account.

MINI AND MAXI AGAIN

In assessing the application of the Proportionality Principle to the scenario of Maxi's occupation of Mini, everybody's good and harm has also to be taken into account. Maxi had occupied Mini, but, it will be recalled, Mini did not resist militarily. Instead, it decided to employ a civilian-based defense strategy in dealing with Maxi. Recall also that, even if Maxi were a liberal society, there would be costs to Mini's population as well as to Maxi's military. This would be especially so if a part of Mini's policies were to sponsor strikes that would paralyze Mini's economy. Indeed, strikes might be counterproductive since Mini's population would likely suffer more than Maxi's military. After all, Maxi could bring in supplies to feed, clothe, and house its military personnel and, as a result, not suffer much from the strikes. But Mini's population would not have such easy access to necessities of life.

In any case, the Proportionality Principle would approve of the civilian-based defense of Mini's government only if the overall benefit to everyone concerned is projected to exceed the harm. Approval then would come if Mini's people and Maxi's military did not suffer excessively and if, in the end, Mini were successful in convincing the Maxi government to withdraw its forces. Presumably, in dealing with a liberal Maxi, the costs to everyone would not be too high and some chance of success might very well be present. What the costs and what the chances of success might be would depend on just how determined Maxi would be in holding on to its gains in occupying Mini.

In dealing with an authoritarian Maxi, however, the calculations of costs vs. benefits and likelihood of success would likely be quite different. Mini could easily be made to pay a high price for its noncooperation both in suffering and in the lesser likelihood of success that it would experience in convincing Maxi to leave. But, like in the other cases above, calculations would not be easy to make—even more so. After all, civilian-based defense policies have to do with attrition. They succeed or fail over the long run, where the more we extrapolate away from the present the less certain we become in assessing what will happen.

There is an additional factor at work that can very well complicate the situation. In dealing with an authoritarian Maxi, Mini's leadership is likely to find it increasingly difficult to control certain segments of its population. As food supplies decrease and children suffer, some could come to feel that they should do more than engage in noncooperation. They might think it proper to take up guns and start fighting a guerrilla war. It is at this point that proportionality and likelihood of success calculations become almost meaningless. How, for example, would those who planned Mini's civilian-based defense policy before the invasion be able to predict when their policy would evolve into guerrilla warfare?

One final point is worth making before leaving the Mini/Maxi scenarios. The Principles of Likelihood of Success and Proportionality are not the only principles of Just War Theory that apply here. The Just Cause Principle, for example, is at work in that Mini can cite that principle to explain why it is reacting the way it is toward Maxi. The Principle of Legitimate Authority is also at work insofar as the civilian-based defense policies that Mini adopted were authorized by the government. Good Intentions is also at work in that Mini is acting in a civilian-based defense way in order to rid itself of the invader. And, finally, the Principle of Last Resort is also at work. The civilian-based defense policies were adopted by Mini only after everything else (including going to war) was considered.

DIVERGENCE BETWEEN SUCCESS AND PROPORTIONALITY PRINCIPLES

Thus far the examples cited in this and the previous chapter suggest that there is a close correspondence between the judgments made with the Principles of Likelihood of Success and Proportionality. Where the one principle says that a nation (or group) should go to war, the other says the same. Where the one recommends no war, so does the other. The only possible exception so far is the case of the Castro revolution in Cuba (discussed in the previous chapter). In that case, it was argued that the Likelihood of Success Principle may not need to be followed. It is unfair to revolutionary movements, whether of the political left or not, religious or not, ideological or not, to hold them to a standard that only nation-states can satisfy.

Nonetheless, it can be argued that Castro and fellow revolutionaries could and should satisfy the Principle of Proportionality. It seemed at the time that more good than harm would follow if the Batista regime were overthrown. After all, that regime had taken away from labor the right to strike, abolished the Cuban congress, abolished political parties, imprisoned and executed many of those who opposed it, and practiced a virulent form of corruption with money flowing into the hands of the regime rather than to the people. Even as early as 1952 and 1953, a reasonable calculation could have been made that the people of Cuba would be better off without having to deal with a corrupt Batista regime. They would be better off, so the calculation of proportionality told them, even if a costly civil war would have to take place. So, in this case, there is no correspondence between the two principles. The one principle is (or should be) silent, while the other says that engaging in war is justified.

World War I gives us a more clear-cut example as to how the two principles fail to converge. If we consider the role of four of the major parties in that war, Germany, Great Britain, France, and Russia, each could conjecture that it could satisfy the Likelihood of Success Principle. Consider Germany first. It had a large, well-trained, and well-equipped army. It had a powerful navy, second only to Great Britain's. It also had the Schlieffen Plan to guide its army into France should the occasion arise for Germany to move in that direction. There were known weaknesses to the plan,[10] yet the German army was formidable enough to have a high likelihood of success even if it had to deal with France and Russia simultaneously.

As to the French army, it was not obviously overmatched in facing its potential enemy from the east.[11] Like the German army, it was large, numbering in the millions, and well trained. It also had an arrangement with Russia so that if either nation were attacked, the other would come to the rescue. As to Russia, its military forces were not so well equipped as the French or German, and maybe not so well trained. However, it had a population that could deliver an almost endless supply of soldiers to the front lines.[12] It also, as Napoleon had discovered and Hitler was to discover later, had a large land body that could easily swallow up an invading army.

As to Great Britain, its army would not go into action without working with the French. Although it was smaller when compared to the major continental armies, it was of high quality. It had been bloodied in the Boer War and knew better than most armies what modern war was about.[13] So all four nations had reason to believe that they could succeed, or at least hold their own, in a major European war. One, possibly two, of them might turn out to be wrong in this assessment. But each nation's assessment at the beginning of the war that it could satisfy the Likelihood of Success Principle was reasonable.

But what about the Proportionality Principle? Could the leaders in these countries have anticipated that the costs of war would be higher than the benefits? Evidently a large number of them did not. Perhaps national pride got in the way of their judgments, perhaps the excitement of war could not be resisted, or perhaps those in charge lost control of events so that one step in the direction of war led to another.

But had those in control of leading their nation to war taken the time to apply the Principle of Proportionality, World War I might not have taken place. There was ample evidence in wars prior to The Great War that modern wars would be extremely costly. The Russo-Japanese War in 1904–1905 showed clearly that modern weaponry, including fast-firing breech-loaded rifles, machine guns, powerful artillery, and large armies and navies can cause a horrendous number of casualties.[14] The Russians certainly learned this lesson, as did the Japanese. But the British, German, and French sent observers to that war. They also could not help but see the trend in war toward more casualties. In addition, the British had recent experiences of combat in the Boer War[15] and other colonial wars. They knew how dangerous modern rifle fire could be and so they entrenched themselves deep into the ground in a way that Belgian, French, and German soldiers eventually did in World War I.

So the handwriting was on the wall. With new and more deadly weapons and millions of soldiers available to use them, an application of the Principle of Proportionality should have given nations pause before they ventured into a major war involving many nations. Each nation might individually calculate that it would be successful if it entered into a major war, but a separate calculation based on the Proportionality Principle should have acted as a warning to the effect that the price of a major war would be too high.

Although the Principles of Likelihood of Success and Proportionality share much in common, they are distinct principles. What they share is taking consequences into account, taking *everyone's* consequences into account, and being difficult to apply. Together they suffer from the measurement problem. It often is not possible to make a reasonable assessment of the likelihood of success or of proportionality. They also share in being secondary principles. Each attempts to measure benefits and harms based on how the Principle of Just Cause has spoken.[16] If that principle speaks in response to aggression, then success is going to be measured in terms of how the aggression has been blunted or defeated. Similarly, proportionality measurements will tell us that the good of going to war has, in part, to do with getting rid of aggressors and deterring them in the future.

But the two principles differ in spite of their points of similarities. The Likelihood of Success Principle is narrower in scope. It is only concerned with reaching the goal (satisfying some just cause) of the war in question. It does not take the overall costs of reaching the goal into account. The Principle of Proportionality does. It focuses on the question: even if we can be successful, are the costs of success worthwhile? And, as we have seen, there are times when the Proportionality Principle will answer this question with a "No" even as Likelihood of Success Principle says "Yes."

NORTH KOREA AND THE BOMB AGAIN

The situation in Korea represents a real-life example of how these principles diverge. In the previous chapter we saw how under certain restrictive conditions South Korea could satisfy the Likelihood of Success Principle. But, as we will see, if it attacks the North, it cannot satisfy the Proportionality Principle. Nor can the North, if it attacks the South.

To see why, consider first the benefits side of the proportionality formula. The principle tells us that estimates of benefits made before the war starts should be at least equal to those of the war's costs. Just War Theory demands that both sides in a war make such estimates. On the North Korean side, the estimates of benefits would be modest at best. The historical record shows that the North Korean people suffered greatly for over a half a century; and that much, but not all, of this suffering can be laid at the feet of the North

Korean government.[17] In contrast, unification under the South Korean flag would likely lead to results that reflect the more robust economy in that country. To be sure, these benefits would be lessened by the difficulties South Korea would have integrating the people of the North into a single economy and society. Still, the projected unification of the North into the South would be expected to have significantly more benefits than the projected integration of the South into the North, at least in the long run.

But, now, consider the other side of the proportionality formula. South Korea is a country with almost 50 million people.[18] Of that total, perhaps about half live in Seoul (between 10 to 11 million), in the nearby city of Inchon (2.6 million), and in the surrounding areas.[19] Because Seoul is partly surrounded by mountains, its citizens tend to live close together in the lowlands. Land is at such a premium that the city has sprouted thousands of high-rise buildings (most are twenty to twenty-five stories high) to accommodate its people. These buildings are often built close together in clusters. If a war started, they would represent a target-rich environment for North Koreans, who admittedly are not averse to attacking enemy civilians. Many of the war's first victims would be the citizens of these two northern cities that are within easy reach of North Korea's rockets, missiles, shells, and bombs.[20] Tens, and very probably hundreds, of thousands of South Koreans would perish before the war got seriously under way.[21] Bridges, roads and highways would quickly be clogged as those who escaped the initial onslaught would flee south. Concentrated together as they inevitably would be, these refugees would present the North Koreans with another target-rich environment. Again tens, perhaps hundreds of thousands of civilians would die. Many more would suffer serious injury.

Beyond that, the fighting between the two armies would create more war victims among South Korean military personnel and the hordes of civilians who could not avoid getting in the way of the shooting, shelling, and bombing. Facing as they would an overly large military machine, South Korean military casualties would undoubtedly be extremely high. Civilian casualties likely would be even higher.

North Korean civilian casualties would be fewer than those of the South for two reasons. North Korea does not have a large metropolitan center near the front as does the South. Second, South Korea and its American ally are more averse to attacking civilian populations.[22] With their smart weapons, civilian casualties would not mount out of control, although they would not be insignificant.[23] In contrast, North Korea's military casualties would be greater than those of the South. With the Americans and high technology on the side of the South, many North Korean units would likely be savaged.

Overall, casualties in a war between the North and the South would probably exceed the horrendous level of the 1950–1953 war.[24] Since that war, the population of South Korea has more than doubled.[25] Today there are more people to target than there were in the past. In addition, the economies of both sides would be devastated for years to come, thus guaranteeing a great deal of suffering following the end of the war. The sophisticated South Korean economy would suffer more than the less developed economy of the North. No doubt, the harm done to those in the way of war would be so great as to lead to the conclusion that a war started by either side would be grossly at odds with the Principle of Proportionality. The good brought about by a war would be overwhelmed by the bad. This point holds even if the reason for starting a war is to keep the North Korean government from developing its nuclear arsenal. Whatever the reasons for war might be, whether they are in accord with Just War Theory or not, horrendous casualties could not be avoided.

Introducing nuclear weapons into a (conventional) war that already fails to satisfy the Principle of Proportionality magnifies the failure. No doubt, the degree of magnification would depend on the power and the number of the nuclear weapons that the North could bring to the battlefield. Yet, the horror of nuclear war would be so great that Just War Theory would reject starting that kind of war under any circumstances. In Korea, Just War Theory tells us that other means should be devised to settle whatever differences exist between the North and South.

It is worth considering what the likelihood is that any nation would actually use nuclear weapons on the Korean peninsula. On the South Korean/American side, that likelihood is very low. The North Koreans, even if they were the aggressors and used these weapons, would be stopped. In the end, they could be defeated with modern and powerful conventional weapons. There would be no need to employ nuclear weapons to defeat a military force that does not possess an overwhelming amount of strength. Although North Korea could be defeated and thus South Korea could satisfy one sense of the Principle of Success, the war would be so horrible that neither side could satisfy the Principle of Proportionality.

On the North Korean side, using nuclear weapons in an aggressive war would be tantamount to committing suicide. As noted already (in the previous chapter), the use of such weapons would simply make its victims even more determined to "get even." There might, at this point, be political pressure to go nuclear in response to a nuclear attack. One would hope this pressure would be resisted. Either way, with or without a nuclear response to their attacks, North Korea's aggressive war would fail.

But then what good does having such weapons do for the North Koreans? One obvious answer is as a deterrent to war. Evidently they do not believe that the threat that their conventional military forces poses to South Korea is great enough to deter aggression against them, especially if the Americans help the South Koreans. The North Koreans seek a further guarantee against being attacked by becoming a nuclear power. Presumably they would consider using their nuclear weapons as a last resort if they were attacked and, most especially, if the attack against them threatens to defeat the present North Korean government. No doubt the Principle of Proportionality would condemn such a use. But the issue here is moot since there is very little likelihood that the South Koreans and their American allies will attack the North. The North may not fully appreciate the deterrent power of its conventional and nuclear weapons, but their potential enemies do. Their enemies realize how disproportional any aggressive war against the North Koreans would be.

So far the argument has been that if either side starts a war, it cannot help but violate the Proportionality Principle. Starting a war, with or without just cause, is just too costly to meet the proportionality requirement. One may still ask, however, about fighting a defensive war. Can, for instance, the South Korean government meet the requirements of proportionality if it fights a defensive war? Initially one would think not. If, as we have argued, the North Korean attack cannot help but be disproportional (more harm than good will come of it), it would seem that the South Korean defense would also have to be disproportional. It is as if we are looking at one side and then the other side of the same coin. But the coin analogy is misleading since we are dealing with two coins. One coin has to do with the decision of the North Koreans to start a war. That decision has the North Koreans choosing war over peace. It is that decision that would count as disproportional if it were actually made.

Once attacked, the South Koreans would have to make a different decision: viz., whether to fight or not. This is the second coin in our analogy. If the South Koreans decide to fight, all the horrors of war described already would fall upon them and that, again, makes it seem as if fighting is the wrong thing to do. But if they decide not to fight, they would face all the horrors of being occupied by a cruel government. So their choice is between two evils. Either they must live (and die) with the consequences of war or the consequences of living (and dying) under the leadership of the North Korean government and its Dear Leader, Kim Jong Il. Should they, as they most assuredly would, choose war over submission, they would satisfy the Principle of Proportionality. As bad as war would be, living under the rule of Kim Jong Il would seem to be something worse both in the short and the long run.

What kind of defensive calculations the North should make if it were attacked is difficult to determine. That country is, after all, run by a very secretive government. Still, it is likely that Kim Jong Il and his associates would argue that a decision to defend the sacred lands and culture of North Korea would be in accord with the Proportionality Principle. Given the unique ideology that supports the North Korean government, it is difficult to know how to mount a counterargument at this point. Perhaps all one can do is grudgingly acknowledge that the North Koreans do indeed satisfy the Proportionality Principle.

All these speculations about a possible war on the Korean peninsula suddenly appear to be moot. As of this writing, all sides seem to be coming to their senses in that they are willing, now, to talk to one another and even make compromises.[26] The North Koreans have agreed to shut down their nuclear reactor and allow inspectors into their country, the South Koreans have sent fuel oil supplies to the North and promise to send more, the Americans have taken steps to relieve North Korea's financial difficulties, and the Chinese and Russians have given their tacit consent to the whole process of cooperation. What remains to be seen is what will happen next. If the next step in the negotiations process is as fruitful as the recent one, talk about various war scenarios will truly become moot.

NOTES

1. *Mo Tzu: Basic Writings*, sec. 19, trans. Burton Watson (New York: Columbia University Press, 1963), 3:52–61.

2. The realist position also allows for the proportionality principle to have a role to play in the decision process concerned with going to war. However, in contrast to the just war version of this principle, the realist version takes into account the gains and losses only of the nation or group making the decision. That is, this is a self-interest version of this principle.

3. Thomas Aquinas, *The Summa Theologica*, 2–2, q. 42, A 2, reply obj. 3, trans. Fathers of the English Dominican Province (Chicago: William Benton Publisher, Encylopaedia Britannica Inc., 1952), 584.

4. Hugo Grotius, *The Rights of War and Peace*, pt. 2, chap. 23, secs. 6–11, trans. A. C. Campbell (Washington, D.C.: M. Walter Dunne, 1901), 274.

5. See Paul Christopher, *The Ethics of War and Peace*, 2nd ed. (Upper Saddle River, N.J.: Prentice Hall, 1999); John Kelsay, *Islam and War* (Louisville, Ky.: Westminster/John Knox Press, 1993); Michael Walzer, *Just and Unjust Wars* (New York: Basic Books, 1977).

6. U.S. Catholic Bishops, "The Just War and Non-Violence Positions," in *War, Morality and the Military Profession*, ed. Malham Wakin, 2nd ed. (Boulder, Colo.: Westview Press, 1986), 248.

7. Sheldon Cohen, *Arms and Judgment* (Boulder, Colo.: Westview Press, 1989), 39

8. Paul Ramsey, *The Just War: Force and Political Responsibility* (New York: Charles Scribner's Sons, 1968), 195.

9. W. V. O'Brien, *The Conduct of a Just and Limited War* (New York: Praeger 1981), 27.

10. John Keegan, *The First World War* (New York: Alfred A. Knopf, 1999), 20–46

11. Hew Strachan, *The First World War* (New York: Penguin Books, 2003) 45–46

12. Strachen, *The First World War*, 143–45.

13. Keegan, *The First World War*, 98.

14. Robert B. Edgerton, *Warriors of the Rising Sun: A History of the Japanese Military* (New York: W. W. Norton & Co, 1997), 179–80.

15. Keegan, *The First World War*, 98.

16. This is true only for the just cause interpretation of Likelihood of Success Principle. See the previous chapter.

17. Stanley Sandler, *The Korean War: No Victors, No Vanquished* (Lexington: University Press of Kentucky, 1999) 269–70. As Sandler points out, there were floods that caused serious food shortages.

18. Wikipedia, "South Korea," at en.wikipedia.org/wiki/South_Korea (accessed June 3, 2007).

19. Wikipedia, "South Korea."

20. Joseph S. Bermudez Jr., "North Korea Takes Wraps off KN-02," *Jane's Defence Weekly*, May 9, 2007, 25. The KN-02 is a solid-fueled surface-to-surface with a range enough to strike well beyond Seoul. Evidently the North Koreans developed this missile with the help of Syria.

21. Scott Stossel, "North Korea: The War Game," *The Atlantic Monthly*, July/August 2006, 96–108. Stossel says: "Pentagon experts have estimated that the first ninety days of such a conflict might produce 300,000 to 500,000 South Korean and American military casualties, along with hundreds of thousands of civilian deaths. The damage to South Korea alone would rock the global economy."

22. This represents a radical change of policy when compared to the 1950–1953 war.

23. Matt Hilburn, "Precision: GPS Kits for Artillery Rounds Would Reduce Collateral Damage," *Seapower*, June 2007, 18–20.

24. Sandler, *The Korean War*, 264. According to Sandler at least 1 million South Koreans (military and civilian) were killed. North Koreans killed were about the same. These figures may be conservative. One writer (Callum A. MacDonald, *Korea: The War Before Vietnam* [New York: 1986], 259) estimates that between 12 to 15 percent of the North Korean population was killed in the war. That means that probably two million or more North Koreans died. As if that were not bad enough, North Korea suffered from an American bombing campaign that leveled every city, and practically every town and village, in that country. In addition to all this suffering and destruction, the Chinese army probably lost another million troops—perhaps as many as a million and a half. See Max Hastings, *The Korean War* (New York: Simon and Schuster, 1987) 329. See also Clay Blair, *The Forgotten War: America in Korea 1950–1953* (New York: Doubleday, 1987). Blair cites Pentagon casualty (dead, wounded, missing, or captured) as follows: military on both sides at 2.4 million; civilian casualties on both sides at 2 million. American dead in the war totaled 4,246 (33,629 in battle; 20,617 from other causes).

25. John M. Collins, "North Korea: The Case Against Preemption," in *U.S. Naval Institute Proceedings*, November 2006, 26–29.

26. David E. Sanger, "North Koreans Say They've Shut Nuclear Reactor," *New York Times*, July 15, 2007, 1, 8.

6

Last Resort

Bruno Coppieters, Ruben Apressyan, and Carl Ceulemans

According to Just War Theory, when conflicts of interest occur between two states the use of force may be justified only as a last resort, that is, only when all nonmilitary means of conflict resolution have been tried. So a party to the conflict may have a just cause, legitimate authority, and right intentions, and have all the other just war justifications for using military force, but still may be prohibited from going to war.

The moral condition that a war can only be considered just if the aggrieved party has given the opportunity for a peaceful settlement is found in Cicero.[1] Roman legal practice, he says, requires a certain time period to elapse between the demand for reparations and the initiation of hostilities.[2] This gives the opponent the opportunity to render satisfaction. War can then be waged justly only when this alternative has been refused. Also, other authors, such as Aquinas, thought of war as a kind of sanction for an injury where no other means of seeking redress is available. Alternatives to war were also explored by Hugo Grotius. He proposed peace conferences and arbitration, and even favored methods for conflict settlement that seem quaint today, such as drawing lots and single combat.[3]

The Principle of Last Resort is not to be discounted entirely even when states are confronted with imminent military aggression. Of course, a large number of factors will then determine to what extent nonmilitary options are still available or if a state has to resort to a preemptive attack. In certain cases, diplomatic channels may still be used to prevent aggression. According to Just War Theory, this option is morally far preferable to the use of force. But it is difficult to define an exact time frame during which alternatives to the use of force should be sought. A long time frame is not reasonable in every case. An enemy may, for instance, preclude all possibility of negotiation with a sudden attack on one's territory.

Applying the Principle of Last Resort may confront political actors with the difficult choice between the evil of war and the burden of injustice. In some cases, the burden of an unjust peace has to be preferred to the horrors of war. In others, instead of preventing war, restraint in the use of force may be taken as a sign of weakness and thus foster aggression, as an aggressor will then have more opportunity for building up its military potential. When this happens we have an erroneous application of the Last Resort Principle on our hands. Famously, such an application took place before the outbreak of World War II. The policies of appeasement of Britain and France toward Nazi Germany led to results that were at odds with their intentions. The Munich Agreements in September 1938 did not constrain Hitler's expansionary military policies, but instead paved the way for his occupation of Czechoslovakia and strengthened his political and military position in Europe.

THE UNITED NATIONS

After World War II, the creation of the United Nations and new developments in international law put severe limitations on the rights of nations to use force. In this institutional context, the Security Council of the UN plays a key role with regard to the application of the Principle of Last Resort. The UN has been given primary responsibility for maintaining international peace and security in accordance with the principles and purposes of the charter.[4] One of its purposes is to investigate any dispute or situation that might lead to international conflict. The UN Security Council may determine the existence of a threat to peace, or an act of aggression, and then recommend action. Before recommending the use of military force, it may issue resolutions that spell out particular measures it wants to see implemented, or decide on coercive measures, such as economic sanctions.

Sanctions are used to persuade an offending state to alter its external or internal policies, and may in this sense be used to signal concern to that state about its role in an escalating conflict.[5] Economic sanctions may take the form of partial restrictions imposed on trade or financial relations with certain parts of a state or, through an economic embargo, for instance, with the state as a whole. Economic sanctions may even be imposed against a warring party.

Imposing sanctions constitutes a significant political action. Sometimes the mere declaration of sanctions will make a state's position clear and force a change in the behavior of another state. The UN Security Council has used sanctions on a number of occasions when other nonmilitary means proved insufficient. They were used against one party to a conflict to force it to comply with particular Security Council objectives. Sanctions were imposed, for instance, in 1977 against the apartheid regime in South Africa (and lifted with the end of apartheid in 1994). To the extent that specific forms of economic sanctions can play an important role in preventing open war, they may be analyzed as an alternative to the use of force, in particular when they are enforced with the legitimate authority of the UN Security Council. There are, however, a number of moral problems involved in their use, which deserve special attention.

The use of economic sanctions involves two main problems that raise questions about their legitimate use. The first has to do with their efficiency. This problem is to a certain degree similar to the problem of "reasonable chance of success" in the use of military force. As with the concept of success in using force, one has to take into account the fact that it is difficult to define precisely what success may mean in this context. UN sanctions can be useful in two ways.[6] First, they signal international disapproval of the actions of a government. Second, they may lead to an alteration of that government's policies, to a deescalation of the conflict, and to the avoidance of the use of force.

The success of economic sanctions may be seen as a delicate balancing of the moral costs and moral benefits to both the sanctioning and the sanctioned states. It is possible to weigh all the factors that need to be taken into account, but this is not an easy task.[7] Sanctions will normally be more successful if the political aims to be achieved are limited. They may be successful if they target, for instance, violations of human rights or particular policies. When assessing their chances of success, it should not be expected that they will achieve reconciliation or a rapprochement between conflicting parties. In many cases, they simply harden positions.

The economic sanctions against Iraq, for example, seemed insufficient to compel Saddam Hussein to withdraw his troops from Kuwait. According to Anthony J. Coates, the sanctions failed to prevent the movement of supplies into Iraq by land. Also, after a decade of hardship during the war with Iran (1980–1988), the regime had become accustomed to privation. The Iraqi regime, moreover, ignored the harsh living conditions of many of its citizens. Economic sanctions thus failed to destroy the political stability of the regime.[8] Economic sanctions likewise failed to force the Iraqi regime to comply with UN resolutions after the Gulf War (1990–1991).

A further major problem with the use of economic sanctions is that they may run counter to the Principles of Discrimination and Proportionality. In some cases the consequences of sanctions have a no less fateful impact on the civilian population than war itself. Sanctions should be thought of as a form of the use of force. Even if the ethical and political problems related to sanctions policies are different from the problems related to war, the price paid by the most vulnerable sectors of the population means that the *jus in bello* Principles of Discrimination and Proportionality have to be taken into account.

These two principles are even more important when the sanctions are effectively implemented by a multilateral regime. UN members have therefore expressed serious humanitarian concerns about the consequences of sanctions on the targeted countries. In particular, the sanctions policies toward Iraq before the 2003 invasion raised widespread concern about the lack of clear ethical criteria when using them as a means of last resort. In the many public debates among experts and diplomats on the use of UN sanctions, it was therefore proposed that "targeted" rather than general sanctions be used. These targeted sanctions can include measures such as halting the transfer of particular technologies, the freezing of leaders' personal bank accounts, or the denial of access to hard currency.[9] In a first resolution in December 2006, the UN Security Council imposed such targeted sanctions against Iran by halting the transfer of some sensitive nuclear technologies. In a second resolution in March 2007, the UNSC also imposed an arms embargo and travel restrictions on a number of individuals engaged in Iranian nuclear enrichment or related activities. The UNSC wanted to persuade Iran to halt its work on uranium enrichment. Unlike the usual trade sanctions, their impact on the most vulnerable parts of the population is negligible. The problem of sanctions thus belongs as much to the moral reflections on *jus ad bellum* as to those on *jus in bello*. For this reason, it will also be discussed in the second part of this volume, in the chapter on the Principle of Discrimination.

NUCLEAR CRISIS MANAGEMENT: THE CUBAN MISSILE CRISIS OF 1962

There are a few classical guidelines or steps that need to be followed in order to prevent the emergence of violent conflict in deteriorating circumstances.[10] First, states should not suspend diplomatic relations—as they often do in case of conflict escalation—but, instead, should keep all lines of communication open. Reliable firsthand information is essential to managing conflict. Second, the parties to the conflict should express their national interests clearly. This information is necessary in order to make clear what they consider to be unacceptable behavior. Citizens at home should also be made to understand the issues at stake when their government is trying to avoid a worsening of the conflict. Clear knowledge about interests in jeopardy also makes it easier for outsiders to mediate in a conflict. Third, the crisis should be put on the agenda of international security organizations such as the UN early enough to permit preventive action. Fourth, the opportunities for quiet diplomacy and dialogue between leaderships should not be neglected.

The key role of these four guidelines for conflict resolution was demonstrated during the Cuban missile crisis of 1962.[11] The fruitful outcome of this crisis gives the most impressive example especially of the role of top-level communication, on both the diplomatic and the informal levels. The crisis itself emerged in the context of worsening American-Soviet relations in 1959–1961. The United States had deployed intermediate-range missiles in Great Britain, Italy, and Turkey. The missiles deployed in Turkey, a neighbor of the Soviet Union, constituted a particularly severe threat to Soviet security. The missiles stationed there could reach the central parts of Soviet territory in a very short time. Furthermore, the United States had a greater number of intercontinental missiles and submarine forces at their disposal than the Soviets.[12]

From the Soviet perspective, these developments constituted a new level of threat. The balance of power between the two superpowers was in peril. The Soviet leaders felt that they had neither the resources nor the time to alter the situation by developing and deploying new weapons technology. Relations between the two states were also strained by other developments, such as the construction of the Berlin Wall in 1961. Meanwhile, the revolutionary regime of Fidel Castro in Cuba, which had overthrown the dictatorship of General Fulgencio Batista in February 1959, became a matter of concern for the United States. Tensions in American-Cuban relations escalated sharply. The American administration applied economic and political sanctions against the island, and even organized subversive actions against the new regime. It is in this context that Fidel Castro strengthened his economic and military links with the USSR.[13] Soviet leaders considered offering massive military assistance to Cuba in order to oppose American pressure on the island and to prevent it from being invaded. At first, the Soviet Union made commitments to supply conventional armaments and munitions amounting to almost $150 million.[14] But in May 1962 the Soviet leader Nikita Khruschev envisaged stationing nuclear weapons in Cuba. Such a move, he thought, would prevent an American invasion of Cuba and reestablish the strategic parity between the superpowers. The Soviet general staff made preparations for transporting significant numbers of troops across the Atlantic. From July to September some 43,000 soldiers were secretly sent to Cuba.[15] The first R-12 missiles arrived in Cuba by the end of September, and 164 nuclear warheads were delivered later.[16]

After receiving information about the deployment of Soviet military forces, the American administration decided to act.[17] On October 22, 1962, President Kennedy made a statement about the gravity of the situation and the necessity of repelling the threat. He announced a blockade of the island. All ships bound for Cuba would be searched. The American military forces at Guantanamo were put on a war footing and American missiles at the bases in Turkey were also prepared for any eventuality. The American president also sent a letter to the Soviet leader in which he pointed out that "the United States would do whatever must be done to protect its own security and that of its allies." He further declared that "the United States is determined that this threat to the security of this hemisphere be removed."[18] For its part, the Soviet government characterized the American actions as "provocative and aggressive" and announced that its troops and those of the Warsaw Pact armies were on a war footing.[19] The Soviet troops in Cuba were made ready to repel an American attack, even if this involved using the atomic weapons under their control.[20] In his reply to President Kennedy, Soviet leader Khruschev characterized the American position as overt interference in the internal affairs of Cuba, the Soviet Union, and other nations. The United States, he said, had no right to control the armaments transported to Cuba for its defense. Soviet arms had only been brought to Cuba to avert aggression.[21] Over the following two days, Kennedy and Khruschev exchanged messages in which the language of ultimatum, confrontation, and threats prevailed.

Cuba and Turkey also played a role in the escalation of the conflict. Castro saw no reason not to shoot down U2 airplanes flying over the island.[22] And Turkey voiced its dissent concerning the proposed removal of American nuclear missiles in Turkey, regarding them as the "symbol of the Alliance's determination to use atomic weapons against a Russian attack on Turkey whether by large conventional or by nuclear forces."[23]

The world was on the brink of a new world war. Fortunately, however, the leaders of the two superpowers did not stop communicating with one another. In a letter to Khruschev on October 25, Kennedy once more explained the American position and expressed regret about the worsening of American Soviet relations. It was as if Kennedy was hinting at certain differences between his own views and those of some of his own military advisers. He seemed to assume that Khrushchev was having similar problems on his side.[24] The Soviet leader understood the message that the Americans were ready for compromise. In a long letter dated October 26 he, in turn, tried to explain the attitude of his government. He did not use the language of confrontation. Instead, he made an appeal to mutual understanding and concluded his letter with the following proposal to Kennedy: "Let us therefore show statesmanlike wisdom. I propose: we, for our part, will declare that our ships bound for Cuba, are not carrying any armaments. You would declare that the United States will not invade Cuba with its forces and will not support any sort of forces that might intend to carry out an invasion of Cuba. Then the necessity for the presence of our military specialists in Cuba would disappear."[?]

But this new language did not lead to an immediate deescalation of the conflict. An American plane was shot down on October 27, killing its pilot

Fidel Castro wrote to Khrushchev that an invasion by American forces was imminent. In order to save time in the diplomatic negotiations, the Soviet government decided to use a rather unusual form of diplomatic communication. Khrushchev's message to President Kennedy was broadcast by Moscow Radio, and a copy sent to the secretary-general of the UN. In this message, the withdrawal of Soviet missiles from Cuba was linked to an agreement concerning the withdrawal of American missiles from Turkey. Kennedy answered in the same unusual way by presenting his letter to the press. This exchange of letters led to positive results.

During the whole negotiation process, two possible compromise solutions had emerged. The first was the removal of nuclear weapons from Cuba in exchange for an American promise not to attack Cuba, as set out in Khrushchev's letter, mentioned above. This proposal was originally made by Aleksandr Fomin (a senior Soviet intelligence officer) to a television reporter, who, in turn, transmitted the message to the American government. The second proposal was to withdraw nuclear missiles from both Cuba and Turkey. This proposal was made by the Austrian Minister for Foreign Affairs, Bruno Kreisky. Both proposals were eventually taken into account in the final settlement. The Soviet Union secured an agreement that Cuba would not be invaded. Each of the great powers also agreed to withdraw its nuclear missiles from near the other's borders. This permitted a peaceful outcome to one of the most serious crises since World War II.

It may be concluded that the American and Soviet leadership applied the principles for successful negotiation indicated above. During the crisis, the two parties did not suspend diplomatic relations but, instead, intensified their contacts. At the same time, they clearly stated what they considered to be the bottom line in a possible compromise. This position was also made clear to the public in their respective countries. The United Nations was also involved in the search for a compromise, while diplomatic negotiations continued behind the scenes. Jonathan Glover notes some further features in the handling of this crisis by Moscow and Washington.[26] Both leaderships, he says, succeeded in keeping their armed forces under control. They both took time to respond cautiously, being aware of the enormous risks they were taking, and of their own fallibility. Provocation was avoided, and the tone of their mutual correspondence remained by and large moderate. They remained aware that only a compromise solution would respect each other's interests and would not lead to a loss of face for each of them.

Secretary of State Dean Rusk, one of the members of the Executive Committee of the National Security Council (Ex-Comm), was convinced of the impact of moral principles on the deliberations. He said: "Moral and ethical considerations play a very important part, even though people don't wear these things on their shirtsleeves or put these things into official memoranda. They play an important part. People act in reference to their basic moral commitments, and they are likely to come to the fore when situations become critical."[27] But the members of Ex-Comm were divided over the question of what role moral principles should play in the management of the conflict.[28] This difference had a direct impact on their perceptions of how the crisis should be handled. The hawks, a minority in Ex-Comm, took only national self-interest into consideration and so were thinking along realist lines. They favored air strikes against Cuba and considered an invasion of the island feasible. They did not believe that the Soviet Union would find any interest in retaliation, and considered the risks of nuclear war generally low. In their view, it was obviously not in the Soviet interest to respond to an invasion of Cuba with nuclear weapons. The doves, including the president himself, were of a contrary view. They considered the risks real and great, and wanted to minimize them as much as possible. They could very well imagine that the Soviet leadership would feel forced to retaliate with nuclear weapons to air strikes or to an invasion of Cuba.

In view of the information about the crisis that was disclosed later on, it seems indeed that the hawks were overconfident in their estimation of the Soviet side's readiness to respond in a way they considered rational and to avoid a nuclear war at any price. The Soviet armed forces were ready to retaliate. Moreover, the confidence of the hawks was based on wrong data concerning Soviet strength. The Americans thought there were only 10,000 Soviet troops in Cuba, whereas their real strength was 43,000. It further became known that there were also 162 nuclear warheads on the island.[29] But the prudential considerations of the doves were not only based on a different interpretation of the dynamics of the crisis and on American national interests. They also used moral principles in their approach to the conflict, and so went beyond considering only national interests. They did not simply assume that the other party would restrain its behavior as the result of rational calculations. These factors had a restraining effect on their position. President Kennedy was well aware of his moral responsibilities, telling Pierre Salinger after an Ex-Comm meeting: "Do you think the people in that room realize that if we make a mistake, there may be 200 million dead?"[30] Robert Kennedy, a brother of the president and an active participant in the management of the crisis on the side of the doves, wrote that Ex-Comm spent a lot of time debating whether the United States had the moral right to strike unexpectedly against Cuba in much the same way that Japan had attacked Pearl Harbor. He added: "We spent more time on this moral question during the first five days than on any other single matter. . . . We struggled and fought with one another and with our consciences, for it was a question that deeply troubled us all."[31] Paul Nitze, assistant secretary of defense and a hawk in Ex-Comm, considered such a moral reflection of the American responsibilities as a waste of time: "Most of the discussion in those early days was way up at the level of morality and this kind of thing and not on the issue of who does what, with what, to whom, and when. I was so annoyed at the failure of the main discussions to deal with who-does-what-with-what-to-whom-when, it wasn't really a planning session, it seemed to me to be rather a sophomoric seminar."[32]

It seems that, contrary to Nitze's assessment, the discussions on the choice of moral principles to follow in handling the crisis had positive political consequences. Jonathan Glover, in his analysis of the American-Soviet nuclear crisis management, comes to the conclusion that the moral code of the doves prevented the American administration from pursuing a policy based on speculative calculations having to do only with the national interest. We may add to this observation that the combination of such a nonmoral position combined with fragmented and incomplete information about the consequences of military actions could very well have led to disastrous consequences for all the parties involved.

Moral considerations also seem to have been prominent in the Soviet policies of self-restraint. Moscow had to oppose the uncompromising position of the Cuban leadership. Moral considerations were made clear in the exchange of letters between the U.S. and Soviet presidents. After the end of the crisis, on October 28, Khrushchev declared to his colleagues in the Soviet Presidium: "Now we found ourselves face to face with the danger of war and of nuclear catastrophe, with the possible result of destroying the human race. In order to save the world, we must retreat."[33]

HUMANITARIAN CRISIS MANAGEMENT: BOSNIA, 1992–1995

A state may use force to impose its will on another political unit. The same goal may be reached by the threat of force. But in terms of international law, threats are severely restricted. According to chapter 1, article 2 of the UN Charter, "All Members shall refrain in their international relations from the threat or use of force against the territorial integrity or political independence of any state, or in any other manner inconsistent with the Purposes of the United Nations." But the UN Security Council itself may threaten to use force for the sake of international peace and security. Such threats are to be found, for instance, in the UN Security Council resolutions concerning the invasion of Kuwait by Iraqi forces in August 1990. The aim of such threats is to strengthen diplomatic pressure, and to force a government or a warring party to acquiesce eventually in the decisions of the Security Council. They provide an effective means of resolving a conflict without actually resorting to the use of force. But such threats will, of course, only be efficacious if there is a real capability and intention to use them if they receive no response.

Consider for example the attitude of the international community towards the war in Bosnia (1992–1995). During this conflict between the three communities in Bosnia (the Serbs, Croats, and Muslims) the Security Council had to decide on several occasions whether it would resort to the use of military force, or try to deescalate the conflict using diplomatic initiatives. The Security Council had great difficulty in applying the Principle of Last Resort when it came to protecting six Muslim enclaves in Serb-dominated territory (Sarajevo, Srebrenica, Zepa, Gorazde, Tuzla, and Bihac). These enclaves had been created to shelter the Muslim population from the policies of ethnic cleansing implemented by the Serb nationalist leadership. They were therefore permanent thorns in the flesh of the Bosnian Serbs (the enclaves in East Bosnia especially), and were in constant danger of being overrun by their troops. A further problem for the international community was the awkward humanitarian situation in these areas. In order to escape being massacred by Bosnian Serb forces, thousands of Muslim refugees sought safety in these as-yet-unconquered "islands."

The international community did not know how to address the problems of overpopulation and lack of sufficient food or shelter for all these people. It feared that an overly military attitude toward the Bosnian Serbs might jeopardize the ongoing diplomatic efforts to find a lasting solution to the conflict. So, how did the international community react to this situation, and more importantly, how can these international reactions be evaluated from the point of view of last resort?

The first important decision by the international community concerning the problem of the enclaves was made in April 1993. In response to severe Bosnian Serb attacks in March 1993 on Srebrenica, one of the enclaves in East Bosnia, the UN Security Council declared on April 16, 1993, that Srebrenica would be treated as a safe area. This meant that it should be free from any armed attack or hostile act. On May 6, the Security Council added five more safe areas: Sarajevo, Zepa, Gorazde, Tuzla, and Bihac. But it had no intention of defending them if they were attacked. The mission of UN-PROFOR (United Nations Protection Force) in these enclaves was at first limited to observing whether the parties to the conflict respected their status as safe areas. But on June 4, the Security Council took additional measures to protect the enclaves. The UNPROFOR mandate was expanded with five more tasks. These were: deterring attacks on the safe areas, monitoring the cease-fire, promoting the withdrawal of military or paramilitary units other than those of the Government of Bosnia and Herzegovina, occupying key points, and protecting the delivery and distribution of humanitarian relief. Security Council Resolution 836 was formulated in robust wording (under the so-called chapter 7 of the UN Charter).

But even if it were meant to deter further attacks against the safe areas, a careful reading of the resolution shows that it looked much tougher than it actually was. It authorized UNPROFOR, "acting in self-defense, to take the necessary measures, including the use of force, in reply to bombardments against the safe areas by any of the parties or to armed incursion into them or in the event of any deliberate obstruction in or around those areas to the freedom of movement of UNPROFOR or of protected humanitarian convoys." A superficial reading gives the impression that it had become possible for UNPROFOR and the member states to defend these safe areas actively. But the text restricted the actual use of force to the defense of UNPROFOR ("acting in self-defense"), if the safe areas should come under attack.

So far the UN measures to safeguard the Muslim enclaves from Serb attacks were essentially noncoercive, in the sense that they appealed largely to the goodwill of the conflicting parties (they were *asked* to respect the requirements of the safe areas). Up to this point, then, the only threat to use military force formulated by the UN had to do with the defense of its own troops. This changed when the Bosnian Serb leadership decided to isolate Sarajevo even further in July 1993 (by conquering Mount Igman). This tighter isolation endangered the already critical humanitarian assistance activities in this safe area. In order to respond adequately to this immediate threat, NATO decided on August 2, in accordance with the UN Security Council resolutions, "to make immediate preparations for undertaking, in the event that the strangulation of Sarajevo and other areas continues, including wide-scale interference with humanitarian assistance, stronger measures including air strikes against those responsible, Bosnian Serbs and others, in Bosnia-Herzegovina."[34] With this decision, the use of airpower was no longer restricted to close air support operations for the UN peacekeeping force. It also became possible to execute air strikes against the military targets of the offending party.[35] This broader interpretation of SC Resolution 836 was undoubtedly an important step toward a more forceful approach to the UN safe-area policy.

But the NATO threat did not make a strong impression on the Bosnian Serbs. So NATO resorted to stronger steps by issuing ultimatums that fell just short of the actual use of force. In February 1994, a mortar attack on a Sarajevo marketplace killed sixty-eight and wounded two hundred. The Bosnian Serbs were considered responsible for this gruesome act by Western public opinion. Now NATO decided to allow air strikes against the Bosnian Serb positions if they did not withdraw their heavy weapons (artillery, tanks, etc.) from a twenty-kilometer exclusion zone around Sarajevo within ten days. This ultimatum was issued at the request of UN Secretary-General Boutros-Ghali. The threat worked. After a ten-day delay, the UN and NATO decided that air strikes were not necessary after all. It was judged that the Bosnian Serbs had made sufficient progress in withdrawing. When in April 1994 another safe area came under fire (this time it was Gorazde),

NATO tried yet again to induce the Bosnian Serbs to comply by confronting them with another ultimatum. Again the Bosnian Serbs were given a deadline for stopping their attack and withdrawing from a twenty-kilometer exclusion zone. This time, however, the threat did not work so well. Although NATO was convinced that the Bosnian Serbs had not fulfilled the requirements of the ultimatum, it did not get the go-ahead from the UN to start air strikes. UN officials considered the progress in withdrawing sufficient and saw air strikes as jeopardizing urgent medical assistance to those in need in the area.

The patience of the international community came to an end, however, in September 1995. The fall of the safe area of Srebrenica in July 1995 led to the murdering of thousands of Muslim men. The international community then came to a position where it could no longer justify measures short of military force—the remaining safe areas required stronger protection measures.[36] What eventually triggered a massive NATO air campaign was yet another murderous mortar attack on a Sarajevo marketplace at the end of August 1995.[37] Operation "Deliberate Force" started on August 30 and the bombing campaign lasted for two weeks. NATO flew 3,500 sorties and managed to destroy most of its selected targets. This operation was considered a success in the sense that it contributed in no small part to the diplomatic breakthrough of the Dayton Agreement of November 1995, which led the foundation for conflict settlement in Bosnia.

So how should the actions taken by the Security Council to safeguard the Muslim enclaves be evaluated? Did the international community reasonably exhaust all means short of war before starting its bombing campaign? Or, on the contrary, had it waited too long before resorting to force? There are strong indications that the international community had indeed exhausted all nonmilitary options. Economic sanctions,[38] a weapons embargo,[39] and a no-fly zone over Bosnia[40] had been put in place at an earlier stage of the war. Diplomatic initiatives to find an overall solution for Bosnia were ongoing at the time of the conflict concerning the enclaves.[41] The more specific measures concerning the Muslim enclaves were basically designed to preserve a status quo with nonmilitary means, pending an overall diplomatic solution. So when NATO finally did start a bombing campaign against the Bosnian Serbs it was, from the last-resort point of view, not a moment too soon.

But, as was frequently asked at the time of the bombing, was it not too late? Had the Security Council not gone beyond the reasonable point of "lastness"? It can be argued that it had. When NATO started operation "Deliberate Force" the safe-area policy had already failed miserably (cf. the fall of Srebrenica). This does not mean, however, that a similar air campaign at an earlier stage of the war would have been an effective answer to the problem. The circumstances in which such an earlier operation would have taken place were far less favorable than at the time operation "Deliberate Force" was carried out. Not only did operation "Deliberate Force" then coincide with a Croat-Muslim military success against the Serbs, but in addition, Serbia proper had finally distanced itself from the Bosnian Serb leadership. There was war fatigue among all parties. These factors, combined with the NATO bombing campaign, made the Bosnian Serbs much less reluctant to accept a diplomatic solution. It is also true that international interventions in complex intrastate wars are very difficult and that easy solutions should not be expected. But it may also be concluded that the Security Council was wrong in giving false hope to the refugee population. It should not have created so-called safe areas in the first place if it had no intention of defending them. And when it did create them, it should have done so with the firm resolution to apply the Principle of Last Resort, which includes the possibility of the use of force. The international community therefore bears its share of responsibility for the thousands of Muslim victims of Srebrenica.

NOTES

1. Paul Christopher, *The Ethics of War and Peace. An Introduction to Legal and Moral Issues* (Upper Saddle River, N.J.: Prentice Hall, 1994), 13.
2. According to Roman law, thirty-three days had to pass between the demand for reparations and the beginning of hostilities. Christopher, *The Ethics of War and Peace*, 13–14, 55.
3. Christopher, *The Ethics of War and Peace*, 95.
4. On the following, see *Basic Facts about the United Nations* (New York: United Nations, 1998); Carnegie Commission on Preventing Deadly Conflict, *Preventing Deadly Conflict: Final Report with Executive Summary* (New York: Carnegie Corporation of New York, 1997), 39, 60–67.
5. On the following: Carnegie Commission on Preventing Deadly Conflict, *Preventing Deadly Conflict*, 52–56; *Basic Facts about the United Nations*, 60; Gary Clyde Hufbauer, Jeffrey J. Schott, and Kimberly Ann Elliott, *Economic Sanctions Reconsidered*, 2nd ed., 2 vols. (Washington, D.C.: Institute for International Economics, 1990).
6. David A. Hamburg and Cyrus R. Vance, "Foreword" to *Sharpening International Sanctions: Toward a Stronger Role for the United Nations: A Report to the Carnegie Commission on Preventing Deadly Conflict* (New York: Carnegie Corporation of New York, November 1996), at www.ccpdc.org/pubs/summary/stremframe.htm (accessed April 5, 2001).
7. D. A. Baldwin, "The Sanctions Debate and the Logic of Choice," *International Security* 24, no. 3 (Winter 1999/2000): 87–92.
8. A. J. Coates, *The Ethics of War* (Manchester and New York: Manchester University Press, 1997), 196.
9. Carnegie Commission on Preventing Deadly Conflict, *Preventing Deadly Conflict*, 55.

10. Carnegie Commission, *Preventing Deadly Conflict*, 49–50.

11. This case was reconstructed on the basis of the following sources: *Karibski krizis 1962 goda v arkhivnykh dokumentakh Rossii, SShA i Kuby: analiz, itogi, uroki. Doklady i tezisy dokladov mezhdunarodnoi nauchnoi konferentsii* (Moscow: Nauka, 1994); Rudolf Pikhoya, "Pochemu Khruschev poteryal vlast'" in *Mezhdunarodnyi istoricheski zhurnal* 8 (March–April 2000), at history.machaon.ru/number_08/analiti4/khrushchev_print/index.html (accessed March 11, 2002).

12. B. G. Putilin and N. A. Shepova, *Na krayu propasti (Karibski krizis 1962 goda)* (Moscow: Obelisk, 1994), 13–15.

13. *"Karibski krizis" i predshestvuyuschie sobytiya*, at www.coldwar.narod.ru/kubacrisis.htm (accessed March 11, 2002).

14. According to P. G. Melian in *Karibski krizis 1962 goda v arkhivnykh dokumentakh Rossii, SShA i Kuby*, 169–70.

15. Rafael Zakirov, "My pokidali Kubu," *Nezavisimaya gazeta*, October 22, 1999, 4, at nvo.ng.ru/history/1999-10-22/cuba.html (accessed March 11, 2002).

16. T. D. Akosta in *Karibski krizis 1962 goda v arkhivnykh dokumentakh Rossii, SShA i Kuby*, 118.

17. "The Cuban Missile Crisis. Document 43. Memorandum for the File (October 24, 1962)," at elsinore.cis.yale.edu/lawweb/avalon/diplomacy/forrel/cuba/cuba043.htm (accessed March 11, 2002).

18. "The Cuban Missile Crisis. Document 44. Letter From President Kennedy to Chairman Khrushchev (accessed October 22, 1962)," at elsinore.cis.yale.edu/lawweb/avalon/diplomacy/forrel/cuba/cuba044.htm (accessed March 11, 2002).

19. Sergey Khruschev, *Nikita Khruschev: krizisy i rakety* (Moscow: Vagrius, 1994), 2:247.

20. A. I. Alexeyev in *Karibski krizis 1962 goda v arkhivnykh dokumentakh Rossii, SShA i Kuby*, 300.

21. "The Cuban Missile Crisis. Document 48. Telegram from the Embassy in the Soviet Union to the Department of State (October 23, 1962)," at elsinore.cis.yale.edu/lawweb/avalon/diplomacy/forrel/cuba/cuba048.htm (accessed March 11, 2002).

22. According to T. D. Akosta in *Karibski krizis 1962 goda v arkhivnykh dokumentakh Rossii, SShA i Kuby*, 212–13.

23. "The Cuban Missile Crisis. Document 75. Telegram from the Embassy in France to the Department of State (Paris, October 25, 1962)," at elsinore.cis.yale.edu/lawweb/avalon/diplomacy/forrel/cuba/cuba075.htm (accessed March 11, 2002).

24. "The Cuban Missile Crisis. Document 68. Letter from President Kennedy to Chairman Khrushchev (October 25, 1962)," at elsinore.cis.yale.edu/lawweb/avalon/diplomacy/forrel/cuba/cuba068.htm (accessed March 11, 2002).

25. "The Cuban Missile Crisis. Document 84. Telegram from the Embassy in the Soviet Union to the Department of State (Moscow, October 26, 1962)," at elsinore.cis.yale.edu/lawweb/avalon/diplomacy/forrel/cuba/cuba084.htm (accessed March 11, 2002).

26. Jonathan Glover, *Humanity: A Moral History of the Twentieth Century* (London: Pimlico, 2001), 224.

27. James G. Blight and David A. Welch, *On the Brink: Americans and Soviets Reexamine the Cuban Missile Crisis* (New York: Farrar, Straus & Giroux, 1989), 78. Quoted in Glover, *Humanity*, 221.

28. On the following, see Blight and Welch, *On the Brink*, 200–233.

26. See James G. Blight and Janet M. Lang, *The Fog of War: Lessons from the Life of Robert S. McNamara* (London and Boulder, Colo.: Rowman & Littlefield, 2005), 59.

30. Quoted in Blight and Welch, *On the Brink*, 220.

31. Quoted in Blight and Welch, *On the Brink*, 221.

32. Blight and Welch, *On the Brink*, 221.

33. Blight and Welch, *On the Brink*, 222.

34. Dick Leurdijk, *The United Nations and NATO in Former Yugoslavia, 1991–1996: Limits to Diplomacy and Force* (The Hague: Netherlands Atlantic Commission, 1996), 38.

35. In close air support (CAS) operations, airpower is used against enemy targets that are in contact with, or in the immediate surroundings of, friendly ground forces. These kinds of air operations are executed on demand and in close coordination with these ground forces. In the context of the Yugoslav conflict, the CAS operations were mainly in support of UNPROFOR. When we talk about air strikes we mean air operations directed against enemy targets that are not in the immediate surroundings of the friendly ground troops, but which do have a significant influence on their operations. During the Bosnian conflict, air strikes were conducted against Bosnian Serb targets in order to deter further attacks against the safe areas. Unlike in CAS operations, the force commander on the ground had nothing to do with the initiation of air strikes. For the use of this kind of airpower, the initiative had to be taken at the highest political levels in the UN and NATO.

36. Laura Silber and Allan Little put it as follows: "The fall of Srebrenica was part of the end game. It was a watershed for Western, in particular, American, policy in the Yugoslav wars. After that, nothing would ever be the same. All reticence about stepping over what General Sir Michael Rose had called the Mogadishu line, which separated peace-keeping from peace-enforcement, was swept aside. The United Nations, led unambiguously now by the United States, in effect went to war with the Bosnian Serbs, all pretence of impartiality now abandoned." Laura Silber and Allan Little, *Yugoslavia: The Death of a Nation* (London: Penguin Books, 1997), 351.

37. On August 29, 1995, one day after the deadly mortar attack, UN Secretary-General Boutros-Ghali stated the following: "The United Nations, after establishing that the deadly attack on the centre of Sarajevo on Monday came from Bosnian Serb positions, yesterday authorized NATO to conduct air strikes against Bosnian Serb military targets. The objective of this action is to deter further attacks on Sarajevo and other UN-designated safe areas in fulfillment of Security Council Resolution 836." See Leurdijk, *The United Nations and NATO*, 79.

38. Although the Security Council imposed economic sanctions on the Federal Republic of Yugoslavia (FRY, constituted by Serbia and Montenegro) in May 1992 (SC Resolution 757) in order to pressure its government not to interfere with internal Bosnian affairs, the Security Council later sharpened its economic sanctions with the intention of getting the FRY to pressure the Bosnian Serbs to be more cooperative during the diplomatic negotiations.

39. From the very beginning of the Yugoslav conflict, the Security Council decided (SC Resolution 713 of September 25, 1991) that all states should immediately implement a general and complete embargo on all deliveries of weapons and military equipment to Yugoslavia, in order to establish peace and stability in the region.

40. The purpose of this ban on military flights in the airspace of Bosnia and Herzegovina (SC Resolutions 781 of October 9, 1992, and 786 of November 10, 1992) was to contribute to the safety of humanitarian assistance on the ground.

41. In the 1992–1995 period the UN and the EU developed a number of peace initiatives within the permanent framework of the "International Conference on the Former Yugoslavia." In 1994 the so-called Contact Group (constituted by the United States, Russia, Great Britain, and France) would take over the lead in the diplomatic process.

II

JUS IN BELLO

A Historical Overview of the *Jus in Bello* Constraints

Guy Van Damme

In Western culture the *in bello* constraints can be traced back to antiquity. Greek warfare (especially in the period of 700 to 450 B.C.E.) was, most of the time at least, conducted according to a number of unwritten conventions.[1] Prisoners of war were not to be killed, but were to be offered for ransom. The pursuit of defeated and retreating enemy was to be limited in duration. Sacred truces, especially those declared for the celebration of the Olympic games, were to be respected. It was also generally agreed that battles should be fought during usual (summer) campaigning season.

Plato was very specific in his prescriptions about what was permitted and what was not. For instance, among the Greeks it should be forbidden to destroy houses or ravage land. Such actions, Plato argued, would only affect the population that had nothing to do with the war. The idea "not to touch those who were not to blame for the conflict," together with the claim that it is absolutely forbidden to consider all the population as the enemy, clearly shows Plato's concern for the noncombatant status of people.[2]

These and other constraints, however, did not have a universal character. Plato's prescriptions only applied to intra-Greek warfare. In this respect Plato distinguishes between a "discord," which is a dispute at home among Greek-brothers, and "war," which is a fight with a foreign enemy.[3] The need to respect a number of rules in a civil strife—such as not to bring fellow Greeks into slavery or to destroy their cities—is obvious to Plato. After the dispute is over, the Greek adversaries will need to continue living alongside each other. They must, therefore, avoid performing those actions that will make reconciliation impossible.[4] As for the barbarians (non-Greeks), they had to be destroyed or enslaved, so there was absolutely no need to be particular about what was, and what was not, permitted in battle. Plato expressed his regret that the Greeks, in waging war against each other, were not behaving according to these rules and was hoping that they would wage war "with barbarians as the Hellenes now deal with one another."[5]

In "De Officiis," Cicero (106 B.C.E.–43 B.C.E.) notes that even in time of war there exist certain duties toward the enemy. One must ensure, for instance, "the protection of those that lay down their arms and throw themselves at the mercy of our generals."[6] Furthermore, one should also distinguish between the guilty and the innocent, and "spare those enemies who were not cruel or barbarous in warfare."[7] In formulating his *in bello* considerations, Cicero was led by the principle of "humanitas," which meant for this Stoic philosopher that all people (and not just those of the own cultural community) were to be considered subject to the principles of natural law and justice. Although Cicero's moral universalism stood in sharp contrast with Greek moral particularism (*in bello* constraints were only to be applied in intra-Greek wars), in practice, military conduct in Roman war had the reputation of being unrestrained.[8]

In Roman society, war, and more specifically the resort to war, was highly formalized. In order to initiate a war justly, a number of legal-religious precepts had to be respected. An example of such a rule was the "repetitio rerum." Before starting the war the offending party had to be offered the possibility of making the necessary reparations in order to avoid war. If there were no reaction within thirty-three days, the "fetiales" or fetial priests would issue the formal declaration of war upon authorization by the Senate and the people.[9] However, once the war had obtained the legal-religious fiat, the actual conduct was no longer submitted to legal or other limitations. On the contrary, as Frederick Russell remarks, the very idea that one was conducting a legally correct war often led to the conviction that it was no longer necessary to respect the rights of the enemy.[10] Reminiscent of this cruelty in Roman military conduct was the way in which medieval theorists spoke about the "bellum Romanum," meaning a category of warfare in which there were no limits and no restraints.

In the early Middle Ages even the Church failed to restrain warfare. In Europe, in fighting among Christians, the distinction between combatant and noncombatant was often ignored. By the end of the eleventh century, some systematic attempts were made to extend noncombatant immunities to the clergy, women, children, and the poor.[11] Unfortunately, these immunities were regularly violated on the battlefield. At about the same time, changes such as the development of heavy armored cavalry led to social, economic, and military changes. A new social order emerged that featured a sharp division between the armed nobles, who were the true soldiers of the day, and the unarmed common people. As Robert Stacy[12] reports, soldiering was considered to be a Christian profession, not a public service. A soldier fought as an individual, not as a salaried servant in the public interest.

Fighting was a noble art for the knights, but was not authorized for other groups of the society. Malham Wakin gives a good example of this point when he retells "the story of those peasants of southern Germany who fought for their emperor in 1078 against knights of the feudal armies, who, upon defeating the peasants, castrated them for daring to bear arms."[13]

Social factors continued to play a prominent role in later centuries in forging rules of combat. Ties of class and family relationships created some obligations and restraints for the upper classes. Thus, during the war against Saxony in 1756, the Prussians had cut off the supplies of the Saxons, but the king of Saxony, who was in the military camp in Pirna, did not suffer because his Prussian relative decided that everything that was destined for the royal table could pass freely. In this example, class and family relationships restrained all-out war. The Principle of Proportionality, one of the two *jus in bello* principles, resulted in part from the same sensibility. One of its purposes is to minimize the consequences of the war on both sides of the battlefield, including the consequences for combatants.

Up to the nineteenth century the "laws" of war remained largely a matter of unwritten tradition. The promulgation in 1863 of the so-called Lieber Code for the U.S. armies was something new in this respect.[14] This code is comprised of 159 articles covering such topics as punishment for crimes against the inhabitants of hostile countries and prisoners of war. Soon after, in 1868, the Imperial Cabinet of Russia initiated an agreement titled "Renouncing the Use, in Time of War, of Explosive Projectiles Under 400 Grammes Weight."[15] Other milestones in the codification of the laws of war (International Humanitarian Law) were the Fourth Hague Convention of 1907[16] and the Geneva Conventions of 1929 and 1949.[17] This body of international law is based on the *jus in bello* Principles of Proportionality and Discrimination. The Red Cross activities have, since its creation in 1864, likewise been oriented toward a respect for those two principles by warring parties.[18]

The concept of *jus in bello* is much older than modern International Humanitarian Law. In the present volume, we are not using this concept—or the complementary concept of *jus ad bellum*—with the same meaning as the one given by lawyers. When using these two concepts, both philosophers and lawyers refer to the protection of fundamental human rights during armed conflicts and more precisely to the humanitarian protection of civilians and civilian objects during such conflicts. Both Just War Theory and International Humanitarian Law are working from the ethical perspective to defend the interests of humankind. But philosophers and lawyers are also working from this universalistic perspective with a different disciplinary approach and with distinct types of argumentation. This is for instance the case when they speak about "proportionality" and "discrimination," or even when using such terms as "military necessity" or "noncombatants." When using these concepts in the analysis of specific case studies, the authors of the following chapters on the two *jus in bello* principles will thus give them a specifically philosphical meaning, which is closely related to but still distinct from the one which derives from the use of a legal discourse.

NOTES

1. Josiah Ober, "Classical Greek Times," in *The Laws of War: Constraints on Warfare in the Western World,* ed. Michael Howard, George J. Andreopoulos, and Mark R. Shulman (New Haven, Conn.: Yale University Press, 1994), 13.

2. Paul Christopher, *The Ethics of War and Peace: An Introduction to Legal and Moral Issues,* 2nd ed. (Upper Saddle River, N.J.: Prentice Hall, 1999), 10.

3. Plato, *The Republic of Plato,* trans. Francis MacDonald Cornford (London, Oxford and New York: Oxford University Press, 1975), bk. 5, 469–70.

4. Barrie Paskins and Michael Dockrill, *The Ethics of War* (Minneapolis: University of Minnesota Press, 1979), 196.

5. Plato, *The Republic of Plato,* bk. 5, 470–71.

6. Cicero, *De Officiis,* bk. 1, 11, quoted in Christopher, *The Ethics of War and Peace,* 15.

7. Cicero, quoted in Bernard T. Adeney, *Just War, Political Realism, and Faith* (Metuchen, N.Y.: Scarecrow Press, 1988), 26.

8. Robert C. Stacy, "The Age of Chivalry," in *The Laws of War,* 27–28.

9. Frederick H. Russell, *The Just War in the Middle Ages* (Cambridge: Cambridge University Press, 1977), 6.

10. Russell, *The Just War in the Middle Ages,* 7.

11. See Keen, Maurice Hugh, *The Laws of War in the Late Middle Ages* (London: Routledge and K. Paul, 1965).

12. Stacy, "The Age of Chivalry," 27–28.

13. Malham M. Wakin, "The Ethics of Leadership I" in *War, Morality, and the Military Profession,* ed. Malham Wakin, 2nd ed. (Boulder, Colo., and London: Westview Press, 1986), 184–5.

14. Francis Lieber, General Orders No. 100 (Instructions for the Government of Armies in the Field) (New York: D. Van Nostrand, 1863). Reprinted in *The Law of War: A Documentary History,* ed. Leon Friedman, 2 vols. (New York: Random House, 1972), 1:158–86.

15. Sidney Axinn, *A Moral Military* (Philadelphia: Temple University Press, 1989), 65.

16. A. Pearce Higgins, *The Hague Peace Conferences and Other Conferences Concerning the Laws and Usages of War: Texts of Conventions with Commentaries* (Cambridge: Cambridge University Press, 1909).

17. *The Geneva Conventions of 12 August 1949,* ed. Jean Pictet, 4 vols. (Geneva: International Committee of the Red Cross, 1952–1960).

18. Christopher, *The Ethics of War and Peace,* 104.

7

Proportionality

Guy Van Damme and Nick Fotion

UNDERLYING ASSUMPTIONS

This chapter returns to the topic of proportionality. The Principle of Proportionality was earlier discussed as one of the criteria that must be met if a state or nonstate group is to resort justifiably to the use of military force. There it was noted that the principle, as a standard of *jus ad bellum*, requires that the anticipated moral cost of fighting the war should not be out of line with the moral benefits. Now it will be applied to actions taken in prosecuting the war, as a *jus in bello* principle. Although the philosophical conception of proportionality, as a principle, has not changed, the environment of its application has.

In the context of *jus in bello*, the term proportionality refers to the total calculus of the balance of goods and evils associated with a particular operation or action in the course of a war. At this point, a clear statement of the principle is needed in order to avoid confusion. Both the principle and theory contain three assumptions.

1. Only consequences count in determining whether an action or kind of action is in accordance with the principle.
2. Among the consequences only *welfare* consequences count. For our purposes, this means that actions affecting directly or indirectly the lives of humans count in the moral calculus. Insofar as humans give them meaning, inanimate objects such as religious buildings and historical sites are also included in this calculus.
3. It is possible to measure welfare consequences.

Together, these assumptions make it possible for actors on the military stage to act reasonably. Roughly speaking, the first two tell these actors, mostly commanders, of course, what to look for in making moral judgments and taking military decisions with a moral meaning. The third assumption reassures these actors that it is possible to make overall assessments so that judgments can be made as to whether one action causes more harm (or benefit) than another.

THE CONDUCT OF WAR

What the Principle of Proportionality itself adds to these three assumptions is a formula that tells those who must make decisions how to make them. One version of the formula is as follows: maximize good and minimize evil. Applied to war, another version says that the destructive effects of an act of war must not be out of proportion to the object sought. The issue is one of weighing the evil of an act of war against the good results to be gained by that same act. According to this guideline, each act, each particular campaign, each specific event of a war must adhere to the Principle of Proportionality. John Rawls makes this same point somewhat differently. He says that: "The means employed must not destroy the possibility of peace or encourage a contempt for human life that puts the safety of ourselves and of mankind in jeopardy."[1] Levels of violence unnecessary to win a war make achieving a lasting peace much more difficult and thus are morally proscribed.

But none of these formulations is detailed enough to explain the Principle of Proportionality fully. For instance, none of them gives guidance to those who make decisions as to how wide ranging the measures of right and wrong are supposed to be. Consider the bombing of Dresden in World War II.[2] Measurements of proportionality that focus on the raids themselves and their immediate consequences to those in and near the bomb area would label these raids disproportional. Viewed narrowly (i.e., viewed tactically), the bombing of Dresden accomplished little militarily, and yet did much harm to many people who had little or nothing to do with the German war effort. The raids may have killed between 35,000 and 135,000 people.[3] A good number were refugees fleeing the advance of the Red Army. Tactically, then, the bombings were immoral. This judgment can be made quite apart from whether these bombings violated the Principle of Discrimination, which says that civilians and certain civilian buildings cannot be directly targeted (see the introduction to this book and the chapter on discrimination).

But, during the war, some argued that the bombing of German cities should be viewed more broadly (i.e., strategically) so as to take account of all its consequences. This means that a military action viewed narrowly (tactically) could fail the proportionality test but yet, viewed more broadly, it could pass the test. Those who defend this broader view could then claim that, in the end, the raids are morally legitimate. This claim presupposes that the Principle of Discrimination can be legitimately overridden by the Principle of Proportionality in certain situations. However, as it turns out, the Dresden raids failed the strategic test as well. These bombings happened so late in the war (on the night of February 13–14, 1945, and during the day of the 14th) that they could not have accomplished much of anything of strategic significance. The raids, then, were immoral through and through.

Still, the principle seems to be telling us that any and all consequences should be taken into account. So in assessing whether a particular military operation is moral or not, one must include in the calculus not only its immediate anticipated consequences but also the anticipated consequences of how this operation might justly help end a war more quickly.

Another example can be cited. We can stipulate that Germany was fighting an unjust war in World War II according the *jus ad bellum* criteria. The conquest of the Low Countries,[4] nonetheless, considered on the level of military operations, generally respected the Principle of Proportionality. Although the Germans were probably respecting the principle of economy of force as much as the constraint of proportionality, their actions were proportionate to the tactical objectives sought. In general, their military invasion aimed at the destruction of those military forces that inhibited the movement of the German tank divisions. Unnecessary killing, suffering, and damage were not excessive for either side. Tactically, individual units behaved in accordance with the principle. The same can be said about these attacks viewed strategically. The individual tank units contributed to the overall "blitzkrieg" strategy that enabled the Germans to defeat France in a matter of weeks in the summer of 1940. So most individual battles in that campaign (on the tactical level), and the campaign as a whole (the strategic level), satisfy the Principle of Proportionality.

A more recent example shows how employing the Principle of Proportionality tactically can, once again, lead to one conclusion, while employing it strategically can lead to another. During the conflict between Argentina and Britain in the Falklands, the *General Belgrano*, a cruiser of the Argentina Navy, was attacked and sunk by the British submarine *HMS Conqueror*.[5] The sinking cost the lives of 368 Argentine seamen. To many, this loss of life seemed out of proportion to the threat posed by the cruiser since at the time it was not being employed against the British fleet that was attempting to recapture the Falkland Islands. A "balanced" judgment (that takes the interests of all sides into account) seemed to indicate that the British had violated the moral constraints of *jus in bello* in conducting their attack on the Argentine ship that was so far from the point of conflict.

Tactically, then, the sinking could be thought of as a moral disaster. No tactical advantage accrued from the sinking. But from the larger strategic perspective it is a different story. The British argued that the loss of one of their carriers or of one of their troopships to the cruiser would have been fatal for their whole operation.[6] Thus, when they ordered the sinking of the *Belgrano*, the British commanders had to consider the deployment of Argentine warships to be a significant threat. That threat made it justifiable for the British Navy to attack the Argentine ships and aircraft before the amphibious landing force was committed. The *General Belgrano* itself posed a particularly lethal threat because it outgunned every British ship in the area and its armor made it resistant to aerial attack. All Argentine warships were given orders to initiate offensive operations in response to an anticipated British landing. The British knew of these instructions. While the *General Belgrano* had turned away from the islands temporarily in order to reduce the risk of falling victim to submarine attack, it remained a legitimate military target. The captain of the *Belgrano*, who declared later that though he was heading his ship toward the mainland, he was doing so in order to get into a position to await further orders, confirmed this judgment.

In these straitened circumstances, the British could not afford to wait to be attacked because that could have made the difference between ultimate victory and defeat. When viewed in a larger perspective, then, the destruction of the *General Belgrano*, terrible though the consequences were, does not appear to be a violation of the Principle of Proportionality. So the first problem one faces in understanding the Principle of Proportionality is dealt with by favoring a more holistic approach in measuring consequences over a more particularistic one. The principle favors the "big picture" approach rather than one that views the battle scene narrowly.

The second problem is more difficult. It has to do with *who* belongs in the moral calculus. If, as the principle suggests, welfare consequences are to be measured, with whose welfare is the commander supposed to be concerned? Is the measurement bilateral or unilateral? With the latter, commanders and soldiers need to be concerned only with their own people's welfare; with the former, they need to be concerned with everyone's.

The insistence that the costs to the enemy should form part of the moral assessment of military action seems counterintuitive to many military decision-makers. As a result, the issue of bilateral judgments measuring the benefits and costs on both sides apparently remains only theoretical for ethical thinkers rather than one to be used by military commanders in the field to guide their decisions. For example, when NATO officials expressed anxiety about the human costs during the Kosovo War they were concerned mainly with the welfare of NATO pilots. That concern expressed itself in the instructions to pilots to fly at such high altitudes that Serb surface-to-air missiles (SAMs) could not easily reach them.[7] At the same time, these instructions meant that, from that height, civilian casualties on the ground inevitably would increase since the pilots could not always tell a military from a nonmilitary target.

The Gulf War (1991) is instructive here as well. When General Norman Schwartzkopf expressed anxiety about the human costs of war, it was clear to every observer that he had the welfare of his own military personnel mainly in mind. He saw the welfare of the Iraqi troops as the concern and responsibility of the Iraqi commanders. This attitude also predominated during the Vietnam War, the Korean War, and World War II. In all these wars, unilateral views on the proportionality of human costs dominated the thinking of the military commanders in the field.

Quite apart from the unilateral tendencies of many commanders (and soldiers in the field), what does the Principle of Proportionality say about this matter? Does it recommend unilateral or bilateral calculations? The answer is clear. The principle makes no provisions for counting only "our side" and thereby excluding the "other side" from the count. Of course, it does not forbid "our side" from shooting at the "other side" while fighting is taking place. But what it tells us is that insofar as *human* suffering is not a good thing, everyone involved in war should take account of the welfare of all who are affected by war.

The Proportionality Principle plays out in the 1991 Gulf War in another way. It was argued by some, in particular Robert McNamara (the former secretary of defense during the Vietnam War) that a war to retake Kuwait from Iraq would yield "thousands and thousands and thousands of casualties" and, of course, would yield even more on the Iraqi side.[8] Evidently, for him and others, deploying a large military force against the fourth-largest military force in the world could not help but do more harm than good. Especially since there were other ways of dealing with the Kuwait invasion, the option of war simply was not worth the price. According to this argument, war in the Gulf would definitely violate the Principle of Proportionality— especially the *ad bellum* version of that principle.

But McNamara's calculations did not carry the day. Others, mostly the military planners themselves, countered that war had changed since Vietnam. They focused attention on how individual battles in a war would go and thus shifted the discussion to the *in bello* version of the Proportionality Principle. New technologies, they said, made it possible that those who possessed these technologies could quickly and cleanly overwhelm those who did not have them. The new war would not be one of attrition. It would not be fought in the jungle with 1970s technologies but fought, instead, in the open desert with 1990s technologies such as smart bombs and missiles, sophisticated sensors, satellites, and computers.

To drive home their point, these planners made a distinction between deploying an overwhelming force and causing unnecessary harm. The former is a causal and the latter an effect (or result) concept. The claim made about an overwhelming deployment is that sometimes it causes unnecessary harm; but at other times it does not. In fact, when an overwhelming high-tech force is properly deployed it can cause less harm than can a smaller force. The claim, then, of those who championed the war to take Kuwait away from the Iraqis was that their version of mounting overwhelming attacks would cause fewer casualties and so would thus be fully in accord with the Principle of Proportionality both on a battle-for battle basis (*in bello*) and an overall war basis (*ad bellum*). As it turned out, these claims were closer to the mark than the claims of McNamara and his supporters.

NUCLEAR ARMS

To most moral theorists, the use of nuclear arms on a large scale is seen as violating the Principle of Proportionality—as well as the Principle of Discrimination. No doubt, the use of these weapons on a large scale would destroy an overwhelming number of "targets" immediately, including people, structures, and artifacts that have no military value. Further, radioactive fallout would have effects on the environment so that present and future generations would suffer lethal consequences for many years to come. The weighing of goods versus evils associated with a massive nuclear strike would seem to lead inescapably to the conclusion that nuclear war would violate the Principle of Proportionality.

However, some argue that the limited use of these weapons could theoretically satisfy proportionality if it did not lead to escalation. In this connection, one may consider the World War II nuclear bombings on the Japanese cities of Hiroshima and Nagasaki.[9] The arguments are well known. At that time, Japan was preparing a desperate defense of their main islands. In response, American officials made the following set of calculations. In the battle of Okinawa in June 1945, U.S. forces suffered almost 40,000 casualties, including over 12,000 dead. Japanese casualties were about 120,000, 110,000 dead among them.[10] It was feared that millions of men and women would be killed in the process of landing on and fighting for the main Japanese islands. In dropping the bombs on two cities, it was estimated that 80,000 to 150,000 Japanese (mostly civilians) would be killed. According to this calculation, there would be fewer people killed by a nuclear attack than by a conventional war that would drag on for several months or even a year. Thus, some see dropping nuclear bombs on Hiroshima and Nagasaki as satisfying the Principle of Proportionality.

Thus, those who took the decision to drop nuclear bombs on Hiroshima and Nagasaki were confronted with the choice doing something that could be thought of as definitely wrong (i.e., deliberately killing civilians) or do ing something else (i.e., invading the country with ground troops) where, quantitatively, the wrong would likely be greater many times over. The American government was convinced that the former option made more sense. They thought that the Principle of Proportionality could justifiably override the Principle of Discrimination. Winston Churchill expressed it as follows: "To avert a vast, indefinite butchery . . . at the cost of a few explosions, seemed, after all our toils and perils, a miracle of deliverance."[11]

The moral legitimacy of this decision has been challenged by many. According to one critical line of thought, the Principle of Discrimination cannot be overridden by the Principle of Proportionality. According to another criticism, the Allies were wrong to make a public ultimatum to the Japanese that included conditions that were unacceptable to them—such as unconditional surrender and the loss of their Emperor.[12] In their view, the Japanese War Cabinet might have accepted a negotiated surrender. It is also said that other ways to end the war could have been tried. The American government could, for instance, have informed the Japanese of the bomb, delivered proof of its terrible destructive power (by dropping a bomb in Tokyo Bay) and, then, offered them a negotiated peace. These options would have been worth trying, even if they did not guarantee an end to the war.

To be sure, ethical thinking concerning warfare has changed profoundly since 1945. The 1949 Geneva Conventions have done much to enhance the respect of the Principle of Discrimination on the battlefield. Furthermore, the use of nuclear weapons is assessed today far more critically than it was in 1945. Much more is known today than at the time about the devastating long-term effects of these weapons.[13] Proliferation has also put an end to a situation where it was possible to use nuclear weapons without having to fear a retaliatory response and total nuclear war. Today, the risk of escalation excludes the possibility of using nuclear weapons under the aegis of the Principle of Proportionality. Thus for an author such as Michael Walzer, "nuclear war is and will remain morally unacceptable, and there is no case for its rehabilitation. Because it is unacceptable, we must seek out ways to prevent it, and because deterrence is a bad way, we must seek out others."[14]

BIOLOGICAL ARMS

Biological arms can be defined as weapons charged with microorganisms such as bacteria, viruses, rickettsia, or fungi.[15] These weapons have been in use for centuries. The best-known early example of such use is during the siege of Caffa in 1346.[16] Caffa[17] (a Genoese seaport) was besieged the year before by the Mongols. But in 1346 a strange deliverance arrived: "The Black Death" struck the Mongol besieging army. "The Black Death" is a disease transmitted to humans via fleabites from rodents.[18] The Mongols were dying by the thousands and, as a result, lost interest in the siege. Neverthe-less, they used catapults to drop many of their plague cadavers into the city. The inhabitants of Caffa could not rid themselves of all the corpses (by dropping them into the sea) and so, soon, the rotting corpses tainted the air and poisoned the water supply. Many inhabitants died. However, a few sur-vivors escaped and, in escaping, contributed to the westward spread of the plague. Constantinople was hit in spring 1347; Messina in October 1347; and Genoa, Venice, and Marseille in January 1348.[19] It was estimated that the population of Europe was reduced by 25 percent within five years.

There are many more examples of biological warfare in history, but this one gives a very clear idea of the main characteristics of this form of war-fare. The biological agents reproduce themselves in the host and, after an in-cubation period, the effects show up. In the meantime, these agents are passed on to others who themselves go through an incubation period and, in turn, contract the disease. Then, once more, the process repeats itself in what is often an uncontrollable fashion.

When we look at what happened in Caffa in terms of the Principle of Pro-portionality, it becomes clear that the uncontrollable and long-term effects of the use of biological arms counts as an overwhelming negative. As a re-sult, these weapons exclude almost any calculation required by this princi-ple. It is also clear that, in the light of the technical capacities of the twenty-first century that make it possible to produce even deadlier biological weapons, weighing the evil of the use of biological arms against the good results gained is not even an option. That is, there is no realistic way that the use of these weapons can satisfy the Principle of Proportionality.

This conclusion is reflected in the steps that the world community has taken to control the use of such weapons. The 1972 Biological Weapons Convention, as an example, prohibits the development, production, stock-piling, and the acquisition of biological weapons.[20] The states that have rat-ified this convention have done so not only because these weapons are seen as violating the Principle of Proportionality but also because they violate the Principle of Discrimination (see chapter 8 on this principle).

Prohibited or not, research with biological weapons has been extensive during the last century. The Japanese conducted research with these weapons earlier in the century. From 1932 till 1945 they built so-called fac-tories of death, most of them in the Chinese province of northern Manchuria. These "factories" made extensive research possible. Not only did thousands of Chinese die from these experiments,[21] even more died from biological agents left behind by the fleeing Japanese troops at the end of the war.[22] Early in the Cold War the United States did research and then conducted tests on some of its own citizens—without their consent.[23] In 1979 it be-come clear that the Soviets had a large program of biological weapons re-search. In that year, a large area around the Urals city of Sverdlovsk was affected by an outbreak of anthrax. The most frightening aspect of the outbreak was that sixty-six people died in a lightly populated area due to the release of less than one gram of anthrax.[24] Since World War II there have been only a few attempts to use these weapons in war. One example occurred during the Vietnam War. Vietnamese forces used bacteriological arms, not against U.S. forces, but against the Hmong tribesman who were, no doubt, in no position to retaliate in any significant way.[25]

THE PRINCIPLE OF DOUBLE EFFECT

In closing this chapter, special mention should be made of what is known as the Principle (or Doctrine) of Double Effect (PDE). Strictly speaking, this principle is not a part of Just War Theory. That is, it is not normally listed as a principle of that theory in the way the Principle of Proportionality and Discrimination are. However, all versions of the principle employ these two principles.[26] Not only that, some who are concerned about the ethics of war prefer to appeal to the PDE since, as we will see, it makes clear which of the two *in bello* principles overrides the other.

The PDE gets its start from the realization that actions often have more than one effect or consequence. War, of course, is like that. Actions performed by a military can lead to the death of enemy soldiers, but also to the death of bystanders, the destruction of buildings such as schools and hospitals, and harm to the environment. Seen in this light the PDE could also be called the Principle of Multiple Effects.

The consequences of a double (or multiple)-effect action can be diagrammed as follows. In this diagram, the *rows* tell of the results of some action. The *columns* of the diagram give an assessment of these results in terms of good and bad. Thus, the cell marked G-I points to the effects of the successful destruction of a munitions factory. This destruction is *both* foreseen and intended by the attacker. The intention and the effects of this action are then evaluated as good (i.e., in accord with the Principle of Discrimination). In contrast, in cell B-I, the foreseen and intended destruction of a whole city is given as an example of an action where the main objective is to terrorize and/or kill much of the civilian population. The effects of this action are evaluated as bad. In cell B-U the effects on an action (e.g., the destruction of houses near the munitions factory) are foreseen but not intended. They represent what is usually labeled collateral damage.

The three claims that constitute the PDE are as follows:

1. Only intended actions that are expected to have good effects (G-I) are permitted. Intended military actions that are expected to yield bad results

Table 7.1. The Double Effect Diagram

EFFECTS OF BOMBING ARE:	GOOD (G)	BAD (B)
INTENDED (I)	e.g., the destruction of a munitions factory in a city G-I	e.g., the destruction of a whole city B-I
UNINTENDED (U)	e.g., the destruction of a munitions dump located near a munitions factory G-U	e.g., the destruction of houses near a munitions factory B-U

(B-I) are forbidden. We see here a direct application of the Discrimination Principle.

2. The intended good effects (G-I) of the military actions should be expected to be greater than the expected, but not intended, bad effects (B-U). Unless G-I is greater than B-U (G-I > B-U), the action is not permitted. We see here a direct application of the Proportionality Principle.

3. The action is not permitted if something else could be done that would have a better ratio of benefits to harm. If, for instance, the munitions factory could be destroyed by a special operations unit, so that there would be little or no collateral damage, then the bombing raid should be cancelled.

It is interesting to see how the Principle of Double Effect speaks to the question of the nuclear bombings in World War II discussed above. On the most obvious interpretation of the principle, claim #1 condemns the bombings straight away. These bombings were indiscriminate and exhibited evil intentions (B-I) rather than good ones (G-I) since the intention of the bomber included the destruction of thousands of civilians. On this interpretation, that ends the discussion. If the bombings were allowable ethically under the PDE, they would have to pass the test of all of that principle's three claims. But such bombings already fail in not satisfying the demands of claim #1.

One might wonder what the PDE would say if the bombers had aimed their nuclear weapons at military targets (counterforce attacks) rather than civilian ones?[27] However, given the power of the bombs, it would be well-nigh impossible to avoid very extensive collateral damage. Expressed in terms of our diagram, the unintended bad effects of the bombing would more than likely have been greater than the intended good effects (B-U>G-I). So now the bombings would be condemned because they violated claim #2 of PDE. In addition, many argued that the bombings also violated claim #3 since the Americans had options available to them other than dropping the nuclear bombs. In sum, PDE could, and did, speak critically about the use of nuclear weapons in 1945.

CONCLUSION

The conception of the Principle of Proportionality as a *jus in bello* criterion is not difficult to understand, but it is a very difficult to employ in concrete situations. In large part this difficulty is because of the uncertainty inherent in war. More often than not, rational calculations are extremely difficult to make. There are, however, times when the principle has application as an instrument for restraining the horrible effects of war. When it is applied properly, it encourages those who make battlefield decisions to consider the costs and benefits impartially and broadly. When it calls for impartiality, the principle tells us not to forget the sufferings of those "on the other side." When it calls for a broad interpretation, it tells us not to make the mistake of looking only for the immediate consequences of our actions. Proportionality in *jus in bello* is a wide-ranging principle that tells us to consider, as best we can, *all* the consequences of our actions as they affect *everyone* who is affected by our actions.

NOTES

1. John Rawls, *A Theory of Justice* (Cambridge, Mass.: The Belknap Press of Harvard University Press, 1971), 379.

2. *The New Encyclopaedia Britannica*, ed. Jacob E. Safra, 15th ed. (Chicago: Encyclopaedia Britannica Inc., 1997), 8:221.

3. *The New Encyclopaedia Britannica*, 221.

4. Richard Holmes, *Army Battlefield Guide Belgium and Northern France* (London: HMSO, 1995), 183–204.

5. Anthony J. Coates, *The Ethics of War* (Manchester: Manchester University Press, 1997), 209–14.

6. M. Hastings and S. Jenkings, *The Battle of the Falklands* (London: Michael Joseph Limited, 1983), 148.

7. Michael Ignatieff, *Virtual War* (London: Chatto and Windus, 2000), 63.

8. *Frontline*, "The Gulf War," a video presentation of WGBH, Boston. First presented on television in the United States on January 9, 1996. McNamara made his casualty estimates before Congress.

9. Winston Churchill, *The Second World War* (London: Cassell, 1949), 557.

10. David Smurthwaite, *The Pacific War Atlas: 1941–1945* (New York: Mirabel Books Ltd., 1955), 130; *The Oxford Companion to World War II*, ed. I. C. B. Dear (Oxford: Oxford University Press, 1995), 836.

11. Michael Walzer, *Just and Unjust Wars* (New York: Basic Books, 1977), 267.

12. See Jonathan Glover, *Humanity. A Moral History of the Twentieth Century* (London: Pimlico, 2001), 93–112.

13. This is also true for nuclear testing. According to an analysis of unreleased government data in the United States, nuclear testing between 1951 and 1962 could cause cancer in an estimated 80,000 Americans. *Financial Times*, March 1, 2002.

14. Walzer, *Just and Unjust Wars*, 283.

15. Erhard Geissler and John Ellis van Courtland Moon, *Biological and Toxin Weapons: Research, Development and Use from the Middle Ages to 1945* (Oxford: Oxford University Press, 1999), 1.

16. Jeanne McDermott, *The Killing Winds, the Menace of Biological Warfare* (New York: Aberhouse, 1987), 21.

17. Now Feodosia, on the Crimean Coast.

18. Mark Wheels in Geissler and van Courtland Moon, *Biological and Toxin Weapons*, 13.

19. Geissler and van Courtland Moon, *Biological and Toxin Weapons*, 14.

20. Paul Christopher, *The Ethics of War and Peace* (New Jersey: Prentice-Hall, 1999), 122.

21. Sheldon H. Harris, *Factories of Death* (London and New York: Routledge, 1995), 51.

22. Harris, *Factories of Death*, 67.

23. McDermott, *The Killing Winds*, 170–88.

24. McDermott, *The Killing Winds*, 36–60.

25. *The New Encyclopaedia Britannica*, 90.

26. For a somewhat different rendering of the principle, see Michael Walzer's *Just and Unjust Wars*, 152–59.

27. See previous chapter for an account of the distinction between counterforce and countervalue attacks. In that chapter see section Nuclear Weapons.

8

Discrimination

Anthony Hartle

Once a state has decided *whether* to fight a war, its leadership and the members of its military will have to make decisions concerning *how* to fight. Within that category of *jus in bello*, one of the most troubling issues in modern war centers on the targets of military weapons and the use of certain weapons that have the potential for indiscriminate effects. Traditional guidance on this topic has commonly been referred to as the Principle of Discrimination. In the broadest sense, the principle maintains that warring parties have an obligation to discriminate between appropriate and inappropriate targets of destruction, a distinction based on the nature of the targets themselves. Historically, most parties to wars have agreed that the destruction of life and property beyond the category of combatants is an evil to be minimized. Accordingly, the lives and property of noncombatants and certain categories of civilian objects should not be the targets of military violence. In the twentieth century, application of the Principle of Discrimination focused on the subordinate but foundational principle of noncombatant immunity. Later in this discussion we will consider the role that constraints on targets play in the terrorist activity and unconventional warfare that mark the opening decade of the twenty-first century.

NONCOMBATANT IMMUNITY

Despite the public agreement concerning the practical and moral importance of protecting civilians during war, noncombatant casualties were a painful feature of every conflict in the twentieth century, a feature that we are certain to observe in the decades to come as well. Minimizing such casualties, a form of "collateral damage" in the euphemistic terminology of high-technology warfare, is the object of the principle of noncombatant immunity. While just war theorists agree that the basis for making the combatant-noncombatant distinction clearly remains a contentious issue,[1] all accept that combatants have a responsibility to minimize "noncombatant casualties." As weapons technology has become increasingly sophisticated, allowing a revolutionary change in the conception of the battlefield, adherence to the responsibility not to injure noncombatants has become increasingly problematic. Sophistication in weaponry, while it has rendered some weapons much more accurate, has extended the battlefield far beyond the horizon and has greatly increased destructive power.

Exercising the responsibility to minimize injury obviously requires that soldiers recognize who qualifies as a noncombatant. The practical rule that enemies in uniform are combatants and subject to attack at any time is a place to start but fails to take us far. Under existing treaties and conventions, soldiers who are wounded and *hors de combat* cannot be targeted; they become noncombatants. Members of the military who are prisoners are no longer combatants, no longer a threat, and thus not subject to attack, whether or not we conclude that they should be technically categorized as noncombatants. That question arises because the Geneva Conventions of 1949 have established elaborate rules for the treatment of sick and wounded members of the armed forces and of those categorized as prisoners of war.

As a practical matter, however, many wars over the last century have involved combatants who do not wear uniforms or any distinctive insignia. Guerrillas, or insurgents using guerrilla tactics, can be farmers by day and assault troops by night. Applying the Principle of Discrimination, while also fighting effectively against irregular forces, poses both practical and moral difficulties.[2] Along with the armies of many nations, United Nations contingents remain firmly bound by the practical and moral necessity of minimizing noncombatant casualties. The practical aspect arises because of UN sensitivity to criticism of mission performance on moral grounds. The moral aspect becomes especially prominent because the protection of human rights remains one of the most common justifications for initiating the use of force under UN auspices. Guerrillas tend to take full tactical advantage of the constraints such considerations impose. They do not wear uniforms and attempt to blend in with the civilian population, using that cover to make them more difficult targets and achieve military advantage.

The challenge to the Principle of Discrimination in irregular warfare thus emerges from the strong tension between effectiveness in military terms and success in political and moral terms. Guerrilla forces and insurgent movements almost always rely on some degree of support from the population of the country whose fate is in question. Insurgents sometimes must make a policy choice between coercing cooperation and developing the willing cooperation of the people of the country. The Principle of Discrimination requires that noncombatant status be respected, outlawing any direct coercion and the use of violence against those not in uniform. One of the most effective means of generating willing cooperation is to demonstrate that the interests of the citizenry are the interests of the unconventional forces. Being scrupulous about not targeting civilians and their property is one of the most effective ways to build such support. If insurgents plan to seize and wield political power with the endorsement of the population, building public support would appear to be their most viable long-term strategy.

In contrast, the choice for counterinsurgency (COIN) forces may be more problematic if the insurgents are fully committed to their cause. If they are so committed, the insurgents may decide that the justice of their goals in turn justifies placing noncombatants at risk by using them as shields, in effect. The risk of such noncombatant injury may restrain the COIN effort. If the COIN forces do react when the unconventional fighters have positioned themselves so that action against them will cause civilian casualties, civilian casualties may turn the population against the government forces. With the justice of their cause in mind, the insurgents may then seek circumstances that will generate civilian casualties. The insurgents clearly have the advantage in such a situation. If the COIN forces reject all actions that would injure noncombatants, the insurgents have a distinct tactical advantage. If the COIN forces inflict noncombatant casualties, the insurgents have a distinct political advantage.

In these circumstances, COIN forces must establish carefully crafted rules of engagement (ROE) for their soldiers. In the conflict in Kosovo, for example, U.S. ground forces operated under the guidance of the following ROE (in the year 2000). Each soldier received a small, pocket-sized ROE card bearing these instructions. The function of KFOR, a NATO-led international force that entered Kosovo on June 12, 1999, with a UN mandate, was to keep the peace and ensure the safety of all parties. Although they did not face organized guerrilla opposition, KFOR elements did have to contend with armed opposition from hostile groups that hid among the general population, much as guerrillas would. The rules provided a point of departure.

Box 8.1. Rules of Engagement

Self-Defense

1. Nothing in these rules prohibits you from exercising your inherent right to defend yourself, KFOR soldiers, and persons with designated special status.
2. Use the minimum force necessary when you use force.

(continued)

3. You may use deadly force to defend yourself, KFOR soldiers, and persons with designated special status from *immediate threat* of serious injury or death.
4. You do not need permission to act in self-defense.

Protection of Property

1. Use the minimum force necessary, which may include deadly force (Five S's), to protect classified documents and property, weapons, ammo, explosives, and property with designated special status. [The section below under "Minimum Force" explains the "Five S's".]
2. Use the minimum force necessary, BUT NOT deadly force, to protect all other KFOR property.

Mission Accomplishment

1. In accordance with command guidance, the senior leader present is authorized to direct the use of force, including deadly force (Five S's), to accomplish the mission.
2. REMEMBER, even in absence of command guidance or orders from the senior leader present, you may always use force to defend yourself, KFOR soldiers, and persons with designated special status from immediate threat of serious injury or death.

Serious Criminal Acts

You may use the minimum force necessary (Five S's), including deadly force, to stop and detain persons committing, or about to commit, in your presence, serious criminal acts upon other persons (murder, rape, serious assault).

Minimum Force

1. Evaluate the threat using Hand-SALUTE.[3] Identify what is in the person's hand, then apply the standard SALUTE factors.
2. Five S's. When possible, use the following degrees of force:
   a. SHOUT verbal warnings to halt! ("STANI")
   b. SHOW your weapons and demonstrate intent to use it.
   c. SHOVE. Use nonlethal physical force.
   d. SHOOT a WARNING shot after issuing a verbal challenge. In English: "NATO. STOP OR I WILL FIRE." In Serbo-Croat: "NATO! STANI EEL LEE PUTSAM!"
   e. SHOOT to eliminate the threat. Fire only aimed shots. Stop firing when the threat is gone.

Respect civilians and their property. Treat all people humanely and with dignity.

In counterinsurgency operations, the safety of noncombatants logically receives high priority. Governments or intervention forces seek to protect civilians and to ensure the support of the general populace. The safety of noncombatants or civilians thus requires the minimum use of force in most situations. The difficulty of identifying insurgent forces, even in situations in which the insurgents display identifying marks (e.g., colored armband, standard clothing item), makes the issue of discrimination a pervasive problem. The experience of recent decades suggests that most guerrilla operations will not include efforts to make participants readily identifiable. That experience requires the carefully targeted use of force by COIN forces. A set of rules of engagement similar to those followed by UN forces in Kosovo thus appears to be a reasonable candidate. Identifying members of the opposing force and thus being able to apply the Principle of Discrimination remains one of the great challenges for forces conducting operations against unconventional forces.

A subjective condition of moral or political innocence also fails as a standard that soldiers can apply to discriminate between combatants and noncombatants. In any reasonable analysis, a conscripted soldier who has determined not to fire a shot in anger would have to be considered morally innocent, even if his country is fighting a war that is unjust under the criteria of *jus ad bellum*. However valid such a distinction might be in theory, opposed combatants have no way of identifying such a person and ensuring that he is not a target. By the same token, a fervid civilian advocate of a clearly unjust war would not be considered morally or politically innocent by most, but as a civilian he is *prima facie* considered a noncombatant not subject to direct attack unless his actions change his categorization. Attitudes cannot be observed.

Alternative explanations of the combatant and noncombatant categories raise further questions. Jeffrie Murphy argues that we should make the combatant/noncombatant distinction by referring to a "chain of agency."[4] If you find yourself in the chain of agency that leads to the application of force by members of the military, then you are a combatant and are liable to be attacked. How do you know if you are in the chain of agency? You are in the chain if you are engaging in any activity that is logically inseparable from war fighting. Participating in any activity that would not take place if it were not for the requirements of warfare places an agent in the chain. Munitions work, for example, is logically inseparable from war fighting. If we did not have wars, we would not need munitions workers. Farming, however, is an activity that is logically separable from war fighting. Even in the absence of war, we still have people farming. Thus, the munitions worker is in the chain of agency; the farmer is not.[5] While this guidance proves useful at some level of decision-making, its application by combat units will leave a prodigious margin for error. Pilots dropping bombs will often find it difficult if not impossible to apply, and they will find it raises further questions as well—including that of how much risk to themselves they should accept in trying to discriminate between those in the chain of agency and those who are not.

Michael Walzer addresses the issue of risk in *Just and Unjust Wars*, claiming that combatants must accept additional risk to themselves to minimize noncombatant casualties. He uses a World War II example to illustrate his point.[6] Free French pilots bombed occupied France, killing French civilians as they attacked targets of value to the Germans. To justify the injury to the very people for whom they fought, the citizens of France, they flew lower and bombed more carefully in order to minimize the civilian casualties. They accepted greater risk in carrying out the bombing raids in order to spare their countrymen as much as possible. We see the actions of the pilots as morally appropriate under the Principle of Discrimination. Military necessity required the bombing. The Just War Tradition, from a humanitarian perspective, required minimizing civilian casualties from both sides. The French pilots also had sympathy for their own, of course. To accommodate the two requirements as much as possible, the pilots accepted greater risk to themselves. Walzer concludes that the pilots had a moral obligation to do so.

The air campaign in Serbia and Kosovo in 1999 illustrates how such accommodation can change. Michael Ignatieff notes that, while NATO pilots used expensive smart weapons and frequently refrained from dropping their bombs when they were unsure of the nature of the target, the NATO military command appeared to be unwilling to risk pilots' lives to the degree accepted by the Free French. NATO's decision not to allow pilots dropping ordnance to descend lower than 15,000 feet certainly minimized the chance that Serbian antiaircraft weapons would succeed in downing NATO's planes. But critics of the NATO effort contended that the chance of bombing noncombatants in error also increased (a claim that NATO's military leaders rejected in news conferences and after-action reports).

The appeal of high-tech warfare is that it saves lives. It presents a way to conduct a war that appears to be governed by two moral constraints: avoiding civilian casualties and avoiding risk to pilots. But the two constraints have turned out to be in direct contradiction. To target ethnic cleansing effectively, you have to fly low. Fly low, you lose pilots. Fly high, and you get civilians. By the second month of the bombing, NATO's priority had become clear: the lives of its professionals were more important than the lives of the innocent foreign civilians.[7]

In Iraq and Afghanistan, American air and artillery strikes have on many occasions caused civilian casualties when attacking what were thought to be insurgent targets. In situations in which the targets are fleeting, the choice is to risk civilian casualties or forgo the opportunity to attack the enemy. A though the authority to make such a decision may be constrained by pushing the level of authorization to higher levels in the chain of command, American policy has permitted such attacks for "high value" targets.

The Principle of Double Effect (PDE), discussed in the previous chapter, provides one of the frequently invoked means of analyzing situations in war involving civilian casualties. Applied to combat situations, the principle claims that unintended suffering of noncombatants is justified if the good effect of a proposed action is morally acceptable, the foreseeable bad effects are not intended or necessary for the good effect, and if the good effects outweigh the bad. Michael Walzer adds one more condition when he applies the principle to warfare, one that incorporates his view of the acceptable balance of risk to combatants compared to risk to noncombatants: "Aware of the evil involved, [the agent] seeks to minimize it, accepting costs to himself."[8]

Thus, in the Kosovo situation, strict application of Walzer's addition to the PDE would probably have required that pilots fly lower and accept greater risk to themselves (and perhaps to the NATO operation, given its political fragility). Without taking that extra step, foreseen but unintended civilian casualties could not be justified under a strict interpretation of *jus in bello* leavened by the PDE.

In addition to the problem of the issue of risk, the chain of agency approach does not provide guidance concerning policies like that of NATO in another area. NATO warplanes attacked oil refining, production, and storage facilities throughout Yugoslavia. Producing fuel is logically separable from war fighting—but it is also clearly necessary to it. When the NATO countries bombed Yugoslavia's industrial capacity, fuel production capability, and power generation capability, they did so primarily to cripple the nation's war machine. In the process, however, they were sometimes attacking targets populated solely by civilians and serving the population in general in addition to the military. As a result, they were attacking not just the military forces, but also the nation as a whole.

In similar fashion, how should attacks against civilian communications facilities be categorized? NATO planes also attacked a television station in Yugoslavia manned only by civilians, claiming that the station was a government organ of propaganda and misinformation that influenced the conduct of the both diplomatic and military activities. Murphy's chain of agency does not stretch far enough to justify those offensive operations, but those executing NATO war plans could claim that there was a link to Serb military activities and that military necessity called for the bombing. Murphy's chain of agency provides a narrower justification than the often-used rationale of military necessity.

With the end of the Cold War and the demise of the Soviet Union, the looming threat of nuclear weapons has subsided somewhat and taken on a different aspect. The proliferation of nuclear weapons firmly establishes such concerns as legitimate still. Along with nuclear weapons, antipersonnel mines now attract wide attention. Examination of these specific weapons systems reveals considerations applicable to any examination of weapons effects under the Principle of Discrimination. We can also identify the close relationship to the other aspect of discrimination, restrictions on targeting.

NUCLEAR WEAPONS

The Just War Tradition concerns limitations on the use of force, or in James T. Johnson's words, the "just war tradition . . . is a moral tradition of justifiable and limited war."[9] The limitations it imposes serve to reduce the likelihood of war and to mitigate the consequences once war begins.[10] As we emphasize in this book, the *jus ad bellum* criteria limit the conditions under which war can justifiably be initiated. Those provisions of just war, applied in conscientious pursuit of moral action, provide guidance that establishes identifiable boundaries for morally acceptable decisions in most cases. Once war begins, however, in addition to specific war conventions, our two mitigating principles constitute the guidance for actions: the Principle of Proportionality and the Principle of Discrimination. The Principle of Discrimination provides clear and specific guidance: combatants are never to target noncombatants directly. The Principle of Proportionality, while clearly stated, is more problematic in application: the level of force applied must be proportionate to the objectives to be achieved. Determining what "proportionate" allows in specific situations calls for judgments that will frequently be subject to considerable debate. When considering the use and the threatened use of nuclear weapons, we find that application of the principles becomes particularly contentious.

For purposes of practical discussion, we believe that we must conclude that nuclear weapons cannot be employed while also adhering fully to the Principle of Discrimination. We can hypothesize unusual scenarios, such as the attack of a military ship at sea far from any inhabited area using a low-yield nuclear weapon in circumstances such that neither the attacked party nor any of its allies will be capable of responding with nuclear weapons. Given such circumstances, we can say that we have established that nuclear weapons could theoretically be used with discrimination. In the same vein nuclear weapons perhaps could be used above the atmosphere in space with full observance of the Principle of Discrimination. Such speculation however, will not satisfy our moral concerns involving the use of nuclear weapons because currently contemplated uses will almost always involve the knowing destruction of noncombatants. Industrial or militarily signifi cant economic targets will normally be found in the vicinity of heavily populated areas or close enough that the effect of fallout will be deadly. In most cases purely military targets will be close enough to civilian population concentrations that even a strict targeting policy, one that demands a restriction to the selection of purely military targets, will have a disastrous impact on civilian life and property.

In 1945, the United States carried out the only atomic bombing of an enemy. The weapon dropped on Hiroshima had the explosive force of 12,000 tons of TNT. Upon detonation, many thousands of people were immediately incinerated. Within seconds, thousands more died from the blast and the consuming firestorm. Within days, radiation effects claimed still more thousands. Contrary to the guidance in the Just War Tradition, the victims were overwhelmingly noncombatants: schoolteachers, newborn babies, priests, and laborers—ordinary citizens. To make the point forcefully, we note that at the close of the Cold War, America's nuclear arsenal featured the Minuteman missile with warheads possessing the explosive force of *1.2 million tons of TNT.*[11] The Hiroshima bomb pales (a thousandfold) by comparison. Any contention that a weapon similar to the Minuteman missile could be used in a manner that effectively discriminates between combatants and noncombatants entirely lacks credibility.

While it is tempting to conclude that the use of modern nuclear weapons is simply unacceptable from a moral point of view if one is to take the restrictions of the Just War Tradition seriously, the issue is not so easily settled. At the heart of this tradition is the idea that the only justifying cause for the use of force is that of preserving and protecting values. The overarching question with respect to the Principle of Discrimination then is whether values may ever be defended by the use of indiscriminate means. In that larger context, the question concerning how to apply the Principle of Discrimination in the context of nuclear weapons requires further examination.

First, Paul Ramsey noted in his discussion of the introduction of "counterforce strategy" (limiting the targets of nuclear weapons strictly to military targets) that the change would not result in completely limiting casualties to combatants, but it would be significantly different in its effects from a "countervalue" strategy.[12] A countervalue strategy is one that threatens to retaliate against a nuclear attack by firing nuclear missiles against high-value targets— the major civilian population centers. Counterforce targeting does observe the prohibition against attacking noncombatants *directly* and *intentionally*. The countervalue strategy simply ignores the Principle of Discrimination. The counterforce strategy, proponents argue, preserves the combatant/noncombatant distinction as much as possible in light of the necessity to preserve fundamental values. Nonetheless, the collateral damage caused by striking military targets is foreseeable.

In balancing the intention of the agent and the regrettable results of an action, the Principle of Double Effect declares that the foreseen but unintended result under moral scrutiny must not itself be a means to the intended result. If the collateral damage that may be caused by counterforce targeting is itself critical to the deterrent effect of a counterforce strategy, even justification under double effect becomes suspect. A pure counterforce strategy, to use Steven Lee's terminology,[13] is not likely to be possible, let alone feasible, in the modern world. Military targets of strategic significance do not sit in splendid isolation in the middle of a desert or an ocean. Only if the bad effect of an action (in this case the collateral damage) is not necessary to achieve the "good" effect will the intended and morally acceptable result (in this case, using the threat of force to preserve the peace) be justifiable based on proportionality. Even with this proportionality consideration in mind, however, we recognize that under the Just War Theory the Principle of Discrimination still applies. When we apply it to the comparison of the counterforce strategy and the countervalue strategy, we find that with respect to the sheer number of casualties that it threatens, the counterforce strategy better serves the value of respect for human beings than does the countervalue strategy, as Paul Ramsey concluded.

Second, if the Just War Tradition is considered not as a legalistic mechanism to determine the justice of war but instead as a means of rendering the activity of war "as nearly just as it can be,"[14] one must weigh the Principle of Discrimination against the Principle of Proportionality. Steven Lee states that, "A concern for avoidance of catastrophic consequences" outweighs a concern for adhering firmly to laws and rules in war.[15] A number of commentators argue that when a state can avoid irreparable harm to the state itself only by violating the Principle of Discrimination, it is morally entitled to do so.[16] That is, if the consequences of a policy or action "necessary to save the nation" include catastrophic alternatives, our normal response is to accept the justifiability of the least disastrous choice. Avoiding nuclear war through deterrence appears to be the least disastrous choice with respect to means of preserving the peace. The Principle of Proportionality appears to outweigh the violation of the Principle of Discrimination. Thus, in practically selecting from the choices available that will avoid catastrophic consequences, our moral responsibility may be reduced to rendering the use of force or the threat of the use of force as just as it can be. That of course is the argument of those who support a version of nuclear deterrence, even though they recognize that the threat to use nuclear weapons is an intentional threat to cause noncombatant casualties. Thus the claim that nuclear weapons make just war thinking irrelevant appears to be reversed: the almost inevitable violation of the Principle of Discrimination makes the issue of just war all the more acute. In that perspective, while recognizing the overriding necessity of preventing nuclear war, we must nonetheless adhere as closely as possible to the requirement to discriminate between combatants and noncombatants.

The purpose of rendering deterrence as just as possible thus becomes a more problematic but also a more pressing issue. If the Principle of Proportionality is given priority over the Principle of Discrimination, one can argue that the critical concern is whether a counterforce strategy makes nuclear war more or less likely than a countervalue strategy. That argument can continue even though one concedes that, in itself, any future use of nuclear weapons will be gravely immoral in light of the Principle of Discrimination. Despite that concession, it may be the case that the Principle of Discrimination would not be *immorally* overridden if the weight of the consequences considered in terms of the Principle of Proportionality were great enough. As Arthur Hockaday notes, a central issue is whether "the extent to which deterrence necessarily involves a conditional intention to commit in certain circumstances actions which will, or are virtually certain or highly likely to, kill noncombatants in numbers disproportionate to the good achieved or the evil abated."[17] From this perspective, the evil abated must be great indeed, but the prospect of nuclear holocaust in the days of the Cold War arguably met that standard.

Since the end of the Cold War, the nuclear standoff between the major military powers has been defused to a large extent. But the continuing proliferation of nuclear weapons in countries such as India and Pakistan and the intense efforts of other nations to acquire nuclear technology continue to be serious concerns for the global community. The dangers of nuclear conflict including issues of deterrence and the discriminatory use of nuclear weapons may again become dominating concerns as the nuclear arms race gathers momentum on a wider scale around the world. In answer to Stephen Toulmin's question, "Given the destructiveness of nuclear weapons, could their use ever be proportionate to a legitimate goal of state action?"[18] we can say that only in the direst circumstances could it be even possible, with moral justification, to contemplate such a step. We can also see that proliferation inevitably makes use more likely, especially in light of the possibility of terrorist groups obtaining nuclear weapons. That prospect should strengthen the moral and practical imperative for reducing nuclear armament.

LAND MINES

Although the discussion of land mines and the problem of civilian casualties assumes almost an academic air in the context of the spreading use of suicide bombers to achieve military and political ends, it remains an important issue. The arsenals of armies around the world include mines of all varieties and pose a distinct threat to noncombatants because of the nature of the weapon. On March 1, 1999, the "Convention on the Prohibition of the Use, Stockpiling, Production and Transfer of Anti-Personnel Mines and on Their Destruction" (henceforth the Mine Ban Treaty) became an element of international law. The treaty resulted from a widespread recognition that antipersonnel mines cause indiscriminate and excessive injury. Over time those most affected are noncombatants. Common estimates claim that over 25,000 people are injured or killed each year by land mines, most remaining from earlier conflicts.[19] As of August 15, 2007, 155 states had taken steps to implement the Mine Ban Treaty.[20] Among the countries that have not yet acceded to the treaty are the United States, Russia, China, Iran, and Cuba, presumably for varying reasons.

The United States has announced that it is fully supportive of the humanitarian purpose of the treaty, and it has established a policy under which it will eliminate all persistent land mines from its arsenal and not use any persistent land mines (to include antivehicle mines) anywhere after 2010.[21] An opponent of the Mine Ban Treaty argues that the treaty is not the way to remedy the violations of discrimination inflicted by the use of land mines. "If the U.S. approves a global ban on all land mines, American soldiers will be put in greater danger and a harmful double standard will be created in arms control: A country not causing the problem—the United States—will disarm while rogue nations proliferating civilian-killing mines will not join the agreement and will not disarm."[22] The argument here is that the focus should be on eliminating all land mines that are not reliable, self-destructing "smart mines."

The driving force behind the land mine campaign clearly invoked the Principle of Discrimination as the foundation stone, however, and overcame security considerations in the arguments that resulted in the Ottawa process that created the Mine Ban Treaty. A recent United Nations report notes "land-mines are uniquely savage in the history of modern conventional warfare not only because of their appalling individual impact, but also their long-term social and economic destruction."[23] The problems posed by land mines and the lack of discrimination in their effects are greatly amplified by the fact that over 100 million land mines remain buried around the world, the legacy of modern warfare.[24] From El Salvador to Angola to Afghanistan to Cambodia, land mines will wreak havoc on unsuspecting civilians for generations to come. Mine-removal programs have made only modest progress. One source reported in 2000 that "the United Nations estimates that it would take 1,000 mine-clearing personnel more than 30 years to discover and disarm the 6 million mines planted in Bosnia and Croatia."[25]

The concern about eliminating land mines invokes a loosely applied version of military necessity to justify continued use. Without the use of land mines, the argument goes, the defense capabilities of a nation would be so weakened that the security of the state would be at risk. At first glance, the argument would appear to be more powerful when wielded by nations with relatively small military forces than when offered by a superpower that presumably has alternative means of defending its service members. More advanced countries that can field "smart mines," for example, would appear to have less justification than others for the use of the less expensive "dumb mines" that can cause death and injury for decades. More broadly, to claim the right to use land mines because they are tactically efficient while admitting their inhumane nature appears to violate both the Principle of Discrimination and the Principle of Proportionality. Most mines now in use will have an effective life of more than fifty years if they are not cleared. Unfortunately, practice indicates that the armed forces most dependent on the use of land mines are the least likely to mark minefields adequately and to remove them when the minefields no longer have a military purpose.

TARGETING

The broad prohibition against directly attacking noncombatants becomes complex in application. While investment, bombardment, and assault of defended places are integral parts of warfare, the attack of undefended towns, villages, or structures is prohibited under Article 25 of the Hague Regulations.[26] That guidance appears clear at first glance, but the following list of exceptions suggests that the rule may not be that easy to apply:

> [F]actories producing munitions and military supplies, military camps, warehouses storing munitions and military supplies, ports and railroads being used for the transportation of military supplies, and other places devoted to the support of military operations or the accommodation of troops may also be bombarded and attacked even though they are undefended.[27]

The Hague Regulation itself appears to allow considerable latitude when it notes that "in sieges and bombardments all necessary steps must be taken to spare, as far as possible, buildings dedicated to religion, art, science, or charitable purposes, historic monuments, hospitals, and places where the sick and wounded are collected, provided they are not being used at the time for military purposes."[28] The qualification "as far as possible" leaves great latitude for interpretation.

The Hague documents and the Geneva Conventions leave many questions concerning the issue of civilians selected as targets. The Protocols to the Geneva Conventions of August 12, 1949, address the many ambiguities at some length and make the protection of the civilian population much more specific. Article 48 of Protocol I states that warring parties will "at all times distinguish between the civilian population and combatants and between civilian objects and military objectives and accordingly shall direct their operations only against military objectives." In turn, military objectives are defined as "those objects which by their nature, location, purpose or use make an effective contribution to military action and whose total or partial destruction, capture, neutralization, in the circumstances ruling at the time, offers a definite military advantage."[29]

Other articles of the Protocols prohibit indiscriminate attacks, providing specific examples after presenting the following definition:

Indiscriminate attacks are prohibited. Indiscriminate attacks are:

    a. those which are not directed at a specific military objective;
    b. those which employ a method or means of combat which cannot be directed at a specific military objective; or
    c. those which employ a method or means of combat the effects of which cannot be limited as required by this Protocol;

and consequently, in each such case, are of a nature to strike military objectives and civilians or civilian objects without distinction.[30]

Additional paragraphs refer to the prohibition of striking works or installations containing dangerous forces, such as dams and nuclear power plants, whose destruction can provide a great danger to civilians.[31] Given the Protocols, the guidelines concerning applying the Principle of Discrimination have reached an unprecedented level of clarity and specificity. Nonetheless, troublesome questions will always arise in applying this half of the *jus in bello* principles. Application becomes particularly challenging when conventional forces conduct operations against groups that totally disregard the strictures of humanitarian laws of war. In the twenty-first century conflicts in Iraq and Afghanistan, insurgent forces used the restrictions of the laws of war to their advantage in fighting against NATO and Coalition forces. Besides direct attacks on civilian targets, they have used the civilian population as shields and religious structures such as mosques as meeting places, fighting positions, and munitions storage sites. The conflicts in the Middle East provide many examples of civilian casualties being employed as a means to tactical and strategic ends. Conventional forces have repeatedly had to make morally difficult decisions about targeting as a result.

ECONOMIC SANCTIONS

As the new century stretches before us, the Principle of Discrimination finds application to activities not included in the traditional scope of the concept.

Economic sanctions, restrictions placed upon economic relations such as international trade and finance, have been applied to change the policies and behavior of states that are accused of violations of international norms. Sanctions include a variety of measures, from broad embargoes to very specific actions, such as the denial of the right to purchase specific goods or services from a particular state. Sanctions can also take the form of denying loans or grants to a state to encourage the adoption of certain actions or a change in certain policies. Sanctions are most effective when they deny a country a critical need, which usually requires that the sanctions be multilateral. Unilateral sanctions by one state will seldom have sufficient effect to persuade the targeted state to change its practices. Multilateral sanctions were effective in helping to end the policy of apartheid in South Africa. Libya felt the pressure of sanctions in making its decision to send the Lockerbie suspects to trial in Scotland and later to abandon its programs to develop weapons of mass destruction. To some extent, it appears that sanctions limited Saddam Hussein's ability to acquire weapons of mass destruction after the Gulf War in 1991. In none of these cases would unilateral sanctions have been as effective as multilateral or United Nations sanctions. Because no one country is a sole supplier, the requirements of the targeted state could have been met elsewhere.

In most cases, a state or states will impose sanctions to influence the behavior of another government, not as a means of punishing the people of the sanctioned state. The issue of discrimination arises when the imposition of sanctions imposes hardships upon the people. Often in the past, the pressure on the government has resulted from the suffering of the people of the state that sanctions have caused. In the case of United States sanctions on Cuba, which included prohibitions on trade involving food and medicine, the citizens of Cuba were directly affected by the sanctions policy.

The United States embargo against Cuba began in 1961 following Fidel Castro's revolution. For many years, the embargo had largely symbolic significance because Communist countries, especially the Soviet Union, could meet Cuba's needs. With the fall of the Soviet Union, however, the sanctions began to affect all aspects of Cuban life. Passage in 1992 of the Cuban Democracy Act by the United States Congress imposed a ban on all subsidiary trade by American businesses, including food and medicines. The United States applied heavy pressure to other countries to stop trading with Cuba. That pressure produced results despite the opposition of the European Union and Russia because of the influence of the United States in the world economy. The result was a progressive increase in public health problems, economic decline, and an overall reduction in the standard of living for the people of Cuba.[32] The sanctions regime directly affected the people of Cuba. Apparently the intent of the United States government was to generate opposition to Castro's rule by making life increasingly more difficult for Cuban citizens and thus persuading them to topple Castro from power. Critics of this policy have raised the issue of moral acceptability.

The Principle of Discrimination prohibits targeting noncombatants directly. If we extrapolate that principle to measures short of war, such as sanctions, it presents a moral argument against a policy such as that of the United States when the sanctions policy intended to influence governmental actions necessarily causes suffering among the civilian population (especially among women, children, the elderly, and the poor). Causes and results are difficult to determine with certainty, but over time trends often become apparent, allowing reasonable judgment of the policies involved. At the same time, the intent of various sanctions is difficult to establish to the degree necessary to ascertain that a specific government policy has violated the Principle of Discrimination by purposefully targeting noncombatants, but ignoring trends that reveal suffering weighs heavily against the moral acceptability of sanctions policy.

As in the case of Cuba, sanctions against Iraq after the Persian Gulf War appeared to cause suffering among Iraqi civilians other than the ruling class, thus encouraging the conclusion that the sanctions were meant to undermine support for Saddam Hussein's government and to foment sufficient discontent to affect government policy. By 2003, critics of the sanctions regime argued that the long-term trends revealed a violation of the Principle of Discrimination and that the sanctions could no longer be justified. The Principle of Discrimination appears to require at a minimum that the imposing authorities carefully consider proportionality. They should examine whether the benefit anticipated can justify the collateral harm done to the civilian populace as a whole with human rights providing the yardstick of justice.

COUNTERTERRORISM

Although we might think of terrorism as a modern phenomenon, its use since ancient times is a matter of historical record. If one were to use a definition that classified as terrorism any act calculated to inspire terror, of course, essentially all acts of war would be classified as terrorism and the term would have little significance. But even the modern sense of terror, violence that in some sense unlawfully targets the innocent (variously defined) for the purpose of coercing governments or specific groups to achieve political or social aims, appears in many early examples. The Roman Empire employed state terrorism to maintain control and oppress conquered populations, just as the Nazis did in the twentieth century. Domestic groups have used terrorist tactics to pressure governments to make concessions or accommodations, as well as to undermine and unseat governmental authorities. Organizations such as the Ku Klux Klan in the United States used terrorist actions to suppress African Americans, and many ethnic groups around the world have suffered in similar ways. We find examples in the Shining Path guerrillas in Peru, the ETA in the Basque region of Spain, and the Tamil Tigers in Sri Lanka. In 1995 in Japan, a religious cult released sarin nerve gas into the Tokyo subway system, killing a dozen people and causing panic. The target of the cult was the Japanese government and Japanese social practices, but innocent subway riders provided the means to achieve the group's ends.

Since the 1990s, terrorism has taken a more ominous turn with the introduction of the widespread use of suicide bombing, a technique that manifests the rejection of any limitation on any use of force that is considered useful in pursuing political objectives when it is employed against the civilian populace in general. In the last two decades, suicide bombers have indiscriminately targeted noninvolved parties, from tourists to small children and the elderly. Terrorist actions of this nature have usually been associated with religious extremism, which is one of the powerful motivators for such extreme behavior. Suicide bombing and other acts of terrorism most often appear in asymmetric conflict that pits a David against a Goliath. Small organized groups cannot defeat the forces of the state in open warfare, but they *can* wage effective guerrilla warfare, especially when they use unconstrained terrorist tactics.

The international terrorist organization al-Qaeda relies primarily on terrorist actions in its pursuit of the demise of the West and the restoration of the Caliphate, the ancient Islamic empire established by Mohammed and his followers. Born in Afghanistan under the leadership of Osama bin Laden in the Soviet-Afghan War of the 1980s, al-Qaeda has become a threat to governments around the world. In Iraq and Afghanistan, Coalition and NATO forces face determined insurgents allied in many cases with al-Qaeda and following its modus operandi.

The struggle against guerrillas or insurgents using terrorist tactics presents major challenges to COIN forces. COIN forces attempt to establish order and security. The insurgent forces attempt to instill fear and acquiescence in the population of a country in order to lay the groundwork for seizing power. For the committed insurgent, no means are proscribed. Only the end matters, and religious terrorists have a ready supply of suicide bombers, one of the most efficient means available in pursuing the weakening and eventual subjugation of populations and governments.

The U.S. Army's *Counterinsurgency* manual emphasizes that COIN operations must "[d]iscredit insurgent propaganda and provide a more compelling alternative to the insurgent ideology and narrative."[33] To accomplish that goal, the support of the civilian population must be obtained. Adhering to the Principle of Discrimination is critical to that effort. If the govern-

ment is to secure the citizenry, build legitimacy through effective governance, isolate the insurgency, and meet the expectations of the people, it
must show that it honors the Principle of Discrimination.[34] Otherwise, the
actions of the government will appear to be no more than a struggle for
power. As the U.S. Army manual notes:

> Combat operations must . . . be executed with an appropriate level of restraint
> to minimize or avoid injuring innocent people. Not only is there a moral ba-
> sis for the use of restraint or measured force; there are practical reasons as well.
> Needlessly harming innocents can turn the populace against the COIN effort.
> Discriminating use of fires and calculated, disciplined response should charac-
> terize COIN operations. Kindness and compassion can often be as important
> as killing and capturing insurgents.[35]

CONCLUSION

Although the Principle of Discrimination may arguably be subordinated to
the Principle of Proportionality in WMD cases, based on the widespread
moral intuition that numbers matter, the Principle of Discrimination remains one of the most important moral guidelines for decision-making in
the context of armed conflict. To the extent that it is recognized and accepted by warring parties, it serves as a prominent constraint on the conduct
of war.

NOTES

1. A. J. Coates, *The Ethics of War* (Manchester: Manchester University Press,
1998), 234.

2. The distinction between guerrillas and insurgents is subtle. Both are categories
of unconventional fighters, members of irregular forces. Insurgents focus their attacks on the government of a country and its agencies. The U.S. Army's new counterinsurgency manual, FM 3-24, defines an insurgency as follows: "[A]n insurgency
is an organized, protracted politico-military struggle designed to weaken the control
and legitimacy of an established government, occupying power, or other political
authority while increasing insurgent control" (page 1-1). The label guerrillas covers
a broader spectrum in that it refers to those in organized groups who practice unconventional or irregular warfare in any environment. Guerrillas may be insurgents,
or they may be participants in combat between states. Most of our discussion will
apply to all forms of unconventional warfare.

3. SALUTE refers to the analysis elements of SIZE, ACTIVITY, LOCATION, UNIT,
TIME, EQUIPMENT. This guidance says to record (when observing what may be enemy forces) what individuals carry in their hands (hence HAND, thinking of immediate threat if weapons are in hand) and then to record the following features of

SALUTE (an acronym long used in the U.S. Army): size (of the enemy force), activity (what they are doing), location (where the observation occurs), unit (report any unit designations discernible), time (when the observation occurred), equipment (that the enemy force possesses, from weapons to vehicles).

4. Jeffrie Murphy, "The Killing of the Innocent," in *War, Morality, and the Military Profession*, ed. Malham M. Wakin, 2nd ed. (Boulder, Colo.: Westview, 1986), 346.

5. The targeting of a munitions factory resulting in the death of munitions workers has been analyzed above from the perspective of Murphy's "chain of agency." It may also be analyzed from the perspective of the Principle of Double Effect (see the preceding chapter on the Principle of Proportionality). If we would consider the munitions workers as noncombatants, the bombing of their factory could then still be justified under certain conditions as a legitimate act, even if the death of civilian workers would inevitably result from it. According to the Principle of Double Effect, the destruction of a military object which would also result in civilian casualties is legitimate to the extent that (1) the Principle of Discrimination is respected which means in this case that these foreseeable casualties are not intended or necessary for the good effect, (2) the Principle of Proportionality is respected which means that the foreseen and intended result of destroying the munitions factory is predicted to do more good than the harm (bad) of the foreseen but unintended result resulting from the death of its workers, and (3) the collateral damages are minimized.

6. Michael Walzer, *Just and Unjust Wars* (New York: Basic Books, 1977), 157.

7. Michael Ignatieff, "Annals of Diplomacy: Balkan Physics," *New Yorker*, May 10, 1999, 79.

8. Michael Ignatieff, "Annals of Diplomacy," 79.

9. James T. Johnson, "Threats, Values, and Defense: Does the Defense of Values by Force Remain a Moral Possibility?" in *Just War Theory*, ed. Jean Bethke Elshtain (New York: New York University Press, 1992), 56.

10. David Fisher, "Priorities in Just Deterrence," in *Just Deterrence: Morality and Deterrence into the 21st Century*, ed. Malcolm McCall and Oliver Ramsbotham (London: Brassey's, 1990), 67.

11. Douglas Lackey makes this comparison in *The Ethics of War and Peace* (Englewood Cliffs, N.J.: Prentice Hall, 1989), 110.

12. Paul Ramsey, *The Just War: Force and Political Responsibility* (New York: University Press of America, 1983), 157–65.

13. Steven P. Lee, *Morality, Prudence, and Nuclear Weapons* (Cambridge: Cambridge University Press, 1993), 150–51. A pure counterforce strategy is one that results in relatively small numbers of civilian casualties; an impure strategy would generate very large numbers of civilians injured and killed.

14. Stanley Hauerwas, "On Surviving Justly: Ethics and Nuclear Disarmament," in *Just War Theory*, 303.

15. Lee, *Morality, Prudence, and Nuclear Weapons*, 61.

16. Michael Walzer in *Just and Unjust Wars*, 269–74, and Gregory Kavka in *Moral Paradoxes of Nuclear Deterrence* (Cambridge: Cambridge University Press, 1987), chap. 1, both support this view.

17. Arthur Hockaday, "The Aim of Just Deterrence: Peace with Justice?" in *Just Deterrence*, 54.

18. Stephen Toulmin, "The Limits of Allegiance in a Nuclear Age," in *Just War Theory*, 282.

19. U.S. Government, White House Press Release, "U.S. Efforts to Address the Problem of Anti-personnel Landmines," 16 May 1996", at www.defenselink.mil/news/May1996/m051796_m102-96.html (accessed May 2, 2000).

20. International Campaign to Ban Landmines, at www.icbl.org/treaty/members (accessed 21 January 2008).

21. U.S. Department of State, "U.S. Landmine Policy," at www.state.gov/t/pm/wra/c11735.htm (accessed January 21, 2008).

22. Baker Spring and John Hillen, "Why a Global Ban on Land Mines Won't Work," at www.nonline.com/procon/html/conMine.htm (accessed May 4, 2000).

23. Graça Machel, "Impact of Armed Conflict on Children," at www.unicef.org/graca/mines.html (accessed May 3, 2000).

24. Machel, "Impact of Armed Conflict."

25. Dan Solomon, "Taking the Initiative on Land Mines," at www.nonline.com/procon/html/proMine.html (accessed May 4, 2000).

26. Annex to the Hague Convention N. IV, October 18, 1907, embodying the Regulations Respecting the Laws and Customs of War on Land.

27. U.S. Army, FM27-10, *The Laws of Land Warfare* (Washington, D.C.: U.S. Government Printing Office, 1956), 19.

28. Article 27, *Annex to Hague Convention No. IV Respecting the Laws and Customs of War on Land, 18 October 1907*.

29. Article 52, Protocol I, *Protocols to the Geneva Conventions of 12 August 1949*.

30. Article 51, Protocol I.

31. Article 56, Protocol I.

32. The impact of sanctions is documented a variety of sources, including H. Kaufman, "The United States-Cuba Policy: A Cuban Perspective," *The Harvard Journal of World Affairs*, 3 (1994): 105–16; A. F. Kirkpatrick, "Role of the USA in the Shortage of Food and Medicine in Cuba," *The Lancet* 348, no. 9040 (1996): 1489–91; and David Kuntz, *The Politics of Suffering: The Impact of the U.S. Embargo on the Health of the Cuban People* (New York: International Health Services, 1994).

33. *Counterinsurgency*, 5–2.

34. *Counterinsurgency*, 5–2.

35. *Counterinsurgency*, 5–12. The manual goes on to emphasize similar points on page 7-7:

In COIN operations, it is difficult to distinguish insurgents from noncombatants. It is also difficult to determine whether the situation permits harm to noncombatants. Two levels of discrimination are necessary:

- deciding between targets
- determining an acceptable risk to noncombatants and bystanders

Page 7-36. Discrimination applies to the means by which combatants engage the enemy. The COIN environment requires counterinsurgents to not only determine the kinds of weapons to use and how to employ them but also establish whether lethal means are desired—or even permitted. (FM 27-10 discusses forbidden means of waging war.) Soldiers and Marines require an innate understanding of the effects of their actions and weapons on all aspects of the operational environment. Leaders must consider not only the first order, desired effects of a munition or action but also possible second- and third-order effects—including undesired ones. For example, bombs delivered by fixed-wing close air support may effectively destroy the source of small arms fire from a building in an urban area; however, direct-fire weapons may be more appropriate due to the risk of collateral damage to nearby buildings and noncombatants. The leader at the scene assesses the risks and makes the decision. Achieving the desired effects requires employing tactics and weapons appropriate to the situation. In some cases, this means avoiding the use of area munitions to minimize the potential harm inflicted on noncombatants located nearby. In situations where civil security exists, even tenuously, Soldiers and Marines should pursue nonlethal means first, using lethal force only when necessary.

The principles of discrimination in the use of force and proportionality in actions are important to counterinsurgents for practical reasons as well as for their ethical or moral implications. Fires that cause unnecessary harm or death to noncombatants may create more resistance and increase the insurgency's appeal—especially if the populace perceives a lack of discrimination in their use. The use of discriminating, proportionate force as a mindset goes beyond the adherence to the rules of engagement. Proportionality and discrimination applied in COIN require leaders to ensure that their units employ the right tools correctly with mature discernment, good judgment, and moral resolve.

III

CASES

9

The NATO Intervention in the Kosovo Crisis

March–June 1999

Carl Ceulemans

PRESENTATION OF THE CASE[1]

On March 24, 1999, NATO Secretary General Javier Solana announced the beginning of an air campaign against Serbia/the Federal Republic of Yugoslavia[2] in order to stop the fighting and the ongoing human rights violations in Kosovo. With these air operations, which would last for seventy-eight days, NATO intervened militarily in a very troublesome region. Kosovo is the southern province of Serbia, and is generally considered one of the most serious trouble spots in the Balkans. This situation can in no small part be attributed to the ethnic makeup of Kosovo. Although Kosovo is a part of Serbia, it contains a large majority (90 percent) of Albanians.

The history of Kosovo is in fact a very complex one of mutual distrust, accusations, and grievances.[3] Because both Serbs and Albanians use their own national myths to justify their territorial claims, it is hard to get a clear picture of the historical background of Kosovo. After some violent protests at the end of the 1960s, the Yugoslav constitution of 1974 granted Kosovo extensive autonomy inside Serbia. However, one of the main differences between the Albanian Kosovars and the Serb and Croat ethnic groups within Yugoslavia was that the latter two had a right to secede whereas the Albanian Kosovars did not. The solution as proposed in the new constitution did not satisfy anybody. The Albanian Kosovars saw themselves as a minority in Serbia and were convinced that Belgrade was responsible for the bad economic situation in Kosovo. In turn, the Serbs thought that Kosovo had been given far too much autonomy and feared Albanian separatism.

In 1981, after Tito's death and the growing economic problems in Socialist Federal Republic of Yugoslavia (SFRY), the Albanians in Kosovo revolted and started a movement to gain republican status for their province. The movement would later develop into a claim for independence. Since then, the situation has worsened for the Serb Kosovars. Thousands had to leave the region because of constant threats and harassment by the Albanian majority.

In March 1989, the Serbian parliament implemented constitutional changes that undermined the rights of the autonomous provinces in Serbia severely. Kosovo and Vojvodina retained the status of an autonomous province, but in reality all decisions were made in Belgrade. The Albanian Kosovar population reacted to these oppressive policies with nonviolent resistance and civil disobedience. On September 13, 1990, the Albanian Kosovar representatives of the Kosovar parliament proclaimed a constitutional law for a "Republic of Kosovo" within the Yugoslav federation. One year later, the Albanians in Kosovo organized a referendum to decide on full independence. It was claimed that about 87 percent of the voters took part, and that about 99 percent voted in favor of Kosovar independence.[4] This result was not recognized by Serbia or any other state, except Albania.

The central figure in the Kosovar struggle for independence was Ibrahim Rugova, the leader of the LDK (Democratic League of Kosovo). He was elected president of Kosovo in May 1992, in an electoral contest that was not recognized as constitutional by the authorities of Belgrade. Rugova was a proponent of nonviolent resistance. He believed that the international community would sympathize with this approach and pressure the Serbs into finding a solution. When no solution developed, an increasing number of Albanian Kosovars began to believe that a more forceful approach was needed. Between 1992 and 1995 a number of sporadic attacks against Serbian policemen occurred in Kosovo. However, from spring 1997 on, when the Kosovo Liberation Army (UCK) began a guerrilla campaign against the Serbian presence, the use of force became more systematic. By the spring of 1998, the confrontations between the UCK and the Serbian police forces escalated into a full-blown war. The UCK tried to force many Serbians to leave Kosovo, while the Serbian forces carried out military operations against Albanian villages in order to destroy the UCK.

At this point, outside observers became very worried. Many feared that the conflict might spread to other sensitive regions, particularly Macedonia and Albania. There was a consensus between Western countries and Russia that Kosovo's autonomy had to be restored (cf. the Yugoslav constitution of 1974) and even enlarged, and that Kosovo had to stay within Serbia. On March 31, 1998, the Security Council voted a resolution (Security Council Resolution 1160) in which it condemned "the use of excessive force by Serbian police forces, as well as all acts of terrorism by the Kosovo Liberation Army." The Security Council also restored the weapons embargo against Yu goslavia that had been lifted after the Dayton Peace Agreement on Bosnia in 1995. This measure was followed by a second resolution (Security Council Resolution 1199) in September 1998 in which the Security Council demanded that all parties cease hostilities and maintain a cease-fire that would allow free and unimpeded access for humanitarian organizations. It also urged Serbia to withdraw its special forces and to start a political dialogue.

On October 13, the Serbian leader Slobodan Milosevic finally signed an agreement with U.S. negotiator Richard Holbrooke. In this agreement he promised to implement the demands stipulated by Security Council Resolution 1199. Milosevic also agreed to cooperate with the OSCE Verification Mission (Security Council Resolution 1203 of October 24) that had to verify whether Yugoslavia kept its promises. Two thousand unarmed verifiers were to be deployed in Kosovo. In order to persuade the Serbs to take the further step of actually withdrawing their troops, NATO threatened the use of air strikes. NATO delayed the deadline several times (the UCK tried to slow down the Serbian withdrawal in order to provoke air strikes), but in the end NATO ordered no military intervention.

The violence flared up again in January 1999, when Serbian forces killed nearly fifty alleged terrorists in Racak.[5] The Serbs and the Albanians were summoned by the international community to start talks in Rambouillet near Paris in February. The negotiations were headed by the United States, the European Union, and Russia. The Western strategy was to offer the Albanian Kosovars interim self-government for three years with no prospect of independence, a NATO peacekeeping force to protect them from the Serbs, and the threat of NATO air strikes to induce Serbian cooperation. The Serbs refused to sign (Milosevic didn't want NATO troops on Yugoslav territory), while the Albanian Kosovars accepted the proposal conditionally (the Kosovar delegation needed further consultation with the Albanian Kosovar people). After the second round of talks in March (these were held in Paris), the Albanian Kosovars finally agreed to sign up. Milosevic kept refusing, and so faced NATO air strikes as a consequence. On March 24, NATO Secretary-General Solana announced the beginning of air operations against Serbia.

The air campaign, dubbed "Allied Force," was conducted on two levels. On a tactical level NATO targeted the Serbian forces in Kosovo. The aim was to destroy these troops and to cut off their lines of supply. On the strategic level the air campaign was conducted against the logistic support system outside Kosovo, the integrated air defense system, the command and control infrastructure, the fuel depots, and other targets that were of vital importance for the functioning of the Serbian/Yugoslav war and security machines. During this bombing campaign NATO pilots flew 37,465 sorties, of which 14,006 were strike sorties.[6] In the first three weeks of the operation,

NATO limited itself to eighty-four strike sorties a day, but after that it increased the number of daily sorties systematically.[7] On June 10, after seventy-eight days of bombing, Serbia's commanders signed a detailed agreement for a complete and rapid withdrawal of their troops from Kosovo, and the swift deployment of a robust Western-dominated force. The Security Council passed a resolution (Security Council Resolution 1244 of June 10) in which it established a UN interim administration (UNMIK) and invited NATO troops (KFOR) to police the peace.

The final destiny of Kosovo was not settled. The Albanian Kosovars were convinced that eventually they would gain independence. In contrast, NATO and the UN still recognized Yugoslavia's sovereignty over Kosovo, while instructing UNMIK to take steps to establish democratic institutions in Kosovo "pending a final settlement." The lack of political agreement meant that the end of the international presence in the region was not in sight. Although Milosevic's removal from power (following his defeat in the first round of the Yugoslav presidential elections in September 2000) and the success of Ibrahim Rugova in the local elections in Kosovo in October 2000 improved the relations with the international community, UN officials remarked that the future of Kosovo is a "process" which has only just begun.[8]

JUST CAUSE

In a press statement following the commencement of the air operations on March 24, 1999, NATO Secretary-General Javier Solana stated that "NATO had the moral duty to stop the violence and bring an end to the humanitarian catastrophe now taking place in Kosovo." In a later press statement in mid-April, Solana was more specific about NATO's objectives. He said that NATO wanted

1. verifiable stop to all military action and the immediate ending of violence and repression;
2. the withdrawal from Kosovo of the Yugoslav military, police, and paramilitary forces;
3. the stationing in Kosovo of an international military presence;
4. the unconditional and safe return of all refugees and displaced persons; and
5. credible assurance of Milosevic's willingness to work on the basis of the Rambouillet framework (i.e., a willingness to reach accords toward a political solution for Kosovo in conformity with international law and the Charter of the UN).

Solana's statements make clear the basis for NATO's claim of Just Cause in the Kosovo crisis. NATO's decision to intervene militarily was a response to what it perceived as gross and massive injustices being committed in the ongoing conflict between the Serbs and the Albanian Kosovars. Although there was and still is much disagreement about the scale of the human rights violations committed in Kosovo prior to the NATO bombing campaign,[9] nobody denies that atrocities took place. Since the spring of 1998, the moment the Serb police forces started a full-blown war against the UCK, Serb actions threatened the lives of thousands of civilians who were forced to leave their homes. In September 1998, the International Committee of the Red Cross (ICRC) stated that "from a humanitarian perspective, it had become apparent that civilian casualties were not simply what has become known as 'collateral damage.'"[10] On the contrary, according to ICRC, civilians had become the main victims, if not the actual targets of the fight.[11] In that perspective, NATO's aims as presented by Solana could legitimately be considered as having a considerable Just Cause quality. Not only did NATO state that its military actions were aimed at stopping the humanitarian catastrophe, it also wanted to make sure that the refugees could safely return to their homes.

Before moving on to the next criterion, it is important to make two related comments. First, in its objectives, NATO wanted to stress clearly the humanitarian and thereby the impartial nature of the intervention. Its primary goal was to "bring an end to the humanitarian catastrophe now taking place in Kosovo." In order to do so, NATO wanted "a verifiable stop to *all* (Serb and Albanian) military action," and the "unconditional and safe return of *all* (Serb and Albanian) refugees and displaced persons." That position did not preclude NATO from saying, however (cf. the second and the fifth NATO objective), that it considered the Serb authorities, and President Milosevic in particular, as the main obstacle to achieving peace.

Second, the scope of the NATO intervention was rather substantial. NATO did not want to limit itself to a quick "in-and-out" delivery of humanitarian assistance, but wanted to create an environment safe for human rights. The Just Cause quality of NATO's aims did not mean that there were no opposing moral claims involved in this particular case. NATO was accused of giving indirect support to the terrorist activities of the UCK and of undermining Serbia's territorial integrity. It was also accused of violating the Principle of Legitimate Authority and other just war principles. In the following sections, we will assess these claims.

RIGHT INTENTIONS

During and after the NATO intervention in the Kosovo crisis, NATO's sincerity was questioned on numerous occasions. The motives that were attributed to NATO were quite diverse. There were those who said that the military intervention had to be understood in the larger framework of NATO's expansion to the east. Others believed that the United States was behind the idea of military intervention because, so the argument went, it wanted to justify the development of new weapon systems programs and because, in turn, it wanted to safeguard its dominant position as the sole superpower in the post–Cold War era. Some saw the decision to go to war in Kosovo as an attempt by President Clinton to divert attention from his domestic problems. An impeachment procedure had just been initiated against him. A further interpretation was that the Western powers were positioning themselves to exploit Kosovo's abundant mineral reserves, which include substantial deposits of lead, zinc, cadmium, silver, and gold. Kosovo also holds an estimated 17 billion tons of coal reserves. The West, so it might be supposed, was also thinking of Kosovo's strategic importance. One of the most imaginative theories about NATO's supposedly hidden agenda, however, was that Western states had failed to solve the "Millennium Bug" problem in the computer programs of their cruise missiles and other smart weapons. So, in order to avoid losing these expensive weapons, they decided to use them in 1999.[12]

Is there any truth to these and no doubt other "hidden agenda" theories? The difficulty with any Right Intentions analysis is that one can never be certain what a person's real intentions are (let alone those of an organization of states). An assessment of intentions is necessarily based on observable (public) indicators of intentions rather than reports of private mental experiences. What did a state say? What did it do? What were the results of its actions? When we look closely at these public indicators, it seems fair to say that NATO's intentions were mixed. When President Clinton was asked whether some moral principle informed the U.S. decision to go to war in Yugoslavia, he answered that "if somebody comes after innocent civilians and tries to kill them en masse because of their ethnic background or their religion, and it is within our power to stop it, we will stop it."[13] A few days later, however, an unnamed administration official modified this pronouncement. This official said that besides clear moral justification, the United States also has strategic interests involved.[14] This was no doubt the case in the Kosovo crisis. The continuing hostilities created heavy instability in the region and posed a threat to international peace and security. Not only were there dangers of a spillover into neighboring countries like Albania and Macedonia, there was also the serious problem of refugees. According to Marc Weller, the number of displaced persons in Kosovo had risen to over 200,000 a few days before the air campaign started.

Furthermore, UK Foreign Secretary Robin Cook admitted in a House of Commons debate on March 25, 1999, that NATO's awareness of the atrocities and the fact that NATO had the capacity to do something about it were not the only justifications for the intervention. Of equal importance was

NATO's credibility. Because our confidence in our peace and security depends on the credibility of NATO, so Cook's argument went, NATO could not have acted differently than it did. His exact words are: "Last October, NATO guaranteed the cease-fire that President Milosevic signed. He has comprehensively shattered that cease-fire. What possible credibility would NATO have next time that our security was challenged if we did not honour that guarantee?"[15]

There is, however, a powerful argument that raises doubt about NATO's intentions. Quite a number of people asked themselves why it was that NATO intervened in Kosovo, but not in other places in the world where similar humanitarian catastrophes had taken place. In 1995, for instance, 200,000 Serbs were expelled from Croatia. Why didn't NATO react in the same way as it did in Kosovo? Another example concerns the Kurd population in Turkey. Over the past fifteen years, Turkey has frequently been accused of human rights violations. Western governments have unsuccessfully pressed Turkey to find a peaceful solution to the Kurdish question. Meanwhile, Turkey retains NATO membership and actually participated in the punishing bombing of Yugoslavia. Some go on to say that in the punishment inflicted on the Albanian population, Serbia trails far behind the savageries inflicted by France in Algeria and the United States in Vietnam. Those who oppose these arguments say that the fact that a government does not apply the same principles in all parts of the world does not necessarily mean that it has no good intentions in applying them in a particular case. NATO's actions in Kosovo have to be seen from this perspective as a precedent for humanitarian interventions, quite apart what was or was not done in the past.

The events that followed the war give support to the argument that NATO had a genuine intention to stop the human rights violations in Kosovo. Indeed, once Milosevic agreed to withdraw his troops, and accept the deployment of an international peace force, NATO stopped the air campaign against the FRY. In the period that followed, NATO also used force to prevent or to stop violent clashes between Serbs and Albanians.

LEGITIMATE AUTHORITY

One of the most controversial issues during the bombing campaign was whether NATO had legitimate authority to use force against Yugoslavia. From a legal point of view, operation "Allied Force" was, to say the least, problematic. The UN Charter identifies only two kinds of settings in which there can be a legitimate decision to use force. First, states have a right of individual and collective self-defense against aggression (Article 51). And second, the Security Council has the authority to decide to use force when there is a threat to the peace, a rupture of the peace, or an act of aggression (Articles 39 and 42). In the latter case it is possible for the Security Council to call on regional organizations in order implement its decisions (Article 53§1). Because Yugoslavia had not attacked or threatened a NATO member, the Alliance could not base its military operation against Yugoslavia on Article 51. And although the Security Council had stated in Security Council Resolution 1199 (September 1998) that the situation in Kosovo constituted a threat to peace and security in the region, it hadn't authorized the use of "all necessary means" to end this threat. Further actions would depend on the situation on the ground. In SC Resolution 1199 the Council "decided that should the concrete measures demanded in this resolution and resolution 1160 not be taken, it would consider further action and additional measures to maintain or restore peace and stability in the region."

Although there was a definite moral consensus to act, the reactions of NATO members toward this legal problem differed greatly.[16] Countries such as Belgium, France, Germany, Greece, Italy, and Spain agreed that there was a moral imperative to act. Yet there was much less agreement among them as to the appropriate legal grounds for the military operation. In contrast, U.S. Secretary of State Madeleine Albright simply stated that the existing UN resolutions (1160 and 1190) were sufficient. Because the Serbs didn't respect the stipulations in these resolutions, and because these resolutions were formulated under chapter 7 (which regulates the use of force by the UN Security Council), NATO, so the U.S. argument went, didn't need any further authorization from the Security Council.

This position is not correct from a legal point of view. The fact that a resolution has been formulated under chapter 7 of the UN Charter doesn't imply automatically that force is authorized. NATO Secretary-General Javier Solana developed a more convincing argument. In order to justify the threat of military action in October 1998, Solana relied on a cluster of reasons.[17] They were:

1. The failure of Yugoslavia to fulfil the requirement set out by resolutions 1160 and 1190, based on chapter 7 of the UN Charter.
2. The imminent risk of a humanitarian catastrophe, as documented by the report of UN Secretary-General Kofi Annan on September 4, 1998.
3. The impossibility of obtaining, in short order, a Security Council resolution mandating the use of force.
4. The fact that resolution 1199 states that the deterioration of the situation in Kosovo constitutes a threat to peace and security in the region.

The first and fourth reasons constitute Albright's argument mentioned above. The second and third reasons take the pure legal argument a step fur ther by offering a moral ground for the exceptional use of force without Security Council authorization. Because of the gravity of the situation in Kosovo, and because the Security Council was immobilized by Russia's and China's threatened use of their vetoes, one could argue that NATO (or any other state or coalition of states for that matter) had a moral right (perhaps even a duty) to take military action unilaterally.

This line of argument shows that NATO's legitimate authority assessment was influenced by Just Cause and, more generally, by other moral considerations. The gravity of the Just Cause (putting a stop to the human rights violations) forced NATO to reconsider the "obvious" Legitimate Authority choice (i.e., the Security Council). Those who questioned NATO's legitimacy to intervene in Kosovo find this argument very troublesome, to say the least. From a Just War Theory point of view, the opponents argue that it is very dangerous to allow the gravity of the just cause to determine the outcome of the Legitimate Authority analysis. Such a maneuver would undermine the Legitimate Authority Principle as an independent principle. For some NATO critics, there is no reason to discuss the matter of Legitimate Authority from a moral point of view when the legal point of view provides us with a perfectly clear solution. These critics conclude that there was simply no legal basis for intervening in Kosovo.

The risks involved in resting the Principle of Legitimate Authority on moral foundations are indeed great. The international security system provided for by the UN and international law could be profoundly destabilized if the legal restraints on the use of force are loosened by an appeal to vague and general moral principles. Thus, for some NATO members such as Belgium there was some reluctance to treat the Kosovo war as a precedent for other forms of intervention.

LAST RESORT

In the spring of 1998, the situation in Kosovo took a turn for the worse. The violent clashes between the Kosovo Liberation Army and the Serb police forces escalated into a full-blown war. In the year that led up to the NATO air campaign against the FRY, the international community took a number of measures in order to find a peaceful solution to the crisis. These measures were a mixture of diplomatic initiatives, nonmilitary sanctions (an arms embargo, a ban on foreign investments, etc.), the deployment of an OSCE-verification team, and the threat of military force. The international efforts to bring the hostilities to an end culminated in the Rambouillet and Paris talks of February–March 1999. From the perspective of a last resort analysis, these talks were crucial because their failure finally led to the NATO decision to go to war against the FRY. The question that needs to be answered is whether the

Western countries had indeed reasonably exhausted alternatives to military strikes. Is it reasonable to presume that, with the failure of the Rambouillet and Paris conferences, NATO could legitimately start its military intervention? Or, is it fairer to say that yet another nonmilitary initiative was justified?

Mark Littman believes that at Rambouillet the possibilities of negotiation, diplomacy, and international pressure were not exhausted.[18] His position is essentially based on two arguments. First, Littman says, it is important to realize that Yugoslavia had accepted the substance of the political proposals of Rambouillet well before the final ultimatum. There was still some discussion on a number of secondary issues, but these could have been resolved later on. Second, and more important, was the nature of NATO's military proposals. Not only were they nonnegotiable, they were also draconian as befitting the military occupation of a country defeated in war.[19] If NATO had been willing to drop the nonnegotiable character of its proposals, so Littman argues, an agreement could have been reached. It was certainly the case that, on February 23, 1999, there were clear signs that the FRY/Serb-delegation was willing to consider "the scope and character of an international presence in Kosovo with a view to implementing the agreement to be adopted at Rambouillet."[20] So, end of discussion? Well, not exactly.

The most one can say about Littman's argument is that it is seriously flawed, and this for a number of reasons. First of all, Littman gives the impression that the Rambouillet conference was the last international diplomatic effort before the bombing started. This is not the case. There was a second round of talks in Paris, on March 15, 1999, the objective of which was precisely to offer the possibility of continued work on the Rambouillet results. Second, Littman seems to feel very strongly that Yugoslavia had accepted the substance of the political proposal of Rambouillet. This impression might be correct if one only looks at the results of the Rambouillet conference. During the talks in Paris, however, the attitude of the FRY/Serb delegation changed drastically. When it became clear to them at the beginning of the Paris conference that the Kosovar delegation was about to sign the Rambouillet proposals, the FRY/Serb delegation immediately presented a counterdraft designed to reopen the talks on a political settlement. In effect, it wanted to take the negotiations back to the beginning.[21] This new FRY/Serb initiative is a strong indication that the earlier Yugoslav acceptance of the substance of the political Rambouillet proposals was nothing but a charade put on to invoke the goodwill of the international community.

Third, and last, there is Littman's argument that NATO's military implementation proposals were nonnegotiable and draconian. This contention is only partly justified. It is true that at the Rambouillet conference, the implementation matter was not offered for discussion, and it is also true that the FRY/Serb-delegation opposed it firmly.[22] However, this was precisely the main purpose of the Paris conference: to talk in detail about the modalities for imlementation, including military implementation. But, as already mentioned, ie implementation issue was never really discussed for the simple reason that ie real Yugoslav objection was not so much about the implementation of the ambouillet proposals, but about the substance of these proposals.

What about the draconian character of the military measures? It is true iat the presence of foreign troops on Serbian territory went against the rinciple of sovereignty. According to the description made by Ivo H. aalder and Michael E. O'Hanlon, these measures were for the Western iplomats "the very crux of the negotiations. The Kosovars were not going ⊃ sign onto an interim agreement unless a substantial military guaranteed ieir safety, while the Serbs were not going to accept an agreement if it re- uired a foreign military presence on their soil. As a senior White House of- cial said at the time, 'the issue is how much force can the Serbs accept and ow little force can the Kosovars live with.'"[23]

So, how must we assess the NATO intervention from the last resort per- ⊃ective? First, based on the diplomatic deadlock in the Paris conference, iere seemed good reasons to believe that further diplomatic action (and so further delay of a military intervention) was no longer justified. When the RY/Serb delegation refused to continue talking about the promising Ram- ouillet results and their implementation, it should have been sufficiently lear that the *threat* of force *alone* would no longer be enough to persuade ie Yugoslav president. In October 1998, for instance, Milosevic had al- ≥ady agreed to comply with the demands of the Security Council Resolu- on 1199 (the so-called Holbrooke agreement) under the threat of the use f force by NATO. But as early as December of 1998, it became apparent iat this agreement would not hold.

Second, because Milosovic did not adhere to these Security Council Res- lution stipulations, the human suffering in Kosovo continued and even in- reased. On Christmas Eve of 1998, Yugoslav forces started new offensives i Kosovo. Belgrade claimed that these actions were necessary to hunt down ie KLA terrorists, but they also generated a new outpouring of refugees.

Third, and closely related to the two previous arguments, NATO credibil- y appeared to be at stake. When all measures short of the use of military ⊃rce had been tried without success, then it seemed that it was time to se- ously consider the next step. Not doing so would have jeopardized the redibility of NATO as an effective military organization, not only in the osovo crisis but also in future conflicts.

LIKELIHOOD OF SUCCESS

ι retrospect we know that after a seventy-eight-day NATO air campaign, 1ilosevic finally agreed to a plan for a complete and rapid withdrawal of

Yugoslav troops from Kosovo and for the swift deployment of a robust Western-dominated force. The nature of the Likelihood of Success Principle, however, does not allow us to judge the probability of success in a "post factum" way. What we need is look for indications that might help us assess the effectiveness of the military operation independently of our knowledge of the final result. The most obvious way to do this is to begin with a comparison of military strengths. If we can establish military superiority for one of the conflict parties, then it seems pretty straightforward where the military advantage, and thus the Likelihood of Success, lie.

No doubt, in the Kosovo case this approach puts NATO in a favorable position. When it comes to military strength, the Yugoslav armed forces, which had been subject to an international weapons embargo for years, were certainly no match for the most successful military alliance of the postwar period. So we might conclude that NATO, which had the military means to impose its will on its adversary, had a clear reasonable chance of success.

But the comparison of military strengths tells only part of the story. When we look more closely, this favorable Likelihood of Success indication seems much less persuasive. First, the nature of some of NATO's objectives need to be considered. When we look at these objectives (see above), it quickly becomes evident that some of them are very hard to reach just by using military force. By damaging their military instruments, you can perhaps induce your opponent to return to the negotiation table, but it is very unlikely that such action will end all the violence and repression. The same goes for the fourth objective. The necessary conditions for a safe return of all the refugees cannot be created simply by a bombing strategy. According to Mark Littman it was predictable that the humanitarian disaster in Kosovo would not be stopped by a NATO air campaign, but would get much worse due to the savage Serb response against the Albanian Kosovar population.[24] Because the Serbs could not retaliate against the high-flying NATO bombers, NATO should have realized that the Serbs would step up their campaign of ethnic cleansing.[25] NATO argued in its defense that such killings and expulsions had been imminent anyway, and that Belgrade had set in motion "Operation Horse Shoe," the plan for the systematic ethnic cleansing of Kosovo, even before the start of the NATO bombing.[26] Whatever the strength of these contentions, Adam Roberts believes that there are grounds for doubting whether, in the absence of the NATO bombing, the ethnic cleansing would have proceeded with such speed and viciousness.[27]

But let us suppose, for argument's sake, that NATO did not know and/or could not have known that the Serbs would react in such a horrendous way. Even in this case one could argue that the likelihood of success was not all that obvious. Despite the fact that NATO had by far a superior military capability, NATO itself limited its considerable advantage in two ways. It too the decision to (1) exclude the use of ground forces from the very beginning of the operation and (2) rely solely on high-altitude bombardment.

These limitations of its military potential were the expression of an uneasy compromise between the necessity to show resolve (the problem of credibility) and the lack of political will to do whatever was necessary to obtain the humanitarian goals that were set. It was clear from the beginning that NATO wanted to avoid the mistakes that the international community had made in Bosnia (1992–1995). After more than three years of failed diplomatic initiatives and half measures, NATO had proven in August–September of 1995 that a firm military stance against the Serb defiance (operation "Deliberate Force") could make a difference. The Dayton Peace Agreement had then paved the way to the postconflict reconstruction of Bosnia. In Kosovo, NATO did not want to waste any valuable time and had the intention to act in a determined manner from the very beginning. Unfortunately, NATO's actions spoke somewhat differently. When one views the intervention, it quickly becomes apparent that NATO, notwithstanding its determination, couldn't help avoiding the same mistakes.

As in Bosnia, there was a deep divide between NATO's high moral ambitions and its actual willingness to do whatever was necessary to fulfill them. At the very beginning of the war, President Clinton's statement that NATO would not use ground forces put serious limitations on the military instruments that NATO could use. This is true especially when one realizes that it was generally believed at the time that the use of airpower *alone* could not win the war. A second and perhaps clearer indication of NATO's military reluctance was its zero-casualty strategy. NATO wanted to bomb Milosevic into submission but was not prepared to make any sacrifices itself. The miraculous result of not losing one pilot during the seventy-eight-day bombing campaign was, according to Edward Luttwak, due to multiple layers of precaution.[28] First, very few strike missions were flown during the first weeks, which meant that the combat risks during these first weeks were rather limited for the allied pilots. Second, in order to minimize allied casualties, the air operation's first and foremost targets were the air-defense systems. Third, NATO avoided the Yugoslav air-defense systems by dropping their weapons from a safe 15,000 ft (5,000 m) altitude and, fourth and finally, NATO restricted its operations when weather conditions were not perfect for high-altitude bombing (although these conditions didn't pose any problems for low-altitude attacks).

The nature of these strategic limitations was clearly detrimental to the effectiveness of the operation. First, by limiting itself to the use of airpower, NATO could only hope that Milosevic, pressured by the air attacks, would decide to call off the military operations in Kosovo. If Milosevic decided to hang in and try to sit out the air campaign (which he did), NATO's likelihood of success inevitably would decrease significantly. The use of air power alone cannot put a stop to the human rights violations. One actually has to send in troops to protect the civilian population (by creating safe areas or humanitarian corridors, etc.). Second, by choosing high-altitude air operations, NATO imposed a high level of risk on the civilian population it wanted to protect. This meant that NATO had to face the possibility of increased accidents, which in the long run, could be very damaging to its image. One simply cannot continue saying that it is one's intention to protect the civilian population and at the same time continue using a strategy that puts these same people in harm's way. More important still is the effect this strategy had on the Serb population itself. There was a significant political opposition in Serbia against Milosevic. By targeting not only pure military objectives, but also mixed military-civilian infrastructure (oil refineries, radio stations, bridges, etc.), NATO had to take into account that the Yugoslav population might very well close ranks with the Milosevic regime and form a united front against NATO.

Adam Roberts gives two explanations for NATO's high degree of reliance on airpower.[29] First, the NATO member states were not willing to risk the lives of their own personnel in the operation. According to Roberts this zero-casualty reflex of Western powers constitutes a basic characteristic of the international interventions in the 1990s. The reason for this reluctance to accept casualties seems obvious. In order not to lose the support of the home front, one must avoid the loss of one's own soldiers in some faraway country (the body-bag syndrome). From a prudential point of view, such restraints were helpful, and perhaps necessary, to obtain the political objectives. The self-imposed limitations were the political price to pay for holding the alliance together. Strangely enough, however, NATO's extreme success in avoiding casualties (not one single combat casualty in eleven weeks of operations) tended, as we have seen, to generate another kind of feeling. Avoiding casualties is one thing; doing so at the expense of the civilian population that one is supposed to protect is quite another.

The second reason for the heavy reliance on the airpower strategy was what Roberts calls "a questionable reading of the history of the Bosnian war."[30] During this war, NATO executed a similar bombing campaign, called operation "Deliberate Force" (August–September 1995), in response to a Serb mortar attack on a Sarajevo marketplace that killed thirty-seven and wounded eighty-four people.[31] Shortly after this campaign, the Serbs agreed to participate in U.S.-led negotiations that ultimately resulted in the Dayton Peace Agreement (November 1995). According to Roberts, NATO thought mistakenly that it could repeat the success of operation "Deliberate Force" in Kosovo. NATO's assumptions were flawed for several reasons. First of all, the successful character of operation "Deliberate Force" had to be understood against the background of a substantial and equally successful ground offensive of the Croatian army against the Krajina Serbs in Croa tia, and against the Bosnian Serbs in Bosnia (the latter in cooperation with Bosnian government forces). In Kosovo the situation was different. Once operation "Allied Force" started, the KLA was not initially able to mount a successful ground offensive as the Croatian army had (this changed, however, toward the end of the air campaign). But besides the lack of a credible land-force component, there was also the fact that the 1995 bombing was not against Serbia proper and thus did not arouse the same nationalist response as would the bombing in 1999.[32]

So how should we assess the likelihood of success of operation "Allied Force"? The least we can say is that the prospects for a successful outcome were not all that obvious. On the contrary, even if we would decide to reformulate NATO's objectives in more military manageable terms such as "the stopping of a humanitarian catastrophe," the NATO air campaign would still remain problematic. There was reason to believe that massive air attacks would likely result in an intensified and accelerated ethnic cleansing campaign by the Serbs. Given the nature of NATO's objectives, this was exactly contrary to what NATO hoped to obtain. Furthermore, the self-imposed restrictions on NATO's military superiority (no use of ground forces and only high-altitude bombing) convinced Milosevic that NATO was not deeply committed to Kosovo's humanitarian cause. NATO, in contrast, was convinced that Milosevic would give in after a few days of bombing.

Both assumptions proved to be wrong. Milosevic didn't cave in, and NATO decided after the first weeks of bombing to intensify its air campaign. It did so not only by stepping up the number of sorties but also by enlarging its scope of targets. The prospects of success for the NATO operation increased significantly once Milosevic began to realize that NATO would not back down and that the Russians would not come to the rescue. In the second half of May, NATO began to move away from Clinton's initial statement of not using ground forces. This changed position was reinforced by NATO's announcement that it would deploy 50,000 troops on the Kosovo border "in order to ensure rapid implementation of any agreement that might be reached."[33] The KLA's major offensive (with the support of U.S. B-52's) on May 26, when it tried to break out of the Kosare enclave on the border with Albania,[34] provided another major factor that contributed to the prospect of a successful outcome.

PROPORTIONALITY (*AD BELLUM*)

Did NATO's decision to go to war against Yugoslavia over Kosovo respect the Principle of Proportionality? In order to answer that question we have to try to establish whether the benefits that could be expected from the execution of operation "Allied Force" outweighed its probable negative effects. Again, as in the Likelihood of Success analysis, the assessment of proportionality does not allow us to profit from our hindsight information. The proportionality analysis is not about comparing the *actual* amount of good with the *actual* amount of damage observed in a "post factum" way, but is essentially about assessing and comparing *possible* benefits and *possible* cost associated with the conducting of a massive air campaign. Let us start with the assessment of the possible benefits of operation "Allied Force."

The main objective of operation "Allied Force" was to force Milosevic to put a stop to the ongoing human rights violations in Kosovo, and, subsequently, to withdraw the Yugoslav forces, so that they could be replaced by an international military presence (cf. the just cause analysis). The benefits associated with these objectives have to be assessed as quite considerable. First of all, putting a stop to hostilities prevents the ongoing humanitarian catastrophe form getting worse. Second, and perhaps more importantly, the end of the hostilities offers the opportunity to rebuild social life. Another important benefit related to the decision to take military action against Yugoslavia was NATO's increase of credibility. By actually carrying out the military threat formulated against Milosevic, NATO rendered the deterrent quality of its threat for the use of military force more credible for future interventions. This, in turn, decreased significantly the likelihood of the actual use of force. But again this credibility bonus must not be assessed as too substantial. NATO was willing to actually do something but was, to put it mildly, prudently cautious in doing so.

What about the possible damages related to operation "Allied Force?" The most direct costs are those related to the actual execution of the operation itself. The strategic choice of high-altitude bombing allows us to assess NATO casualties as small. By executing their mission from a 15,000-ft (5,000 m) altitude, NATO pilots were relatively safe from the Yugoslav air defense systems. The safety of the NATO pilots had to be paid for, however, by imposing a relatively higher risk on the civilian population. This casualty risk increased even more when NATO decided to start bombing targets in densely populated areas like Belgrade. The material component of the damage has to be assessed in a more differentiated way. With a gradual strategy, as NATO used, there is always the possibility that the opponent would cave in during the first low-intensity stage of the operation. In such a scenario, material damage would most probably be limited to military installations, the primary NATO targets. However, that same incremental strategy could very well have the opposite effect. Low-intensity bombings could very well create the image in the mind of the opponent that the attacks are not all that bad and that he could possibly to sit out the air campaign. To counteract such an image, NATO would have to accelerate its air operations to an extreme by attacking "borderline" targets and by increasing its intensity significantly. In that last "protracted war" scenario, the ma terial damage would most probably be greater than the damage that would have been done by adopting a more decisive military strategy from the very beginning. The fact that Milosevic was not a person who would cave in easily made the protracted war scenario more likely.

But the probable costs related to operation "Allied Force" have a more indirect component. The decision to intervene militarily in the Kosovo crisis implied a serious risk of a geographic escalation. There was a real possibility that the conflict would spill over into Albania or Macedonia (the problems of Kosovar refugees pouring into both Macedonia and Albania, the border-crossing weapons traffic from Albania to Kosovo, etc.). But that was not the only escalation risk. The eventual success of the NATO action might inspire communities within the Yugoslav borders (cf. Hungarians in Vojvodina), as well as communities within other multinational states (like Russia), to try the same thing the Albanian Kosovars did. Another foreseeable effect of operation "Allied Force" was the risk of entering into a new Cold War. There was already for Russia the very troublesome fact of NATO expansion. Poland, Hungary, and the Czech Republic became full members of the alliance a few days prior to the beginning of the air campaign. The decision to bomb Russia's fellow Slavs further added to a strained relationship. A clear indication of this increased tension was President Yeltsin's statement that the use of NATO ground troops in Kosovo could draw "Russia into the fighting on Serbia's side, possibly provoking a wider conflict in Europe or even a 'third world war.'"[35] Despite these blustering words, the risk that such a scenario would actually take place should not be exaggerated. Not only did Moscow need the West for financial reasons,[36] it probably did not desire that its relations with the West be jeopardized because of the intransigence of the Milosevic regime.[37]

Was the chosen strategy a proportionate one then? When we put all the considerations about costs and benefits together, operation "Allied Force" appears to have been an acceptable trade-off between effectiveness and keeping direct and indirect risks in check. NATO had no choice but to take military action (Milosevic no longer reacted to NATO threats) if it intended to stop the atrocities and keep its credibility. By choosing a gradually escalating high-altitude bombing campaign, NATO perhaps did not choose the most effective strategy. Given the fact that Milosevic was not willing to accept the loss of sovereignty over Kosovo, one could argue that a more decisive use of force, combined with a threat to use ground forces, might have been more effective. Such a more decisive strategy, in comparison with the strategy of gradual escalation, would probably not have led to a new Cold (or even hot) War. Even if NATO had chosen to start massive air operations from the very beginning, Russia would still have needed financial support from the West. The crucial factor that justified the choice of the gradual rather than of the more decisive approach was that the latter probably would not have been accepted by all NATO members. For instance, when NATO decided to step up the intensity of its bombings during the campaign, a number of allies began to have second thoughts (e.g., Italy and Greece) or experienced strong opposition at home (e.g., Germany and France). Therefore, the loss of effectiveness by not choosing the more decisive approach was probably balanced by the fact that NATO succeeded in starting and continuing a military operation, and thereby saving its credibility.

DISCRIMINATION

To what extent did NATO's air campaign exercise discrimination? In order to realize its goals, NATO intended to paralyze and destroy the Yugoslav military potential. The nature of the military objective (to incapacitate a Yugoslav military establishment that was scattered all over Yugoslavia) brought NATO to a situation where it was often pushed to the extreme in the sense that it was often sharply confronted with two important problems involving discrimination.

The first was that it was not always possible for NATO to identify combatant targets with certainty. On the decision and information gathering level, for instance, there was always the possibility of basing the target list on erroneous information (cf. the bombing of the Chinese embassy in Belgrade on May 7, 1999). On the pilot's level there were a number of factors that could complicate the search and recognition process of the proper targets considerably. Poor weather conditions limited proper visual contact of the target. Pilots often returned to their base without expending their ordnance.[38] A second important element was the required bombing altitude. The 15,000 ft (5,000 m) altitude made it very hard for the pilots to be certain whether what they were aiming at was a legitimate target. On April 14 in the neighborhood of Djakovica, a U.S. F16 pilot fired on what he thought was a military convoy. Unfortunately, he hit a tractor and wagons carrying Albanian Kosovars, thereby killing sixty-five people.[39] Another element that contributed to the complexity of the air operation was that the Yugoslav police and military did all they could to make NATO's task difficult, if not impossible. They did this by submerging military targets in a clear civilian environment (e.g., hiding tanks and other military material in villages, dressing military personnel in civilian clothes, mixing with civilian convoys, etc.).[40]

The second problem had to do with the questionable moral character of some NATO targets. In response to the continued defiance of Milosevic, NATO was pushed to include "borderline cases" on its target list. Especially after mid-April 1999, it became increasingly clear that NATO was no longer limiting itself to pure military targets (defense infrastructure, fielded troops, tanks, etc.). Bombing expanded to oil refineries, fuel dumps, bridges, roads, railroads, etc. These elements of infrastructure were of vital importance to those actively involved in the process of human rights violations. The Yugoslav police and military could not properly function for instance without the regular resupply of fuel. With the widening of the target list, NATO wished to incapacitate the Yugoslav military by cutting off its resupply lines. But were these mixed or dual installations (a military and civilian utility) proper targets for military attack?

In this context, the Double Effect Principle offers a way out on condition that the damage to the mixed infrastructure is solely intended to affect the capability of the Yugoslav armed forces. If NATO's intention was to demoralize the Yugoslav population in order to generate additional pressure for the Milosevic regime to give in, then the double effect principle no longer provides justification for these actions in the combatant/noncombatant gray zone. The principle forbids the use of the noncombatants as a means for achieving legitimate objectives. In this regard, many people questioned the legitimacy of NATO's use of the so-called soft bombs against the Yugoslav power plants. These bombs explode in the air above power plants, showering splinters of graphite onto the electrical transformers below. The result is a power shutdown as the graphite splinters create short circuits. Although NATO stated that these power shutdowns were intended to incapacitate the Yugoslav military establishment ("If a command and control system has no electricity to turn it on," NATO spokesman Jamie Shea said, "it is just wire, metal and plastic, not a functioning military system"), the discomfort to the Yugoslav population was all too obvious. Still, one can interpret NATO's use of these "soft bombs," which create no substantial material damage, as an important indication that NATO had no real intention of destroying Yugoslavia's economic potential. Furthermore, the satisfaction of the Double Effect Principle's condition of necessity (in order to obtain the good, we cannot avoid doing the evil) seems obvious in the case of targeting mixed installations like power plants. The mixed character of the targets implies *per definition* that there will be at least some nonmilitary damage.

PROPORTIONALITY (*IN BELLO*)

The level of proportionality (*in bello*) during operation "Allied Force" has to be assessed in a differentiated way. Most attacks on purely military targets appeared proportional. On the one hand, the expected benefits related to the bombing of military targets could be considered as real and immediate, and, on the other, one could assess the probability of significant collateral damage as quite limited because of the use of precision guided high-tech devices. One has to be prudent, nonetheless, and not exaggerate the risk-free character of these high-tech weapons. First, there is always the possibility of human error or a mechanical defect. Second, the capacity to bomb in a more discriminate way does not necessarily imply that this capacity will be put to a good use. Often the risk reduction provided by these weapons induces unwarranted confidence, and the selection of targets results in unacceptable collateral damage when any error occurs. And third, in the case the adversary tends to blur the distinction between the military and nonmilitary targets (e.g. putting tanks in factories with a sole civilian purpose), one is often pushed to perform military actions that, high-tech weapons or not, carry a considerable risk of being disproportionate. It goes without saying that those who deliberately create such confusion not only carry a great deal of responsibility for the collateral damage; they also threaten to undermine the very idea of discrimination in the long run.

The proportionality of the attacks on the so-called mixed or dual targets was much less obvious. The benefits of dual-attack targeting have to be considered at the strategic level. By destroying roads, bridges, railroads, fuel dumps, and so on, NATO wanted to slow down and eventually immobilize the Yugoslav war machine. The probability that this policy would actually succeed had to be assessed as high. In the long run no army or police force can continue its operations when it lacks sufficient logistical support. A clear disadvantage, however, is the fact that its effects would not be felt right away. In contrast, the bombing of dual targets like power plants and telecommunication centers has a more direct impact for the simple reason that it will almost immediately affect the functioning of the military command, control, and communication systems.

The collateral damage related to the bombing of dual installations has to be assessed as both certain and substantial. The certainty of the collateral damages follows, as we already remarked, from the very nature of the dual targets. The substantial amount of damage can in large part be attributed to the fact that the destruction of a significant number of dual targets has implications on a macro and micro level. The bombing of power plants, bridges, and roads, for instance, did not only affect the functioning of the Yugoslav military machine but also undermined the economic potential of the Yugoslav society as a whole and thereby affected the well-being of the noncombatants. On a micro level we have to consider not only the actual destruction of the dual installations themselves, but also (like in the case of the bombing of the pure military targets) the unintended casualties and material damage in the immediate proximity of the objective. Other micro-level related collateral damage that deserves special mention is the bombing of the power plants. Although NATO tried to minimize the direct damage to these installations by using so-called soft bombs (cf. discrimination), some of the indirect consequences were, to say the least, problematic from a moral point of view. Hitting electricity plants meant, for instance, that power would be cut off in hospitals, babies' incubators, and water-pumping installations.[41] In fact, in one specific instance, the military lawyers who were responsible for assessing the acceptability of the potential targets actually rejected an electricity plant. For the proportionality condition to be respected, the military character of the dual target has to be *clear*. A bridge that we know will probably never be used for military purposes (because of its remote location, for example) has little military significance and can therefore not be considered as a legitimate target.

CONCLUSION

Although the scale of human rights violations in Kosovo prior to the air campaign is still uncertain, it can hardly be denied that NATO had a defensible just cause in stopping the humanitarian crisis. NATO's intentions, however, were at best mixed. NATO wanted to show resolve by taking the appropriate military actions at the right time. Yet, the Alliance limited itself from the very beginning to a high-tech, risk-free gradual air campaign, a choice that, from a likelihood of success point of view, appears problematic. One just can't stop ethnic cleansing by bombing from a 15,000-ft altitude. The problem, however, was that the chosen strategy was—taking into account the domestic policy constraints of NATO governments— probably the only one available. Politically it was this kind of self-limited operation or no operation at all. From the perspective of proportionality, this suboptimal solution could be defended as an acceptable trade-off between effectiveness and keeping direct and indirect risks in check. The most troublesome "*ad bellum*" principle, however, was legitimate authority. From a legal point of view, NATO didn't have a leg to stand on. Morally speaking, however, NATO could be considered as a legitimate authority, because of the extreme gravity of the situation and the probable immobilization of the Security Council should action in Kosovo come to a vote. Although NATO used weapons and rules of engagement with high discrimination and a measured proportionality (accidents couldn't be avoided entirely, of course), operation "Allied Force" became highly problematic when NATO started to include so-called dual targets in its bombing lists. The collateral damage generated by this kind of bombing was both certain and substantial. NATO entered the war thinking that Milosevic would give in after a few days of bombing, only to learn that Kosovo was not Bosnia. In the end, it took a seventy-eight-day air campaign, during which Milosevic pushed the world's most powerful military alliance to the most difficult choices.

NOTES

1. The two chapters on NATO's intervention in Kosovo have been written in 2000/2001.

2. After the de facto dissolution of the Socialist Republic of Yugoslavia (SFRY) in 1991, the two former republics of the SFRY, Serbia and Montenegro, continued to be united under the name Federal Republic of Yugoslavia (FRY).

3. For more details on the Kosovo history, see Ivo H. Daalder and Michael F. O'Hanlon, *Winning Ugly: NATO's War to Save Kosovo* (Washington, D.C.: Brookings Institution Press, 2000), 224; Raymond Detrez, "The Rights to Self-Determination and Secession in Yugoslavia: A Hornets' Nest of Inconsistencies," in *Contextualizing Secession: Normative Judgements in a Comparative Perspective*, ed. Bruno Coppieters and Richard Sakwa (Oxford: Oxford University Press, 2003); Tim Judah, *Kosovo: War and Revenge* (New Haven, Conn., and London: Yale University Press, 2000), 348; Noel Malcolm, *Kosovo: A Short History* (London: Macmillan, 1998), 492; Miranda Vickers, *Between Serb and Albanian: A History of Kosovo* (London: Hurst and Company, 1998), 348.

4. Malcolm, *Kosovo. A Short History*, 347.

5. There were, and still are, many questions about what exactly happened in Racak. Some say that at least one group of men found at the place of the massacre were not civilians, but KLA combatants who had been killed during earlier military actions with the Serb forces. Others claim that there are no indications to suggest that those who were found killed there were not unarmed civilians. Tim Judah, *Kosovo: War and Revenge*, 194.

6. Wesley K. Clark, "When Force is Necessary: NATO's Military Response to the Kosovo Crisis," *NATO Review* 47, no. 2 (Summer 1999): 16.

7. Stephen P. Aubin, "Operation Allied Force: War or 'Coercive Diplomacy'?" *Strategic Review* (Summer 1999): 7.

8. *Economist*, "State in Embryo," (November 27, 2000), 37.

9. Authors like Noam Chomsky argue that the humanitarian catastrophe that NATO used to justify its air campaign only really began after the NATO bombing started. See Noam Chomsky, *The New Military Humanism: Lessons from Kosovo* (London: Pluto Press, 1999), 16–17.

10. Marc Weller, *The Crisis in Kosovo 1989–1999: From the Dissolution of Yugoslavia to Rambouillet and the Outbreak of Hostilities* (Cambridge: Documents & Analysis Publishing Ltd., 1999), 258.

11. Weller, *The Crisis in Kosovo*, 258.

12. Adam Roberts, "NATO's "Humanitarian War" over Kosovo," *Survival* 41, no. 3 (Autumn 1999): 107.

13. James Kitfield, "A War of Limits," *National Journal*, July 7, 1999, 2155.

14. Kitfield, "A War of Limits," 2155.

15. Roberts, "NATO's 'Humanitarian War' Over Kosovo," 107.

16. Catherine Guicherd, "International Law and the War in Kosovo," *Survival* 41, no. 2 (Summer 1999): 26.

17. Guicherd, "International Law and the War in Kosovo," 27.

18. Mark Littman, *Kosovo: Law & Diplomacy* (London: Centre of Policy Studies, 1999), 8–13.

19. Littman, *Kosovo*, 10.

20. Littman, *Kosovo*, 12.

21. Weller, *The Crisis in Kosovo*, 475.

22. Weller, *The Crisis in Kosovo*, 475.

23. Ivo H. Daalder and Michael F. O'Hanlon, *Winning Ugly*, 80.

24. Mark Littman, *Kosovo: Law & Diplomacy*, 16–17.

25. Within one month of the start of the bombing, over half a million people had fled from Kosovo into neighboring countries, and many thousands more were displaced within Kosovo itself. By the end of the campaign 1,400,000 persons were displaced.

26. Roberts, "NATO's 'Humanitarian War' over Kosovo," 110.

27. Roberts, "NATO's 'Humanitarian War' over Kosovo," 110.

28. Edward Luttwak spoke in this perspective of the NATO-intervention in Kosovo as the first "post-heroic" war. Edward Luttwak, "Give War a Chance," *Foreign Affairs* 78, no. 4 (July/August 1999): 40.

29. Roberts, "NATO's 'Humanitarian War' over Kosovo," 108.

30. Roberts, "NATO's 'Humanitarian War' over Kosovo," 108.

31. Dick A. Leurdijk, *The United Nations and NATO in Former Yugoslavia, 1991–1996: Limits to Diplomacy and Force* (The Hague: Netherlands Atlantic Commission / Netherlands Institute of International Relations "Clingendael," 1996), 78.

32. Roberts, "NATO's 'Humanitarian War' over Kosovo," 108.

33. Ivo Daalder and Michael O'Hanlon, "Unlearning Lessons of Kosovo," *Foreign Policy* (Fall 1999): 131.

34. Judah, *Kosovo: War and Revenge*, 284.

35. *Economist*, April 17, 1999, 17.

36. The visit of IMF director Michael Camdessus to Moscow for talks on further loans almost coincided with the commencement of operation "Allied Force."

37. M. A. Smith, *Russian Thinking on European Security after Kosovo* (London: Conflict Studies Research Centre, July 1999), 6.

38. During the first twenty-one days of the operation NATO had only seven days of good weather.

39. According to Michael Walzer's version of the "double effect" principle, as described in *Just and Unjust Wars*, this course of action would have been morally questionable. In the framework of this doctrine Walzer introduces what he calls "the civilian's right to due care." (See Michael Walzer, *Just and Unjust Wars: A Moral Argument with Historical Illustrations* [New York: Basic Books, 1992], 156–9.) In that perspective one could argue that the Albanian Kosovars enjoyed a right to due care and that thereby NATO pilots had to accept a greater risk for themselves by bombing the military targets at a lower altitude. The use of Apache helicopters would no doubt have been a positive step in this respect. These combat helicopters operate at low altitude, thereby decreasing the probability of collateral damage, but at the same time increasing their own vulnerability to enemy attack.

40. Judah, *Kosovo: War and Revenge*, 259.

41. Michael Ignatieff quoted in Tim Judah, *Kosovo: War and Revenge*, 258.

10

NATO's Intervention in the Kosovo Crisis

Whose Justice?

Boris Kashnikov

The legitimacy of NATO's war against Serbia in March 1999 has been widely debated. In the previous chapter, Carl Ceulemans concludes that justice is on the side of NATO's military campaign. But his analysis is not the only one possible within the framework of Just War Theory. In the following, a different analysis is presented. It shows that while operating within the framework of Just War Theory one can arrive at quite different conclusions from his.

JUST CAUSE?

The core of the Just Cause argument provided by the proponents of NATO intervention in Kosovo concerns the "gross and massive human rights violations" committed primarily by Serbian military and paramilitary in that region. It seems, however, with the hindsight knowledge we have after the war, that the scale of those violations was grossly exaggerated. Editorial comments in Western newspapers spoke about huge numbers of civilian victims and some even referred to the risk of genocide against the Albanian population of Kosovo. NATO justified its use of military force by arguing that there was a need for humanitarian intervention. NATO did so without knowing the exact figures of the alleged violations. Indeed, it seems that there were human rights violations, but that the number of victims were fewer than claimed. Also, there were far fewer mass graves than was claimed before and during the war by Western media and government officials.

In order to assess the scale of the human rights violations before the war started, it is necessary to understand the nature of the conflict in which the

Serbs and Albanian Kosovars were involved. The scale of human rights violations and the number of war crimes is generally strongly related to the nature of war and the moral attitudes of the belligerents. And among all types of wars, civil wars and wars of secession are the most vicious. For Albanian Kosovars and all Serbs (both those living in and outside of Kosovo) this region is part of their sacred homeland. The fact that the Serbs constitute a minority in Kosovo does not mean that this land has less value to them. In Serbian history Kosovo is a sacred place, the cradle of national statehood, to be compared with the significance of Jerusalem for the Jews. Serbs cannot, therefore, lightly abandon that region to the Albanian Kosovars. This is especially true for the Serb Kosovars, who, in addition, did (and do) not want to abandon their country and homes. The Serb people had therefore a strong right, and the Serb authorities a strong duty, to oppose the separatist activities of the Kosovo Liberation Army (KLA).

It is true that the military operations pursued by both by the Albanian Kosovars and the Serbs had horrible consequences for the civilian population of the region. But these consequences should not be considered as higher compared to other wars of this type, and surely did not justify a new war with additional civilian victims. Civilian casualties took place in Kosovo in the context of a guerrilla war against the Serb authorities. The tactics that this implies (e.g., the Serb army had to respond to firing coming from villages in densely populated areas) have indeed to be taken into account. But the number of victims was not so high as claimed by NATO officials. Ivo Daalder and Michael O'Hanlon, who defend the legitimacy of the NATO operation, estimate the number of people killed in Kosovo in 1998 as high as 2,000. This figure includes KLA fighters and civilians of both Serbian and Albanian origin.[1] When compared with the number of civilian victims in the military actions of the Turks against the Kurds (who are seeking autonomy) or of the Russians against the Chechen government of Dzukhar Dudayev in 1994–1996,[2] it becomes clear that NATO's presentation of its case is severely flawed. The way the war between the Serb authorities and the KLA was fought may be considered as unjust and did justify the concern of the international community. But the degree of injustice did not reach the level that justified military intervention.

There was thus no Just Cause for NATO's war against Yugoslavia. In responding to the question concerning the Principle of Proportionality we will see, later in this chapter, that NATO may have created more victims as a result of the "collateral effects" of its bombings of Yugoslavia than the 1998 civil war itself did. According to Ivo Daalder and Michael O'Hanlon, NATO bombings killed 500 civilians during 78 days of war, whereas the number of Serbian servicemen killed was likely about 1,000. According to some Serbian sources, the number of civilians killed may, however, have been as high as 5,700.[3] The humanitarian consequences of the destruction of the social and medical infrastructure have also to be taken into account.

Denying that NATO had just cause in waging this war does not mean that the Serb authorities and military did not commit sordid war crimes. It remains to be seen to what extent the government had plans to force the Albanian population out of its homes, and who precisely was responsible for these crimes. The hundreds of thousands of civilians who were expelled from cities and villages were perceived by Western media as the victims of "ethnic cleansing." Such activity needs to be severely condemned and prosecuted. But it does not justify the extraordinary exaggerations made by NATO concerning the scale of human rights violations during this war and the additional victims that were created as a consequence of NATO's military intervention.

LEGITIMATE AUTHORITY?

The roles of the Western governments, and particularly the United States, should not be neglected in assessing moral responsibilities. Quite apart from the issue of Just Cause in Kosovo, NATO's threats to use force and its use of force cannot be reconciled with the present regime of international law. The UN Charter bans every appeal to the threat of force, and the use of force itself, except in self-defense (including collective self-defense) or when it is explicitly authorized by the Security Council.

The American administration started to threaten Serbia without any such authorization as early as 1992. In a letter to Slobodan Milosevic of December 1992, President Bush warned that "in the event of conflict in Kosovo caused by Serbian action, the United States would be prepared to employ military force against the Serbs in Kosovo and in Serbia proper." This so-called Christmas warning was reiterated by the Clinton administration in 1993.[4] Such threats were understood by Albanian radicals as clear signs that it was to their advantage to escalate armed conflict in the area and then to blame the Serbs for using military force. The American policies strengthened the position of the Albanian proponents of a violent solution. At the same time they were costly to many segments of the Albanian Kosovar population that supported nonviolent resistance and the strategy of compromise.

The Kosovo debacle should be regarded largely as the result of an interventionist doctrine that was encouraged by Bill Clinton.[5] This doctrine made it possible for the KLA to acquire NATO support by demonstrating "Serbian atrocities." Thus the KLA did its best to prevent, for instance, a Serbian withdrawal from the region—a withdrawal that was a condition of the Milosevic/Holbrooke agreement in 1998. In this way, it became possible for the KLA and the Western countries to label Serb authorities the culprits for their failure to deescalate the conflict.

NATO members and NATO itself claimed that they were entitled to use force unilaterally to prevent massive violations of human rights. Such claims have serious negative repercussions on the development of an international regime of human rights. First, it is difficult to find universal and objective criteria of human rights violations that are commonly agreed upon by all states and that are equally applicable to all situations in every part of the world. The United States and NATO would furthermore hardly agree that other states, such as Russia or China, have the same right of final judgment in the sensitive matter of human rights violations. Discrimination, denial of citizenship rights, and other human rights violations of the Russian population in Latvia, for instance, still remains a major concern for the Russian government. It would hardly be acceptable for Western countries if Russia claimed a right to intervene in this matter. And what should the Chinese government do were it confronted with severe human rights violations against members of the Chinese communities in certain countries of Southeast Asia? Fortunately, both the Russian and Chinese governments have shown great restraint when they have faced such problems by acting in accord with international law. In contrast, the NATO alliance claimed for itself a right to interfere in Kosovo that it would not acknowledge to other countries.

After the end of the Cold War and the dissolution of the Warsaw Pact, NATO underwent a serious transformation. In 1999, its eastward expansion led to the inclusion of Hungary, Poland, and the Czech Republic in the NATO alliance, and to the creation of an extensive program of military cooperation, called the Partnership for Peace (PfP). Military cooperation was forged with all Organization for Security and Cooperation in Europe (OSCE) countries—except Tajikistan—and was presented as supporting OSCE efforts to stabilize the whole of the Euro-Atlantic region. The high number of participant countries and the intensity of the cooperation made it possible for NATO Secretary-General Javier Solana to state in September 1996 that PfP was the most successful military cooperation program in Europe's history.[6] This program was supplemented in December 1996 by a political body, the Euro-Atlantic Partnership Council (EAPC), where the countries participating in the PfP could discuss issues related to the construction of a new security architecture for Europe. Through these kinds of activities, NATO performs a number of tasks that have been traditionally performed by OSCE. This transformation of NATO, and its competition with OSCE, have created substantial problems for Russia. Whereas the political cooperation in the framework of OSCE is based on the principle of equality between all member states, this is far from being the case in such a cooperation framework as EAPC. At the time of the Kosovo intervention, NATO and

Russia already had great difficulties in finding common ground for cooperation. The intervention only made matters worse.

During the Kosovo crisis, the NATO Alliance went a significant step further in carving out a new role in the European security order. In justifying its military action, NATO Secretary-General Solana claimed that NATO had the duty to use force without the authorization of the UN Security Council because this UN institution proved unable to act appropriately in the given circumstances. Already in October 1998, he justified the threat of NATO's military action with the impossibility of obtaining, in short order, a Security Council resolution mandating the use of force.[7] This means that NATO started to present itself not as a complementary organization to OSCE but rather as a substitute for the authority of the United Nations. Other countries, especially Russia and China, are extremely concerned about this evolution. NATO seems to have forged a new doctrine of international relations, in which it claims to play a leading role and which is likely to make the world a much more dangerous place. If such unilateral decision-making in matters of war and peace becomes normal practice, the issue of human rights may become a justification for any type of intervention by states that have the military capabilities of doing so.

RIGHT INTENTIONS?

The NATO alliance is not a homogenous bloc. Not all its members joined the military intervention against Serbia enthusiastically. When all were eventually convinced to support this decision, each did it with its own intentions. But among the NATO member states, the intentions of the United States have to be taken into account more than the rest. Its position was indeed decisive in triggering the war. The following list of intentions is based on public and academic debates on the war, where someone or some group of people referred to each intention in one or another of the NATO countries as having been decisive in starting the war. It was said that the war started in order to:

1. impose the will of the NATO alliance on the Serb government;
2. weaken the Serbian military forces;
3. take hold of a strategic position in the Balkans;
4. give credibility to NATO's use of the threat of force;
5. unite NATO and strengthen the level of its strategic interaction;
6. take hold of strategic mineral resources of the region;
7. test new weapons and military know-how in real action;
8. utilize older missiles and weapons systems before they become out of date;

9. provide humanitarian relief to all the inhabitants of Kosovo and put an end to the violent ethnic conflicts in that region.

Among those various intentions only the ninth is a good one. This means that it is the only one directly related to what was officially proclaimed as NATO's just cause. Some of these intentions are strikingly immoral (6, 7, and 8). If it could be proven that any one was decisive in the decision to wage war, the whole military operation would have to be considered unjust. The remaining reasons (1–5) are by themselves neither moral nor immoral. Their moral character depends on their relation to the declared Just Cause. They are legitimate only to the extent that they are related to its realization. If such a relation cannot be demonstrated, for instance by proving that NATO had no real intention to provide humanitarian help or that such a good intention was not decisive in its decision to use force, then they have to be considered immoral or bad as well.

Of course, NATO always claimed that its primary intention was to provide humanitarian aid to Kosovo. And indeed it received much public support in NATO countries for having this intention. But it is surely not an easy task to prove that this was NATO's primary intention. It is, however, possible to see if NATO had such an intention in similar conflicts. And it is quite easy to prove that it did not. NATO did nothing to save the Serbian population of Krajina in Croatia from their plight. The entire Serbian population of more than half a million people were expelled by Croat forces, and many of their houses leveled to the ground in 1995. This ethnic cleansing was done in violation of Security Council resolutions. NATO countries put strong diplomatic pressure on Croatia to reverse this policy, but they did not implement sanctions or take similar measures as those that were directed against Serbia. It is not realistic to assume that NATO had entirely changed its moral standards in four years' time, and that in 1999 it was following humanitarian policies that were entirely absent before. It is far more probable that the intention to provide humanitarian relief was not of vital importance but rather a disguise for more powerful intentions.

The lack of a strong humanitarian commitment can also be demonstrated by the way the war itself was waged and how NATO addressed the issue of postwar reconstruction. NATO's use of military force led to gross and massive human rights violations. Once an agreement with the Serb government was finally signed, NATO failed to disarm the KLA. Nor did NATO provide for the safety of the remaining Serbian population. The killings and expulsion of Serbs, and of members of other minorities, continued after NATO took control of Kosovo. Further, Serb historical and cultural sites were damaged or destroyed by radical Albanian Kosovars. Also, NATO did not have the intention to act as firmly as it had done only a few months earlier against Serbia.[8] It may therefore be concluded that the intention to provide humanitarian relief was—if existent at all—weak and irrelevant to the decision to wage war. The other intentions mentioned above were far more powerful, which makes it possible to state that the Principle of Right Intentions was not respected.

LIKELIHOOD OF SUCCESS?

When it comes to the Principle of Likelihood of Success, some proponents of NATO intervention feel at ease. Serbia was hardly a match for Allied forces. Such a focus on NATO's military supremacy is, however, far too restrictive. The Principle of Likelihood of Success requires a broader view of success than military supremacy on the battlefield. Also NATO had given a broad political characterization of the objectives it wanted to reach with the use of force. According to the Rambouillet framework document and its military provisions, the main aims of the NATO operation were

1. a verifiable stop to all military actions and the immediate end of violence and repression;
2. the withdrawal from Kosovo of the Serb military, police, and paramilitary forces;
3. the stationing in Kosovo of NATO troops and their free access to the whole Yugoslav territory;
4. the unconditional and safe return of all refugees and displaced persons to Kosovo;
5. credible assurance of Milosevic's willingness to work on the basis of the Rambouillet framework in order to reach a political solution;
6. a political process aimed toward establishing an interim political framework agreement providing for substantial self-government for Kosovo, with respect to the territorial integrity of Yugoslavia and the minority rights of the whole Kosovar population;
7. a comprehensive approach to the economic development and stability of Kosovo.

There was no likelihood of success for NATO to defeat Serbia in a ground war. This was so not for military, but mainly for political reasons. A ground war, because it would have resulted in many casualties on both sides, would have created strong opposition in many NATO countries, including the United States. This would then have led to sharp differences among the members of the Alliance, the lack of the necessary consensus, the ending of the military operations, and a NATO defeat. Consequently, NATO chose to use airpower exclusively. This strategy contradicted its proclaimed humanitarian aims. In turn, this policy facilitated the ethnic cleansing of Albanian

Kosovars by the Serbs during the war, and of Serb Kosovars after the war. NATO cannot, therefore, be seen as having successfully fulfilled the humanitarian objectives that it had put forward.

If, after the war's end, one were to make a balance sheet of achievements in terms of NATO's own objectives, one would have to arrive at negative conclusions. Only some diplomatic and humanitarian objectives, such as the return of the Albanian Kosovars to their homes, were achieved (although there is every reason to believe that they could have been more easily realized by other means than the use of force). Some other objectives, such as the implementation of an effective civilian administration, have not been realized. Nor has the objective of effectively protecting minority rights.

The presence of NATO even under UN auspices does not solve the problems of the region. It creates demands among the Albanian population that their region may soon become independent. Radical Serb nationalists are planning to take revenge as soon as NATO troops are withdrawn. Violence and crime have not stopped in the meantime. Whereas the Albanian Kosovars have been allowed to return to their homes, the Serb Kosovars are now being victimized. The safe return of the more than 100,000 refugees (Serbs, Romany, and other minorities) is out of the question. The ethnic cleansing of these minorities makes free elections and the principle of self-government for Kosovo a mockery. As it was stated by the Orthodox Bishop of Raska and Prizren in a letter of protest concerning the role of KFOR (NATO's Kosovo Force): "Now the Albanians are oppressing Serbs and are committing the same crimes against Serbs and other non-Albanian communities which were committed against the Kosovo Albanians in the time of Milosevic's regime. But these recent crimes occur in the time of peace and with the presence of KFOR, very often just in front of their eyes."[9]

NATO has been unable to prevent an escalation of the ethnic conflicts in other countries. In April 2001, the Macedonian president Boris Trajkovski stated in an address to the UN Human Rights Commission in Geneva that instability is also threatening his own country, as a "direct export from Kosovo." He called for the "urgent and systematic" disarmament of the population in Kosovo and for the immediate punishment of terrorists and "armed extremists." It is estimated that 30,000 refugees resulted from the clashes in the area at the time.[10] The situation in southern Serbia, subject to attacks by Albanian insurgents, was hardly any better. Since early 2000, ethnic Albanian guerrillas have been using some parts of the buffer zone between Kosovo and Serbia proper—that had been demilitarized at the end of the war—as a sanctuary from which to attack security forces in southern Serbia's Presevo Valley Region.

There are various types of peacekeeping operations. In assessing the chances of success of NATO's operation in Kosovo, it is important to identify what type of peacekeeping operation it is. The chances of success of any such an operation without the full support of the warring parties themselves is minimal. Unfortunately, this is the type of peacekeeping operation found in Kosovo. About this, Charles Krauthammer says: "The logical end of all humanitarian intervention is peacekeeping. And the lesson of the last half-century is that peacekeeping works if the parties have had enough and merely want an outsider to provide reassurance—Sinai is the classic example—but that peacekeeping in the absence of these conditions is an exercise in futility."[11] Deploying peacekeeping operations without having a clear mandate from the warring parties themselves includes, as part of this futility, the risk that the peacekeepers themselves will be seen to be partial and thus soon will become the targets of the local forces. This happened in Somalia, Nagorno-Karabakh, and other places where peace has been enforced, and it is happening now again in Kosovo. Not only Russian but also American military have been the victims of violent attacks of radical Albanian Kosovars. It is clear that NATO took the decision to intervene militarily in great haste, without realistic goals or a clear policy as to how to pacify the region and without an exit strategy.

LAST RESORT?

Respecting the Principle of Last Resort means that all nonmilitary means to settle the crisis have been used first. NATO did not respect this principle. Negotiations based on mutual compromises still had a chance. But NATO claimed that all negotiations including the Rambouillet talks failed before it took the decision to start its air campaign. But, on the contrary, there were no negotiations in a strict sense. In February 1999 the first round of negotiations in Rambouillet under the auspices of the Contact Group (United States, Britain, France, Germany, Italy, and Russia) started.[12] On February 6, the conference was supposed to discuss the general principles for solving the problem including the status of an autonomous Kosovo that had been worked out by the contact group. But the delegations were given only the so-called "Temporary agreement on peace and autonomy in Kosovo and Metokhia (Framework document)" and three supplements dealing with the Constitution of Kosovo, the elections of local bodies, and the judicial system. The Serb delegation accepted all the conditions of the agreement, insisting only on guarantees of territorial integrity. On February 23, the contact group declared that progress had been made in the negotiations and that a political settlement would be reached soon.

But the final text of the agreement was presented to the parties only on the final day of negotiations. As it happened, about two-thirds of this text was completely new to the Serb delegation. In addition, two supplements to the text were not composed by the contact group but by NATO. The Russian representative refused to sign these supplements. According to the draconian supplements, NATO's military forces were to be deployed in Kosovo unconditionally, with no indication of terms. The text of Rambouillet document gave NATO further "free and unimpeded access throughout the Federal Republic of Yugoslavia," including Serbia. The Serb delegation stated that these conditions were simply nonnegotiable. Serbia faced an ultimatum of agreeing either to what it rightly considered an occupation by foreign military force of its territory, or air strikes. Nevertheless, Serbia agreed to sign the political part of the agreement as a result of the threats. It also agreed to an international presence, the nature of which was to be specified later. After that agreement was made, Serbia was ready to discuss the scope and terms of the international military presence in Kosovo. The second round of negotiations in Paris began on March 15, 1999. But the proposal of the Serb delegation was rejected. Albanians were permitted to sign the document alone. The Russian delegation refused to give its support to this type of negotiations.

All these events make the United States and NATO responsible for disabling the negotiations. Mark Littman rightfully concludes that NATO did not make every necessary effort to find a compromise. He adds that "at a critical point in the discussions at Rambouillet, NATO abandoned diplomacy in favor of a package of non-negotiable demands contained in a document described by Dr. Kissinger as 'a terrible diplomatic document,' 'a provocation' and 'an excuse to start bombing.' And it is likely that, if the terms which were agreed at the end of the campaign had been put forward at Rambouillet, then the ethnic cleansing and the war could have been averted."[13]

Indeed, Littman considers that the following provisions, which were accepted by NATO and the Serb government at the end of the war, contained significant concessions to the original demands by NATO. These provisions are that

1. any international force stationed in Kosovo would have to be authorized by the United Nations Security Council;
2. such an international force would, besides NATO, also include Russian troops;
3. the civilian administration to be installed would be under the control of the United Nations Security Council;
4. the force should have no access to any part of Yugoslavia outside Kosovo.[14]

The scope of the NATO concessions shows that its previous objectives were unreasonable. Indeed, the terms on which the bombing ended included important departures from Rambouillet that amount to concessions to the Serbs. The United Nations Security Council, instead of NATO, received ultimate authority for Kosovo, thereby giving Russia, a country friendly to the Serbs, a power of veto. And whereas Rambouillet gave NATO forces unimpeded access to all of Yugoslavia, including Serbia, the June settlement allowed the alliance free rein only in Kosovo. Related to these matters, Michael Mandelbaum comments as follows: "Whether such modifications, if offered before the bombing began and combined with a more robust OSCE presence in Kosovo, could have avoided what followed can never be known. What is clear is that NATO's leaders believed that concessions were unnecessary because a few exemplary salvos would quickly bring the Serbs to heel."[15] That was an evil assumption that paved the road to war. It means that the NATO alliance had chosen to discard serious attempts at finding a diplomatic solution in favor of the use of force.

PROPORTIONALITY (*AD BELLUM*)?

Was the decision to launch a military operation proportional to the scale of the problems to be solved in Kosovo? In order to answer this question, an attempt will be made to establish whether the benefits that could be expected from the operation outweighed its negative effects. Only moral benefits should be taken into account, of course, not geopolitical advantages for NATO or the enhancement of its credibility. In the following, this problem is approached from a postwar perspective, with the hindsight information we now have.

On the positive side, the scale of violence that took place before March 1999 was indeed diminished, thanks to NATO's intervention. And Albanian refugees were permitted to return to their homes. On the negative side, as already argued above, violent ethnic conflict itself was not halted. Further, the end of the war marked the beginning of new waves of ethnic cleansing, but now of Serb Kosovars. Further costs of the war include the horrors of war for the civilian population in Serbia and Kosovo. People were wounded and killed, and severe damage was done to the economy and to the environment. NATO's intervention also weakened the global international system of crisis management based on the exclusive authority of the UN Security Council concerned with military intervention, and the threat to intervene, in internal ethnic conflicts. But such a quick overview of costs and benefits requires further elaboration.

The Principle of Proportionality takes into account both what NATO and the Serbs did, even though NATO, in fact, precipitated the war. With respect to what the Serbs did, they are most responsible for the policies of their military and paramilitary forces that were used to expel the Albanian Kosovar population from their homes. These are breaches of the laws of war referring to *jus in bello*. But those who opposed NATO's decision to start the war pointed out beforehand that such criminal policies should be expected from the Serb authorities and paramilitaries if a war were to start. This point was made even by General Wesley Clark, supreme commander of the NATO forces in Kosovo. Serbian terror and violence, he said, would intensify with the onset of the NATO bombing campaign. Together, both the Serbs and NATO brought about the following unfortunate consequences:

1. the death of at least 500 civilians as a direct result of NATO bombings;[16]
2. the death of 10,000 Albanians killed by Serbian military and paramilitary and the expulsion of hundreds of thousands of Albanian Kosovars;
3. the death of 1,000 Serb servicemen, killed by NATO in the war;[17]
4. the destruction of a large part of Serb and Kosovar economy;
5. the death of 300 Serbs, killed in Kosovo by Albanians in first nine months after the war;[18]
6. the expulsion of almost 200,000 Serbian Kosovars and members of other minorities;[19]
7. environmental consequences, whose scale is not yet known;
8. the delegitimation of the UN Security Council and the creation of a historical precedent for similar interventions;
9. a continuing instability in the region;
10. the turning of Kosovo into a stronghold of organized crime.

This list would be even longer, if we would include the indirect consequences of the war. First, the severe damage done to the Chinese embassy (by U.S. planes) and the death of three of its citizens was an enormous shock to Chinese leaders and to public opinion. It also led to a severe conflict among NATO members. Second, NATO based its intervention on its military superiority over Serb forces. One of the main indirect consequences of such a policy was an increase in military spending in various parts of the world. Nations came to feel that their military arsenals needed to be upgraded. In particular, this happened in poorer countries, at the cost to needed investments in social services, supplies, equipment, and construction. A third indirect consequence of the war was (and is) the strengthening of secessionist movements all over the world. It reinforced radical Albanian forces in neighboring Macedonia striving for unification with Albania. Expectations for an international recognition of the independence of Kosovo have further strengthened forces in Chechnya who were striving for a new confrontation with Russia. The secessionist leadership of Abkhazia declared independence in 1999 and refused to negotiate a federal arrangement with

Georgia. The Abkhazian leadership hoped that the international recognition of Kosovo would pave the way to the international recognition of its own independence.[20] Fourth, it also strengthened forces in governments that are confronted with secessionist conflicts to abandon the difficult search for negotiations and compromise solutions, and so to use force instead. Russian policies toward Chechnya (the war against Chechnya started in September 1999, a few months after NATO's Kosovo campaign) are one example. Another concerns Georgian policies toward Abkhazia. The president of Georgia, Eduard Shervadnadze, made repeated appeals for support from NATO so as to be able to follow the Kosovo example and, thereby, enforce a solution in Abkhazia.

Quite obviously, all these indirect results of the Kosovo war on ongoing conflicts in Europe are not in the interest of the Atlantic Alliance. As a consequence, the NATO governments have had to make strenuous diplomatic efforts to explain that their own actions should not be thought of as constituting a panacea for solving secessionist conflicts; and that they consider the path of negotiations generally still the most viable solution.

WINNING UGLY: DISCRIMINATION AND PROPORTIONALITY (*IN BELLO*)

There is a considerable amount of agreement among observers, quite apart from whether they are proponents or opponents of the war, that the NATO operation was far from ideal in terms of the *jus in bello* Principles of Proportionality and Discrimination. One of the major results of the operation was that it hardly matched the claims of humanitarian nature of the war.

There is no denying that NATO tried to act in accordance with these two principles. The target list was carefully checked and military drift kept under control. This was due, in part, to pragmatic considerations. The NATO Alliance had to take the public opinion of its member states into account, and particularly those currents of opinion opposed to the war. The criticism of states, such as Russia or China, and their principled opposition to the war, also had to be taken into account. All these factors constituted strong constraints on NATO's activities.

But two major factors contributed to the lack of full respect of these two principles. First, the refusal of the Serb leadership to surrender was followed by a military escalation in the bombing campaign. This led to placing so-called borderline cases on its target list. The bombing expanded to oil refineries, fuel dumps, bridges, and roads. All these facilities can be used by the military, but they are of vital importance for civilians as well. They only have a minor military significance, and are therefore not proper targets for military attack.

Second, the NATO strategy of zero casualties was hardly helpful in terms of enforcing discrimination. The pilots had to bomb from an altitude of 15,000 feet. Not surprisingly, this led to numerous mistakes whose consequences were fatal for the civilian population. On April 14 in the neighborhood of Djakovica, a U.S. F16 pilot hit a tractor and wagons carrying a group of Albanian Kosovars by mistake, thereby killing sixty-five people. On another occasion a NATO pilot inadvertently fired two missiles into a train crossing a bridge at Grdelicka Klisura in southern Serbia, killing twenty people.

Some even more serious examples concern the use of cluster bombs (that the United States, according to Human Rights Watch, stopped using in May[21]) and depleted-uranium weapons. Although the scale of the effects of this latter weapon on the health of the population are not precisely known at this point, they could be considerable. After analyzing the environmental impact of depleted-uranium ammunition used in Kosovo in 1999, the United Nations Environment Program (UNEP) recommended on March 13, 2001, that precautionary measures be taken in the areas struck by this ammunition.[22]

The Human Rights Watch report of February 7, 2000, concluded that a third of all the incidents and more than half the deaths occurred as a result of intentional attacks on illegitimate or questionable targets. Nine incidents were a result of attacks on targets without military function. This includes a heating plant and seven bridges that were neither major transportation routes nor had any military function.[23]

A great number of civilian assets were hit as a result of the increased number of borderline items on the target list, NATO's refusal to take risks with its pilots, and the deliberate decision to increase the economic and social costs of the war for Serbia. Many of the borderline targets included roads, railroad tracks, bridges, power plants, factories of many kinds, food and sugar processing plants, cigarette factories, central heating plants for civilian apartment blocks, a radio and television tower, post offices, nonmilitary government administrative buildings, governmental residences, oil refineries, civilian airports, gas stations, and chemical plants. Bombs fell in national parks and preserves. Many religious and cultural sites were severely damaged, among them churches and monasteries.[24] Water pumps were hit and water reserves slashed. Electricity to pumps was cut. As a result, seventy percent of Belgrade's 2 million people were without running water, and the city was down to 10 percent of its water reserves.[25]

Some of those targets were destroyed as the result of deliberate acts (e.g. the destruction of the radio television tower in Belgrade) while others were destroyed by accident. It is remarkable that no in-depth investigation has taken place in order to determine whether and to what extent some of those civilian assets were targeted deliberately. But it is clear that depriving a civilian population of water, by bombing water supplies, is a textbook example of a violation of International Humanitarian Law. According to Just War tradition, one of the main reasons war should be avoided to the maximum extent possible is that mistakes made by political leaders or military commanders almost always have dramatic consequences for the civilian population. Such mistakes may in certain cases even be considered as war crimes. Extensive damage to property not justified by military necessity should be considered as such. According to Robert Hayden, it is therefore not a sign of impartial justice that the Prosecutor of the International Criminal Tribunal for the Former Yugoslavia (ICTY) has brought such charges of destruction of property to the fore against the Bosnian Serb leaders Ratko Mladic and Radovan Karadjic, but failed to do so against NATO.[26]

The arguments of Ivo Daalder and Michael O'Hanlon, that these violations of the Principles of Discrimination and Proportionality are minor in nature, are not convincing.[27] As has been argued above in analyzing the various principles of *jus ad bellum*, the war could not be justified in terms of humanitarian reasons. The way the war was waged gives a further confirmation of this judgment. The principles of *jus in bello* were also not respected. If the war is justified as a humanitarian effort, the means should be appropriate to that end. A contradiction between both was on starkest display in Kosovo.

CONCLUSION

The people in the Balkans emerged from the war considerably worse off than they had been before. But what is probably even more important is that the world had to face instability again because the NATO alliance simply rejected the norms of international law and chose to project its military power instead. The world has since then become a more dangerous place in which to live, in particular for weaker states. The security order based on the legitimate authority of the UN Security Council gives militarily weaker states some limited protection from predatory states. However, the long-term consequences of NATO's breaching international law threatens this limited protection.

The violation of the Principle of Legitimate Authority is probably most striking in NATO's decision of March 1999. But the other principles of the Just War tradition were not respected either. The "humanitarian intervention" in Kosovo turned what had been a brutal repression of a brutal armed uprising into a humanitarian catastrophe, and led to the first massive bombings of a European country since World War II. At the same time, NATO transformed itself from a defensive alliance into the first proud aggressor in Europe since the Soviet Union's invasions of Hungary in 1956 and of Czechoslovakia in 1968. Seen from this perspective, the term "humanitarian intervention" as used by those who want to justify NATO's actions is out of place.

NOTES

1. "Certainly the levels of violence in Kosovo before March 24,1999, were modest by the standards of civil conflict and compared to what ensued during NATO's bombing campaign." Ivo H. Daalder and Michael E. O'Hanlon, *Winning Ugly: NATO's War to Save Kosovo* (Washington, D.C.: Brookings Institution Press, 2000), 12.

2. The number of people killed during the first Russian-Chechen war has never been firmly established, but is far higher than in Kosovo. According to Anatol Lieven, it may have exceeded 20,000 lives. Anatol Lieven, *Chechnya: Tombstone of Russian Power* (New Haven, Conn., and London: Yale University Press, 1998), 108.

3. Daalder and Hanlon, *Winning Ugly*, 240.

4. Daalder and Hanlon, *Winning Ugly*, 9.

5. John B. Roberts, "Roots of Allied Farce," *The American Spectator* 16, no. 12 (1999): 35–38.

6. Bruno Coppieters, "Between Europe and Asia: Security and Identity in Central Asia," in *Security and Identity in Europe Exploring the New Agenda*, ed. Lisbeth Aggestam and Adrian Hyde-Price (London and New York: Macmillan and St. Martin's Press, 2000), 196.

7. Catherine Guicherd, "International Law and the War in Kosovo," *Survival* 41, no. 2 (Summer 1999): 27 and the analysis of Carl Ceulemans, in this volume.

8. The excuses Daalder and O'Hanlon are finding for the killings and expulsion of the Serb Kosovars after the victory of the united KLA-NATO forces in June 1999 are amazing. The Albanian Kosovars "can be forgiven a certain paranoia, even if their revenge attacks against Serbs cannot be condoned" Daalder and O'Hanlon, *Winning Ugly*, 16.

9. Mark Littman, *Kosovo: Law and Diplomacy* (London: Centre for Policy Studies, 1999), 45.

10. www.un.org/peace/kosovo/news/kosovo2.htm#Anchor27 (accessed May 4, 2001).

11. Charles Krauthammer, "The Short, Unhappy Life of Humanitarian War," in *The National Interest* (Fall 1999): 8.

12. Elena Guskova, "Dinamika Kosovskogo krizisa i politika Rossii," in *Kosovo: Mezhdunarodniye aspekty krizisa* (Moscow: Gendalf, 1999), 57–66.

13. Littman, *Kosovo: Law and Diplomacy*, v.

14. Littman, *Kosovo*, 13. This agreement further reconfirmed the principle of territorial integrity of Yugoslavia and the will of all parties to disarm the KLA, which had already been expressed by the NATO members before the war.

15. On a description of the Kosovo war as an unintended consequence of political mistakes, see Michael Mandelbaum, "A Perfect Failure," *Foreign Affairs* 78, no. 5 (September/October 1999): 2–8.

16. According to Human Rights Watch report at least five hundred Yugoslav civilians died in ninety separate incidents during the seventy-eight-day bombing cam-

paign. The report also finds that NATO committed violations of International Humanitarian Law in its targeting and bombing practices. The report was released on February 7, 2000, at www.hrw.org/press/2000/02/nato207.htm (accessed May 5, 2001).

17. Daalder and O'Hanlon, *Winning Ugly*, 154.

18. Daalder and O'Hanlon, *Winning Ugly*, 196.

19. Daalder and O'Hanlon, *Winning Ugly*, 177.

20. Interview of Bruno Coppieters with the Abkhaz president Vladislav Ardzindba in Sukhum on November 13, 2000.

21. The Human Rights Watch report of June 1999, at www.hrw.org/reports/1999/nato2/index.htm (accessed May 5, 2001) and its report of February 7, 1999, www.hrw.org/press/2000/02/nato207.htm (accessed May 5, 2001).

22. www.un.org/peace/kosovo/news/kosovo2.htm#Anchor27 (accessed May 5, 2001).

23. The Human Rights Watch Report, at www.hrw.org/hrw/press/2000/02/nato207.htm (accessed May 5, 2001).

24. Guskova, "Dinamica Kosovskogo Krizisa i politika Rossii," 65–66.

25. Robert Hayden, *Humanitarian Hypocrisy*, at jurist.law.pitt.edu/hayden.htm (accessed March 11, 2002).

26. The Bosnian Serb leaders were accused by the prosecutor of the International Criminal Tribunal for the Former Yugoslavia (ICTY) of "extensive destruction of property": "that they individually and in concert with others planned, instigated, ordered or otherwise aided and abetted in the planning, preparation or execution of the extensive, wanton and unlawful destruction of . . . property, not justified by military necessity or knew or had reason to know that subordinates were about to destroy or permit others to destroy . . . property or had done so and failed to take necessary and reasonable measures to prevent this destruction or to punish the perpetrators thereof." Hayden, *Humanitarian Hypocrisy*.

27. Daalder and O'Hanlon, *Winning Ugly*, 182–227.

11

Kosovo and the Question of a Just Secession

Bruno Coppieters

THREE DEBATES ON KOSOVO

Kosovo raised three international debates. First came NATO's decision in March 1999 to go to war over Kosovo. The main arguments in this debate on a humanitarian intervention without UN Security Council authorization are to be found in the two preceding chapters. The second debate arose over the creation of an international administration for Kosovo, and the third concerned the international status of the territory.

The six *jus ad bellum* principles are traditionally applied to war settings in order to assess the legitimacy of the use of force. They have been used in the two preceding chapters to answer the question: to what extent was the forceful external involvement in a secessionist crisis with severe humanitarian consequences justified? The present chapter shows that these principles can also be of heuristic value for examining the legitimacy of the creation of an international administration in Kosovo and assessing Kosovo's right to unilateral secession and its recognition by other states.

After the surrender of Serbia in June 1999, the main international actors agreed that the first priority for the region was international support for regional stability. According to UNSC Resolution 1244 (1999), Belgrade had no right to exercise its authority over the territory of Kosovo, even though formally this territory remained part of the Federal Republic of Yugoslavia:[1] a decision on its future status would be taken at a later stage. NATO troops—and, up to 2003, also Russian troops—were deployed as peacekeepers in Kosovo. The formal authority over this region was a UN-led administration (United Nations Mission in Kosovo, UNMIK), coordinating the work of international agencies—a form of governance not to be found in any other secessionist crisis.

At the time, the ethical debate over the legitimacy of this international administration focused largely on the Proportionality Principle, which weighs the positive and negative consequences of political decisions. The reconstruction of Kosovo entailed a number of successes and failures. One of the positive consequences of the creation of an international administration was that Kosovo Albanians no longer had to fear being forced out of their homes, as had happened to more than 700,000 of them in 1999.[2] But the military intervention leading to its creation had been followed by new forms of injustice that the international administration was unable to redress or prevent. NATO KFOR troops deployed in Kosovo and UNMIK international civilian police failed to give sufficient protection to its Serb population.[3] The first wave of Kosovo Serbs left the region out of fear, but many were physically driven out of their homes. Ethnically motivated crimes were inadequately prosecuted. Kosovo Serbs also left for economic reasons: postwar reconstruction did not provide the institutional environment needed for economic growth. In 2003, some 130,000 of Kosovo's Serbs—roughly two-thirds of its prewar population—were still there, but a great number of them remained displaced within Kosovo and unable to return to their original homes.[4] The positive and negative consequences of the creation of an international administration were thus substantial, and it was difficult to make a clear-cut proportionality calculation of its moral costs and benefits.

Where the democratization of Serbia was concerned, Slobodan Milosevic, already weakened by his defeat in the war and the loss of Serb control over Kosovo, was ousted from power in October 2000. Regime change in Belgrade paved the way for a constitutional agreement between Serbia and Montenegro, the two constituent entities of the Federal Republic of Yugoslavia whose relations had been severely strained during Milosevic's rule. It also led to a normalization of relations with the international community. Serbia could even look forward to membership of the European Union, on condition that it pursued state reforms. All these elements contributed to the stabilization of the Balkan region.

But the international consensus on UNSC Resolution 1999 and the creation of an international administration for the territory did not mean that there was agreement on how to resolve the Kosovo problem. The future status of the territory was the subject of the third international debate over Kosovo. Western countries favored recognizing it as an independent country, whose transition to full independence would be supervised by the international community. Russia and China opposed this option, declaring themselves in favor of the existing form of international administration. But on February 17, 2008, Kosovo proclaimed its independence unilaterally with EU and U.S. support. All three debates on Kosovo had repercussions that went far beyond the region itself. The main issues concerned the resolution of secessionist conflicts in general. The questions at stake, in effect, created three different Kosovo models:

1. To what extent did the Kosovo conflict provide a political model for forceful external involvement in a secessionist crisis with severe humanitarian consequences?
2. To what extent did the Kosovo conflict provide a political model for solving secessionist conflicts by having the UN or other international organizations administer breakaway territories?
3. To what extent did the Kosovo conflict provide a political model for a unilateral right to self-determination, up to the right to independence, for the people of a territory who have suffered severe injustice?

In the view of the Western countries that were involved in NATO's intervention in Kosovo and in its international administration, and that have been supporting its right to unilateral[5] independence, these decisions were based on a complex constellation of factors, at both the domestic and the international levels. They reasoned that secessionist conflicts in other parts of the world should be regarded as the product of entirely different factors, so the set of principles adopted to resolve the Kosovo conflict—by military intervention, the creation of an international administration, or the recognition of a unilateral declaration of independence—would never constitute legal precedents or political models for resolving other secessionist conflicts.

This line of argument, denying the exemplary character of these three Kosovo experiences, is far from convincing. First, emphasizing the uniqueness argument in relation to Kosovo could lead to an interpretation whereby the questions of military intervention, international administration, or international status cannot be decided by universal principles but only by ad hoc criteria that are drawn up to fit the circumstances of each particular situation. This type of argument would make it impossible to claim any legitimacy for the decisions taken on Kosovo, or even to have a rational discussion on the legitimacy of any decision concerning a secessionist conflict.

Second, any attempt to resolve a particular conflict may become part of a political model for discussing how to resolve other conflicts. This does not necessarily mean, however, that all secessionist crises should be resolved by following that model.

Third, since 1999, in a number of secessionist conflicts, Kosovo has already been turned into a series of political models on all three issues mentioned above: the use of force in secessionist conflicts, the internationalization of such a conflict, and the right to unilateral secession. Players draw lessons from the Kosovo experience to strengthen their own positions in the conflicts they are themselves involved in. The first Kosovo model, on military humanitarian intervention, was applied by the Georgian government in 1999 in an attempt to find international support for the use of force against Abkhazia. The second, on the creation of an international administration, was followed by the secessionist Chechen leadership in 2003 in an attempt to persuade the international community to give Chechnya a UN-led administration. The third Kosovo model, on the right to secession, has been referred to in several secessionist conflicts, even before Kosovo's unilateral declaration of independence on February 17, 2008.

The *jus ad bellum* principles are traditionally applied to war settings in order to assess the legitimacy of the use of force as an exception to the rule that public authorities have to preserve peaceful relations between one another and with their citizens. But they can also be of heuristic value for dealing with the legitimacy of the creation of an international administration, or with the right to unilateral secession and its recognition by other states. These are exceptions to the general rule that the international community has to preserve the territorial integrity of states and not withdraw part of a territory from the control of its central government. The six *jus ad bellum* principles take on a specific meaning in the systematic examination of the justification for such exceptions (see boxes 11.1, 11.2, and 11.3).[6]

MILITARY INTERVENTION: THE CASE OF ABKHAZIA

These principles are useful for gaining a better understanding of the application of the first Kosovo model (on military intervention) to other secessionist conflicts. Georgian president Eduard Shevardnadze was the first to follow the Kosovo model by calling for the use of force against a breakaway state in his own country, shortly after NATO's military intervention in 1999. Abkhazia, a territory that had been formally part of Georgia before the dissolution of the Soviet Union, seceded in 1993. This separation was the result of a Georgian military defeat. In August 1992 the Georgian authorities had attempted to resolve an ethnic conflict in Abkhazia, between their community and the Abkhaz, by using military force. But North Caucasus volunteers and Russian troops sided with the Abkhaz, leading to the defeat of the Georgian troops and the flight of nearly the entire Georgian population from the territory. Russia deployed troops to separate the conflicting parties, with UN peacekeepers in a monitoring role. The UN was given the further role of mediating between the parties. The UN regarded Abkhazia as part of Georgia, and was striving for a federal solution based on the principle of territorial integrity, but the negotiations on the reunification of the territory with Georgia produced no concrete results. All Georgian appeals to the

Box 11.1. Criteria for Military Intervention in a Conflict on Sovereignty

1. A war should have a just cause: the injustice to be prevented or remedied should be serious enough to justify the use of military force. In the case of a secessionist conflict, the central government will often invoke territorial integrity as a just cause for the use of force. But the secessionist party may likewise invoke the Just Cause Principle in defending itself against the central government. External players may invoke humanitarian reasons, such as genocide or the threat of genocide, to justify their right or even their duty to intervene using military means.

2. The decision should be guided by right intentions: a war about secession should be fought primarily for motives consistent with a just cause. External military intervention for predominantly geostrategic motives, for instance, would be unjust.

3. Only a legitimate authority may launch a war to uphold a just cause: persons or institutions that do not represent the public interest cannot be regarded as legitimate authorities when it is being decided to resort to force in a secessionist crisis. To what extent the central government or the secessionist party may constitute such a legitimate authority has to be examined in each particular case. The conditions on which the UNSC may act as a legitimate authority in deciding on the use of force in secessionist conflicts are specified in the UN Charter.

4. A reasonable chance of success in upholding the just cause is a prerequisite for starting military operations. In a secessionist crisis, the probability of military defeat, or the impossibility of redressing or preventing injustice by using force, precludes the legitimacy of resorting to military means.

5. The Proportionality Principle must be respected: the anticipated cost of fighting the war for the just cause should not be disproportionate to the expected benefits. This cost-benefit calculation refers to both moral and material benefits for the populations concerned and for the world community at large.

6. Violence may be used only as a last resort: force is the last of the options for remedying or preventing injustice in a secessionist crisis. Before this step is taken, it must be very clear that all efforts to uphold the just cause by negotiations have proved fruitless. In a conflict on sovereignty, lack of formal status by the secessionist party may render negotiations difficult.

UNSC for forceful international intervention to crush "de facto" Abkhaz statehood were in vain, mainly owing to Russian opposition to any move in that direction. Only a minority of the Georgian population expelled from Abkhazia were able to return to their homes.

The Kosovo war then showed that it was possible for Western states to intervene forcefully in a secessionist crisis. In Shevardnadze's view, the ethnic cleansing of the Georgian population from Abkhazia constituted a just cause for intervention, as had been the case in Kosovo.[7] For Shevardnadze, the fact that NATO had intervened in support of a population that wanted to secede and create an independent state was secondary. More important was the idea that the use of military force remains the most effective instrument for ending the contest of wills in a secessionist conflict. The lesson the Georgian president was drawing from Kosovo was thus presented as an alternative to a peaceful resolution of the conflict over Abkhazia. But there were no strong arguments to bring this alternative option into line with the Last Resort Principle. This option was also in breach of other Just War Principles. Shevardnadze himself conceded that, contrary to what had happened in Kosovo, here the use of force would require the consent of the UNSC. Without Russian support, such intervention would create a new international conflict, which NATO members were unwilling to engage in. This meant that the application of this particular Kosovo model to Abkhazia was not in line with the Legitimate Authority and Likelihood of Success Principles. For all these reasons, NATO countries have never taken seriously the suggestion to apply this Kosovo model to Georgia.

INTERNATIONAL ADMINISTRATION:
THE CASE OF CHECHNYA

NATO's war on Kosovo ended in June 1999. Just a few months later, in August, the Russian government under the leadership of Prime Minister Vladimir Putin decided to enforce a military solution in Chechnya, a territory in the Northern Caucasus that was under the control of secessionist forces. The Chechen forces suffered a decisive military defeat, and had to confine themselves to isolated acts of military resistance. In numerous cases, Chechen fighters even resorted to terrorist acts.

In 2003, the proindependence Chechen government came up with its own interpretation of the Kosovo model. Its plan for "supervised independence" for Chechnya was based explicitly on the Kosovo experience.[8] UNSC Resolution 1244 was the main reference in the appeal to the international community to give this war-torn territory an international administration.

The Chechen government argued that the correction and prevention of injustice required full sovereignty and independence. Chechnya was in

Box 11.2. Criteria for an International Administration for a Breakaway Territory

1. In order to prevent injustice in secessionist conflicts, the creation of an international administration for a breakaway territory should have a specific just cause. Attempts to secede may be either illegitimate or legitimate. In the first case, an international administration may be helpful for guaranteeing a transition toward the reunification of a country in accordance with the principle of territorial integrity. In the second case, an international administration aims to redress or prevent serious injustice, such as genocide or other forms of severe oppression, perpetrated by a central government.
2. The creation of an international administration should be guided by right intentions that are consistent with a just cause, and not by the particular geopolitical interests of certain outside powers.
3. Only a legitimate authority may create such an international administration for a breakaway territory. It may be agreed with the central government, or imposed by the UNSC. The European Union does not in itself have the legal authority to create such an administration for nonsovereign entities. It may be involved in one, however, on the basis of an authorization from the central government or the UNSC.
4. A reasonable chance of success in upholding the just cause is a prerequisite for such an option. The ineffectiveness of an international administration in overcoming the secessionist crisis through either reunification or independence would go against this option. The nonsustainability of the new institutions or the inability of the administration to prevent an escalation of the violent conflict would negate the legitimacy of such an arrangement.
5. The Principle of Proportionality must take into account the anticipated benefits, which refer to the correction or the prevention of injustice, and the costs. The external imposition of an international administration on the central government or on the population of the breakaway territory may negatively affect the self-sustainability of state institutions and the principle of democratic representation.
6. The creation of an international administration against the wishes of one (or both) of the parties has to be a last-resort solution for remedying or preventing injustice, in cases where consensual alternatives respecting the principle of the territorial integrity of states cannot be found.

principle considered to have a unilateral right to secede from the Russian Federation, but the Chechen authorities agreed that the UNSC would play a crucial role in the supervision and final recognition of independence. Chechnya would be given a UN-appointed administration to prepare the ground for democratic state reform and, ultimately, Chechen independence. The Principle of Legitimate Authority was central to this idea.

The plan received support in some political circles, particularly among European Parliament members, but it never became part of the negotiations on a solution for Chechnya. Russia would never support the deployment of UN troops to secure its own national borders. The plan, therefore, had no real likelihood of success.

Box 11.3. Criteria for Unilateral Independence

1. Secession should have a just cause. This means that the injustice to be prevented or remedied should be severe enough to justify a unilateral declaration of independence, and the recognition of a new independent state by the UNSC and the international community against the will of the central government, or its partial recognition.
2. A unilateral declaration of independence and its recognition should have a reasonable chance of success in achieving its aims. These are threefold. First, the declaration and/or unilateral recognition of independence are unjustified if there is no reasonable chance of translating the just cause into reality. Secondly, there should be a reasonable chance of having the new state recognized in the long run by a substantial section of the international community. Thirdly, a declaration or recognition of independence is unjustified if it does not result in new state institutions that are sustainable.
3. A unilateral declaration of secession and/or its recognition can only be a last-resort solution. Before resorting to such a decision, it should be reasonably clear that all other options—including minority rights, autonomy, and federalism—are powerless to remedy or to prevent injustice and that it is impossible to obtain the central government's agreement to the creation of the new independent state.
4. A unilateral declaration of independence has to be made or recognized through a legitimate authority. This principle has two different meanings in this particular context. First, it refers to the legitimate authority of the secessionist movement. This should represent the entire population of the seceding territory. It should be able to enforce legislation over the whole territory and to act with respect for international human rights and minority rights. The need for a distinct and clearly identifiable national identity, and for a majority (perhaps even a special majority) of referendum votes in favor of in-

dependence, may also be approached from the Legitimate Authority Principle. Secondly, it refers to the process of recognizing a state through a legitimate authority on the international scene. A limited number of states may confer partial recognition. Full recognition by the world community of states generally means entry into the UN.
5. The principle of proportionality should be respected. The anticipated costs and benefits should be calculated at both the domestic and the international levels.
6. The decision to seize independence or to recognize a state that has seceded unilaterally should be guided by right intentions. This means that the unilateral declaration or recognition of its independence—either by the UNSC or unilaterally by some states—should be motivated primarily by considerations consistent with the just cause for independence.

UNILATERAL INDEPENDENCE: THE CASE OF KOSOVO

Before Kosovo's declaration of independence on February 17, 2008, five options were envisaged for the future status of Kosovo (see box 11.4). With the exception of the first one, they were based on the assessment that Kosovo had a just cause for independence. Each of these options needs to be examined further in the light of the remaining just-secession Principles of Likelihood of Success, Last Resort, Legitimate Authority, Proportionality, and Right Intentions.

Box 11.4. Five Options in the Negotiations on the Status of Kosovo

1. An agreement between Belgrade and Pristina on autonomous status.
2. An agreement between Belgrade and Pristina on independence for Kosovo.
3. An agreement within the UNSC on supervised independence for Kosovo, paving the way for the full implementation of the Ahtisaari plan (see p. 248 for more information on this plan).
4. A decision on the question of sovereignty and independence is put on hold, pending a resolution by the UNSC on supervised independence. This option may include a reform of Kosovo's state structures with the consent of the UNSC.
5. Kosovo's unilateral declaration of independence is partially recognized.

A Just Cause for Independence?

The international authority established by the UN for Kosovo ruled out the exercise of state authority over this territory by Belgrade, pending a decision on its final status. The Western states who supported this SC resolution in 1999 were strongly motivated by a just cause argument. In their view, the Serb state was responsible for the massive violation of human rights in the 1998–1999 period. An international administration would prevent the Kosovo Albanians from being in such a situation again. The same just cause argument in favor of the establishment of a provisional international authority over Kosovo was also used to justify the definitive loss of sovereignty over this territory by Serbia.

The Serb government, for its part, likewise argued from the just cause perspective. It considered that the secession of Kosovo would violate its sovereignty and the principle of territorial integrity. It has strong historical ties to the region. From the Serb point of view, the independence of Kosovo was a direct threat to the rights of the Serbian minority of this territory. Belgrade did not accept the argument that the past crimes of Slobodan Milosevic justified the future independence of Kosovo, maintaining instead that the democratic Serbia that emerged from the overthrow of the Milosevic regime in October 2000 gave sufficient guarantees to prevent such injustice from ever being repeated again.

It may be stated that the massive scale of the human rights violations created a just cause for Kosovo's independence, despite the principle of territorial integrity. The injustice was so severe that it has delegitimized Serbia's sovereign rights over the territory to which this principle of territorial integrity is tied.

Does Independence Have a Likelihood of Success?

The first option would have given Kosovo autonomy within Serbia, while the four remaining options aimed at its independence. What were their chances of success, with respect to (1) upholding the just cause, (2) achieving independence, and (3) creating sustainable state institutions?

Where the option on autonomy is concerned, the Serb government argued that the war crimes committed against the Kosovo Albanians could not be repeated in a democratic Serbia. Constitutional guarantees, they said, were to be given to the Kosovo Albanians in the form of broad autonomy for Kosovo.

The likelihood of success of the autonomy option in preventing fresh injustice had to be strengthened by European integration. Serbia had a reasonable long-term chance of becoming fully integrated into the European Union, and such integration is generally considered to have positive conse-

quences for conflict resolution.[9] State reform in line with European democratic and legal standards would have strengthened the guarantees of the
autonomy of Kosovo Albanians within Serbia. Integration into the EU, in
particular, would have increased the likelihood of shared sovereignty within
a federal framework. The transfer of power from the Serbian state and the
Kosovar substate levels to the European level of governance would have decreased the points of friction between the communities, and the significance of international boundaries. The Europeanization of Serbia was thus
an additional argument in favor of autonomy for Kosovo.

Those who did not believe that autonomy could succeed in preventing
fresh injustice against the Kosovo Albanians argued that the Serbian constitution provides only limited forms of self-governance for the autonomous
provinces, including Kosovo (Articles 182–187). Autonomous provinces
can regulate "matters of provincial interest" in accordance with Serbian law,
but the central government and the Constitutional Court of the Republic of
Serbia keeps them under the close supervision.[10]

Serbia agreed to looser links between Belgrade and Pristina than those
stipulated in the present constitution. The autonomous status of Hong
Kong within the People's Republic of China was mentioned by Serb nego-
tiators. But there was no guarantee that such autonomous status would be
democratic or sustainable. Serbia had undergone thorough democratic reform, but it did not enjoy sufficient political stability or multiethnic toler-
ance to secure autonomy for Kosovo or power sharing between the Serb majority and the Kosovo-Albanian minority at the central state level.[11] For
these reasons, the Kosovo Albanians did not feel that Serbia had become
trustworthier since the overthrow of the Milosevic regime. They were therefore unwilling to enter into negotiations on alternatives to independence.

In the previous section on the Just Cause Principle, we concluded that the
severity of the injustice suffered by the Kosovo Albanians before NATO's intervention in 1999 justified independence from the perspective of a just
cause. Independence was also justified from the perspective of the Likelihood of Success Principle. Autonomy within Serbia and other federal alternatives did not offer sufficient security guarantees to the Kosovo Albanians.

The four remaining options aimed at achieving Kosovo's independence
through different means. Their likelihood of success in achieving recognition had to be assessed separately. The second option—Serb consent to
Kosovo's independence—was not likely. Kosovo is crucial to Serb national
identity. The government's hands were tied by a constitution that considers
Serbian territory "inseparable and indivisible" (Article 8).[12] The Serb constitution (Article 114) further prescribes that the Serbian president has to
swear that he will devote all his efforts to preserving "the sovereignty and
integrity of the territory of the Republic of Serbia, including Kosovo and
Metohija as its constituent part."[13]

The European Union and the United States had expected Serbia, which had put great faith in its expectation of membership in the European Union, to cave in to their diplomatic pressure. This incentive, however, was not sufficient to persuade the main political parties to give up Serbian rights over Kosovo.

It was asserted that Serb consent to independence could be achieved by making far-reaching concessions, such as territorial adjustments to the advantage of Serbia. Serbian-populated Northern Kosovo could be attached to Serbia. At first, this kind of partition was deemed unacceptable by Western governments. The creation of ethnically homogeneous territories would have been in breach of the principle of multiethnic coexistence, and undermining this principle was seen as a threat to the multinational Bosnian federation and the multinational Macedonian state.[14] But in the face of Serb and Russian intransigence, Western diplomats softened their position on that question—without, however, being able to break the deadlock in the negotiations.

The second option thus fulfilled the Likelihood of Success Principle defined as the successful upholding of a just cause, but it did not fulfill the same principle when it is defined as the likelihood of achieving independence. It could be added here that this option was again in accordance with the same principle when defined as the creation of sustainable state institutions.

A third option was a unilateral decision taken by the UNSC—against the will of Serbia—on independence for Kosovo under international supervision. In March 2007, the UN secretary-general presented a "Report" and a "Comprehensive Proposal for the Kosovo Status Settlement" to the UNSC. Both documents had been prepared by his special envoy, Martti Ahtisaari.[15] After abandoning all hope of reaching agreement between the parties, he pleaded in favor of a decision by the UNSC in favor of supervised independence. Ahtisaari received support from Western countries, but Russia and China remained firm in their refusal to accept a UNSC proposal that would run counter to the Serb position on territorial integrity.[16]

Since 2006 the UN mediation process was extended repeatedly in order to broaden international support for an agreement. Each postponement was coupled with the setting of new deadlines, with still no breakthrough in the negotiations. But a last-minute compromise between the permanent members of the UNSC could not reasonably be ruled out. It may thus be concluded that the third option fulfilled the Likelihood of Success Principle as far as the implementation of just cause was concerned, and as a reasonable strategy for achieving independence, despite the immense difficulties confronting international diplomacy.

Furthermore, the third option met the same Likelihood of Success Principle with respect to the creation of sustainable institutions. A UNSC resolution in favor of supervised independence would have created the necessary legal framework for efficient governance in Kosovo. Expressing a view widely shared among Western diplomats, Ahtisaari stated that "economic development in Kosovo requires the clarity and stability that only independence can provide."[17]

A fourth option available was to put the decision on hold, at least where sovereignty and independence are concerned. This option would have given Western powers more time to persuade Russia and China not to oppose a SC resolution in favor of supervised independence. But even though this option fulfilled the Likelihood of Success Principle in terms of just cause and as a strategy for independence, it created a series of sustainability problems of its own. A lengthening of the decision-making process could have led radical Kosovo Albanians to resort to force. Violent riots had already taken place (back in March 2004), directed against the Serbian population of Kosovo. Hundreds of citizens belonging to the Kosovo minorities were injured in mobilizations across the territory that involved more than 50,000 people.[18] A repetition of such events could have necessitated the use of force by the local police and by NATO's KFOR troops, without any guarantee, however, that this would have stabilized the situation. An escalation of violence would have entailed the risk of a spillover into other Balkan states, including neighboring Macedonia and Bosnia. But not all international actors appeared to be worried by this eventuality. Russian diplomats did not seem particularly impressed by this argument against postponing a UN decision on final status.[19]

There were also substantial legal and economic arguments against postponement. As the clarification of the final legal status of Kosovo was intended to enable large-scale economic aid and investment to flow in from abroad, any delay made economic recovery more difficult, particularly in a situation where economic indicators were worsening.[20] For these reasons, the option of leaving Kosovo in a legal and political limbo for an indefinite period encountered strong opposition from Western states, and postponement would not have met the Likelihood of Success Principle in its specific meaning of the creation of sustainable institutions.

The fifth alternative was a unilateral declaration of independence by Kosovo and its recognition by major countries.[21] The likelihood of success of this option was strengthened by the reasonable expectation that Kosovo's independence would have been recognized by a substantial part—and in the long run, even the whole—of the international community. This was mainly thanks to Western support. To gain acceptance from the international community was difficult, but the combined diplomatic leverage of the United States and the European Union gave Kosovo far greater diplomatic support than that enjoyed by any other breakaway state.[22] This option also fulfilled the Likelihood of Success Principle defined as the creation of sustainable institutions, even if the main measures proposed by Special Envoy Ahtisaari had to be implemented without the legal basis provided by authorization from the SC.

Is Independence a Last Resort Option?

The first two options—autonomy or independence—were based on an agreement between the conflicting parties, so the question of independence as a last resort did not arise. The Western governments, faced with Russia's opposition to the third option of a UNSC decision on supervised independence, decided in favor of the fifth option—partial recognition of a unilateral declaration of independence. This option was not in line with the Last Resort Principle, contrary to the fourth option. To put the decision on hold left some room for seeking agreement at the international level.

Is Independence Based on a Legitimate Authority?

In a just secession analysis, the Principle of Legitimate Authority refers first of all to the legitimacy of the process of recognizing independence and secondly to the legitimacy of the new state institutions that are to be created within the framework of supervised independence. The latter involves assessing their sustainability, representativeness, and respect for minority rights.

The Kosovar institutions that came into being after the 1999 war were weak and incapable of taking on the responsibilities normally assumed by state authorities. The failure to integrate the Serbs and other minorities, opposition to the return of Serb refugees, lack of qualified personnel, and widespread corruption were among the main problems found in the post-1999 context.[23] The principle of "standards before status," adopted by the UN in 2002, was intended to create democratic institutions based on the rule of law. State reforms preceded the present international discussion on the supervised independence of Kosovo, as a necessary condition.

Ahtisaari's "Comprehensive Proposal" of 2007 contained a list of general principles, such as the aim of creating a multiethnic society with Albanian and Serbian as official languages, respect "for the highest level of internationally recognized human rights and fundamental freedoms, as well as the promotion and protection of the rights and contributions of all its Communities and their members." It further ruled out unification with Albania and, as part of the supervised nature of Kosovar independence, proposed a comprehensive international framework to "supervise, monitor and have all necessary powers to ensure effective and efficient implementation of this Settlement." The decentralization of state power to the municipal authorities was designed to strengthen the multiethnic character of self-governance.

The active involvement of the EU, the appointment of an International Civilian Representative with wide powers, and an international military presence all constituted strong guarantees that human rights and democratic standards would have been upheld in the new state, particularly with respect to its minorities—or rather, the non-Albanian "communities," as they were termed in the Ahtisaari plan.

Unlike the autonomous institutions to be created for the Kosovo Albanians within Serbia under the first option, the Ahtisaari plan gave broad guarantees of the sustainability, representativeness, and respect for minority rights of the state institutions. In principle, the last four of the five options mentioned above could have addressed these issues, but only the second (through Serb consent) and the third (through a UNSC resolution) were able to implement the Ahtisaari plan in full. Both options would thus have met the Legitimate Authority Principle in its two different meanings: as regards the legitimacy both of the process of recognition and of the creation of state institutions.

In the fourth option—the suspension of the sovereignty issue—the state institutions would still have been regarded as legitimate, being based on the 1999 UNSC resolution on the creation of an international administration. Where the Legitimate Authority Principle in relation to the process of recognition is concerned, this option would have been based on the assumption that in the future an agreement could be found within the UNSC. It was thus also in accordance with both meanings of the Legitimate Authority Principle.

The fifth option, on the contrary, was not in line with the Legitimate Authority Principle in its first meaning, as it only referred to partial recognition, ruling out acceptance by the Serb central government and the UNSC as a whole. Full legitimacy would be lacking even if Kosovo were to be recognized by a substantial part of the international community. Furthermore, lack of UN supervision of the process leading to independence created serious legal problems for the EU in its reconstruction and state-building efforts. But this did not make the new independent state institutions less legitimate in terms of their representativeness or respect for minority rights. The fifth option was thus in accordance with the Legitimate Authority Principle in its second meaning.

Is Independence in Accordance with the Proportionality Principle?

The moral costs and benefits of each of the five status options had to be calculated at both the domestic and the international levels. Where autonomy was concerned, with the first option the costs were higher than the benefits at both levels, as autonomy could not prevent renewed domestic conflicts with international implications. Where the four other options were concerned, one benefit of independence was to lift Kosovo out of the legal limbo to which it has been relegated since the military intervention in 1999. The consequences for the non-Albanian minorities in Kosovo—primarily the Serb population that has not left the territory—also had to be assessed. International monitoring and control of the new state had to give strong guarantees of minority protection in Kosovo. But it must also be acknowledged that the presence of international peacekeeping forces in Kosovo in the postwar period had not been sufficient to secure the rights of the Serb minority, who fled the region in great numbers. The chances that the Serb population remaining in Kosovo would be ready to participate in electoral contests and public life in an independent Kosovo were slim, particularly in view of their abstention during local elections in the past. At the international level, the first concern was the potentially destabilizing repercussions on other conflicts.

The costs and benefits were directly proportional to the type of outcome and the degree of international legitimacy the modus of supervised independence would receive in the various options in favor of independence. An agreement between the two parties on independence for Kosovo, in line with the second option, would have resulted in a positive proportionality calculation at both the domestic and international levels.

Despite being based on an endorsement by the UNSC, the third option would still have had significant negative consequences for the mediation of other conflicts. The establishment of a legal framework for supervised independence in the noncolonial world would have constituted a novelty in secessionist conflicts. The UN had traditionally regarded the application of federal and other power-sharing techniques as the best approach to resolving violent ethnic conflicts and achieving the reunification of divided states and nations. If the UNSC would have endorsed the third option, it would have been more difficult for this organization to convince the leaders and populations of breakaway territories that there are viable last-resort alternatives to full sovereignty.

The fourth option—postponement of the status issue—could have had substantial negative consequences for domestic security, and the fifth for international security. A split in the international community over the recognition of a new state, following the fifth option, was detrimental to resolution of other secessionist conflicts.

Russia pointed out the importance of envisaging all the potential repercussions on international security of a unilateral Western decision on Kosovo. In its view, any decision had to be consistent with the management of other secessionist conflicts. Unilateral steps by the Western states leading to a recognition of Kosovo's independence could very well have been followed by unilateral steps (not necessarily involving the recognition of their independence) on the part of the Russian government concerning Abkhazia, South Ossetia, and Transnistria.

Unilateral recognition of a Kosovar declaration of independence did not only set Russia and China against the EU and the United States but also created dividing lines within the EU. In one way or another, Spain, Slovakia, Cyprus, Greece, Hungary, and Romania are all confronted with secessionist conflicts. The remaining EU members had the greatest difficulty in convincing these countries that the replacement of UN and OSCE activities by a large-scale EU mission without the endorsement of the UNSC was not detrimental to their own interests. In spite of these efforts, some of these countries declared in February 2008 that they would not recognize Kosovo.

Are the Motives for Independence Based on Right Intentions?

There is no reason to believe that the true intentions of the Serb or Kosovar authorities diverged from their justification of their respective positions on secession. They both defended ideological positions that were in line with their views on nationhood and on their legitimate interest in a just world order. The Kosovo Albanian authorities were convinced that refusing them independence would constitute a severe injustice, while the Serb government argued that breaching the territorial integrity of its state was unjust. Other motives undoubtedly existed, but they were of secondary importance in this respect. As far as the Right Intentions Principle is concerned, both parties were thus defending what they subjectively regard as a just cause.

The positions of the external actors were more complex. Western governments, in particular the European Union, were directly involved in the management of Kosovo's affairs, and were thus far more concerned about the consequences of any status decision for stability in Kosovo itself than either Russia or China, which did not have to carry the burden of the nonresolution of this conflict. Some EU members were likewise fearful of the indirect consequences of the option of partial recognition of Kosovo for secessionist conflicts within their own territory (Spain and Cyprus) or on the territory of one of their allies (Greek concerns about Cyprus). Russia had similar concerns in relation to the North Caucasus, but in a Western unilateral decision it also saw certain opportunities for strengthening its position on Abkhazia, South Ossetia, and Transnistria. Despite these very different interests and perspectives, however, all the external parties—including Russia—were primarily defending a position that they subjectively considered to be in line with their view of nationhood and just cause. In this respect, the Right Intentions Principle was respected in all the positions that have been taken concerning the future status of Kosovo.

CONCLUSION

In March 2007 Martti Ahtisaari argued in his proposal that Kosovo constituted "a unique case" which required "a unique solution."[24] The case of Kosovo is indeed exceptional in many respects, including the circumstances of the conflict, but the option of supervised independence for the territory nonetheless remains based on a number of principles that have universal value. In 1999 the Georgian government proposed to apply the Kosovo model on the use of force in a secessionist conflict to Abkhazia. In 2003, the Chechen secessionist leadership defended the necessity to apply the Kosovo model on the creation of an international administration for breakaway territories to its own country. These two applications, however, were unconvincing and have never been taken into account by external mediators. It is unlikely that the Kosovo model on unilateral independence—resulting in the recognition of a breakaway state by a large part of the international community—will be applied directly to another conflict, but in future negotiations on conflicts over sovereignty this particular Kosovo model will very probably have a greater impact than the two previous ones.

Five options were at stake in the status debate: (1) autonomy; (2) independence with the agreement of Serbia; (3) supervised independence under the authority of the UNSC; (4) the postponement of the final decision on independence in the expectation that this would be decided consensually within the UNSC at a later stage; (5) the unilateral recognition of Kosovo's independence by a number of states.

The first option was an agreement between Serbia and Kosovo on autonomy. This option was not in line with the Just Cause Principle, as it would have failed to guarantee the correction and prevention of severe injustices. So, this option did not meet the Likelihood of Success Principle, understood as the successful upholding of a just cause and as a reasonable chance of building sustainable institutions. The option of autonomy contradicted likewise the Principle of Legitimate Authority, in that it requires the creation of legitimate state institutions. For all these reasons, autonomy was not in line with the Principle of Proportionality, taking into account the costs and benefits at the domestic and international levels. The fact that this option accords with the Principle of Right Intentions (which is also the case with all the other options described below) did not make it any more just or feasible[25] —it merely demonstrates that this particular principle is quite irrelevant in making a just choice among the various status options.

An attempt to achieve an agreement between Serbia and Kosovo on independence fitted in with the Just Cause Principle and all the others, with the exception of the Likelihood of Success Principle understood as a reasonable strategy for achieving independence.[26] Such an attempt had indeed every chance of failing, thanks to the Serbs' uncompromising position on the principle of territorial integrity.

A UNSC decision on supervised independence was in line with all the principles. As a strategy for achieving independence, it had a far greater likelihood of success than the previous option, mutual agreement. Kosovo was a singular case among secessionist conflicts owing to the widespread support among Western governments for the idea of its supervised independence. This had created the reasonable hope that Russia and China may have had to agree to this option in the long term. The deadlock in the UNSC negotiations on the international status of Kosovo never meant that this option was definitively off the negotiating table. Sooner or later, the permanent members of the UNSC had, in their own interest, to find a compromise solution concerning to the problem of Kosovo.

As the choice of a UNSC resolution in favor of supervised independence for Kosovo could not be materialized in the short term, putting the decision on sovereignty and independence on hold may have been a reasonable alternative, despite its significant moral and political costs, notably the risk of domestic instability. This risk meant that the option was not in line with the Likelihood of Success Principle when it refers to the sustainability of state institutions, or with the Proportionality Principle when it refers to consequences at the domestic level. It was in line with the Proportionality Principle, in terms of its consequences for international diplomacy, with the Last Resort Principle, and with the Principle of Legitimate Authority, insofar as it entails a legitimate process for achieving recognition. And in terms of the second meaning of the Legitimate Authority Principle, this option would not have affected the domestic legitimacy of the state institutions.

Finally, the Western choice for option 5—namely, the recognition of Kosovo's unilateral declaration of independence causing a split in the international community—was not fully justified either, despite its attractiveness as a strategy for achieving independence by the creation of a fait accompli. Such a unilateral act might have been in line with the Just Cause Principle and the Principle of Likelihood of Success, in its implementation of a just cause, its strategy for achieving independence, and the building of sustainable independent state institutions. But it was not in accordance with the Principle of Legitimate Authority (in terms of the process of recognition) or Proportionality (owing to the costs and benefits at the international level).

International status for Kosovo had to guarantee that the type of massive injustice suffered by the Kosovo Albanians under Serbian rule would not be repeated and that a similar fate would not be in store for the Kosovar minorities. An internationally supervised form of independence, met this criterion. But the strong support of Western countries for this status option has

Table 11.1. Five Options and Six Criteria in the Kosovo Negotiations

	Agreement between Serbia and Kosovo on autonomy	Agreement between Serbia and Kosovo on independence	UNSC decision on supervised independence	Final decision on independence on hold	Partial recognition
Just Cause	No	Yes	Yes	Yes	Yes
Likelihood of Success:					
– in implementing a just cause	No	Yes	Yes	Yes	Yes
– as a strategy for achieving independence	Not applicable	No	Yes	Yes	Yes
– in building sustainable institutions	No	Yes	Yes	No	Yes
Last resort	Not applicable	Not applicable	Yes	Yes	No
Legitimate authority:					
– of the process for achieving independence	Not applicable	Yes	Yes	Yes	No
– of the state institutions	No	Yes	Yes	Yes	Yes
Proportionality:					
– domestic	No	Yes	Yes	No	Yes
– international	No	Yes	Yes	Yes	No
Right intentions	Yes	Yes	Yes	Yes	Yes

not been sufficient to guarantee its full international acceptance. The choice of partial recognition by Western governments seemed capable of strengthening Kosovar state institutions at the domestic level, but it raised questions about their international legitimacy and their access to international institutions. Putting the decision on the final status option on hold seemed to entail severe risks for domestic stability, but it would have remained in line with international law and with the principles applied by Western governments in other secessionist conflicts. A suspension of the sovereignty question would, in particular, have had the advantage of leaving the door open for further diplomatic negotiations, notably within the UN Security Council.

Western governments made their decision on the basis of deep concern about domestic stability in Kosovo, in the hope that it would not have detrimental long-term effects on the resolution of secessionist conflicts elsewhere. The denial that Kosovo could constitute a universal model was based on this hope. The question of full recognition may, however, have to come back before the UNSC to be resolved in common by the great powers.

The deadlock in the negotiations has led to mutual accusations. The main actors have been accusing each other of seeking strategic advantages that are at odds with the security interests of the region and of the populations concerned. In terms of the just secession principles, they accused each other of going against the Principle of Right Intentions. But this criticism is open to challenge. Strategic interests did undoubtedly play a role, but they do not fully explain the parties' difficulty in reaching agreement on common principles for resolving the question of a just secession. In the case of great powers such as Russia or China, such interests remain subordinate to their view of what constitutes a nation and, in particular, to their fear of secessionist crises erupting on their own territory. The very concept of a divided state has a different meaning for them than for the United States. Like Spain, or Cyprus, Russia and China frame the problem of Kosovo in terms of their own national identity. It may be concluded that it is perhaps unfortunate that the search for geopolitical advantages not in line with the Right Intentions Principle does not play a greater role in such conflicts on sovereignty. It would make it easier to find compromises.

NOTES

1. Since 1992, Serbia and Montenegro have constituted the Federal Republic of Yugoslavia. In 2003 this federation was reconstituted as the State Union of Serbia and Montenegro, and the two constituent republics became fully independent in 2006.

2. See International Crisis Group (ICG), "Kosovo: Toward Final Status," *Europe Report* 161 (January 24, 2005), at www.crisisgroup.org/home/index.cfm?id=3226&l=1 (accessed February 3, 2008), 2. Extensive use has been made of this report in the present

analysis. The various just war principles referred to here are not used in the ICG report, however.

3. The inability of KFOR and UNMIK to protect the Serb and Romany communities was glaringly obvious during the riots that erupted in March 2004, where hundreds of houses belonging to minorities were destroyed. See Human Rights Watch, "Failure to Protect: Anti-minority Violence in Kosovo," March 2004, at hrw.org/reports/2004/kosovo0704/ (accessed February 3, 2008).

4. See the introduction to "Failure to Protect," at hrw.org/reports/2004/kosovo0704/3.htm#_Toc77665973 (accessed February 3, 2008) and International Crisis Group, "Kosovo: No Good Alternatives to the Ahtisaari Plan," *Europe Report* 182 (May 14, 2007): 4, at www.crisisgroup.org/home/index.cfm?id=4830&l=1 (accessed February 3, 2008).

5. In the context of this discussion, "unilateral" means that the decisions on the use of force or on the international status of the secessionist territory were opposed by the central government.

6. The just war principles are applied to the Georgian-Abkhaz and the Chechen conflicts in Bruno Coppieters, "Secession and War: A Moral Analysis of the Russian-Chechen Conflict," *Central Asian Survey* 22, no. 4 (December 2003): 377–404 and Bruno Coppieters, "War and Secession: A Moral Analysis of the Georgian-Abkhazian Conflict," in *Contextualizing Secession: Normative Studies in Comparative Perspective*, ed. Bruno Coppieters and Richard Sakwa (Oxford: Oxford University Press, 2003), 187–212.

7. See Floriana Fossato, "Georgia: President Supports NATO Air Campaign; Draws Parallels With Abkhazia," Radio Free Europe/Radio Liberty, *News & Analysis*, 11 May 1999, at www.rferl.org/features/1999/05/f.ru.990511133219.asp (accessed February 3, 2008). On the positions of Georgian officials on how the Kosovo example should be followed by Georgia, see also Grigory Alexeyev, "CIS States Claim New Savior—NATO," *The Russia Journal*, August 30, 1999, at www.cdi.org/russia/sep0399.html (accessed February 3, 2008). See also *The Army and Society in Georgia*, December 1999, 9, at www.cpirs.org.ge/Archive/AS_12_99.pdf (accessed February 3, 2008).

8. The plan, entitled "The Russian-Chechen Tragedy: The Way to Peace and Democracy," published in February 2003 by the Ministry of Foreign Affairs of the Chechen Republic of Ichkeria, was reproduced in *Central Asian Survey* 22, no. 4 (December 2003): 481–509.

9. On the consequences of European integration for secessionist conflicts at the European periphery, see Bruno Coppieters et al., *Europeanization and Conflict Resolution: Case Studies from the European Periphery*, special issue, *Journal on Ethnopolitics and Minority Issues in Europe* 1 (2004), at www.ecmi.de/jemie/special_1_2004.html (accessed February 3, 2008). Also published as a book by Academia Press, Ghent, 2004.

10. "Constitution of the Republic of Serbia," at www.parlament.sr.gov.yu/content/eng/akta/ustav/ustav_1.asp (accessed February 3, 2008).

11. "Kosovo: Toward Final Status," 15.

12. "Constitution of the Republic of Serbia."

13. "Constitution of the Republic of Serbia."

14. "Kosovo: No Good Alternatives," 10–15.

15. Letter dated March 26, 2007, from the secretary-general to the president of the Security Council. Addendum. Comprehensive Proposal for the Kosovo Status

Settlement, UN Security Council, S/2007/168/Add.1, at www.unosek.org/unosek/index.html (accessed February 3, 2008). This document includes the report and the comprehensive proposal. The concept of independence is mentioned in the former but not in the latter—a difference that is important in the search for international diplomatic support for the ideas present in both documents. See ICG, "Kosovo: No Good Alternatives to the Ahtisaari Plan," 3, n. 17.

16. On Russia's position, see Oksana Antonenko, "Russia and the Deadlock over Kosovo," *Survival* 49, no. 3: 91–106.

17. "Report of the Special Envoy," 3.

18. Human Rights Watch, Human Rights News, Kosovo: "Criminal Justice System Fails Victims," May 30, 2006, at hrw.org/english/docs/2006/05/30/serbia13441.htm (accessed February 3, 2008). See also Human Rights Watch, "Not on the Agenda: The Continuing Failure to Address Accountability in Kosovo Post-March 2004," May 30, 2006, at hrw.org/reports/2006/kosovo0506/ (accessed February 3, 2008).

19. "Kosovo: No Good Alternatives," 6.

20. "Kosovo: Toward Final Status," 1, 5.

21. This option is analyzed in depth in International Crisis Group, "Breaking the Kosovo Stalemate: Europe's Responsibility," *Europe Report* 185, August 21, 2007, at www.crisisgroup.org/home/index.cfm (accessed February 3, 2008).

22. Turkey remained diplomatically isolated when it recognized the independence of the Turkish Republic of Northern Cyprus (TRNC) in 1983. Russia would likewise be unable to gain a significant following in the international community if it were to recognize the unilateral declarations of independence made by Abkhazia, South Ossetia, or Transnistria. This lack of likelihood of success largely explains why the Russian government has so far refrained from granting such recognition.

23. "Kosovo: Toward Final Status," 8–9.

24. "Letter dated 26 March 2007," 4.

25. Unlike independence, the option of autonomy cannot be considered a last resort. Nor may the Likelihood of Success Principle, understood as the achievement of recognition for Kosovo's independence by the international community, or the Legitimate Authority Principle, in its meaning as a legitimate process for achieving recognition, be applied in such a case.

26. The last resort criterion is not applicable to the option of achieving independence on the basis of an agreement between the parties.

12

Terrorism

Nick Fotion

THE NATURE OF TERRORISM

More than likely, terrorism has been around as long as humans have been using violence as a way of settling disputes among themselves. We can imagine cavemen terrorizing (frightening, intimidating, etc.) other cavemen by grunting loudly and screaming in order to protect their food supply. In early history, we find the Assyrians ruthlessly suppressing insurrections in their empire in order to send a message to others who were considering rebellion.[1] The Mongols killed everyone in cities who resisted their invasion and then sent word ahead about what had happened.[2] Terrorized, the authorities and the people in that next city often did not put up a fight. Before them, the Huns did the same thing.[3] Before either group, the Jewish Zealots had their own version of terrorism.[4] They used daggers on those Jews who were cooperating with the Romans. Other Jews of a more moderate stripe were terrorized into siding with the Zealots. Much later, the Muslim (Shiite) Assassins also used daggers in a similar way.[5] They terrorized by stabbing a leader who had strayed from the true path of Islam. Usually, the Zealots and the Assassins paid with their lives shortly after performing their deeds.

As we know it today, terrorism is as varied as it was throughout history. States can practice terrorism as can nonstate groups. State terrorists can practice their way of fighting against other states, or against people inside their own state. Nonstate groups can practice terrorism against other states, their own state, or various groups both outside and inside their own state.

In addition, there is variation in what happens to terrorists when they perform their deeds. Whether they are state or nonstate terrorists, some can be classed as escape terrorists. Either before, during, or after they perform their deed, they endeavor to escape from the scene. But some are suicide (or, as they are sometimes called, martyr) terrorists[6] who die directly as they perform their victimizing act or, as with the Assassins, die moments later at the hands of others.

There is also variety in how one terrorizes an opponent. It can be done through threat or by presenting the enemy directly with a frightening experience (e.g., by showing off the vast numbers of tanks the enemy will face). But the most familiar form of terrorism today is a three-stage affair. First, the terrorist picks out a group of victims. The victims might be killed, tortured, wounded, raped, or harmed in some other way (e.g., by having their homes burned). Second, others associated with the victims see for themselves or are told what has happened (e.g., via melodramatic television reports), and so are terrorized. This can be called the primary effect of terrorism.[7] Third, in their state of terror they might flee, they might implore their government to do what the terrorists want, or they might lose faith in their government and thus contribute to its fall. These are the typical secondary effects of terrorism.

Terrorizing one's enemies sometimes get results, sometimes not. The effort to terrorize may fail as it did in World War II during the bombing of London and other cities in Britain. Rather than giving up (a possible secondary effect), the British became more determined to resist Hitler's Germany.[8] Later, the Germans responded to Allied bombing in a similar manner. Their morale was never crushed by the bombing.[9] Beyond that, they were able to sustain and actually increase military production even as the bombing reached unheard-of levels of intensity.[10] Still, in other settings, terrorism often brings about effects in peoples' lives that are welcomed by the terrorists and are unwelcomed by those they are targeting.[11]

It is no surprise, therefore, that those in charge of fighting in war and in warlike settings consider using the tactic of terror when facing their enemies. They could use other tactics. If they have large enough forces, they might just smash their opponents with a frontal assault. Or they might encircle their enemies and strike them from the rear. They might even resort to siege warfare if their enemies are well entrenched. At other times, if they are relatively disadvantaged in numbers and equipment, they might resort to guerrilla warfare. All these tactics might contain elements of terror, but their main thrust is elsewhere. However, there will be times when the preferred tactic will be where terrorism is dominant. It is a tactic that could be used against "innocents" in war and also against those who are not so innocent, such as governmental officials, the police, and even enemy military personnel.

Many writers on the topic dispute this last claim. Terrorism, they argue, is restricted, *by definition*, to attacks on those who are variously described as innocents, noncombatants, civilians, or those who are not involved directly with the military.[12]

No one argues that those who are innocent are, in fact, the ones most often terrorized. However, the definition issue is concerned with whether terrorists are still terrorists when they terrorize those who are not quite innocent.[13] Against the claim that terrorism can be defined by drawing a sharp line between innocents (i.e., civilians, nonparticipants in war, etc.), on the one side, and military and police personnel, on the other, the argument here is that no such line should be drawn. The reason is obvious. The behavior of the attackers who come to be labeled terrorists when they attack innocents often is exactly the same as when they attack those who are not so innocent. In both cases the attackers aim to terrorize and, often, they aim as well to achieve some political result from the terrorism they have triggered (i.e., some secondary effect). In both cases, to put it in another way, the attackers are engaged in a special kind of psychological warfare triggered by acts of violence against a group of victims. The argument here is that it is a kind of warfare that can, in principle, work on anybody.

To appreciate the point better, imagine the following scenario. A guerrilla organization or a cell of rebels identifies a group of people as their targets. Imagine that this group is composed of ethnics living in the same country as the guerrillas. Imagine, as well, that the guerrillas want to bring about ethnic cleansing of these people. They begin their cleansing operations by killing a few of the ethnics in close-by villages. They spread the word to the ethnics that they should get out or more will be killed. Almost immediately, after the first killings, there is a second round of killing, but this time of both "innocent" ethnics *and* ethnic policemen. The remaining ethnics along with their policemen are terrorized (the primary effect of the victimizing process) enough that members of both groups move across the border into a neighboring country (the secondary effect). As indicated above, the pattern can vary as when the terrorists victimize at random the citizens (or the military) of a country and terrorize the people and its government into freeing prisoners who are sympathetic to the terrorists. Or, the pattern can vary by being more focused. The victims can be government workers, and the terrorized are other government workers who either resign or change their policies because they are terrorized. The pattern can vary even more, as in Iraq, when an attack on a target sometimes victimizes both civilians and police and, at other times, primarily victimizes members of the police force. Another possibility, as in Greece in the 1970s, is when a group of terrorists go out of their way to avoid killing innocents.[14] The Greek terrorists claimed that they were fighting on behalf of the people and, in effect, were honoring the principle of discrimination. So instead of attacking ordinary Greek civilians, they attacked governmental officials who, they claimed, had committed crimes against the people during the days of the Greek dictatorship. They also attacked foreign military attachés, embassy officials, and politically powerful (right-wing) businessmen.[15] The point here is that it makes no sense to call those who merely attack innocent terrorists, but then refuse to call those who terrorize noninnocents such as the police by that same name. It isn't as if, when the police are attacked, that the attackers are doing anything different than when they are attacking innocents. In both cases, certain individuals are made into victims, others are terrorized (the primary effect) and, as the result of the terror, some sort of secondary effect takes place (e.g., the government hands over its political prisoners to the terrorists).

Given what has been said about (the most familiar form of) terrorism so far, the following concepts can now be understood better. A *terrorist act* is one whose primary intent is to psychologically affect people (or an individual) by frightening, terrorizing, etc. them so as to lead to a result (most likely a political one) desired by the terrorists. *Terrorism* is the regular production by some group or individuals of terrorist acts (i.e., a policy of engaging in a series of terrorist acts). *Terrorist* is one who practices terrorism as his or her *main* tactic in a war or warlike conflict. One does not earn the label of terrorist if he or she engages in regular military activity that has some terrorizing elements in it most of the time. He or she also does not earn the label if he or she engages in terrorism on occasion. However, note that one can be called a terrorist if he or she joins the terrorist group one day and, a few days later, kills a number of people by setting off a bomb strapped around his or her waist. That one person's single attack constitutes the whole of what that person did in the war or warlike struggle.

Strictly speaking, these accounts of "terrorist act," "terrorism," and "terrorist" do not represent definitions. Rather, they are rough characterizations (descriptions) of concepts that are probably impossible to define.[16] Fortunately, however, no strict definitions are needed since these rough characterizations are sufficient to allow the discussion of terrorism to continue. [17]

THE MORALITY OF TERRORISM

Keeping in mind that these characterizations of "terrorist act(s)," "terrorism," and "terrorist" are broad enough to allow for both civilians (innocents, etc.) and noncivilians to be either victimized and/or terrorized, it follows that terrorism is not necessarily immoral. Or, putting it differently, not all terrorism goes against Just War Theory. Assuming for the moment that a war between a nation and a terrorist group is already under way, the theory does not necessarily forbid terrorism aimed at military personnel, police, and certain governmental officials. As a tactic of war, such terrorism is no more immoral than many other tactics employed by military personnel or any other group engaged in conflict. None of these actions (against military personnel, etc.) violate the Principle of Discrimination. To the ethics of war, it makes no difference if the enemy forces are defeated by being shot, bludgeoned, starved, worn down by fatigue, or terrorized. All these means of bringing about enemy defeat are cruel, but they are not necessarily immoral. It may be that, as a matter of fact, terrorism has limited application when dealing with military personnel. More than likely, the training such personnel receive makes them more immune to terrorist tactics than civilians. But that fact does not change the judgment that terrorism is not *necessarily* immoral when it is used against noncivilians such as military and police personnel.

However, the judgment tends to change as the targets of terrorism change. With the most familiar form of terrorism (see above), for example, at least some doubt enters into the judgment when the victims are mainly officials of government. To be sure, doubt is not an issue with certain officials. Those in charge of the military (e.g., the defense minister) can be treated in the same way as the terrorists treat soldiers. But what of the mayor of a village? A local official in charge the city's water supply? A schoolteacher? A nurse who works for the government?

As the aim of the terrorist attacks gradually moves away from military and police targets, doubt about the morality of the attacks increases.[18] When that aim finally is on shopkeepers, carpenters, secretaries, mothers, and children; or the aim is on grocery stores, restaurants, shops, schools, medical clinics, and religious edifices, doubt about the immorality of what is happening vanishes. One can now ask: what else could the terrorists do to act in a more immoral way? And the answer seems to be "Probably nothing." At this point the terrorists have apparently gone to the limit against the Principle of Discrimination. In effect, when terrorists intentionally victimize and terrorize civilians (innocents), they take upon themselves a moral burden that can be overcome only with the strongest reasons.

TERRORIST ARGUMENTS

To overcome this burden, terrorists can argue that the evil they do is justified because of some greater evil perpetrated upon them and their people by their enemies. This is exactly how many terrorists argue. They refuse to portray themselves as evildoers. Instead, they take on the mantle of righteousness.[19] They may concede (although most do not) that they are terrorists. But they justify their actions by presenting arguments taken from both the *jus ad bellum* and the *jus in bello* side of Just War Theory (as they understand the theory). Thus they may try to keep the debate about their actions within the moral domain rather than move it to the self-interest domain of Realism.

Focusing the discussion that follows mostly on Islamic terrorism (and thus on nonstate terrorism), consider the following argument presented by none other than Osama bin Laden in his famous 1996 declaration-of-war statement.

> The people of Islam had suffered from aggression, iniquity, and injustice imposed on them by the Zionist-crusaders alliance and their collaborators, to the extent that the Muslims' blood became the cheapest and their wealth loot in the hands of the enemies. Their blood was spilled in Palestine and Iraq. The horrifying pictures of the massacre of Qana, Lebanon, are still fresh in our memory. Massacres in Tajikistan, Burma, Kashmir, Assam [in India], the Philippines, Fatina, Ogadin, Somalia, Eritrea, Chechnya, and Bosnia-Herzegovina took place, massacres that send shivers in the body and shake the conscience.[20]

Others argue along the same lines.[21] They have, they say, just cause for engaging in war against any and all of those nations that are guilty of aggression against Islamic people. They also have just cause to engage in civil war (a *jihad*) against followers of Islam who have strayed from the true path. This is made clear by Abd Al-Salam Faraj in the following passage from his *The Neglected Duty*.

> The rulers of this age are in apostasy from Islam. They were raised at the table of imperialism, be it Crusaderism, or Communism, or Zionism. They carry nothing from Islam but their names, even though they pray and fast and claim to be Muslim.[22]

Of course, merely having just cause is not enough to fully justify any nation or group going to war. It certainly does not justify use of terrorist tactics against civilians (innocents) even when war is viewed from an Islamic perspective.[23] So it is not surprising that supporters of terrorism provide arguments that go beyond the Just Cause Principle of Just War Theory. The following example is typical.

> If bombing London [7 July 2005] was evil, then greater evil was to bomb Iraq for decades with far greater intensity and loss of life! The former may be excusable but the latter certainly is not. But we live in a world where state-terrorism can be excused, but not the minor "terrorism" of just retaliation. Thus the victims are portrayed as aggressors, and the aggressors are portrayed as victims.[24]

This particular argument shifts attention away from *jus ad bellum* issues to those of *jus in bello*. It presupposes a defense of the Principle of Discrimination on the part of Islamic warriors.[25] Indeed, the charge that the enemies of Islam create (innocent) victims in large numbers makes no sense unless these enemies are seen as violating the Principle of Discrimination. What the author implies is that even his terrorist friends are doing wrong by victimizing ordinary citizens. But he adds that that wrong is excused because of the circumstances. Without looking at the circumstances, what terrorists do in killing women, children, and so on, certainly looks blatantly immoral. However, when what terrorists do is viewed as a response to the enemy's extensive immoral state terrorism, things look different. Now, the circumstances show that what the terrorists are doing is retaliating.

Retaliation is not identical with revenge. Revenge has no purpose beyond giving those who practice it a personal or cultural sense of satisfaction.[26] But in one important meaning of the term at least, retaliation has a purpose. Its goal is to stop the enemy from engaging in certain kinds of harmful behavior. So, one interpretation of the above argument can be characterized as follows: "We engage in this seemingly bad behavior of terrorizing innocents in order to encourage our enemies to stop their *gross* forms of (immoral) terrorism that they started in the first place."

There is another interpretation of retaliation that may be what is moving some Islamic terrorists into action. It is not always clear from their writings, but they may be retaliating as a way of punishing their enemies. If their enemies kill, maim, exploit, or subvert the culture of their people, it is only right that these enemy people suffer for their crimes. But, however retaliation is interpreted, and it is possible to interpret it both ways, terrorists see themselves as acting within the bounds of ethics. They are acting morally. According to them, it is their enemies who are immoral.

So casting their own terrorism as a form of retaliation represents one argument that terrorists give to avoid the charge that what they do is immoral. Some terrorists use a second argument. As will become clear shortly, this one is not fully compatible with the retaliation argument. Interestingly enough, a version of this second, so-called collective-responsibility argument is used by the same author who employs the first one.

> Everyone takes it for granted that the civilians in the UK are innocent, but are they really disconnected from the UK foreign policy? Especially, as the civilians have voted for the Labour Party and therefore endorsed the war in Iraq, endorsed the killing of innocent civilians in Iraq? Surely, if innocent Iraqis as a whole could be punished for its dictator, then this should apply even more to a democracy where the people's voice dictates policy and manifesto. Hence, the Labour government, the Labour voters and the silent spectators are clearly guilty in the major state-terrorism, and genocide against Iraq.[27]

As against the first argument, now in this second argument there is no implied admission of doing something wrong. No longer is it a matter of even seemingly acting against the Principle of Discrimination. The reason for this is simple. There are only a few innocents around. Since most everyone is not innocent (and so are responsible collectively), attacking most anybody in a train, bus, restaurant, or wherever, is much the same as attacking enemy soldiers. So with this argument, there is no need for apologies or excuses. To be sure, children in the United Kingdom, the United

States, and elsewhere are innocent. But against the vast majority of adult cit-izens in these countries who are not innocent, what children terrorists de-stroy can count as collateral damage. In effect, what those who present this argument have done is narrow the meaning of "innocent" so that it applies only to a few people. This manipulation of meaning makes life easier for the terrorists, and death more probable for most everybody else.

Contemporary nonstate terrorists have another argument that suppos-edly excuses the killing of innocents. It is sometimes called the argument from necessity. Briefly, this argument tells us that in an asymmetric struggle between a nonstate group and a state with a powerful military establish-ment, the former has no choice but to resort to terrorism. With only small weapons in hand, the nonstate group cannot hope to fight a state's military establishment and survive. It can only survive by engaging in terrorism. Its options are closed much in the way that British options in World War II were closed when, if it were desirous of harming Germany late in 1940 and during most of 1941, it could do so only by engaging in a civilian bombing campaign against German cities.

It is worth noting that these three arguments (revenge/retaliation, collec-tive responsibility, and necessity) do more than allow those who present them to make exceptions to the Principle of Discrimination. It is not just that these arguments *permit* targeting civilians. They create *duties*.[28] Follow-ers of radical Islam are obligated to do what they can to rid their state, their society, and/or their culture of the evils that plague Islam. Minimally these duties range from giving support to Islamic terrorists, from there to becom-ing escape terrorists, all the way to becoming martyr terrorists. Understand-ably, the latter are the true heroes. Martyrs will, of course, be rewarded in paradise. Still, choosing to become a martyr is difficult, especially for those in their youth who lose the whole of their life on earth. So it is proper that they and what they do are celebrated by the *umma* (the Islamic commu-nity).[29] It is also proper for the *umma* to recruit new martyrs until that time that the *umma* is secure.[30]

ASSESSING THE ARGUMENTS

Many terrorists and their sympathizers present us with other arguments to support their cause. They tell us that since they are already under attack, an appeal to the last-resort principle is moot. Or they say that others on their side have tried negotiations, boycotts, and demonstrations, but that all these efforts have failed. So when they make the move to terrorism, their side has truly arrived at their last resort. They also tell us that their inten-tions are good. They are fighting, they say, to undo the military, economic, and cultural aggressions of the West. But these arguments are secondary to the main ones already discussed. It is the main arguments concerned with just cause, revenge/retaliation, collective responsibility (also meaning change), and military necessity that need to be looked at closely. These are the arguments to which the terrorists themselves pay the most attention.

First, then, what about the just cause argument? In the Osama bin Laden quote above, note should be taken that his declaration of war is not aimed just at the United States, or even just the United States and the United Kingdom. The immoralities against Islam that he cites are committed by the Indian, Philippine, Russian, and Serb governments among others as well as the United States and United Kingdom. But more than that, bin Laden makes it clear that establishment Islamic states such as Saudi Arabia and Egypt need to be overthrown since they are corrupt, they practice intimidation, and, worst of all, they deviate from the true laws of Islam.[31]

It is difficult to imagine a more improbable declaration. It certainly would be improbable for one state, no matter how powerful it is, to declare war on a whole host of states scattered throughout the world for a whole host of different reasons. But bin Laden's al-Qaeda, an amorphous nonstate group, is doing just that. It can declare worldwide war because its weakness is its strength. Its weakness is that it lacks land to call its own and lacks large military assets as well. But these weaknesses turn into strengths because, lacking a fixed landmass to protect, al-Qaeda becomes hard to locate. The lack of large military assets similarly turns into an advantage. Large military assets are easy to locate and destroy; small ones, like those belonging to al-Qaeda, cannot be easily located and therefore not easily destroyed.

But the bravado of such a worldwide declaration aside, how justified are his many declarations of war? Do he, his followers, and other Islamic terrorist groups really have just cause on their side?

It seems that they do. Going back to the eighteenth, through the nineteenth, and well into the twentieth century, most Islamic states suffered from colonialism.[32] Speaking in very general terms, these states were heavily exploited most especially by England and France. But even when the colonized states were liberated in the latter part of the twentieth century, many were still dominated by the economic power of their former colonial masters and also by the United States. It didn't help any, from the (fundamentalist) Islamist point of view, that many of the liberated Islamic states (e.g., Egypt, Iran—during the Shah's reign, Iraq, Pakistan, Saudi Arabia, Syria) became secular dictatorships of one kind or another. As secular rather than sectarian, Islamic states, these dictatorships cooperated either with the Western capitalists or the communists from Eastern Europe. The result was that the way of Islam was subverted by ideologies foreign to it. The subversion extended to cultural concerns.[33] For example, Islamic peoples were now encouraged to view and admire mostly underdressed "liberated" Western women. They were also encouraged to view alcohol consumption and other Western practices foreign to Islam as acceptable. To make matters worse, Islamic states suffered from more than occasional invasions by the "Crusaders." The most recent examples of course are the invasions of Afghanistan and Iraq by mainly U.S. and UK forces. But perhaps the worst invasion of all from the Islamist point of view occurred in Palestine. In that country, the Zionist invaders saw, and see, themselves as permanent occupiers of lands that truly belong to them. As bad as the U.S. and UK invaders are, they at least see themselves as "coming and going." But the Zionists are in Palestine to stay in the form of the new state of Israel.

According to the dissidents, then, Islam has been and is being aggressed against by all sorts of forces in all sorts of ways. That being the case, the dissidents, and really all true members of Islam, are fully justified in fighting a defensive war. They are justified both in accordance with Western Just War Theory and the corresponding theory of Islam. One can agree with this claim even if, at the same time, arguing that many of the claims of aggression against Islam are grossly exaggerated. For instance, it is claimed that American aggression against Iraq since the 1991 war has caused the death of 600,000 children.[34] The claim is a strong one in that it puts all the blame for the loss of these children on the Americans. It is as if it were not possible for the Iraqi regime to divert money and resources from its military program and its corrupt practices to mitigate the problem. For propaganda purposes, evidently, it is better to put the full blame on somebody else. Another example of exaggeration, not atypical of radical Islamist writings, is seen in the following "Letter to Bill Clinton."

> You have bombed Baghdad, oh master of the world, with more than 250,000 cruise (missiles) to destroy it, [knocking it down] on the heads of its children, women, and elderly. To destroy the playgrounds of its youth and the dolls of its little girls. You have no specific target to bomb and no one you aimed at, [just] a blind crazy bombing.[35]

Aside from the fact that the U.S. military would have been delighted to ever have possessed 250,000 cruise missiles, let alone expend that number of the very expensive missiles on Iraq, the last thing one can accuse the U.S. air forces of doing since the early 1990s is engage in indiscriminate bombing. More than any other military establishment, the United States has invested billions of dollars in smart weaponry in part to make the wars it fights more discriminating. No doubt, accidents of one kind or another will happen even with the smartest of weapons.[36] But it makes only propaganda sense to claim that the United States engaged in "blind crazy bombing."

Still, in spite of these exaggerations, and looking at it from the radical Islamist point of view, what the United States, the United Kingdom, Israel, and the established Islamic nations are engaged in is aggression. It is aggression of the military variety on the part of the United States, the United

Kingdom, and Israel. It is also "aggression" via corruption on the part of the established Islamic nations. Islam is being threatened by all these governments in several ways and, so, just cause does seem to be on the side of the Islamist rebels.

However, even if the rebels can be given the benefit of the doubt with respect to the Just Cause Principle, and with respect to the other *jus ad bellum* principles (e.g., such as last resort and right intentions), that is not enough to warrant the approval of indiscriminate forms of terrorism. At most what the application of the *jus ad bellum* principles permit the rebels to do is to go to war. Additional arguments are needed to justify the use of indiscriminate terrorism as a tactic in that war.

That, as has been made clear already, is why the argument concerned with revenge/retaliation is introduced by the rebels. They think that the terrible evils their enemies have committed against them, especially against innocents in the Islamic community, warrant a strong retaliatory response. Thus it only seems fair that Western innocents should be targeted to counter the targeting by the West of Islamic innocents. But in view of the wildly exaggerated propaganda claims of Western evildoing against Islamic innocents, it is not clear that the terrorists have ample justification for the way they are fighting. Some other response seems to be more appropriate since, after all, it has been granted that the Islamists have just cause (and presumably some of the other principles of Just War Theory) on their side. They could, as they did, attack the Pentagon since that institution clearly does not fall under the rubric of innocence. They could also attack other U.S. and UK military facilities and personnel as they are doing in Iraq. They might even be justified in attacking a wide variety of U.S., UK, and other Western governmental facilities throughout the world (e.g., embassies, information agencies). These attacks could be terroristic or not. But, as a general policy, it is difficult to justify deliberate attacks on women, children, and so on, in Western countries especially since the West is not deliberately and systematically attacking Islamic women, children, and so on.

If the retaliatory argument against "innocents" fails to fully justify terrorist attacks, the collective-responsibility argument might be thought to fare better. According to that argument, few "innocents" are to be found in Western democratic countries. In these countries, ordinary citizens vote for and support their evil leaders and so are as (or almost as) responsible for the wrongs that their governments do. They too, then, can be attacked just as their military forces can be.

The force of this argument comes from the nature of the concept of innocence as it is applied in war settings by many terrorists. "Innocence," they suppose, is an analog (i.e., a degree) concept. On this conception, one can be more or less innocent. Some humans, children for example, are completely innocent with respect to matters that would interest most terrorists.

Others, who oppose the political party that sponsors the "war on terrorism," are close to being innocent. According to this way of thinking, their "guilt" grows a bit more if they, in general, support their government in most of its policies and laws even if they don't support the "war on terrorism" effort. The "guilt" grows still more if they support the war but did not vote for the war party, and grows even more when they both support and vote for that party. It grows still more when compared with those who work in factories that directly support the war effort and those who are in the military.

If, as many terrorists suppose, innocence can be treated as an analog concept, it will not likely be easy to apply the Principle of Discrimination and then say that these people over here can, but those over there cannot, be attacked. Where the line is drawn will be a function of a variety of factors such as how serious the war is. If a war is long and protracted, munitions workers would be subject to legitimate attack. But if a war is about over, attacking those same workers (who, let us say, are far from the front) would not be legitimate. So there is some slack as to where the line should be drawn. In terms of what was said earlier in our chapter on the Principle of Discrimination, the rules of engagement (for either side) will vary somewhat from situation to situation. Take another example, should a bridge that is used equally by civilians and the military be subject to attack? If it is close to the front, and the war is long and protracted, Just War Theory would probably countenance an attack; otherwise not.

Still, it should be clear that it is a radical departure from the Just War Tradition (of both east and west) to move the discrimination line all the way over so that only those who are at the extreme are innocent. In effect, this radical moving of the line changes the meaning of "innocence" (and related concepts such as "nonparticipants") in war from an analog to a digital (i.e., an on/off rather than a degree) concept in a rather arbitrary fashion. One is now either totally (completely, purely) innocent like a child, or one is totally not innocent. And, since on this digital interpretation, there are now very few who are innocent, the terrorists are free to attack just about anyone they please.

Unfortunately, for the terrorists, changing the meaning of "innocence" (and related concepts), thus allowing the collective responsibility argument to work, has what might be called a backfire effect. If all that is needed to make the enemies' people subject to attack is that they are barely touched by their military establishment, then the same argument can be applied to the other side. Terrorists also have relatives, friends, supporters, voters, and so on. Consistency demands that if it is proper to attack just about anyone in the camp of those opposed to terrorism, it is proper to attack just about anyone in the terrorists' camp. Putting it differently, if it is wrong to attack women and children on the terrorists' side (as the terrorists insist it is), it must be wrong to attack their enemies' women and children.

So far, it appears that terrorists have just cause and perhaps some other justice-of-the-war principles on their side. They, possibly, can start a war justly. But, so far, it appears that they have no good arguments for fighting an indiscriminate war. The retaliation and the collective responsibility (i.e., the redefining) arguments they present on their behalf do not work. However, their third, and final, major argument pertaining to the discrimination principle might work. The radical Islamist version of this military-necessity argument goes something like this.[37]

> We rebel groups do not possess sophisticated and expensive military equipment. In this regard we are disadvantaged in ways that rebels of the past were not. Their equipment was often as good as that used by those they rebelled against. But now the equipment gap between our enemies and us has grown and continues to grow. Our rebellion to end the enemy's occupation cannot, therefore, take the form of face-to-face battles. We would lose such battles every time. But our cause is desperate. Indeed, our plight is such that we can only succeed if most of our attacks are aimed at non-military targets. And our plight is such that we must include martyr terrorists in our arsenal. Either we attack so-called innocents with martyrs, if necessary, or we give up on our rebellion. And we cannot do that. The purpose of our rebellion is to save Islam, true Islam, from the military, political and cultural encroachments of the West. If these encroachments were allowed to continue, they would not just harm Islam, they would destroy this sacred institution completely.

Those who approve of this argument are not telling us that they have no respect for the Principle of Discrimination. You can tell that they do since, once again, they are often quick to attack their enemies for violating that principle. When *their* children and grandparents are attacked, these attacks are called gross immoralities. That is one part of their argument. In the other part, they say that Islam is in such desperate and serious straits that its (radical) defenders should seriously consider making an exception to that principle. They might not have to make an exception since they just might possess the means to save Islam and still keep to the principle. But, in fact, they say that, given the desperate straits Islam is in, they have no other option but to attack (so-called) innocents. Given that they are technologically disadvantaged, their options essentially shrink to one: viz., attacking innocents. So they must not just consider the possibility of attacking these innocents in the enemy camp, they must actually attack them.

What can we make of this argument? It is best in making an assessment to look at its two parts separately. What of the claim that Islam finds itself in a distressing situation that Michael Walzer calls a supreme emergency?[38] When we think of such an emergency we imagine two things. One, a nation such as Great Britain in 1940 and 1941 facing a most serious and imminent invasion. Two, if its invasion succeeds, the enemy intends not just to act as an occupier but as a force that aims to dismember totally the culture and institutions of the land being occupied.

One has to ask whether anything close to that is happening to a large number of the Islamic nations in the world. To be sure, some have been recently occupied for a time by Western powers. But such occupations do not involve efforts to systematically dismember the Islamic religion or the culture found in them. Other Islamic nations have not even been occupied recently. Rather, they are Islamic states (e.g., Egypt) but they are, in the view of the rebels, corrupt. One can grant that the "invasion" by the West need not be purely physical in nature. According to the rebels, Western financial resources and its media further the corruption of the Islamic religion and culture in every Islamic nation. But, unfortunately, for the radical Islamist argument, none of these threats rises to the level of creating anything like a supreme emergency. Serious though they are, they are all reversible by a variety of means other than attacks on women, children, old people, the sick, and the lame.

This point brings us to the other part of the radical Islamist argument. It just is not the case that the only option available to the rebels is to attack so-called innocent people in the West or the innocents in the corrupt Islamic states. For one, the rebels can sponsor revolutions to overthrow the corrupt Islamic states. Iran is an example of what is possible. For another, they can develop programs within their religion to root out the influence of Western culture. For still another, they can directly attack Western military forces with guerrilla warfare and suicide volunteers. Still another option is to participate in the political process of one and then another Islamic state. No doubt this option is not always a real one in those countries run by strong dictatorships. But as more of the Islamic nations become at least somewhat democratic, this option in fact will become more real.

In sum, this third argument (pertaining to the Discrimination Principle) of the Islamic rebels is no better than the other two that are used to justify attacks on innocents or so-called innocents. So in applying Western *and* Islamic Just War Theory to the actions of Islamic rebels, attacks on the general population to further the cause of rebellion are not easy to justify. Attacking a population as a whole, that is, attacking "innocents," seems to be more a matter of expediency rather than ethics. There is no question that such attacks are relatively easy to execute and do, in fact, yield results. But granting these points says nothing about the ethics of these policies. It has been granted that in many settings throughout the world rebels have just cause on their side and probably can justify "going to war" with their enemies based, as well, on the other *jus ad bellum* principles. It has also been granted that terrorism can be used, as it was in Greece in the 1970s, in a way that is compatible with the Discrimination Principle. But radical Islamists cannot so easily justify their terrorist policies aimed at the vast majority of a population that has little to do with their grievances. That is, they cannot discount the status of their enemies' civilian population so easily as they think they can. Their arguments are too weak to effect such a discounting. In the end, then, Just War Theory condemns most forms of terrorism simply because these forms violate the Principle of Discrimination in such a gross manner.

NOTES

1. Arther Ferrill, *The Origins of War: From the Stone Age to Alexander the Great* (London: Thames and Hudson, 1985), 67–69.

2. Kim Stubbs, "Facing the Wrath of Khan," *Military History*, May 2006, 31–37. See also *The Mongol Conquests: Time Frame AD 1200–1300*, ed. Tony Allen (Alexandria, Va.: Time-Life Books, 1989), 18–19.

3. Henry Woodhead, ed. *Empires Besieged: Time Frame AD 200–600* (Alexandria, Va.: Time-Life Books, 1988), 41–43, 110.

4. Mia Bloom, *Dying to Kill: The Allure of Suicide Terror* (New York: Columbia University Press, 2005), 8–11.

5. Bloom, *Dying to Kill*, 4–8.

6. There is no neutral vocabulary available to talk about these matters. The expression "suicide terrorism" is preferred by some because of its double negative meaning. "Suicide" carries negative meaning since it describes actions that are forbidden by many ethical stances and "terrorism" carries negative meaning since it is mainly associated with killing innocent people. So to call some actors in war suicide terrorists is to have a convenient label that quickly and effortlessly condemns them. In contrast, "martyr" is a commendatory word. Most of us admire martyrs. If, in addition, one avoids using the word "terrorist" to characterize these actors, a much more favorable image of them emerges. In short, it is well-nigh impossible to come up with terminology that pleases everyone. Perhaps the best one can do is to use "suicide" and "martyr" interchangeably even though these expressions do not carry exactly the same meaning.

7. "Terrorized" (and its derivatives) are not the only words that can be used to characterize the primary effect. We can also speak of those affected by the victimizing process as being frightened, intimidated, or shocked. Any word or expression that conveys the idea of a profound negative psychological reaction will do.

8. Gerhard L. Weinberg, *A World at Arms: A Global History of World War II* (Cambridge: Cambridge University Press, 1994), 148–50.

9. James L. Stokesbury, *A Short History of World War II* (New York: William Morrow and Company, Inc., 1980), 279.

10. Weinberg, *A World at Arms*, 480, 616-619.

11. Robert A. Pape, *Dying to Win: The Strategic Logic of Suicide Terrorism* (New York: Random House, 2005), 39–41.

12. For example, see Igor Primoratz ("What Is Terrorism") and Tony Cody ("Defining Terrorism") in *Terrorism: The Philosophical Issues*, ed. Igor Primoratz (New York: Palgrave/Macmillan, 2004), 15-27 and 3-14 respectively. See also David

Rodin, "Terrorism without Intention," *Ethics* 114 (2004): 751–71. See as well Lionel K. McPherson, "Is Terrorism Distinctively Wrong?" *Ethics* 117 (2007): 524–46.

13. Alissa J. Rubin, "Sunni Insurgents in New Campaign to Kill Officials," *New York Times*, September 26, 2007, A1, A11.

14. "Revolutionary Organization 17 November," at en.wikipedia.org/wiki/Revolutionary_Organization_17_November (accessed October 17, 2007).

15. So, in attacking certain businessmen, the Greek terrorists did not follow the Principle of Discrimination to the letter. Still they followed it far more than vast majority of modern, and not-so-modern terrorists do.

16. Walter Laqueur, *The New Terrorism: Fanaticism and the Arms of Mass Destruction* (New York and Oxford: Oxford University Press, 1999), 5. Laqueur points out that there are over one hundred definitions of terrorism in the literature. We can speculate that one reason for this abundance of definitions is the complexity of the concept. But another reason, perhaps more important, is that many of these definitions are infected with politics. Thus one group defines terrorism such that even though it engages in activities that involve terrorism, it is excluded from being called terrorist. Rather, they say, they are freedom fighters. Others define terrorism in such a way that those who oppose them are all called terrorists.

17. Strict definitions give us the necessary and sufficient conditions for identifying an object or phenomenon. As Laqueur's comments in the previous endnote suggest, it may not be possible to give a strict definition of such a complex and politically charged concept as terrorism. In place of a definition a characterization describes a concept in piecemeal fashion so that a reader has at least a rough idea what is being talked about.

18. See Anthony Hartle's chapter on the Principle of Discrimination in this edition of *Moral Constraints on War*.

19. Michael Moss and Souad Makkhennet, "The Guidebook for Taking a Life," *New York Times*, June 10, 2007, secs. 4, 1, 3.

20. Osama bin Ladin, "Declaration of War (August 1996)" in *Anti-American Terrorism and the Middle East*, ed. Barry Rubin and Judith Colp Rubin (Oxford: Oxford University Press, 2002), 137.

21. Ayatollah Ruhollah Khomeini, "Islam Is Not a Religion of Pacifists (1942)," in *Anti-American Terrorsm and the Middle East*, 29. In the same volume, see also Sheikh Muhammad Sayyed Tantawi, "Suicide Operations Are Legitimate Defense (April 8, 1997)," 36–37. More recently, see Shanin, "Blame It on Blair!!" at articles@hotmail.com July 7, 2005 (accessed October 8, 2005).

22. Abd Al-Salam Faraj, "The Neglected Duty," trans. Johannes G. Jansen, *The Neglected Duty: The Creed of Sadat's Assassins and Islamic Resurgence in the Middle East* (New York: Macmillan, 1986), 169. See also Max Rodenbeck, "The Truth about Jihad," *The New York Review of Books*, August 11, 2005, 52.

23. John Kelsay, *Islam and War: The Gulf War and Beyond* (Louisville, Ky.: Westminister/John Knox Press, 1993). See chapters 2 and 3.

24. Yamin Zakaria, "London Bombings: A Plea for Honesty," at yaminz@yahoo.co.uk July 11, 2005 (accessed August 10, 2005). See also Even Thomas and Stryker McGuire "Terrorism at Rush Hour," *Newsweek*, July 18, 2005, 29–36.

25. John Kelsay, *Islam and War*, 36.

26. Mohammed M. Hafez, *Suicide Bombers in Iraq: The Strategy and Ideology of Martyrdom* (Washington, D.C.: United States Institute of Peace Press, 2007), 44–45.

27. Zakaria, "London Bombing."

28. Osama bin Laden, "Interview with Usama bin Laden (1996)," in *Anti-American Terrorism and the Middle East*, 147.

29. There is another reason for celebration. It turns out that martyr terrorism is the most effective form of terrorism. See Ayman Al-Zawahiri, "Why Attack America (January 2002)," in *Anti-American Terrorism and the Middle East*, 133. See also Pape, *Dying to Kill*, 61–76. Pape puts the ratio of martyr killings to killings by ordinary forms of terrorism at more than twelve to one.

30. Mia Bloom, "Mother, Daughter, Sister, Bomber," *Bulletin of the Atomic Scientists*, November/December 2005, 54–62. Women, as well as men, are recruited from among members of the Muslim community. One reason they are is because they can get by checkpoints more readily by being "charming" and by feigning pregnancy. However, using women as martyrs (suicide bombers) is not restricted to Muslim rebel movements. Famously, LTTE (Liberation Tigers of Tamil Eelam) in Sri Lanka, secular movement, has used women bombers. So have various groups in Chechnya. It is estimated that between 15 percent to 30 percent of all martyr terrorists are women.

31. Osama bin Laden, "Declaration of War," 138.

32. Farhad Khosrokhavar, *Suicide Bombers: Allah's New Martyrs* (London and Ann Arbor, Mich.: Pluto Press, 2005), 28–32.

33. Oliver Roy, *Globalized Islam: The Search for a New Ummah* (New York: Columbia University Press, 2004), 14.

34. Osama bin Laden, "Declaration of War," 141.

35. Atallah Abu Al-Subh, "Letter to Bill Clinton (December 3 1998)," in *Anti-American Terrorism and the Middle East*, 130.

36. Carlotta Gall and David S. Cloud "Afghans Say U.S. Airstrikes Killed 21 Civilians," *New York Times*, May 10, 2007, A10. Even when no mistakes are made, civilians die on a regular basis simply because they are a part of the target area. These deaths cause bad feelings between the American government and the people that government is supposed to be protecting.

37. Robert A. Pape, *Dying to Kill*, 29–30.

38. Michael Walzer, "Supreme Emergency," in *Just and Unjust Wars* (New York: Basic Books, Inc. 1977), 251–68.

13

The War in Iraq

2003 and Beyond

Nick Fotion

BACKGROUND

Saddam Hussein was a power in Iraq long before he became president of that nation in 1979. He had risen to power as a member of the Ba'athist party.[1] He had become the vice president of the Revolutionary Command Council, the second most powerful political position in the country.[2] The Ba'athist president just before Saddam Hussein was Hasan al Bakr, to whom he exhibited great loyalty. However, Bakr was not a strong leader. For the ambitious Saddam, the vacuum of leadership at the presidential level gave him the opportunity to assume important responsibilities. In the Ba'athist tradition, he played an important role in modernizing Iraq. He led the way by improving transportation and by building hospitals, schools, radio stations, and other public facilities. On the social level, he took steps not only to abolish illiteracy but also to raise standards to the point that Iraq was a leader in education in the Middle East. These liberal policies extended to women. Women were given official status equal to men, and so had the opportunity to receive advanced degrees at universities in Iraq and abroad. They were also allowed move about freely and to seek employment outside the home.

Once he assumed power as president in 1979, there seems to have been a change in his priorities. It is not that he abandoned the progressive social and secular policies that inspired the Ba'athist movement. Rather, now, what was more important to him and his administration was Iraq's place as a political and military power in the Middle East. A military buildup had actually started before he became president. Iraq had purchased airplanes from France and armored equipment from the USSR. But the buildup increased as problems developed with Iraq's neighbor, Iran. Under the leadership of the

Shah, Iran had created a powerful military.[3] It possessed a military establishment that was twice the size of Iraq's. Part of that establishment included
extremely modern and powerful F-14 fighter planes bought from the United
States. But when the Shah was overthrown in 1979, and replaced by Ayatollah Khomeini, Saddam saw an opportunity to attack Iran and settle some
old scores. The opportunity was there because Khomeini, in the process of
establishing a sectarian government in Iran, had severely damaged his nation's military establishment.[4] Always prone to settle disputes by force, Saddam could not resist starting a war with Iran. He did so in September of
1980.

Rather than being a quick and dirty war, as Saddam expected it would be,
the Iran/Iraq War was not quick but it was dirty. Its dirtiness involved,
among other events, "the war of the cities" with Iraq using Scud-B missiles
to attack Teheran and the Iranians responding by attacking Baghdad.[5] By
1988, Saddam had gained the upper hand. But the cost in lives was great.
Iraqi casualties were in the hundreds of thousands. Further, the cost in treasure was backbreaking. To pay for the war, Iraq had to borrow hordes of
money from neighboring Islamic states. In a sense, this borrowing did not
bother Saddam. He thought that in attacking Iran he would be seen as protecting the Sunni nations to the west and south from the fundamentalist
Shiite religious movement centered in Iran. He thought he was doing Syria,
Saudi Arabia, Kuwait, Egypt, and other smaller nations in the region a favor. He thus thought that they should be grateful to him and to Iraq. Indeed, he thought that they would forgive the debts that Iraq had incurred.

But they did not. Kuwait and other nations insisted on being paid back.
To make matters worse, Kuwait and some of these other countries in the region were pumping oil at such a high rate that oil prices took a tumble.[6]
This meant that Iraq could not generate enough income to pay back its
debts. Saddam argued that Iraq was being strangled economically and that
unless something was done to alleviate the situation, he might resort to
force. He threatened to use force as well since negotiations over Iraq's border disputes with Kuwait were not going well.

Frustrated over these and other issues, Saddam ordered the invasion of
Kuwait that started on August 2, 1990.[7] In a matter of hours, Iraq occupied
the whole of that small country. Saddam even positioned some of his troops
so they could quickly occupy the oil-rich northeast corner of Saudi Arabia.[8]
Had he been allowed to do this, he would have been in control of far more
than the 20 percent of the world's oil production that he now possessed after having invaded Kuwait. Needless to say, given such an oil bonanza, Saddam's and Iraq's financial difficulties would have quickly vanished.

It is at this point that coalition forces led by the United States intervened.
UN resolutions were passed condemning what Iraq had done; and by the
middle of January 1991, a force of more than one-half million coalition

soldiers, airmen and sailors was ready to take Kuwait away from Saddam. Once the war started, Iraq did not use chemical weapons as it, in fact, did in the Iran/Iraq war. It was evidently fearful of massive retaliation. However, with or without these weapons, it was clear almost from the beginning that the Iraqi military was grossly overmatched.[9] As a result, the war lasted only a few weeks. In the process, Kuwait was liberated and a large portion of Saddam's military machine was destroyed.

The period following the Gulf War of 1991 was an uneasy one. For one thing, the Shiites in the south rebelled against Saddam's government. Saddam brutally suppressed the rebellion using, among other weapons, armed helicopters that the Americans had unwisely allowed him to keep. For another, Saddam and his regime faced pressure from the UN to allow inspectors into Iraq to check for weapons of mass destruction. Saddam succumbed to this pressure and a representation from UNSCOM (United Nations Special Commission on Disarmament) came to Iraq in 1991 headed by Dr. David Kay. Under his aggressive leadership, the Iraqis were forced to destroy many mass-destruction weapons. Unfortunately, by the time the UNSCOM team left Iraq, it could not certify that all of these weapons had been destroyed.[10] Still another series of events that made the situation in Iraq uneasy were the "no fly" policies of the United States and Britain.[11] Their airplanes flew over Kurdish-held territory to prevent Iraqi aircraft (and ground forces) from attacking Kurdish civilians. From time to time, the guardian airplanes were challenged by Iraqi radar. These challenges led to attacks on the offending Iraqi radar stations. This off-and-on struggle gave the impression that the 1991 Gulf War was still continuing. In a way, this impression was confirmed when, belatedly, a no-fly zone was established in the south to give the Shiite community some measure of protection against Saddam and his regime.

The unease in Iraq increased after 9/11. It increased especially after the war in Afghanistan led to the fall of the Taliban regime in that country. To the Iraqis, it appeared that the Americans and their British allies were looking around for an enemy in order to continue their war against terrorism. They did not have far to look. Iraq was there, seemingly guilty of a variety of sins, seemingly involved in terrorism, seemingly not fully cooperative with UN efforts to check for mass destructive weapons, and seemingly representing unfinished business from the 1991 war. After a flurry of activity in the UN (see below) and in their national legislatures, the Bush and Blair administrations decided that it was time to go to war. They did so in March of 2003. Importantly, they did so with significantly smaller forces than those used in the 1991 Gulf War. Using "minimal" forces was part of Secretary of Defense Donald Rumsfeld's military transformation policy.[12] By using more and better smart weapons, advanced sensors, improved communications, and more mobile forces than were available in 1991, Rumsfeld felt that the

U.S. military could do "more with less." How that policy played out later in the war will be evident shortly.

About that war, two questions need to be answered. Did the United States, Great Britain and their allies go to war justly? And, did they fight justly?

JUST CAUSE

The just cause in the First Gulf War is fairly clear-cut. Saddam's attack on Kuwait constituted an act of aggression against a country recognized as sovereign by the rest of the world. The coalition formed to respond to this aggression could not respond as the attack took place. But it responded as soon as it was militarily possible to do so. In contrast, just cause in the Iraq War of 2003 is not so clear-cut. At the time the war started, there was no ongoing or recent act of aggression to respond to. It is true that there was the ongoing "war" against terrorism in various parts of the world. It was in that connection that the war in Afghanistan could be justified. But try as it may, the Bush/Blair team could not assign the label of terrorist to Saddam.[13] Saddam was obviously sympathetic to at least some terrorist acts, especially those aimed at Israel. He was reputed to be rewarding the families of martyr terrorists in Palestine and Israel. But there was no evidence that he was actively involved in planning, organizing, or even sponsoring acts of terrorism. So it is wrong to say that there is just cause for starting a war because of Saddam's involvement with terrorism.

However, there was a second reason, one related to terrorism, that both Bush and Blair presented as a just cause for war. They claimed that Saddam possessed weapons of mass destruction. It was said that he could either use these weapons himself or hand them over to terrorist groups. What was known about these weapons is that he had possessed some in the past. He had, after all, used chemical weapons against Iranian forces during their war in the 1980s; and used them as well against the Kurds.[14] Further, he had bought Scud missiles that he used in the war of the cities during the Iran/Iraq war. Further still, it was known that he had made efforts in the past to build nuclear weapons. Indeed, the Israelis destroyed the nuclear facility at Osirak in 1981 to keep him from developing these weapons.[15] Finally, when UNSCOM (United Nations Special Commission on Disarmament) came to Iraq and actually destroyed many of his mass destruction weapons, Saddam and his subordinates behaved in ways that led many to believe that he was still hiding (in his palaces where UNSCOM could not tread) a good number of these weapons.

Now whether everyone in the Bush and Blair administrations believed that Iraq still had these mass-destruction weapons is in dispute. What is clear is that some did believe. For one, Colin Powell, then secretary of state, most likely did.[16] His presentation before the UN (February 5, 2003) was, at the time, quite convincing.[17] He cited evidence and showed pictures indicating that Iraq had these weapons, and was making strenuous efforts to hide them. Also, much of the military believed that Saddam had mass destruction weapons. This was clear when one considers the orders the troops were given once the war started. They were instructed on many occasions to take precautions against chemical attacks. They fully expected to be attacked with these weapons.[18] They were quite surprised when such attacks did not take place.

But even if one gives the Bush and Blair administrations the benefit of the doubt about the existence of these weapons, just cause for going to war was not there. That is, even if they had sound evidence that Iraq had these weapons, that would not have been a sufficient to constitute a just cause for war. The reason should be clear from what was said in chapter 1. In that chapter, a distinction is made between preemptive and preventive wars. The former are wars started because the threat of war is serious and imminent. The enemy is about to attack, perhaps in a matter of hours. If the nation about to be attacked preempts the threat by striking before it is struck, Just War Theory countenances such a strike. In contrast, a preventive war is one that deals with a future threat, one that might be realized several years down the road. Just War Theory does not countenance starting such a war because there is time to take other steps short of war to prevent the future threat from being realized. Dealing with the threat of Iraqi mass-destruction weapons was clearly a preventive, not a preemptive move. No one presented evidence that the Iraqis were getting their logistics in order so as to be ready to attack anyone. No troops were massing on the border of a neighboring state, and there was no evidence that Iraq was moving their mass destruction weapons into position for some sort of attack on some neighboring nation. There was only the claim that Iraq had such weapons. So even if the threat from the existence of these weapons was sincerely seen as real, and even if in fact it was real, Just War Theory tells us that that was not enough to present the Bush and the Blair administrations with a just cause for starting the Iraq war.

The mass-destruction argument fails especially because the Iraq military never recovered from the damage done to it in the 1991 Gulf War and the additional damage that UNSCOM did to it after the war. A weakened Iraq was in no position to pose a serious threat even to such a near neighbor as Israel. At worst, Iraq would have been left with only a few Scud missiles and essentially no air force to deliver its mass-destruction weapons. But even if it could mount some sort of limited attack, Saddam had to know that the counterattack against his country would have been devastatingly far greater.

So both the terrorism and the weapons of mass destruction arguments fail in producing a just cause for the Iraq war. But there was another argument available to provide a just cause. One of the accepted reasons for going to war is to intervene when a humanitarian disaster is taking place. It was said by some in the Bush administration that Saddam is a cruel dictator and that he had a long history of brutalizing various ethnic groups. We saw that during the Iran/Iraq war, he attacked the Kurds for allegedly cooperating with the Iranians. We also saw that he brutalized the Shiites in areas in and around Basra right after the 1991 war. But in 2003, he and his administration were not involved in any general humanitarian catastrophe. No doubt he was brutalizing a certain number of citizens, if they were suspected of forming an opposition program to his administration. But there was no large-scale humanitarian disaster taking place or looming on the horizon. So that reason also fails by way of providing a just cause for war.

However, there was still another argument that was presented as a just cause. It is a kind of stealth argument. It did not receive much public attention prior to and during the early days of the war. It was as if the Bush administration felt that the terrorism and mass-destruction arguments had more of a public face than this stealth argument. That argument had its origins in neoconservative thinking.[19] It held that the world, and particularly the Middle East, would be better off if governments were democratic, rather than autocratic, and that it is the duty of the United States as the dominant power in the world to sponsor and promote such governments. In full bloom, such thinking is committed to a version of the domino theory. Once one country become more democratic, other countries will follow suit—with or without the help of the United States. That is the argument.

Iraq was chosen to experience democratization first. The reasons for receiving such an honor are not completely clear. Some speculate that Bush wanted to attack Iraq first in order to take care of the unfinished business of his father. Saddam and his military were beaten in the 1991 war, but they managed, somehow, to stay in power. Now, it is said, is the time to remove them. Others argued that Iraq was first in line for democratization simply because it continued to be the "bad boy" in the block. Whatever the reason, the justification for starting the war, the real justification was to democratize Iraq. That at least is how the stealth argument was, later, presented to the public when the other arguments for war failed.

It may be that this is the real reason that motivated the neoconservatives in the administration to convince Bush that it is time to go to war. But if it is, it should be clear that that the democracy reason also cannot serve as a just cause within the framework of Just War Theory. It may be a noble reason to go to war to rid the world of one and then another dictator; and then replace each one with a democratic or democratic-like regime. But Just War Theory specifically forbids going to war for ideological reasons. It is not a just cause to go to war in order to promulgate Catholicism, Protestantism, communism, socialism, or any other such ideology, including a democratic one. By and large, just wars are fought when there is some sort of large-scale

violence taking place, usually in the form of aggression; and the nation acting justly does what it can to suppress that violence.

From this analysis of the Just Cause Principle, there appears to be, in summary, no just cause for the war in Iraq. In its own way, each of the four arguments (terrorism, mass-destruction weapons, humanitarian issues, and
democracy) presented fails to meet the standards of just cause as they have
been traditionally interpreted.

RIGHT INTENTIONS

A large part of what constitutes right intentions concerns acting in accordance with a just cause. Thus, if some aggression takes place, a nation that
goes to war primarily in an effort to undo that aggression is said to have
good intentions. But such a way of looking at right intentions obviously
poses a problem for those responsible for starting the war in Iraq. If they
have no just cause, that is, if they have no good (moral) reasons for going
to war, how can they exhibit right intentions in fighting that war?

Logically speaking they cannot. But their intentions can be measured
against their *beliefs* that they had just cause. Did the "coalition" forces fight
in such a way that (they believed) would contribute to harming terrorism?
Did they fight in such a way as to bring about the destruction of mass-
destruction weapons? Did they fight in such a way as to correct a humanitarian disaster problem? And did they fight in such a way as to help bring
about democracy in Iraq?

It is no argument against their right intentions that they failed to bring
about the good effects of their intentions. The coalition, for example, might
have believed they were suppressing terrorism by going to war when, in fact,
they were doing exactly what it would take to make it flourish. Still their intentions, even if misguided, most likely were geared to harming the terrorist movement. There is little or no evidence to suggest otherwise. Similarly,
their intentions were to destroy the mass destruction weapons that all
(most?) of them believed existed. Again it makes no difference in assessing
right intentions that these weapons were, later, not found. Also, again, it
makes no difference that no humanitarian catastrophe was taking place at
the time the war started. If the U.S. government and its military believed
that humanitarian work was needed, their behavior once the war started
suggests that their intentions were to do such work.

Finally, the intentions of the Bush-led U.S. government were clearly
aimed at democratizing Iraq. This "right intention" in fact is the most
clearly present intention. It is backed by the whole ideology of the neoconservative movement that was then entrenched in the Bush White House.[20]
That ideology may have had such a hold on those who were committed to

it that they were tempted, both consciously and unconsciously, to distort the intelligence that was available to them at the time.[21] As mentioned above, this intention did not receive much publicity especially prior to the war. But as the other just causes were shown to be flawed in one way or another, greater reliance was placed (in retrospect) on the just cause of bringing about a democracy in Iraq and of implementing that (alleged) just cause with the right intentions. Indeed, many of the Bush policies in Iraq (e.g., encouraging elections, establishing a constitution, encouraging the Shiites not to run roughshod over the minority Sunnis) make clear their intention was to promote democracy.

Granting then that the Bush and Blair administrations cannot, strictly speaking, exhibit right intentions because they do not have just cause on their side, it still seems proper to say that they had right intentions before and as the war started. Many people in these two administrations probably had "wrong" intentions. Some very likely wanted war to secure oil at low prices for the Western world.[22] Still others had other "bad" intentions, ones found more in the realist tradition, such as to put the Islamic radicals in their place by presenting them with an overwhelming show of force.[23] However, when war is the issue, intentions are almost never purely good. It is enough, as we said in chapter 3 on Right Intentions, that a nation's right intentions be in place with enough force to make a difference. And it seems that that is the case in the Iraq War. So we can take it that although the just cause principle was not satisfied in that war, the Right Intentions Principle was.

LAST RESORT

The Last Resort Principle should not be interpreted literally. Resorts to action can be identified as "first," "second," "third," and so on, but there is no marker to identify any particular resort as the last one. All we can expect from those who are making decisions about going to war is that they make a series of serious efforts before they send their military in harm's way. What we want leaders to do is start the war only after they have reached and failed to get satisfaction from their last *reasonable* resort (however vague "reasonable" might be).

Well, did the Bush/Blair team reach the last reasonable resort before they invaded Iraq? It is true that several resorts were tried before the war started on March 20, 2003. For one, the "no fly" policy was in place. This policy's purpose, in part, was to force Iraq to comply with UN and U.S. wishes not to act in a threatening way against other nations and people. For another, various sanctions policies were (more or less) in place to keep Iraq from resupplying its military and from stockpiling weapons of mass destruction. For still another, the Bush and Blair team supported Resolution 1441 that

was passed unanimously by the UN on November 8, 2002.[24] This resolution demanded that Iraq allow UN inspectors to return to Iraq and demanded as well that these inspectors be given unfettered access to all sites
where such weapons might be found.[25] The Bush/Blair team also attempted
to have an additional UN resolution passed that would allow U.S. and
British forces to enter Iraq. They failed in this endeavor.

Nonetheless, other reasonable steps could have been taken. It was quite
clear, in spite of the heavy war rhetoric just before the war started, that there
was no special urgency to start a war on March 20. There was no immediate threat that Iraq posed to its neighbors so as to make starting a war appropriate. So, more patience could have been tried. Further, Saddam had
agreed to let UN inspectors back into Iraq and they, in fact, entered the
country. Later Saddam complied with the request of the UN to supply documents showing clearly that the weapons Iraq had in the past no longer existed. It is true that the inspectors were too few to do an adequate job, and
Hans Blix was not the preferred choice of the Americans and the British to
lead the inspection team. It is also true that the documents Saddam sent to
the UN did not contain much information that was new and so did not re-
assure many that Iraq had no weapons of mass destruction. Still, there
seemed to be enough people around monitoring what Saddam and his administration were doing to keep them in check. Irritating though Saddam
might have been in his delays and deceptions, he was not in a good position to threaten anyone in 2003 even if he had a few weapons of mass destruction in hand. Nor would he have been in position to attack anyone in
2004 or even 2005. So, one must conclude that the Bush/Blair team decided
on war before reaching the point of last *reasonable* resort.

LIKELIHOOD OF SUCCESS

One way of employing the Likelihood of Success Principle in the Iraq War
is in terms of the success or failure of military operations.[26] It can refer to
more than that. It can also encompass the success or failure of the political
maneuverings to establish a democratic government after a war is over—
one of the alleged just causes of the war. Evidently the neoconservatives in
America believed that the likelihood of success of this larger project was
quite high. They believed that the Iraqi military could be defeated easily, the
people of Iraq would welcome Saddam's overthrow and then quickly em-
brace democracy. To say the least, these assessments diverged radically from
reality. But the problem for Just War Theory is not to make an assessment
of how things turned out in the end, but how things looked at the beginning. Nor is the problem to identify the prior-to-war assessments that were
actually made by those who were authorized to start the war. Rather, it is to

assess what the actual likelihood of success of the war is and/or of the political aftermath of the war.

Dealing with the war first, it is clear that the likelihood of success was quite high. The Iraqi military never really recovered from the 1991 war. Instead of commanding a force of more than a half a million as Iraq did in 1991, its military numbered more like 200,000 in 2003. Not only that, they were less well equipped.

> In 1991 it [Iraq] had over 5,000 tanks, but in 2003 it had only 2,000; nearly 7,000 armored personnel carriers in 1991, in 2003 less than 2,000; self-propelled artillery equipment 500 in 1991, 150 in 2003; towed guns 3,000 in 1991, under 2,000 in 2003. Most of the Iraqi equipment, moreover, largely Soviet but some French in origin, was old, even antiquated. [27]

To be sure, the American forces were smaller too. But they were far better equipped and trained than the Iraqi military. By any measure, it was clear from the beginning that the Iraqi army was overmatched. So as a war between two traditional military forces, it was obvious which side would be successful. No one doubted what the final results would be of the nation versus nation war.

But what of the likelihood of success of a war with insurgents that might, and of course did, develop after the traditional-style war was over? Notoriously, the Bush/Blair team, and their corresponding military forces, underestimated the possibility and the potential seriousness of such a war. That represents a serious flaw in their planning.[28] Any overmatched military force will be tempted to fade away from regular-battle scene and, later, reappear as an insurgency. Given that possibility, a larger force should have been deployed by the American and British military to occupy, as against merely bypass, those population centers and other areas where insurgents might assemble, organize, and gather stray military equipment. Had such a larger force been deployed, the likelihood of successfully fighting the insurgents would have increased. Exactly how much it would have increased is anybody's guess. But as viewed before the war started, the increase would likely have been great enough to warrant saying that the Likelihood of Success Principle is satisfied or, at least, could have been satisfied.

The issue of democratizing Iraq is another matter. To be sure, as conceived by President Bush, his administration, and the neoconservatives in his administration, success would be easy to come by.[29]

But there were warnings that administering and converting Iraq into a democracy would not be easy. Some of these came from Colin Powell, who at that time was secretary of state.[30] There were others. Had they been listened to, it would not have been obvious that Iraq, a country cobbled together of various ethnics groups by the British early in the twentieth century,[31] could be turned into a democracy over a reasonable period of time. Thus, if the ultimate goal of the war was to make Iraq a democracy, the Principle of Likelihood of Success (i.e., in the just cause sense) was not satisfied.

PROPORTIONALITY (*JUS AD BELLUM*)

So the coalition forces satisfied the Likelihood of Success Principle in two senses. In advance of the war, they could have figured that the Iraqi army would be defeated and an insurgency would be suppressed before it even got started. But they did not satisfy the Success Principle in a third sense that had to do with bringing democracy to Iraq.

The results of applying the Proportionality Principle are similarly mixed. On the one side, it can be argued that even though the coalition forces fought an unjust war insofar as they could not satisfy the Just Cause Principle, they could still project that they could do some good in precipitating the war. The good comes from overthrowing a dictatorship that harmed many in the past and most likely would continue harming others in the future. Had the mistake of "minimalism" not been made, enough troops and police would have been available to properly occupy the country, Allied forces just might have been able to get "in and out" in short order.

In parallel with the "minimalism" mistake was the mistake of disbanding the existing Iraqi police and military forces. The result of these two mistakes was to create a power vacuum that the insurgents quickly filled. But these mistakes need not have been made. Had they not, the planners of the Iraq war could have figured that more good would come from the war than not. In advance of the war, then, it can be argued that, in one sense, the Principle of Proportionality was satisfied.

However, in another sense, it was not satisfied. Given the complex social and political conditions found in Iraq, it is not clear what overall good or harm would come about by overthrowing Saddam's regime. Even if the coalition forces were stronger than they actually were, and even if the coalition forces' political leaders had acted wisely, it is not clear that chaos could have been prevented. So in this overall sense the Principle of Proportionality was not satisfied.

LEGITIMATE AUTHORITY

There is likely to be an interminable dispute in applying the Legitimate Authority principle to the Iraq War. The main reason is that there is no general agreement as to which authority represents the final authority. Some argue that the United Nations is the final authority and so most wars must receive the blessing of the UN before they can be legitimized. Those who hold to this view claim that Resolution 1441 was not worded in such a way as to authorize making war on Iraq. It is true that it did threaten Iraq with serious consequences if it did not prove that it no longer possessed weapons of mass destruction. It also demanded that Iraq cooperate fully with any UN inspection team sent to Iraq to verify that these weapons no longer existed in Iraq. But 1441 did not explicitly threaten Iraq with war should it not comply. As such, another resolution was needed, one that said that the UN would use all necessary means to achieve compliance.

Because of the objections of France, Germany, and other nations, that second resolution was never passed.[32] As a result those who claim that the UN has preeminence with regard to the principle of legitimate authority say that the war in Iraq was not properly authorized.

The other side, championed by the United States, argued that UN approval is a sufficient but not a necessary condition for authorizing war. If the UN had sanctioned war, the Unite States would have been happy to say that the war is legitimate. But UN approval is not necessary. There are, according to this view, other ways of legitimizing war that, in effect, bypass the UN. One of these ways is to seek legitimacy by forming a coalition with other nations (e.g., of NATO partners as in Kosovo). But the foremost way is to have the institutions in charge of war-making matters in one's own nation declare that a particular war is legitimate. That, of course, is what the United States, the United Kingdom, Australia, and a few other nations did. They claimed that the war is legitimate because the proper institutions in each of these nations declared it so.

So the answer to the question concerning the legitimacy of the war in Iraq is not obvious. "No" it is not legitimate if one leans on the UN; "Yes," it is legitimate if one leans instead on one's national institutions.

PROPORTIONALITY (*JUS IN BELLO*)

In discussing the Proportionality Principle it is convenient to divide the war, as was done in the discussion on likelihood of success, into two parts: the traditional-style war and the war against the insurgents. The discussion starts with the former.

The British forces' main assignment was to capture the southern city of Basra. They approached their task cautiously. They surrounded the city, reconnoitered with care, and moved into a part of the city when they felt it was ready to be occupied. Little by little, then, they finally occupied the city. These tactics guaranteed that casualties among the Iraqis and their own forces would be minimal. In effect, that guaranteed that they operated well within the framework of the Principle of Proportionality.

The American assignment was quite different. The Americans had to move from their starting point in Kuwait all the way to the north so as to capture such cities as Baghdad, Tikrit, and Mosul. Originally, they had planned to attack both from Kuwait in the south and from Turkey in the north. However, for a variety of reasons, the Turks refused to give the Americans access to their land and bases.[33] Having, then, to deploy their major forces exclusively from the south (i.e., Kuwait) the Americans could not adopt the cautious tactics of their British compatriots. Instead, they were forced to move with speed so that they would cover over three hundred miles in about three weeks. The speed they employed so surprised the Iraqis that they were often not prepared for battle. As far as the Americans were concerned, then, there was no need to employ excessive force to achieve their goals. Speed did the job for them. As a result, the battles fought that led to the downfall of Saddam's regime also fell well within the framework of the Principle of Proportionality.

It is more difficult to assess whether this principle is satisfied when discussing the war against the insurgents. As do most insurgents, the Iraqi insurgents often fought in urban centers by locating themselves in homes, schools, hospitals, and religious edifices. They also used improvised explosive devices (IEDs) planted in roads and streets to create casualties among the occupying forces (mostly American, of course). And they employed terrorist tactics in attacking civilians, Iraqi police, and military recruits as well as regular Iraqi police and military forces.

In responding to these attacks, the charge can easily be leveled that the Americans, and their British allies, used excessive force. This charge was made most forcefully late in 2004 when American, British, and Iraq forces fought in Fallujah to quell the Sunni rebellion in that city. After the battle, it was evident that much of the city was destroyed.[34] But what was not evident was that excessive force was responsible for this destruction. Restraint (combined with indecision[35]) was used when, on several occasions, the allied forces waited for negotiations to work (generally they did not) before attacking. Commanders were keen not to attack mosques, for example, even when bullets were flying at their military units from these locations. And when these units attacked, they did not use large bombs to excess to root out stubborn resistance. Very likely, in the heat of battle, certain units attacked with excessive force, but there is little evidence that excess was part of the general strategy aimed at returning Fallujah to the authority of the Iraqi government. This claim can be generalized. By and large, the American forces fought and are fighting the war against the insurgents with restraint. They therefore cannot be charged with violating the Principle of Proportionality in either a general or a systematic way.

DISCRIMINATION

Focusing first on the traditional-style battle to unseat the Saddam regime, the Allied forces deserve high marks for keeping within the framework of the Principle of Discrimination. There are several reasons for saying this. First, Allied air forces focused more on military targets in this war than they did in 1991. In the 1991 war, these forces spent considerable effort attacking Iraq's infrastructure that both the military and the civilian population depended upon.[36] In contrast, there was less damage done to these "dual-purpose" Iraqi facilities in the 2003 war. Second, more smart weapons were available in 2003 as compared to 1991. Roughly 10 percent of the bombs dropped in the 1991 war were "smart." In 2003, 70 percent were.[37] Three, the Allies did whatever they could to avoid pitched battles in cities and towns so as to avoid civilian casualties. They did not always succeed in this endeavor. But, generally, by adopting a policy of moving quickly toward Baghdad, Tikrit, and other locations, they managed to keep the Iraqi forces off balance and so managed as well to keep both military and civilian casualties to a minimum. Four, the Allied forces were given strict rules of engagement to avoid harming civilians. In preparation for the war, their training placed great emphasis on how important it was to act in accordance with these rules.

So the record of the Allied forces in the traditional-style portion of the war with respect to discrimination was exemplary. Unfortunately, blemishes in that record suddenly appeared when insurgents rather than soldiers became the enemy. Part of the problem was that the insurgents were more persistent than the Allies supposed they would be. At first the insurgents were not particularly well organized. But gradually both their organization and tactics improved. In addition, their explosive devices became more powerful, their ambushes more surprising, and their terror attacks on the civilian population and Iraqi police more frequent. One other result of their developments was that Allied (mainly American) casualties began to rise. At first there was one soldier killed each day, then two and at times three or more.

To stop this rise, high officials in Washington and in Iraq began to pressure those in charge of prisoners captured in the course of both the traditional and the insurgency wars. Prisoners had information about the insurgency, and the high officials wanted this information to save the lives of American, British, and Australian military personnel. But many of these prisoners could not be persuaded or bribed to talk. So the only recourse, the last resort as it were, seemed to be to use some form of coercion.[38] That might mean that prisoners would be interrogated for long periods of time, deprived of sleep, kept in an uncomfortable environment (e.g., room temperatures well below normal), frightened by large and vicious dogs, humiliated, slapped, and abused physically both in nonlife- and life-threatening ways. Evidence has now emerged that this coercion that, often, turned into torture, was not restricted to the infamous Abu Ghraib prison. It was widespread in many prisons throughout Iraq.[39] Further, evidence suggests that the Americans outsourced some of this coercion.[40] Thus if a prisoner were an Egyptian, he might be sent to his home country. There, presumably, the coercion would be of a kind that the Americans themselves would be reluctant to indulge in.

But the coercion the Americans themselves practiced in Iraq was bad enough. One reason for this is that it was not well supervised by officers at the various prisons. Another reason is that lower level noncommissioned officers, enlisted personnel, and nonmilitary types (e.g., CIA officials), were often responsible for extracting the information that their superiors were anxious to receive. Many of these lower-level military personnel were trained, officially, in the ethics of war and how prisoners should be treated. But evidently that training did not take root. As to the nonmilitary coercers, it is not clear that they ever received serious training in issues pertaining to the ethics of war. In any case, there was always the pressure from above to "get that information." One can even speculate that some of these prison guards and officials in charge of coercing prisoners had psychological problems that made abusing prisoners "entertaining" to them

Whatever the case, it was clear that matters soon got out of control in many of the prisons. Behavior that deviated widely from that countenanced by Just War Theory became quite common. It was so common that it was inevitable that the public would learn about it. When it did, it was like handing the insurgency a major military/political victory. If fighting in Iraq is in part a struggle to win the hearts and minds of the Iraqi people, the publicity of the coercion, including torture, taking place in the many prisons in Iraq and elsewhere, helped lose that struggle. As bad as the coercion was, it was made to seem worse by the insurgency's rhetoric. Putting it differently, the bad publicity of the coercion probably hurt the American (Allied) cause more than the information gained by coercing the prisoners helped it. But even if the gains were greater than the losses, it remains true that the behavior the American military and intelligence people engaged in was contrary to Just War Theory.

A second blemish appeared during the insurgency war. Actually, it was in place from the beginning of the war. Ever since the American military became an all-volunteer force, it suffered from a shortage of personnel. Bringing volunteers into the military is expensive since their salaries have to be competitive with civilian salaries. But even when the military is well paid, there are some who simply do not like military life. It is also expensive to train these volunteers properly. So a shortage of soldiers, sailors, and air personnel is almost inevitable. To compensate for this shortage, the American military contracts with private companies to deliver food, construction, transportation, security, and other services to the military.[41] These companies often hire ex-military personnel, but also many who have never been in the military.

A good number of these private contractors found themselves in Iraq. Their numbers reached more than 125,000.[42] Given the work they were asked to do, they were frequently in contact with Iraqi civilians. Indeed, they were in contact in such a way as not to be firmly under the control of the military. U.S. military and governmental supervision was lax and often nonexistent. As a result, some of the contract workers acted as if they had the right to "play by their own rules." Not surprisingly, the rules they adopted led to a variety practices such as the mistreatment of Iraqi civilians and to a great deal of corruption.[43] Although many of these private contractors behaved honorably, others did not.[44] As a result much harm was done to the programs of defeating the insurgents and establishing a democratic government in Iraq.

But what of the actual fighting with the insurgents? Can the American and other allied forces be accused of behaving in such a way as to add another blemish to their war effort? That is, can they be blamed for indiscriminate, careless, or deliberate attacks on civilians?

These are difficult questions to answer because reports of what has happened, and is happening, in Baghdad, Basra, Tikrit, and hundreds of other places vary considerably. To hear it from the Muslim press, almost any shooting incident where Iraqis are killed and wounded is described as "unprovoked" and "mindless." Further, the American troops especially are charged with behaving in a crude and rude manner when they break into homes in their attempts to capture insurgents. In contrast, to hear it from the allied military, soldiers are said to behave in accordance with strict rules of engagement that prevent them from firing indiscriminately. American officials also talk about the extreme difficulties of dealing with insurgents who fire at them from almost any concealed location including heavily populated areas, schools, medical facilities, and mosques. In response, the allied military forces (again, mainly American) say that when they fight back, the civilian casualties that result are not wholly, or even mainly, their fault. They claim that they use much discretion before they fire so they are acting, as much as is humanly possible, in accordance with the Principle of Discrimination.

Concerning these two contrasting accounts, evidence suggests that, in general, the truth is closer to the Allied, rather than the Muslim, accounts. Unlike the "loose cannon" private contractors, U.S. and British military forces are under tight control of commissioned and noncommissioned officers who have been trained to fight under the rules of Just War Theory. There is also a heavy echelon of military lawyers to advise those in command about what can and cannot be done with respect to attacks that affect civilians. Further, the mass media often have reporters "embedded" with individual units. These reporters keep an eye on what soldiers are and are not doing. Of course, inevitably there are lapses when the pressure of battle is too much for certain commanders and soldiers. There also has been, and will be, lapses with soldiers who never follow the ethical and legal rules of war unless someone is watching them. Yet, on the whole, the U.S. and UK military have invested much time and effort to encourage their military forces to act in an ethical manner.[45]

LATER DEVELOPMENTS

Wars never stand still. The Iraq War is no different. Three important changes took place in 2006 and 2007. The first did not directly concern the "occupying" forces but, instead, had to do with sectarian violence mainly between Sunnis and Shiites. Even before 2006, such violence was on the rise. But a single event, the February 2006 bombing of the Askariya shrine in Samarra, radically escalated that violence.[46] The shrine is Shiite in a predominantly Sunni community, and so is vulnerable to attack. The bombing triggered retaliations, which in turn triggered retaliations to the retaliations. In effect, the sectarian violence turned the war in Iraq into two wars. One was against the "occupiers," the other was Iraqis against each other.

The second change was political than rather than military. It occurred in the United States. In the November 2006 elections, the Democratic Party took control of Congress. With their newfound power, and with public opinion polls showing President Bush and the war becoming increasingly unpopular, the Democrats were emboldened to criticize the war effort seriously for the first time. Some Democratic candidates running for the presidency in the 2008 elections began to argue that the United States should withdraw its military forces as soon as possible. Even Republican politicians, including some of that party's presidential candidates, backed off supporting Bush in his determination to "stay the course."

The third change was more military than political. President Bush, encouraged by the recommendations of General David Petraeus, the top military commander in Iraq in 2007, decided to send more troops to Iraq.[47] For the most sanguine, this "surge," if given time to take effect, was supposed to save the war for Bush. The surge was to be a necessary step toward eventually bringing victory once certain sectors of Baghdad and other cities were made safe for ordinary people ("through constant policing and patrolling"[48]). To the somewhat less sanguine, the surge was supposed to give the Shiia-dominated Iraqi government time to make political agreements with the aggrieved Sunni population, but ones still acceptable to the Shiia population. Given enough time, it was hoped that a stable and strong central government would take shape; and Iraq would finally be on its way to recovery.

Even with these developments in place, the "occupiers" found themselves able to move in any one of three directions. The first involves a reaffirmation of Bush's "stay the course" policy. The argument here is that the surge is working in that the level of violence in Iraq has diminished.[49] Anbar Province has been pacified and that, finally, the United States has, in David Petraeus, a general who has a rational plan for dealing with the insurgency.[50] All that is needed is time for the plan to play out. Eventually, of course, there would be a withdrawal, but it would take place only after the Iraqi military and police forces are in better order than they were even as late as 2008, and after the Iraqi political structure is reformed. All these changes might take years to implement.[51]

However, as has already been pointed out, a major problem with this "stay the course" policy is public opinion in the United States. For this option to work the administration and its allies would have to mount a major public relations campaign to convince the people and the politicians to change their views (once again).

It should be noted that it is no objection to the "stay the course" policy that it cannot meet the *jus in bello* standards of Just War Theory. Under Petraeus's leadership, the "occupiers" can, if they choose to do so, act in such a way that more good than harm might come by following his policy and choosing as well to fight in such a way as to protect "innocents." So the "stay the course" policy is compatible with both the Principles of Proportionality and Discrimination. That is, this policy is not inherently immoral in these respects.

The second path the "occupiers" could take is to depart the scene precipitously or within a matter of months. This policy would most obviously result in an end to American (and British) casualties and also an end to a drain on the U.S. national treasure. What effect it would have on Iraq is anybody's guess. Many scenarios suggest that the civil war in that country would escalate, and that both civilian and military casualties would mount significantly. Thus, it is not clear that this path is compatible with either the Proportionality or Discrimination Principle.

The third path falls between the other two. One variation (among many) of this policy envisions only a partial withdrawal. There would be a complete withdrawal from the Shiia areas of Iraq. However, the remaining American forces would retire into the more friendly Kurdish portions of Iraq. While there, they would be in place to protect the new "democratic" Kurdish nation from Turkish incursions.[52] Retaining a presence in "Kurdistan" would serve another purpose. It would help to contain Iran. One unintended consequence of the Iraq War is the growth of Iranian power in the region.[53] American presence in Kurdistan, it is alleged, would act as a deterrent to further Iranian expansion.

According to those who prefer this option over the other two, Iran, not al-Qaeda, is the major threat to the welfare of the region. Although al-Qaeda has proven that it can cause all kinds of trouble, it does not possess the kind of political and military clout that Iran has. An extended version of this partial withdrawal policy would likely also involve containing Iran by supplying certain Sunni nations such as Saudi Arabia with advanced military equipment.[54]

Another variation of the "partial withdrawal" policy would have some American forces stay behind in provinces controlled by the Sunnis. They would stay behind at the invitation of the Sunnis.[55] One reason this invitation might be forthcoming is to help the Sunnis control the influence of al-Qaeda. Already, in Anbar province, American Sunni cooperation has been successful in diminishing the influence of al-Qaeda. Similar success also seems to be taking place in Diyala Province.[56] Moderate tribal leaders evidently are frightened enough by al-Qaeda's violent ways and its radical Islamic ideology that they are, reluctantly, willing to work with the "occupiers."

Like the first path, the path of partial withdrawal probably can live within the framework of Just War Theory. It is a deterrent path that ends a portion of the Iraq War and, to that extent, does not challenge either the Proportionality or the Discrimination Principle. The only problem with this path is the other portion of the war. Partial withdrawal does not settle the sectarian tensions between the Sunnis and the Shiias. If the Americans were to leave all of Iraq except for the Kurdish portions, the Shiias and the Sunnis might indeed find themselves killing one another on a much larger scale than they have done in 2006, 2007, and 2008. Because of such killing, the two *in bello* principles might not be easily satisfied.

CONCLUSION

When all is said and done, a straightforward application of Just War Theory shows that the war in Iraq is unjust. Recall that for a war to be just it has to satisfy all of the theory's *jus ad bellum* criteria. Failing one is enough to earn those who started that war the "unjust" label. The coalition satisfied the Principles of Proportionality and Likelihood of Success partially at best. Debatably, it also satisfied the Right Intentions and possibly the Legitimate Authority Principles. But it clearly failed to meet the standards of two of the theory's principles. No good case in terms of Just Cause was made for going to war. Nor does it seem possible to make a good case. Similarly, no good case was made, or could be made, for going to war with respect to the Last Resort Principle. It seems that other options than war were available to the Bush/Blair team in 2003. Instead of trying to identify these options, the team, but most especially the Bush part of that team, seemed to be looking for a fight as a third or fourth rather than a last reasonable resort.

With respect to the justice in the war, the Allies (but most especially the Americans) garner a mixed record. Their policies concerned with the treatment of prisoners early in the war represented a gross lapse away from meeting the standards of the Principle of Discrimination. To a lesser extent, another lapse resulted from the contractor policies adopted by the U.S. military. Frequently these contractors were not terribly concerned to act in the spirit of Just War Theory. Their motivation, understandably, was with turning a profit rather than with following the principles of just war.[57]

The record of the American (and British) military is more positive even as they were eventually forced to engage in urban warfare. These soldiers, marines, sailors, special forces, and air personnel are well trained not only to do their military work but also to do their work in accord with Just War Theory.

However one assesses the ethical record of the "occupiers," the war itself has not gone well for them. As of this writing, it appears that they will be forced to leave all or some of Iraq by 2009. A complete and fairly quick withdrawal probably would lead to long period of chaos and so to consequences not compatible with the *jus in bello* principles of Just War Theory. A partial withdrawal (into the Kurdish part of Iraq as suggested above) would likely put some limits on the chaos and, insofar as it did that, would be more in accord with the *in bello* principles. Following the "stay the course" policy does not (necessarily) violate either one of the two, but it does not seem to be feasible because of negative public opinion about the war in the United States.

NOTES

1. John Keegan, *The Iraq War: The 21-Day conflict and Its Aftermath* (London: Random House, 2005), 40–51.

2. Dilip Hiro, *Saddam Hussein: About the Man*, at www.bbc.co.uk/education/Walden/sad_about3.shtml (accessed October 15, 2006).

3. Keegan, *The Iraq War*, 58–59.

4. Keegan, *The Iraq War*, 59–61.

5. Michael R. Gordon and General Bernard E. Trainor, *The Generals' War: The Inside Story of the Conflict in the Gulf* (Boston: Little, Brown and Company, 1991), 240.

6. James F. Dunnigan and Austin Bay, *From Shield to Storm* (New York: William Morrow and Company, 1992), 40–41.

7. Anthony Hartle, "The Gulf War, 1990–1991," in *Moral Constraints on War*, ed. Bruno Coppieters and Nick Fotion, 1st ed. (Lanham, Md.: Lexington Books, 2002), 161–76. This material is partly reproduced in the Just Cause chapter in this volume (pp. 30–31).

8. Dunnigan and Bay, *From Shield to Storm*, 41–43.

9. Dunnigan and Bay, *From Shield to Storm*, 269–70.

10. SIPRI, "Iraq: The UNSCOM Experience," at www.sipri.se/pubs;Factsheet/ UNSCOM (accessed November 15, 2006).

11. Todd S. Purdum, *A Time of Our Choosing: America's War in Iraq* (New York: Times Books, 2003; New York: Henry Holt and Company, 2004), 15, 32.

12. Purdum, *A Time of Our Choosing*, 96–97.

13. George Packer, *The Assassins' Gate: America in Iraq* (New York: Farrar, Straus and Giroux, 2005), 40–41.

14. Keegan, *The Iraq War*, 66, 70,

15. Keegan, *The Iraq War*, 70.

16. Purdum, *A Time of Our Choosing*, 69–72.

17. Michael R. Gordon and General Bernard E. Trainor, *Cobra II: The Inside Story of the Invasion and Occupation of Iraq* (New York: Pantheon Books, 2006), 131–34.

18. Yossef Bodansky, *The Secret History of the Iraq War* (New York: Regan Books, 2004), 207–8.

19. Keegan, *The Iraq War*, 95–98. See also Mark Danner, "Iraq: The War of the Imagination," *New York Review of Books*, December 21, 2006, 81–88, 94–96. Also see Packer, *The Assassins' Gate*, 15–32. Packer has an excellent account of neoconservative thinking (how it developed and how it influenced President Bush).

20. Keegan, *The Iraq War*, 95–98.

21. Gordon and Trainor, *Cobra II*, 134.

22. Jim Holt, "It's the Oil, Stupid," *London Review of Books*, October 18, 2007, 3–4. Holt suggests that there were some in the White House, who were not necessarily neoconservatives, who wanted to go to war because of Iraq's vast, and largely unexplored, oil resources. As evidence for his claim, Holt notes that draft laws pertaining to Iraqi oil have been written by the United States to favor American (and other Western) oil companies. He also notes that the United States is building very large and permanent bases in Iraq that would help protect its oil interests.

23. Danner, "Iraq: The War of the Imagination," 82.

24. United Nations, Resolution 1441, at www.un.int/usa/sres-iraq.htm (accessed January 12, 2007).

25. Keegan, *The Iraq War*, 106–7.

26. See chapter 4.

27. Keegan, *The Iraq War*, 129.

28. Michael R. Gordon and Bernard E. Trainor, "Dash to Baghdad Left Top U.S. Generals Divided," *The New York Times*, March 13, 2006, A1, A8.

29. Gordon and Trainor, *Cobra II*, 72–73.

30. Gordon and Trainor, *Cobra II*, 71.

31. Keegan, *The Iraq War*, 13–21.

32. Keegan, *The Iraq War*, 106–15.

33. Yossef Bodansky, *The Secret History of the Iraq War*, 31–32. See also Gordon and Trainor, *Cobrra II*, 115.

34. Bing West, *No True Glory: A Frontline Account of the Battle for Fallujah* (New York: Bantam Books, 2005), 315–16.

35. West, *No True Glory*, 319–21.

36. George A. Lopez, "The Gulf War: Not So Clean," *The Bulletin of the Atomic Scientists*, September 1991, 30–35. As the title of his article suggests, Lopez is critical of

the air campaign against Iraq for being too robust. For a somewhat different view see, in the same issue, Nick Fotion, "The Gulf War: Cleanly Fought," 24–29.

37. Keegan, *The Iraq War*, 142.

38. *Frontline*, "The Torture Question," at www.pbs.org/wgbh/pages/frontline/torture/view/ (accessed December 21, 2006). See also Eric Schmitt and Tim Golden, "Pentagon Plans Tighter Control of Questioning," *New York Times*, November 8, 2005, A1, A20.

39. Human Rights Watch "Torture in Iraq," *New York Review of Books*, November 3, 2005, 67–70, 72.

40. Raymond Bonner, "The CIA's Secret Torture," *The New York Review of Books*, January 11, 2007, 28–31.

41. *Frontline*, "Private Warriors," at www.pbs.org/wgbh/pages/frontline/shows/warriors/contractors/ (accessed November 12, 2006).

42. Amy Klamper, "Hold Them Accountable," *Seapower* July 2007, 14–18. Klamper reports that 80 percent of the contractors in Iraq are "locals." She also reports that between five to eight thousand nonlocals are "toting guns in and around Baghdad" some of whom have used their guns indiscriminately.

43. T. Christian Miller, *Blood Money: Wasted Billions, Lost Lives, and Corporate Greed in Iraq* (New York: Little, Brown and Company, 2006), 287–93.

44. John F. Burns, "The Deadly Game of Private Security," *New York Times*, September 23, 2007.

45. For a darker view of how the Iraq war was fought, see Michael Massing's "Iraq: The Hidden Human Costs," *New York Review of Books*, December 20, 2007, 82–87. Massing argues that the American reliance on firepower leads to many civilian casualties. He (and Human Rights Watch) cites a figure of 10,000 (at a minimum) civilian deaths during the weeks of the invasion alone. Massing argues that, for a variety of reasons, these deaths are underreported. The result is that Americans have a sanitized view of the war and how their soldiers behave.

46. John F. Burns, "Revered Mosque in Iraq Is Bombed for Second Time," *New York Times*, June 14, 2007, A1, A11. The second bombing took place June 13, 2007.

47. Peter W. Galbraith, "The Surge," *New York Review of Books*, March 15, 2007, 4, 6, 8.

48. Arthur Herman, "How to Win in Iraq—and How to Lose," *Commentary*, April 2007, 23–28.

49. Michael E. O'Hanlon and Kenneth M. Pollack, "A War We Just Might Win," *New York Times*, July 30, 2007, A19.

50. Babak Dehghanpisheh and John Barry "Brainiac Brigade," *Newsweek*, September 17, 2007, 38–40. The authors claim that Petraeus is not following his original plan (as expressed by him in the government's field manual 4-23). In FM 4-23, Petraeus envisions winning the hearts and minds of a (foreign) population with the help of its strong central government. But no such government exists in Iraq. So Petraeus and his brain trust have adapted by giving support to local groups, tribes, etc. who are keen on fighting al-Qaeda-in-Iraq.

51. Solomon Moore and Richard A. Oppel Jr., "Attacks Imperil Iraqi Militants Allied With U.S.," *New York Times*, January 24, 2008, A1, A8. Moore and Oppel point to one reason why making Iraq more tranquil will be difficult. They report that leaders of the Awakening movement (and members of other groups) who are cooperat-

ing with American forces are under attack by Sunni (and possibly Shiia) extremists. Over one hundred leaders have been assassinated. These attacks have shaken the various communities and groups that are intent on ending the fighting in Iraq.

52. Peter W. Galbraith, "The Way to Go," *New York Review of Books*, August 16, 2007, 4, 6, 8.

53. Peter Gailbraith, "The Victor?" *New York Review of Books*, October 11, 2007, 6–12.

54. Mark Mazzetti and Helene Cooper, "U.S. Arms Plan for Mideast Aims to Counter Iranian Power," *New York Times*, July 31, 2007, A6.

55. One scenario here has the Americans staying behind by building superbases away from major urban centers. According to Holt, the Americans are already building five such bases. Balad Air Base, forty miles north of Baghdad is one such base. See Holt, "It's the Oil, Stupid," 3–4.

56. Thomas L. Friedman, "Watch the Sunni Tribes," *New York Times*, August 29, 2007, A23.

57. Ginger Thompson and Eric Schmitt, "Graft in Military Contracts Spread from Kuwait Base," *New York Times*, September 24, 2007, A1, A22. Corruption seems to range from the beginning of the war to the present, and to infect not only private companies but also military officers who come into contact with these companies.

14

Concluding Comments

Nick Fotion and Bruno Coppieters

REALISM, PACIFISM, AND MILITARISM REVISITED

This study of the ethics of war has focused primarily on Just War Theory, one of four basic positions concerned with war and its horrors. But, having looked at this theory at length, we unavoidably paid attention to, and profited from having looked at, Realism, Pacifism, and Militarism as well. We dealt with these positions especially when we applied the principles of Just War Theory to concrete historical cases. Some of our cases were concerned with German policies in the years preceding and during World War II. These policies were without a doubt inspired by militarist motives. Others dealt with political choices where realist motives played a role. To be sure, it was sometimes difficult to identify countries or leaders with one or the other of these positions since they often shifted their viewpoint over time. For example, as a member of the Republican administration under Nixon, the American ambassador to the UN, George H. W. Bush, condemned the Indian intervention in Eastern Pakistan (now Bangladesh). In so doing, he defended a foreign policy line strongly embedded in a realist view of the world. Pakistan, as an ally of the United States, had to be defended against India, an ally of the Soviet Union. This support to the Pakistani authorities was fully independent of the fact that the Indian intervention of 1971 put an end to the massacres of the civilian population of Eastern Pakistan. But twenty years later, as president of the United States, he justified the military actions against Iraq with just war arguments.

In other cases, parties in conflict justified their actions with both realist and just war motives. This may have been because public opinion needs to be given a sense of direction by the leaders of the state. The analysis of one of the cases reviewed in this volume illustrates this point. During the Kosovo crisis in 1999, President Clinton declared that only humanitarian considerations were at stake in the decision to use force. But such pronouncements were moderated by other official pronouncements saying that the United States also had strategic interests involved. This addition was clearly meant to calm the worries of those Americans who feared that NATO might sacrifice American national interests in the name of a humanitarian mission.

Our book describes the resistance by the Czechoslovak population to Soviet occupation in 1968. This is a good illustration of the potential of a popular mobilization using exclusively nonviolent means. One could further point to the Indian national liberation movement, led by Mohandas Karamchand Gandhi, to demonstrate that the practical importance of Pacifism should not be neglected.

Our policy of mostly, but not exclusively, focusing on Just War Theory yields certain other dividends. It throws light on Just War Theory *as a theory*, on the one hand, but also on the positions of Realism, Militarism, and Pacifism, on the other. Consider Pacifism as an instance. Pacifism, it was said, is the main response on one side of Just War Theory. Most pacifists defend an absolutist attitude. Compared to Just War Theory it should now be evident that this position is simply not so complicated as Just War Theory when it comes to application. Absolute Pacifism takes moral claims about violence in general and violence in war in particular to have no exceptions. That is, it claims that rules such as "War is not permitted" allow for no exceptions. Pacifism is certainly complicated when it comes to *justifying* the position philosophically or morally. The arguments needed to make a convincing theoretical case for the position itself are difficult to present and understand. In addition, rationally convincing others not to use violence in the real world, especially in the face of direct threats to their lives or the lives of their relatives, friends, and group, is certainly difficult. This is so even after people have come to accept Pacifism on rational grounds.

However, once accepted, Pacifism provides a straightforward means of deciding if force should be used in this or that situation. If exceptions that allow for the use of violence in one or another setting are forbidden, then absolute pacifists can look at any situation where war is threatened and say "No." They might add, "All wars are immoral." In saying "No" to war pacifists may, once again, be challenged to defend their overall stance, and they might find it difficult to live by the doctrine they have accepted. But, once the position is accepted, there is no need for absolutist pacifists to work their way through a set of criteria the way just war theorists do in determining whether they should or should not be involved in war.[1] This does not mean, however, that this position is easy to apply, when it comes to the search for alternatives to the use of force. Chapters 4 and 5 on the Principles of Likelihood of Success and Proportionality illustrate the difficulties of applying the nonviolent methods of Civilian-Based Defense.

On the other side of the just war position, realists do not have the luxury of offering one and only one answer when war is knocking at the door. Like pacifists, realists face a difficult task of justifying their theoretical position.[2] But unlike most pacifists, realists are not absolutists or near absolutists. They do not say "Yes" to war automatically just as the pacifists say "No" automatically. Rather, most realists (and most militarists as well) say "Yes" to war sometimes and "No" at other times. This means that when it comes to applying their theory to any particular war setting, realists will (one would hope) be going through a process of reasoning not unlike that of the just war theorists.

Here is how it might go. Facing the possibility of war, realists would, first of all, try to uncover some good reason for going to war. This "good reason" would not necessarily be the same as just cause is for just war theorists. On the face of it they might be the same. The good reason may for instance be the protection of the territorial integrity of an allied or friendly state or the reestablishment of international peace and security. But for realists these good reasons would apply only to the extent that they, in turn, involve protecting the realists' national interest. As such, humanitarian considerations do not enter into their calculations.

A more direct formulation of a realist argument would be along the lines of "We will profit immensely if we invade our neighbor since there is much oil (coal, fertile land, factories for making airplanes, etc.) over there." This line of thought would also weigh the possible disadvantages of such an invasion. Rather than articulating their good reasons for going to war in terms of ethics, realists would do it in terms of self-interest. For them, then, a proposed war to help an ally who is a victim of aggression or to invade another nation could pass their good-reasons test if the oil supply in that country's wells is huge, but fail the test if the supply is small.

But assuming the good-reasons test has been passed, realists would likely want to satisfy other tests as well. Interestingly enough, these tests would also be similar to those found in Just War Theory. For one, there is the test concerned with right (good) intentions, only now "right intentions" would mean not acting in accordance with "just cause" but, rather, acting in accordance with the interests of one's own state. Similarly, realists would apply a Likelihood of Success Test, as it is done in Just War Theory. Realists and just war theorists would agree that a first meaning of this principle is that a decision to go to war has to be based on reasonable chances to be successful on the battlefield. They would thus both apply what we called in chapter 4 the military interpretation of the principle. But both currents would differ insofar as a second meaning of the principle is concerned. Just war theorists will then give an interpretation of this principle according to a moral purpose. According to this second meaning, they would understand this principle as the "likelihood of success in satisfying a just cause." In contrast, for realists this principle would mean something like "likelihood of success in satisfying our nation's self-interests." Both traditions would entirely disagree in their interpretation of the Principle of Proportionality. Proportionality in Just War Theory is a consequentialist test concerned not just with the welfare of one side in a war but of all the sides that might be affected by the war. It is, therefore, by nature an ethical test. It follows that realists who see no direct role for ethics in war will adapt the Principle of Proportionality to their self-interest purposes. For them, proportionality must then mean something like, "We will go to war if the overall good of doing so is proportional (e.g., greater overall) to the bad *for our side.*" Even the Last Resort Principle can be applied to the realist position. If the assumption is made that war is a very costly way of satisfying one's self-interest, the strategy of realists would necessarily be one where other means of getting what they want need to be tried before resorting to war.

So the parallel of Just War Theory and Realism insofar as deciding when to go to war is quite close. It is not quite so close when it comes to fighting a war. To be sure, there is somewhat of a parallel when applying a version of the Proportionality Principle. Realists are concerned with costs and benefits of fighting battles and campaigns but, again, their cost/benefit analysis is restricted to their own side. But it is different with the Principle of Discrimination. Realist theory shows no respect for the lives of noncombatants on the other side except for public relations purposes or in cases where the state has to take International Humanitarian Law into consideration. The view is very different from the Just War Theory perspective, which makes the moral judgment that everyone's interests need to be taken into account even if, at times, one's own self-interest suffers to some extent.

Since both realists and just war proponents have a theory to help them think through their problems, the similarity between the two positions is much closer than is often supposed. Foremost, what they share in common are procedures. Both theories say that when it comes to making decisions about war certain procedures need to be followed. With the Last Resort Principle, for example, the procedures are that alternatives to war must be tried first and, with the Legitimate Authority Principle, only certain officials representing political communities are allowed to take the steps that lead to war.

But if we view these theories about going to war as a combination of a set of procedures *and* a set of value judgments, we see that the Realist and Just War Theories differ from one another mainly with respect to the latter. Realism uses many of the same procedures as does Just War Theory, but it commits to different values, and thus interprets the principles differently. It values the interests of the nation making the decision whether to enter a war or not, and how it should fight it once the war starts. It does not directly value anyone or anything outside the nation's interests. In contrast, Just War Theory values all humankind. Behind many of the principles that make up the theory, but most especially the Just Cause, Proportionality, and Discrimination Principles, is the notion that everyone touched by what happens in war should receive consideration. Taking account of everyone does not exclude giving one's own people privileged status in some circumstances. A nation, any nation, after all has special duties to protect its own citizens. It defends its borders and its people in ways that, often, it does not do for other nations. But giving equal consideration to all means that it will not put enemy civilians at risk any more than it would its own, that it treats enemy wounded the same way it treats its own, that it treats enemy prisoners the same way that it wishes the enemy would treat its own, and the like.

Much of what has been said about Realism applies to Militarism. Not being an absolutist position the way Pacifism tends to be, it too requires criteria to help it make decisions about when war should start and when it should not. Thus militarists also need a version of the Just Cause Principle. Recall (from the Introduction) that what is particular about the militarist conception of just cause is that it is not framed in universal terms. So when militarists speak about injustice, they do not do so from the perspective of humankind but from that of a particular group or community. It is moreover generally done from the specific perspective of the moral superiority of their own ethnic group or religious community. Hitler, for instance, spoke about the cultural superiority of the Germans of Sudetenland over the other peoples of Czechoslovakia when he called for the destruction of that country and framed the cause of the world war he was preparing in terms of "racial community" and "living space for Germany." He spoke openly about the necessity of submitting the Slavic peoples to the yoke of the Aryan race. This interpretation of a just cause has nothing to do with the humanitarian perspective of Just War Theory. It also differs from Realism, as Realism does not state that the interests of one particular group, community, or state are morally superior to the interests of another.

But militarists also need the criteria of legitimate authorization, right intentions, likelihood of success, and proportionality, whose meaning they would interpret according to their ideology. What they probably do not need is a Last Resort Principle. Since, for militarists, war is generally a fruitful activity, they do not need to try very hard to avoid it the way just war theorists do. These theorists would speak about moral constraints on every type of decision concerning war, whereas militarists would only consider prudential constraints. They consider indeed that war is as such a virtuous activity. It is as if militarists make peace in order to prepare for war, while just war theorists and realists make war in order to prepare for peace.

JUST WAR THEORY AND EXCESSIVE OPTIMISM

Although comparing the various ethical positions on war to one another helps improve our understanding of Just War Theory, it is still tempting to make mistakes in applying this theory. Of the many mistakes that can be made, two are more basic. The first is triggered by excessive optimism. With this mistake, too much is expected from ethical theory in general, and Just War Theory in particular. The overly sanguine followers of the theory suppose that it will yield definitive answers to all ethical problems pertaining to war. To be sure, they acknowledge that our knowledge of facts available for making judgments is limited. If a nation just does not know what the situation is on the other side of the border, it cannot arrive at rational answers about what it should do. But these sanguine just war theorists insist that if ample facts were available and if those facing the prospect of war understood the nature of Just War Theory and, further, if they were rational, answers concerning what they should do would be forthcoming in every case.[3]

The model these thinkers use in theorizing comes from the so-called hard sciences and engineering. They see that in many areas of physics and chemistry, a combination of theory and the facts yields precise answers. Thus, in these fields, predictions can be made as to the exact location of some object or the exact amount of a particular fluid in a flask. Supposing, then, that all theories must be like the typical theories in the hard sciences, these sanguine theorists come to expect that ethical theories must yield similar precise outcomes. Their attitude is that either Just War Theory and other ethical theories will yield precise results once the facts are in, or they are worthless.

A clue that there is something wrong with this sanguine view of theory comes from the many cases discussed in this volume. Recall the hesitant nature of the judgments we made concerning the Soviet invasion of Poland in 1939 (chapter 3). The present volume contains two contradictory views on NATO's war in Kosovo (chapters 9 and 10). Even if there is a fair amount of agreement about the facts in these cases, no automatic judgment follows once the theory is applied. We can see why if, once again, we take a closer look at Just War Theory and at the way the elements of the theory interrelate.

As we have seen, the *jus ad bellum* portion of that theory contains six criteria (viz., Just Cause, Legitimate Authority, Right Intentions, Likelihood of Success, Proportionality, and Last Resort Principles). The various elements of that theory connect with one another, and the meaning of the principles cannot be completely assessed independently of one another. Right intentions, for one, is measured against just cause. To be good, intentions must be such as they help to satisfy the Just Cause Principle (e.g., by returning the land liberated from an oppressed people). In a similar way, Likelihood of Success and Proportionality Principles both count the benefits and costs of war against what the purpose of going to war (in most cases, just cause) was in the first place. Even last resort can be understood only against the background of just cause. The very last resort, for instance, might be that last attempt to undo some aggression against an ally. Although some criteria or principles are dependent upon others, when applying the theory, they are treated as if they were independent. As such, each principle needs to be applied to a war setting serially. To be justified in going to war, then, a public authority needs to overcome each of six separate hurdles. Failing any one, the war is thought not to be just.

But why should we suppose that judgments will be hesitant and that disagreement in applying these theories not uncommon? Why not suppose that the optimist about Just War Theory is right? As we have seen, quite simply because none of the principles can be stated with precision. Take the Just Cause Principle. The violation of a state's political sovereignty and territorial integrity, an act we commonly label as aggression, is injustice in one form. If a nation is aggressed against, it has successfully negotiated the hurdle of the Just Cause Principle and is on its way to justifying its entry into war. But, as was made clear in chapter 1 in the discussion of this principle, there are various forms of aggression so it is possible for two nations involved in a war to accuse each other of being the aggressor. "Yes we sent our troops over the border so in one sense we are the aggressors, but we 'aggressed' against the real aggressor who, some twenty years ago, seized the land we are now trying to reclaim." So who is the aggressor here? This is not to say that because "aggression" in this case is ambiguous (i.e., has two or more distinct meanings), it is always ambiguous. There are also situations where there is neither ambiguity nor vagueness present, that is, no sharp line separating one concept from another or no major problem in knowing how to apply a certain principle to particular circumstances. In these cases there will be no doubt as to who the aggressor is. But there is enough lack of clarity to the concept to cause trouble in any number of situations. This in turn will cause trouble for anyone who thinks that Just War Theory, combined with the facts, will automatically yield answers as to how a nation should behave when faced with the possibility of war.

If not aggression, just cause may have to do with humanitarian needs. But vagueness is here as well. If some nation causes serious harm to a large segment of its own people, either deliberately or through neglect, just how serious does that harm have to be before intervention is justified? How many people need to be harmed? The theory does not tell us because this subprinciple within Just War Theory is stated in very abstract, that is, vague, terms. The two contributions on Kosovo in this volume present, for instance, different views on this issue and, thereby, show vagueness at work.

So it goes with the other principles. If right intentions are generally defined as supporting just cause, the answer to the question as to when the Principle of Right Intentions is satisfied may vary widely. Some will say that right intentions should not be mixed with intentions that are not directly related to satisfying just cause, even if no intention to act unjustly or immorally is involved. Others will say that the principle can be satisfied in cases involving mixed intentions, if those intentions not directly related to the realization of a just cause are not the main reasons for going to war. A third group will apply the Principle of Right Intentions in a still more flexible way. They will say that the mere presence of right intentions among the various intentions in the decision-making process will already be sufficient to consider the principle as being satisfied. This position comes close to Realism, but is not identical with it, as the presence of a just cause is a *conditio sine qua non* for the just war perspective.

Last resort we noted in chapter 6 can mean last *reasonable* resort. How many resorts does a nation have to test before it says that it has exhausted all the reasonable alternatives? The principle is easier to use in some contexts than in others. Imminent attack by enemy forces may preclude, for instance, any possibility for negotiation. But in other cases some vagueness is present. The Principle of Proportionality is no better off. As we noted in chapters 5 and 7 on these principles of Just War Theory, this principle does not make it clear whether proportionality between good and bad means 50/50, 75/25, or what. As we will see below the same point can be made with respect to the Likelihood of Success Principle.

Even the Legitimate Authority Principle causes problems. This principle works well when we think about international war in a world consisting of sovereign states. When two or more states approach war, the principle of Legitimate Authority can be applied with relative ease. Nations know who their leaders are and specify by law which of these leaders is responsible for declaring war. The UN Charter has established clear legal rules on the use of force. But—as we have seen in various case studies throughout this book—these rules are often violated or challenged on political grounds. NATO's decision to intervene in Kosovo without the proper authorization of the UN Security Council has led to heated debates among just war theorists. Things are even more complicated when dealing with intrastate war. Under which conditions may anticolonial, secessionist, or revolutionary movements satisfy the Principle of Legitimate Authority? International lawyers are debating complex borderline cases, and this is no less the case in the ethics of war.

The source of this problem is easy to understand. Just War Theory is the product of a long historical tradition. Just War Theory and the Principle of Legitimate Authority developed in the writings of St. Augustine in one of the parts of the Roman Empire. Augustine distanced himself from the pacifist Christian tradition through a reinterpretation of the scriptures. His Principle of Legitimate Authority was one among the principles meant to legitimate and to restrict the use of force by political authorities, without rejecting the religious obligations of a Christian toward God and humanity. The emergence of the Westphalian system of sovereign states in the seventeenth and eighteenth centuries expressed a shift in loyalty away from the religious authority of the Church toward the political authority of the state. This shift found a further expression in the secularization of the Just War Tradition. Whereas the Christian doctrine of the legitimate use of force addressed the question of how to resolve the tension between political and religious loyalties, the Just War Tradition in its secularized form addressed the question of how allegiance to the state could be brought into conformity to an allegiance to humankind.

Since then, Just War Theory became a theory to help one nation deal with the threat and the reality of war when facing another nation. It became generally perceived as a theory on interstate conflicts. But, as we have seen, the theory may also be applied to intrastate conflicts. Most of the criteria will then not change since they are applicable to all war and warlike settings. A secessionist movement, for instance, can cite Just Cause (e.g., in the form overcoming oppression and exploitation by a colonial power) just as easily as a nation-state can (e.g., in the form of overcoming aggression which has taken place in the past). Similarly a rebel group can cite Last Resort just as a nation-state does. It will not be justified in entering into a guerrilla and/or civil war unless it has tried (all) other means of overcoming the injustices it is trying to overcome. The same will be the case with Proportionality and Right Intentions. They will apply to rebel wars just as they do to international wars. But the criterion of Likelihood of Success may have to be relaxed some (see chapter 4 on the discussion of Cuba). That is, a rebel group may not have to show to the same extent as a regular government that it has a reasonable hope of success before it can begin to use force. Still, since it can still apply most of the *jus ad bellum*, as well as the *jus in bello* criteria, any rebel group will face basically the same hurdles that any nation-state faces. Even though it is modified somewhat, rebel, guerrilla and other nonstandard military groups can still be judged as operating within the most important constraints of Just War Theory. Finally, in the chapter on terrorism (chapter 12), it became even clearer that there is no barrier to applying Just War Theory to nonstate groups of various kinds. The theory was applied freely to both the states that were attacked by terrorists and the terrorists themselves.

The situation is in principle no different in the *jus in bello* portion of Just War Theory. The Principles of Discrimination and Proportionality have been codified in International Humanitarian Law, which provides for some clear legal rules and the possibility to prosecute war crimes. But in some cases, the application of the *jus in bello* portion of Just War Theory still remains affected by ambiguity and, sometimes, even vagueness. NATO's war on Kosovo has been justified with political arguments drawing on the Just

War Tradition, but this tradition also provides strong arguments for a critical assessment of the way the war has been fought. Chapter 8 on the Principle of Discrimination and the chapters 10 and 11 on Kosovo point to the contradiction between a justification of the war in humanitarian terms and the political decision taken by NATO leaders to have their pilots fly safely high in the sky. In a contradictory way, this policy puts at risk the very people NATO was trying to save. But this criticism is based on a particular interpretation of the duties of soldiers on the battlefield, which is not necessarily shared by all just war theorists. If, then, a certain vagueness and ambiguity are found throughout Just War Theory, it becomes obvious that this theory cannot be applied to all or almost war settings as if the application were scientific (i.e., in the spirit of physics and chemistry) in nature.

EXCESSIVE PESSIMISM

Once the flaws of excessive optimism are exposed, it is tempting to react in the opposite direction. Instead of expecting too much from the theory, now too little is expected. The vagueness and ambiguity of the just war principles lead some thinkers to suppose that these principles are like putty. Rather than yield definitive answers when applied, they are subject to being molded in whatever shape their users want them to be. In its extreme form, this pessimism about Just War Theory leads to skepticism or even cynicism.

But the degrees of vagueness and ambiguity found in any ethical theory, including Just War Theory, should not be exaggerated. The terms used in ethics are never as precise as those in some of the sciences. Aristotle told us as much when he said in his *Nicomachean Ethics*.

> Our discussion will be adequate if it has as much clearness as the subject-matter admits of, for precision is not to be sought for alike in all discussions, any more than in all the products of the crafts. . . . for it is the mark of an educated man to look for precision in each class of things just so far as the nature of the subject admits; it is evidently equally foolish to accept probable reasoning from a mathematician and to demand from a rhetorician scientific proofs.[4]

Saying that there is vagueness and ambiguity in the terms we use when dealing with ethical questions is not the same as saying that they are totally ambiguous and vague. Much of ordinary language contains vagueness and ambiguity but we do not, as a result, abandon it. To grant, for example, that our ordinary color words are vague so we cannot say whether a particular patch of color is red or orange does not mean that other patches cannot be seen as clearly red or clearly orange. Indeed, it makes no sense to say that red and orange are totally vague. The reason we know that a color patch is near the border separating red and orange (and thus concept we use to talk about it is vague) is just because some other color patches are not near the (vague) border. The same is true about national borders. A border dispute triggered by a vague or unclear border is understood because we know that the two nations are composed of other territories that are not under dispute. Vagueness, then, can take the edge off a concept and thereby prevent those who wish to use it from making precise judgments all the time. But that does not necessarily keep them from using that term effectively to make moral judgments most of the time.

What this discussion means for Just War Theory is that such theory has not been rendered useless by vague and/or ambiguous terminology. Rather, the theory falls somewhere between the way those who are extremely sanguine and those who are pessimistic view it. It is not the case that there is no vagueness and ambiguity present (optimist position), nor that vagueness and ambiguity pervade all of our thinking (pessimist position). It is a theory whose primary function is to organize our thinking about war in such a way as to tell us when we should and should not go to war. By encouraging those who are considering going to war to ask themselves a series of questions (e.g., "Do you have a just cause?" "Have you tried to negotiate your problems?"), the theory slows the onset of war and sometimes even prevents it. Beyond that, by asking questions once the war starts (e.g., "Are these people legitimate targets?" "Are you overreacting in blasting an opponent who is about to surrender?"), Just War Theory helps make war less horrible and cruel than it might otherwise be. Jumping over these hurdles may not help in every case (as the optimists hope it would), but it can help in a wide variety of cases (as the pessimists deny it does).

Just War Theory thus delivers support for making more rational, prudential, and conscientious choices. It is interesting to note that Realism has the same purposes. Insofar as that theory encourages its followers to articulate what the good (self-interest) reasons are for entering war, what the likelihood of success of war is, what the proportionality calculations are, and so on, realists also face hurdles that slow the process of going to war and possibly prevent war. They too can profit from reviewing past cases of war. And they too profit from the way their theory organizes their thinking and makes it more rational so that they approach and participate in war knowing that they have systematically thought about whatever decisions they make.

In spite of having said some reassuring things about dealing with the Error of Excessive Pessimism, some might think that more needs to be said. The pessimist view is triggered, paradoxically enough, by excessive optimism. Here is how this triggering mechanism works. Those who are pessimists about applying Just War Theory to wars between state and nonstate groups or to other nontraditional settings realize that these sorts of application pose special problems for the theory. Dwelling on these problems, these pessimists become convinced that these special problems are beyond resolution. One reason they become so convinced is that they often have high expectations as to what Just War Theory should be able to do. That is, initially, these pessimists have the same high expectations of Just War Theory that the optimists have. Both groups look at theories in ethics as if they must be as successful as theories in physics and chemistry. Demanding much of theory, and seeing that theory cannot deliver what is demanded, these thinkers lapse into a deep pessimism about Just War Theory, in general, but more specifically about the application of that theory to wars between states and nonstate groups.

What we have done in this work in order to avoid this pessimism (skepticism) is adjust our expectations. Not expecting too much of Just War Theory, it is possible, we argue, to use that theory productively in all sorts of wars including those fought between a state and a nonstate group.

A UNIVERSAL THEORY?

Even allowing a certain amount of slippage in the form that Just War Theory takes, it is remarkable how universal the theory remains. Why this is so is not easy to explain. But a plausible account can be given as follows. As mentioned above, Just War Theory has a two-part structure. One part has to do with procedures, the other with values. With respect to the former, the universal nature of Just War Theory is understandable. When, as Last Resort does, we are told to identify all our choice options, we are being asked to do something very basic: to behave in a rational way. Reason tells us not to choose a very costly option until other options have been examined. Similarly, when the Principle of Proportionality (in *jus ad* bellum and *jus in bello*) tells us to assess the costs and benefits (whatever they might be), we are again being asked to think rationally. Likelihood of Success likewise urges us to behave rationally as well by, again, reminding us that we need to make cost/benefit assessments of a certain sort before we act. Even the Principle of Legitimate Authority urges us to behave rationally by encouraging the society to let only those who are authorized (hopefully the best qualified) to make the important decisions about war. Since, then, much of Just War Theory is based on procedural considerations that are heavily tied to reason, prudence, logic, and clear thinking that are universally recognized as valid, it is understandable that this theory has a tendency to have universal status.

But what of the value portion of Just War Theory's structure? How can it be said to be universal? Recall that this values portion in Just War Theory is humanistic. It says that all humans should be given consideration without exception. All count for something in the vast moral calculus; and no one is supposed to be discounted as less a person than any other. This is the portion of Just War Theory that has less than universal acceptance. Terms such as "humanism," "humanistic," and "humanitarian" trigger, for many, thoughts of Marsilio Ficini, Michael de Montaigne, Desiderius Erasmus, and Thomas More among others—all of them modern Western thinkers.

However, humanism viewed widely as the doctrine that all humans are worthy of concern has a much broader history. Christianity originally was (and still is in many of its forms) humanistic in its notion that each of us is the child of God. According to this doctrine, it matters not whether we are rich or poor; old or young; black, red, white, or yellow, we all count for something (of value) in the eyes of God. Ancient Greek culture is not especially known for its humanistic outlook. It did very little, for example, to discourage slavery. Yet, even in this culture, the Stoics managed to transcend Greek ethnicity and see each person as having a unique role to play in the Cosmos. In India, Buddhism was universal in its thinking of human beings as well. Because of this thinking, it had a special appeal to the poor. It also proved to be transportable as a doctrine because it taught salvation not just for one particular group, but for all people. In addition, humanistic thinking can be found in China. Confucius and Mo Tzu developed the notions of humanheartedness (*jen*) and universal love, respectively. Humanheartedness explicitly shows concern for everyone. All are welcome to Confucius's school to learn, whether they be from his province or not; and whether they be rich or poor. Mo Tzu's notion of universal love literally means what it says. We are to show equal concern for everyone. Indeed, for Mo Tzu, we are supposed to be as concerned for other people's parents to the same extent that we are concerned for our own. The Muslim religion is here as well. Muhammad had a special concern for the poor and preached a doctrine of salvation that applied to all.

So although humanistic notions are not universal, in the sense of being held by everyone, they have a place in many cultures and at many different times. Insofar as they are, and insofar as Just War Theory rests on these notions, the theory's foundations are as firm as any ethical theory can be. Given such firm foundations, Just War Theory deserves the increased attention it has been receiving of late when states and nonstate groups engage in violent struggles to settle their disputes.

NOTES

1. On conditional Pacifism: see the introduction to this volume.
2. We are using here the concepts of "Realists," "Pacifists," and "just war theorists" in order to clarify theoretical differences. It is, however, clear that in practical life, individuals may use arguments from various currents in ethical thought.
3. A variation of this sanguine outlook insists that the proper application of Just War Theory (along with the facts) would resolve all conflict or disagreement. Thus

if two just war theorists were in a disagreement about whether to go to war, what would be needed is a conference between the two of them. Once they talked things over, it is supposed that the theory would be able to resolve the conflict (assuming of course that the two who disagree are open-minded).

    4. Aristotle, "Nicomachean Ethics," bk. 1, para. 3, in *The Basic Works of Aristotle,* ed. Richard McKeon (New York: Random House, 1941), 936.

Index

Abkhazia. *See* Georgian-Abkhaz conflict
Abu Ghraib, 293
Afghanistan, x–xi, xiv, 15–16, 34, 39, 57, 117–20, 124n39, 176, 182, 184, 187, 270, 281–82
Ahmadinejad, Mahmoud 40, 51–52n52
Ahtisaari, Martti 245, 248–51, 254
Albania, 196, 200, 209, 211, 230, 250. *See also* Kosovo
Albright, Madeleine, 202
Algerian War (1954–1962), 62–65, 71n25, 201
al-Qaeda, xi, 34, 36–37, 108, 118, 120, 187, 269, 297, 300n50
Ambrose, St., 11
Andréani, Gilles, 16
Angola, 182
Annan, Kofi A., 202
Aquinas. *See* Thomas Aquinas, St.
Argentina. *See* Falklands War (1982)
Aristotle, 11, 312
asymmetric warfare, 109, 121, 187, 268
Augustine, St., 11, 23n34, 27, 70, 75–76, 101, 126, 310
Australia, 115, 290
Austria, 83

Bangladesh. *See* Indian-Pakistan War (1971)
Batista, Fulgencio, 62, 106–7, 121, 130, 143
Belgium, xii, 29, 58, 103–5, 128, 202–3
belligerent status, 15, 62, 64
Belorussia, 87
Bhutto, Zulfikar Ali, 80
Bin Laden, Osama, 187, 266, 269
biological weapons, 37, 72n32, 89–93, 96, 165–66
Blair, Tony, 68, 88, 281–83, 286–88, 297
Blix, Hans, 287
Boer War (1899–1902), 131
Bolivia, 62
Bosnia, xii, 46–47, 53nn77–80, 147–51, 153nn35–39, 15nn40–41, 182, 196, 207–9, 215, 248–49, 266
Boutros-Ghali, Boutros, 149, 153n37
"Brezhnev" doctrine, 112
Buddhism, 315
Bull, Bartle, 17
Bull, Hedley, 19
Bush, George H. W., 31, 82, 89, 91, 93, 96, 221, 284, 303

Bush, George W., xi, 16–17, 36–38,
    51n52, 88–96, 118–20, 281–88,
    295–98, 299n19

Caroline incident, 31–32
Carr, Edward Hallett, 3
Castro, Fidel, 107–8, 130, 143–45,
    185–86
Catholic Bishops (U.S.), 48–49, 77, 126
Catholicism, 57, 284
Ceaucescu, Nicolae, 61
Chamberlain, Neville, 84
Chechnya, xii, 220, 230–31, 234n2,
    240, 242, 244, 254, 266, 277n30
Che Guevara, Ernesto, 62
chemical weapons, 39, 72n32, 89–91,
    93, 96, 281–83
Cheney, Dick 95
China, xii–xiii, 41, 67, 114–15, 127,
    136, 137n24, 166, 182, 212,
    222–23, 230–31, 238, 247–49, 253,
    255, 257; ancient China 11, 126,
    315
Chirac, Jacques 40, 119
Christianity, 8, 11, 45, 75–76, 126,
    156, 310–11, 315. *See also* pacifism;
    religion
Christopher, Paul, 44
Churchill, Winston, 59–60, 165
Cicero, 11, 28, 139, 156
civilian-based defense (CBD), 10,
    22n29, 23n30, 110–11, 113,
    129–30, 305
civil war. *See* war
Clark, Wesley, 230
Clausewitz, Carl von, ix
Clinton, William J., 69, 200, 207, 209,
    221, 270, 304
Coates, Anthony J., 141
Cohen, Sheldon, 126
colonialism/anticolonialism 12, 15–16,
    31, 55, 58–60, 62–65, 70, 73,
    105–6, 131, 269, 310–11
Conference on Security and
    Cooperation in Europe (CSCE). *See*
    Organization for Security and
    Cooperation in Europe (OSCE)

Confucius, 315
Cook, Robin, 200–201
counterinsurgency. *See*
    insurgency/counterinsurgency
Croatia, 46, 182, 195, 201, 208–9, 224
Cuba, 62, 106–7, 121, 124n40, 130,
    142–47, 182, 185–86, 311
Cuban Missile Crisis (1962), 142–47
Cyprus, 253, 257, 259n22
Czechoslovakia: in the period
    1933–1945, 83–85, 140, 307; Soviet
    occupation of Czechoslovakia
    (1968), 57, 111–14, 121, 233, 304
Czech Republic, 211, 222

Daalder, Ivo H., 205, 220, 233, 234n8
discrimination principle, xi, xiv, 13, 15,
    18–19, 76, 141–42, 157–58,
    160–61, 164–68, 171–91, 212, 215,
    231–33, 263–68, 272–75, 276n15,
    292–98, 306–7, 311–12
double effect principle (PDE), 167–69,
    177, 180, 189n5, 213, 217n39
Dresden, bombing of, 160–61
Dubcek, Alexander, 112
Dudayev, Dzukhar, 220

Egypt, 32–33, 43, 50n71, 65, 269, 274,
    280, 293
Erasmus, Desiderius, 7, 315
ethnic cleansing, 48, 263; in Abkhazia,
    242; in Bosnia 46–47, 148; in
    Croatia, 224; in Kosovo xii, 69, 176,
    206, 209, 215, 221, 225–26,
    228–29. *See also* responsibility to
    protect (concept)
Europe, x–xi, 65, 95, 108, 113, 120,
    131, 185, 222, 269; and intrastate
    conflicts, xii, 197, 223, 231, 233,
    238, 243–44, 246–49, 253;
    Medieval Europe, 56–57, 156, 166;
    and weapons of mass destruction,
    xiii, 7; and World War II, 58–59,
    84–85, 140

Falklands War (1982), 16, 161
Ficini, Marsilio, 315

Fomin, Aleksandr, 145
France, xi–xii, 56, 63–66, 269; and
   Iran, 40, 42; and Iraq, 95, 119–20,
   279, 288, 290; and Kosovo, 202,
   212, 227; in the period 1933–1945,
   58–61, 65, 67, 83–84, 103–6, 117,
   128, 140, 161, 176; and weapons of
   mass destruction, xi, 40; in World
   War I, 29, 130–31. *See also* Algerian
   War (1954–1962); Vietnam War:
   First Indochina War (1946–1954)

Gandhi, Mohandas, 9, 304
Gaulle, Charles de, 59–61, 65, 117
Geinlein, Konrad, 83–84
Geneva Conventions, 15, 64, 157, 165,
   183. *See also* International
   Humanitarian Law
genocide, xii, 12, 48, 69, 73, 77, 82,
   219, 241, 243, 267
Gentilis, Albericus, 44
Georgian-Abkhaz conflict, 230–31,
   240, 242, 252–54, 258n7, 259n22
Germany, xi, 157; and Iraq 67, 95,
   119–20, 290; and Kosovo, 69, 202,
   212, 227; in the period 1933–1945,
   6, 58–60, 71n14, 83–87, 103–4,
   117, 121, 128, 140, 160–62, 176,
   262, 268, 303, 307; in World War I,
   29, 130–31
Glover, Jonathan, 145, 147
Greece: and Kosovo 202, 212, 253; and
   terrorism 263, 274
Greenspan, Alan, 94
Grotius, Hugo, 11, 28, 44, 52n72, 76,
   88, 101, 126, 139
guerrilla. *See* war
Gulf War (1990–1991). *See* Iraq

Hacha, Emil, 85
Hadley, Stephan, 17
Hague Conventions/Regulations, 157,
   183
Hayden, Robert, 233
Hehir, Bryan, 45
Hezbollah, 39–40, 43, 108–10, 122,
   123n19

Higgins, Rosalyn, 47
Hiroshima and Nagasaki, bombing of,
   123n33, 164, 179
Hitler, Adolf, 6, 83–86, 131, 140, 262,
   307
Hockaday, Arthur, 181
Holbrooke, Richard, 197, 205, 221
Holmes, Robert L., 9, 22n20, 23n34, 77
Hosking, Geoffrey, 112
humanitarian intervention. *See*
   responsibility to protect (concept);
   war
human rights, x, xiii, 44–45, 63–64, 69,
   73, 77, 89–91, 93, 96, 141, 157,
   172, 186, 195, 199, 201, 203, 208,
   210, 213, 215, 219–24, 244, 246,
   250–51
Human Rights Watch, 232
Hundred Years' War (1337–1453), 56
Hungary, 57, 85, 211, 222, 233, 253
Hussein, Saddam, xi–xii, 30, 37, 39, 67,
   79, 90, 93–94, 118–19, 141,
   185–86, 279–84, 287, 289, 291–92

Ignatieff, Michael, 176
India, 9, 11, 42, 80–83, 181, 266,
   303–4, 315
Indian-Pakistan War (1971), 80–83
insurgency/counterinsurgency, 18, 173,
   175, 187–88, 188n2, 191n35,
   288–89, 292–93, 296
interest, national and security, xi, 1–7,
   10, 15, 30, 39–40, 55–57, 61, 64,
   68–69, 74, 79, 82, 84–85, 88,
   90–92, 95–96, 106, 112–13,
   124n44, 139, 142, 145–47, 157,
   200, 231, 241, 243, 253, 255, 257,
   299n22, 304–7, 313. *See also*
   realism; right intentions principle
International Atomic Energy Agency
   (IAEA), xiii, 38, 41–43. *See also* Iran;
   nuclear weapons
International Humanitarian Law, xiv,
   15, 110, 157, 184, 233, 235n16,
   306, 311. *See also* discrimination
   principle; Geneva Conventions;
   Hague Conventions/Regulations

international law, xiii, 7, 15, 18, 29, 31–34, 44, 62–63, 69, 76–77, 90, 124n40, 140, 147, 157, 182, 198, 203, 221–22, 233, 257, 310

Iran, x–xi, xiii, 34, 37–43, 52n52, 108, 120, 124n44, 141–42, 182, 269, 274, 279–82, 284, 296–97. *See also* Ahmadinejad, Mahmoud

Iran/Iraq War (1980–1988), 39, 141, 280–82, 284

Iraq, x–xii, xiv–xv, 15–16, 34, 36–37, 39–42, 67–69, 72n32, 88–96, 117–20, 124n39, 124n44, 279–98, 299n22, 300n36, 300n42, 300n45, 300nn50–51, 303; and the definition of a civil war, 17–18; and the Gulf War (1990–1991), x–xi, 30–31, 78–79, 141, 147, 163–64, 280–83, 303; and *jus in bello*, xi, xiv, 141–42, 163–64, 176, 184, 186–87, 263, 266–67, 270–71, 290–95; and the Six Day War (1967), 32–33

irredentism, 98n28

Islam: Islamic terrorism and radicalism, 16, 51n52, 187, 261, 265–75, 286, 297; Islamic tradition of just war (*jihad*), 76, 82, 108–10, 117, 123n19, 266. *See also* al-Qaeda

Israel: and Hezbollah 108–9, 122; and Iran, 39–40, 42–43, 52n52; and Iraq 89–93, 96, 282–83; and radical Islamism 270–71; Six Day War (1967), 32–33, 50n21, 50n23

Italy, 6, 84, 143, 202, 212, 227

Japan, 6, 40–41, 105–6, 116, 131, 146, 164–66, 187. *See also* Russo-Japanese War (1904–1905)

jihad. *See* Islam

Johnson, D. P., 102

Johnson, James T., 178

Jordan, 17, 32–33

just cause principle: and the Afghanistan war (2001–), 118–19; and the Gulf War (1990–1991), 30–31, 78–79, 282; history and definition, 11–12, 27–30, 49, 49n4,

56, 63, 73–80, 102, 126–27, 132, 241, 305–11, 313; and humanitarian intervention, 43–48, 242; and the Indian-Pakistan War (1971), 82; and Iran's nuclear program, xiii, 38–43; and the Iraq War (2003–), 36–37, 67–68, 88, 90, 92–95, 118–20, 124n39, 282–87, 289, 297; and Kosovo, 198–99, 203, 210, 215, 219–21, 224, 243–49, 253–56; and the Munich Agreement (1938), 85; and terrorism, 18, 34–35, 266, 269, 271, 273–74

Kant, Immanuel, 7

Karadjic, Radovan, 233

Katyn Forest Massacre, 87

Kay, David, 281

Keegan, John, 17

Kennedy, Edward, 81

Kennedy, John Fitzgerald, 143–46

Kennedy, Robert, 146

Kerry, John, 93

Khan, A. Q., 38

Khan, Fazal Muqeem, 81

Khan, Yahya, 81

Khomeini, Ayatollah, 280

Khruschev, Nikita, 143–44

Kim Il Sung, 114

Kim Jong Il 114, 135

Kissinger, Henry, 228

Korean War (1950–1953), 114, 127, 163. *See also* North Korea

Kosovo: international status of Kosovo, xiv, 20, 58, 237–59; Kosovo Force (KFOR), 173–74, 198, 201, 226, 238, 249, 258n3; Kosovo Liberation Army (UCK, KLA), 196–97, 199, 203, 205, 209, 220–22, 224, 234n8, 234n14; 1999 intervention in Kosovo, x, xii–xv, 16, 67–69, 162, 173, 175–77, 195–238, 310–12. *See also* NATO; Rambouillet, negotiations in; United Nations

Krauthammer, Charles, 227

Kreisky, Bruno, 145

Kuwait. *See* Iraq: and the Gulf War (1990–1991)

last resort principle: and Bosnia (1992–1995), 147–51; and Cuban Missile Crisis (1962), 142–47; history and definition of the principle, 13, 18, 76, 139–40, 305–11, 314; and Iraq, 67, 141–42, 286–87, 292, 297; and Kosovo (international status), 243–45, 250, 252, 255–56, 259n25; and 1999 Kosovo intervention, 203–5, 227–29, 241; and preventive and preemptive war, 35, 68; and terrorism, 268, 271; and the United Nations, 140–42, 145
League of Nations, 7
Lee, Steven, 180
legitimate authority principle: and the Algerian War (1954–1962), 62–65; history and definition of the principle, 11–12, 47, 55–57, 70, 75–76, 108, 306, 310, 314; and the French resistance, 58–61; and the Iraq war (2003–), 67–69, 289–90, 297; and Kosovo (international status), 243–45, 250–51, 254–56, 259n25; and 1999 Kosovo intervention, xiii, 68–69, 199, 201–3, 215, 221–23, 233; and revolutionary movements, 61–62; and the UN Security Council (UNSC), 66–70, 141, 233, 241–42
Lewis, Bernard, 51–52n52
Libya, x, 39, 185
Lieber Code, 157
likelihood of success principle: and Afghanistan (2001–), 117–20; and Belgium (1940), 104–5, 128; and Civilian-Based Defense, 110–11, 129; and Cuba in the 1950s, 106–8; and Czechoslovakia (1968), 111–14; and Hezbollah, 108–10, 129; history and definition of the principle, 12, 47, 76, 101–2, 127, 130, 241, 305–8, 310–11, 313–14;

and the Iraq war (2003–), 17–18, 41, 68, 117–20, 123n36, 124n39, 287–90, 297; and Kosovo (international status), 244–49, 254–56; and 1999 Kosovo intervention, 205–10, 215, 225–27, 245–49, 254–55; and Luxembourg (1940), 103–4, 121, 128; and North Korea, 114–17; and sanctions, 241; and terrorism, 36; and Thailand (1940 and 1941), 105–6
Littman, Mark, 204, 206, 228
Luttwak, Edward, 207
Luxembourg (1940), 103–4, 121, 128

Macedonia, 196, 200, 211, 226, 230, 248–49
Mandelbaum, Michael, 229
martyrdom, martyrs/self-sacrifice, 103–4, 109–10, 120–22, 207, 262, 268, 273, 275n6, 277nn29–30, 282
McNamara, Robert, 163–64
Mearsheimer, John J., 92
media, 7, 16–17, 50n21, 84, 88–89, 95, 113, 219, 221, 274, 295
Mencius, 11
Middle Ages, 45, 56, 70, 156
militarism, xiv, 5–7, 303–4, 307
military necessity, 158, 176–77, 182, 233, 235n26, 269, 273
Mill, John Stuart, 46
Miller, France, 85
Milosevic, Slobodan, 9, 197, 199, 201, 205, 207–15, 221, 225–26, 238, 246–47
mines, 178, 181–83
Mladic, Ratko, 233
Molotov, Vyacheslav, 87
Mongols, ix, 165, 261
Montaigne, Michael de, 315
Montenegro, 153n38, 216n2, 238, 257n1
Morgenthau, Hans, 3
Morocco, 65
Mo Tzu, 11, 126, 315
Munich Agreement (1938), 84–85, 140

Murphy, Jeffrie, 175, 177, 189n5;
    Murphy's chain of agency, 175–77,
    189n5
Mussolini, Benito, 6

Nagasaki, bombing of. *See* Hiroshima
    and Nagasaki, bombing of
Nagorno-Karabakh, 227
Napoleon, 57, 102, 131
Nasser, Gamal Abdel, 33, 50n21
NATO: and Afghanistan, 184, 187; and
    Bosnia, xii, 53n77, 149–51, 153n35,
    153n37; and Kosovo, x, xii–xv, 16,
    67–69, 162, 173–74, 176–77,
    195–215, 216n9, 217n28,
    217nn38–39, 219–34, 234n1,
    234n8, 234n14, 235n16, 237–40,
    242, 247, 249, 290, 304, 308,
    310–12
neoconservatives, 92, 284–85, 288
Netherlands, 103–4, 128
Nitze, Paul, 146–47
Northern Alliance, 117
North Korea, I –xi, 37, 39, 43, 94,
    114–17, 123n33, 127, 132–36,
    137n20, 137n24. *See also* Korean
    War (1950–1953)
nuclear weapons: and France, 40; and
    Iran, 38–43, 52n52, 52n58, 142;
    and Iraq, 37, 89–91, 93–94, 96,
    282; and *jus in bello*, 134–35,
    164–65, 168–69, 170n13, 178–81;
    and North Korea, 43, 94, 114–16,
    122, 123n33, 134–36; Nuclear
    Non-proliferation Treaty (NPT),
    xiii, 38, 41–43, 52n58;
    proliferation of, xiii–xiv, 7, 35,
    37–43, 52n52, 52n58, 89–91, 93,
    96, 177–78, 282. *See also* Cuban
    Missile Crisis (1962); International
    Atomic Energy Agency (IAEA);
    war: preventive and preemptive
    war

O'Brien, W. V., 126–27
O'Hanlon, Michael E., 205, 220, 233,
    234n8

Organization for Security and
    Cooperation in Europe (OSCE), 67,
    197, 203, 222–23, 229, 253
Organization of African States (OAS),
    67

pacifism, 6–11, 20, 22n20, 22n22,
    23n34, 75–76, 303–5, 307, 310.
    See also civilian-based defense
    (CBD)
Pakistan, 38, 42, 80–83, 119, 181, 269,
    303. *See also* Indian-Pakistan War
    (1971)
Panama, 57
Parsons, Anthony, 30
peacekeeping operations, x, 14, 46,
    149, 153n36, 173–74, 197–98, 201,
    226–27, 237, 240, 252. *See also*
    NATO
Pétain, Philippe, 58–59, 61, 117
Petraeus, David, 295–96, 300n50
Phibun Songkhram, 106
Phillips, Robert, 46
Plato, 11, 155–56
Poland, 85–87, 113, 211, 222, 308
Powell, Colin, 72n32, 282, 288
preventive and preemptive wars. *See*
    war
proportionality principle (*ad bellum*),
    12–13, 35, 47, 50n20, 67–68, 76,
    101, 125–32, 136n2, 241, 305–8,
    310–11, 313–14; and the creation
    of an international administration
    238, 243; and Iraq 67, 163–64, 289,
    297; and Kosovo, 209–10, 215, 220,
    229, 238, 241; and North Korea,
    116, 132–36; and the right of
    secession 245, 251–52, 254–56
proportionality principle (*in bello*), 13,
    15, 76, 141–42, 157–69, 183, 186,
    189n5, 191n35, 306–7, 311, 314;
    and Iraq, 163–64, 290–91, 296–97;
    and Kosovo, 213–15, 231, 233; and
    nuclear war, 164–65, 178, 180–81,
    188. *See also* double effect principle
    (PDE); nuclear weapons
Putin, Vladimir, 119, 242

Qassem, Naim, 108–10

Rahman, Sheikh Mujibur, 80–81
Rambouillet, negotiations in, 197–98, 203–5, 225, 227–29. *See also* Kosovo
Ramsey, Paul, 67, 126–27, 179–80
Rawls, John, 160
realism, xiv, 1–6, 10, 20, 21n7, 32, 77, 79, 92, 106, 136n2, 146, 265, 286, 303–7, 310, 313, 315n2
Red Cross (International Committee of the Red Cross, ICRC), 64, 72n25, 157, 199
religion, 8, 17, 20, 22n22, 45, 52n52, 57, 73, 75–76, 108–10, 120, 130, 156–57, 159, 183–84, 187, 200, 232, 261, 265–66, 268–70, 273–74, 280, 291, 307, 310–11, 315. *See also* Christianity; Islam; pacifism; war
responsibility to protect (concept), 48
retaliation, 146, 266–69, 271, 273, 281, 295
revenge, 18, 55, 73, 75, 226, 234n8, 267–69, 271
revolution. *See* war
Ribbentrop, von Joachim, 87
Rice, Condoleezza, 14–15
Rieff, David, 47
right intentions principle, 12, 19, 73–99, 126, 139, 305, 307–11; and the Gulf War (1990–1991), 78–79; and Hitler's policies, 83–86; and the Indian-Pakistan War (1971), 80–83; and the Iraq war (2003–), xv, 68, 88–96, 285–86, 297; and Kosovo, 199–201, 223–25, 241, 243, 245, 253–57; and Soviet policies, 86–88. *See also* interest, national and security
Roberts, Adam, 206, 208
Roman Empire, 11, 70, 156, 186, 310
Rugova, Ibrahim, 196, 198
rules of engagement (ROE) 173–75, 191n35, 215, 272, 292, 294
Rumsfeld, Donald, 281–82
Rusk, Dean, 145
Russell, Frederick, 156

Russia, x, xiii, 7, 18, 61, 130–31, 136, 157, 182, 185, 220, 222, 240, 242, 244, 259n22, 269; and Iran's nuclear program, 41; and the Iraq War (2003–), 67, 119; and Kosovo (international status), 238, 248–50, 252–53, 255, 257; and 1999 Kosovo intervention, xii–xiii, 196–97, 203, 209, 211, 222–23, 227–31, 237; and North Korea, 114–15, 136. *See also* Chechnya; Georgian-Abkhaz conflict; Russo-Japanese War (1904–1905); Soviet Union
Russo-Japanese War (1904–1905), 131
Rwanda, xii

Sahnoun, Mohamed, 48
Salinger, Pierre, 146
sanctions, 13, 33, 66, 140–42, 184–86, 203; against Cuba, 143, 185–86; in former Yugoslavia, 150, 153n38, 224; against Iran, 43, 142; against Iraq, x–xi, 94, 141–42, 185–86, 286. *See also* United Nations
Saudi Arabia, 43, 94, 120, 269, 280, 297
Schwartzkopf, Norman, 163
secession, 12, 15, 20, 58, 73, 82–83, 98n28, 220, 237–59. *See also* Algerian War (1954–1962); Bosnia; Chechnya; Cyprus; Georgian-Abkhaz conflict; Indian-Pakistan War (1971); Kosovo; Nagorno-Karabakh; NATO; South Ossetia; Spain; Transnistria; United States: American Civil War (1861–1865); war
self-determination, principle of /right to national, 12, 46, 62–63, 65, 85, 87, 239. *See also* Algerian War (1954–1962); Bosnia; Chechnya; Czechoslovakia; Georgian-Abkhaz conflict; Indian-Pakistan War (1971); Kosovo; Nagorno-Karabakh; NATO: intervention in Kosovo; secession; Transnistria; war: of secession

Serbia. *See* Kosovo; NATO
Shea, Jamie, 213
Sherman, William Tecumseh, 4
Shevardnadze, Eduard, 9, 240, 242
Shiite 17, 40, 108, 117, 261, 280–81,
 284, 286, 295–97, 301n51. *See also*
 religion
Six Day War (1967), 32–33
Slovakia, 85, 253. *See also*
 Czechoslovakia
Solana, Javier, 195, 197–99, 202,
 222–23
Somalia, 227, 266
South Africa, 141, 185
South Korea, 114–16, 132–34, 137n21.
 See also Korean War (1950–1953);
 North Korea
South Ossetia, 252–53, 259n22
sovereignty, x, 15, 21n3, 29, 31, 43–45,
 48, 57–58, 60–62, 66, 70, 70–71n8,
 79, 198, 205, 211, 241–42, 245–47,
 249, 251–52, 254–55, 257, 309
Soviet Union, xii, 39, 83–84, 86–87,
 113, 143–46, 177, 185, 233, 240,
 303. *See also* Afghanistan; Chechnya;
 Cuban Missile Crisis (1962);
 Czechoslovakia; Korean War
 (1950–1953)
Spain: and Kosovo 202, 257; and
 secession 187, 253
Sparta, 6
Spykman, Nicholas J., 2
Sri Lanka, 187
Stacy, Robert, 157
Stalin, Josef, 86
Suarez, Francisco, 28, 44, 52n72
Sudan, x
Sudetenland, 83–85, 307
Sunni, 17, 117, 280, 286, 291, 295,
 297, 301n51. *See also* religion
Sun Tzu, ix, 3, 5
Syria, x, 17, 32–34, 120, 137n20, 269,
 280

Tajikistan, xii, 222, 266
Taliban, 34, 117–19, 281
Tamil Tigers 187, 277n30

territorial integrity, 20, 29, 33, 43–44,
 64, 81, 147, 199, 225, 227, 234n14,
 240–41, 243, 246, 248, 253, 255,
 305, 309. *See also* secession; war: of
 secession
terrorism, xi, xiii–xv, 16–18, 35–36, 89,
 91, 93, 96, 124n40, 186–87, 196,
 261–77, 281–85, 311
Thailand, 105–6
theory (just war theory as a theory), x,
 xiv, 11, 19–20, 24n51, 167, 304,
 308–15
Thirty Years' War (1618–1648), 57
Thomas Aquinas, St., 11, 27, 126, 139
Tito, Jossip Broz, 195
Tolstoy, Leo, 8–9
torture, 64, 293
Toulmin, Stephen, 181
Trajkovski, Boris, 226
Transnistria, 252–53, 259n22
Trotsky, Leon, 55
Turkey, 30, 43, 120, 143–45, 201,
 259n22, 291, 296

UCK. *See* Kosovo
United Kingdom: and the Falklands
 War (1982), 16, 161; and Iraq, xi,
 30, 40, 67–69, 92, 118, 267,
 269–70, 281–82, 290; and Kosovo,
 68, 227; in the period 1933–1945,
 6, 58–59, 83–84, 103–6, 140, 262,
 273; in World War I, 130–31
United Nations: and Afghanistan, 118;
 and Bosnia, 46–48, 53nn77–80,
 53n82, 147–51, 153nn36–38,
 154n41; International Criminal
 Tribunal for the Former Yugoslavia
 (ICTY), 233, 235n26; and Iran,
 42–43, 142; and Iraq, x–xii, 30–31,
 36, 67–69, 118–19, 141, 185,
 280–83, 286–87, 289–90; and *jus in
 bello* questions, 142, 172, 182; and
 the just cause principle, 32–33,
 62–63, 70, 118–19, 310; and
 Kosovo, xiii, 69, 173, 198, 201–3,
 221–23, 226, 228–29, 232–33,
 237–59; and the principle of last

resort, 140–42, 145; and the question of legitimate authority, 12, 30, 32, 35, 48, 62, 66–70, 118, 201–3, 221, 223, 228, 230, 233, 237, 250–51, 253, 289–90; responsibility to protect (concept), 48; and Rwanda, xii; and the Six Day War (1967), 33; UN High Commissioner for Refugees (UNHCR), 17, 46; UNICEF, xi; UNMIK (United Nations Interim Administration Mission in Kosovo), 198, 238, 258n3; UNPROFOR (United Nations Protection Force), 53n80, 53n82, 148–49, 153n36; UN security system, x, xii, 7, 15, 45, 48, 58, 70, 140, 310. *See also* Cuban Missile Crisis (1962); Indian-Pakistan War (1971); International Atomic Energy Agency (IAEA); legitimate authority principle; NATO

United States: and Afghanistan, xi, xiv, 16, 117–20, 176; American Civil War (1861–1865), 4, 18, 127; and Bosnia, 153n36, 208; and Iran, xi, 38–39, 42, 52n52, 296; and Iraq, xi, 16–18, 31, 41–42, 67, 88–96, 117–20, 124n44, 176, 270, 281–82, 285–88, 290–98; and *jus in bello* principles, 157, 164–65, 168, 173, 177, 182, 185, 187–88, 188n2, 189n3, 212, 232, 270, 292–95, 298, 300n45; and Kosovo, 173, 177, 197, 200, 202, 209, 212, 221, 227, 230, 232, 238, 304; and North Korea, 133–36, 137n24; and Panama, 57; in the period 1933–1945, 6, 60–61, 164–65, 168; and rogue states, x–xii, 57, 185; and terrorism, xiv, 16–17, 34–35, 37; and weapons of mass destruction, 164–66, 178–79, 182. *See also* Bush, George H. W.; Bush, George W.; Clinton, William J.; Cuban Missile Crisis (1962); Iraq, and Gulf War (1990–1991); Kennedy, John Fitzgerald; Korean War (1950–1953); NATO:

intervention in Kosovo; terrorism; Vietnam War: Second Indochina War/Vietnam War (1964–1973)
universalism (universal values and principles), 3, 8, 24n51, 44–45, 57, 92, 155–57, 222, 239, 254, 257, 307, 314–15
utilitarianism, 20, 126

Vattel, Emmerich de, 28
Vietnam War: First Indochina War (1946–1954), 63–64; Second Indochina War/Vietnam War (1964–1973), 16, 163, 167, 201
Vitoria, Francisco de, 27–28, 44, 52n72, 97n13

Wakin, Malham, 157
Walt, Stephen M., 92
Walzer, Michael, 32–33, 35, 38, 43–44, 50n21, 67, 165, 176–77, 217n39, 273
war: anticolonial war (*see* colonialism); *bellum Romanum*, 156; civil war, xii, 4, 15, 17–19, 108, 120, 127, 130, 220, 266, 296, 311; declaration of, 14–16, 86, 156, 266, 269; definition of, 19; guerrilla and antiguerrilla war, xiv, 13, 23n30, 62, 64–65, 82, 106–8, 117, 172, 175, 187, 188n2, 196, 220, 226, 262–63, 274, 311; humanitarian intervention, 43–45, 47–48, 52n72, 66–67, 69, 73, 90, 201, 219, 227, 233–34, 237, 240; nuclear war, 7, 38, 43, 52n52, 122, 134, 146, 164–65, 180–81; preventive and preemptive war, 28, 31–38, 68–69, 73, 79–80, 86, 88, 90, 93–95, 139, 283; religious war, 45, 73, 76; revolutionary war, 12, 58, 61–62, 70, 73, 107–8, 121, 130, 143, 310; war of secession, xii, 12, 15, 70, 73, 82–83, 220, 230–31, 237–44, 253–54, 257, 258n5, 310–11. *See also* Algerian War (1954–1962); Bosnia; Chechnya; Falklands War

(1982); Georgian-Abkhaz conflict; Indian-Pakistan War (1971); Iran/Iraq War (1980–1988); Iraq; Kosovo; Nagorno-Karabakh; NATO; Russo-Japanese War (1904–1905); secession; terrorism; Thirty Years' War (1618–1648); Vietnam War
weapons of mass destruction, x–xiii, 34–37, 39, 42, 67–69, 88–91, 93–94, 96, 118–19, 185, 188, 281–87, 290. *See also* biological weapons; chemical weapons; nuclear weapons
Weber, Max, 55
Weiss, Thomas, 47
Weller, Marc, 200
Westphalia, Peace of (1648), 45, 57, 70n7, 311
Wolfowitz, Paul, 88, 94, 96

Yeltsin, Boris, 211

About the Contributors

Ruben Apressyan is head of the Department of Ethics at the Institute of Philosophy, Russian Academy of Sciences, and professor of ethics at Lomonosov Moscow State University. He is a member of COMEST (the World Commission on the Ethics of Science and Technology, set up by UNESCO) and the author of *Ideia morali i bazovye normativno-eticheskie programmy* [*The Idea of Morality and Fundamental Normative-Ethical Programs*] (1995). With Abdusalam Gusseinov he has published the textbook *Etika* [*Ethics*] (1998), and *Etika: entsiklopedicheskii slovar* [*Encyclopedic Dictionary of Ethics*] (2001).

Carl Ceulemans is associate professor in the Department of Philosophy at the Belgian Royal Military Academy, Brussels. He obtained a PhD in political science at the Vrije Universiteit Brussel. His fields of research are military ethics, ethics, and international relations. He is the author of *Reluctant Justice: A Just-War Analysis of the International Use of Force in Former Yugoslavia (1991–1995)* (2005). Other recent publications are "War Against Terrorism. Some Ethical Considerations from the Just War Perspective," in *Just War and Terrorism: The End of the Just War Concept?* (2005); and "Moral Equality of Combatants," in *Parameters* (Winter 2007–2008).

Bruno Coppieters is professor of political science at the Vrije Universiteit Brussel (Free University of Brussels). He holds a PhD in Philosophy from the Freie Universität Berlin and teaches courses on the history of political thought, conflict resolution, and the ethics of war and secession. His published works deal mainly with federalism and conflicts over sovereignty in the Caucasus and the Balkans. He has coedited the following books: *Statehood* *and Security: Georgia After the Rose Revolution* (2005) and *Contextualizing Secession: Normative Studies in Comparative Perspective* (2003).

Nick Fotion is professor of philosophy at Emory University, Georgia. At Emory, he teaches courses and seminars in ethical theory, military ethics, biomedical ethics, and logic. He also taught at Yonsei University in Seoul, Korea, as a Fulbright Scholar, in 1984, 1988, and 1990–1991. During the 1991–1992 academic year he was a visiting professor at the U.S. Air Force Academy. His publications include over one hundred articles in such fields as ethical theory, military ethics, biomedical ethics, and philosophy of language. In 2002 he published *John Searle*. In addition, he has authored or edited ten other books.

Brigadier General (Ret.) Anthony Hartle is the former head of the Department of English at the United States Military Academy, West Point, New York. He began his military career on Okinawa as an infantry officer with the 173d Airborne Brigade, followed by two tours of combat duty in Vietnam. He later commanded a battalion in the 101st Airborne Division (Air Assault). He was a staff member of the presidential commission investigating the accident to the space shuttle *Challenger*, and he served for many years as the chairman of the Executive Committee of the Joint Services Conference on Professional Ethics. General Hartle is the author of *Moral Issues in Military Decision Making*, 2d ed. (2004), and coeditor of *Dimensions of Ethical Thought* (1987). He has published a variety of articles and chapters in military and academic publications.

Boris Kashnikov is professor in the Department of Practical Philosophy at the Moscow Higher School of Economics. He is a retired colonel of the Russian Ministry of Internal Affairs (MVD). In 1989 he served in the Soviet peacekeeping forces in Nagorno-Karabakh and in 1993–1994 took part in a UN mission in Croatia as civil police station commander. With Nick Fotion and Joanne Lekea he coauthored *Terrorism: The New World Disorder* (2007). Among his Russian publications are a book on liberal theories of justice and Russian political practice, *Liberalnie teorii spravedlivosti i politcheskaya praktika Rossii* (2004). He is the coeditor of a book on the social and philosophical aspects of organized crime in Russia: *Organizovannaya prestupnost v Rossii: filosofskie i sotsialno-politicheskie aspekty* (1999).

Guy Van Damme is associate professor and head of the Department of Philosophy at the Royal Military Academy of Belgium. He obtained a PhD in philosophy at the Vrije Universiteit Brussel. He was formerly a commissioned officer of the Belgian armed forces. His fields of research include logic, social philosophy, and applied ethics, with a particular interest in business ethics and military ethics. His publications include articles on globalization, the arms race, and military obedience. He recently published *Logique et argumentation* with Lt Jordy Deneweth (2007).